Reinterpreting the Borderline

New Imago: Series in Theoretical, Clinical, and Applied Psychoanalysis

Series Editor: Jon Mills, Adler Graduate Professional School, Toronto

New Imago: Series in Theoretical, Clinical, and Applied Psychoanalysis is a scholarly and professional publishing imprint devoted to all aspects of psychoanalytic inquiry and research in theoretical, clinical, philosophical, and applied psychoanalysis. It is inclusive in focus, hence fostering a spirit of plurality, respect, and tolerance across the psychoanalytic domain. The series aspires to promote open and thoughtful dialogue across disciplinary and interdisciplinary fields in mental health, the humanities, and the social and behavioral sciences. It furthermore wishes to advance psychoanalytic thought and extend its applications to serve greater society, diverse cultures, and the public at large. The editorial board is comprised of the most noted and celebrated analysts, scholars, and academics in the English speaking world and is representative of every major school in the history of psychoanalytic thought.

Titles in the Series

Reinterpreting the Borderline: Heidegger and the Psychoanalytic Understanding of Borderline Personality Disorder, by Paul Cammell
Transgenerational Trauma and the Aboriginal Preschool Child: Healing through Intervention, edited by Norma Tracey
The Ethics of Remembering and the Consequences of Forgetting: Essays on Trauma, History, and Memory, edited by Michael O'Loughlin
Fragments of Trauma and the Social Production of Suffering: Trauma, History, and Memory, edited by Michael O'Loughlin and Marilyn Charles
Relating to God: Clinical Psychoanalysis, Spirituality, and Theism, by Dan Merkur
The Uses of Psychoanalysis in Working with Children's Emotional Lives, edited by Michael O'Loughlin
Psychodynamic Perspectives on Working with Children, Families, and Schools, edited by Michael O'Loughlin
Working with Trauma: Lessons from Bion and Lacan, by Marilyn Charles
In Freud's Tracks: Conversations from the Journal of European Analysis, edited by Sergio Benvenuto and Anthony Molino
Desire, Self, Mind, and the Psychotherapies: Unifying Psychological Science and Psychoanalysis, by R. Coleman Curtis
Hypocrisy Unmasked: Dissociation, Shame, and the Ethics of Inauthenticity, by Ronald C. Naso
Searching for the Perfect Woman: The Story of a Complete Psychoanalysis, by Vamık D. Volkan with J. Christopher Fowler

Reinterpreting the Borderline

Heidegger and the Psychoanalytic Understanding of Borderline Personality Disorder

Paul Cammell

ROWMAN & LITTLEFIELD
Lanham • Boulder • New York • London

Published by Rowman & Littlefield
A wholly owned subsidiary of The Rowman & Littlefield Publishing Group, Inc.
4501 Forbes Boulevard, Suite 200, Lanham, Maryland 20706
www.rowman.com

Unit A, Whitacre Mews, 26-34 Stannary Street, London SE11 4AB

Copyright © 2016 by Rowman & Littlefield

All rights reserved. No part of this book may be reproduced in any form or by any electronic or mechanical means, including information storage and retrieval systems, without written permission from the publisher, except by a reviewer who may quote passages in a review.

British Library Cataloguing in Publication Information Available

Library of Congress Cataloging-in-Publication Data

Names: Cammell, Paul, 1973– author.
Title: Reinterpreting the borderline : Heidegger and the psychoanalytic understanding of borderline personality disorder / Paul Cammell.
Other titles: New imago.
Description: Lanham : Roman & Littlefield, [2016] | Series: New imago : series in theoretical, clinical, and applied psychoanalysis | Includes bibliographical references and index.
Identifiers: LCCN 2016032727| ISBN 9781442252844 (cloth : alk. paper) | ISBN 9781442252851(electronic)
Subjects: | MESH: Heidegger, Martin, 1889–1976. | Borderline Personality Disorder--therapy | Psychoanalytic Theory | Philosophy, Medical
Classification: LCC RC569.5.B67 | NLM WM 190.5.B5 | DDC 616.85/852—dc23
LC record available at https://lccn.loc.gov/2016032727

∞™ The paper used in this publication meets the minimum requirements of American National Standard for Information Sciences—Permanence of Paper for Printed Library Materials, ANSI/NISO Z39.48-1992.

Printed in the United States of America

"The borderline is never a secure place, it never forms an indivisible line, and it is always on the border that the most disconcerting problems of topology get posed. Where, in fact, would a problem of topology get posed if not on the border? Would one ever have to worry about the border if it formed an indivisible line? A borderline is, moreover, not a place per se. It is always risky, particularly for the historian, to assign to whatever happens on the borderline, to whatever happens between sites, the taking place of a determinable event"

          Jacques Derrida, *Resistances of Psychoanalysis* (1996, p. 77).

Contents

Acknowledgements		ix
Introduction		1
PART I: PHILOSOPHICAL FRAME		**25**
1	Heidegger's Project of *Being and Time* (1928)	29
2	Ludwig Binswanger: Dilemmas Relating Heideggerian Thought to the Human Sciences	47
3	Relationality: Individuation, Dialogue, Alterity, and Ethical Care	67
4	Embodied Affectivity: Body, Affect, Impulse, and Alterity	77
5	Temporality: The Timeless Unconscious, *Nachträglichkeit*, and the Shattering of Time	93
6	Technology and Science: Exteriorization, Interiorization, and Becoming	103
PART II: DEVELOPMENTAL FRAME		**115**
7	Relationality: Transition, Transformation, and Differentiality	121
8	Embodied Affectivity: Desire and Becoming	133
9	Temporality: Seduction, Integration, and Translation	153
10	The Origins of Borderline Personality: Scientization, Technologies of the Self, and Cultural Disavowal	161

PART III: CLINICAL FRAME — 177

11 Relationality: Relations Within and Without — 183

12 Embodied Affectivity: Borders, Bordering, and the *Abject* — 201

13 Temporality: Play, Care, and the Work of Trauma — 209

14 Technicity and Technique: Conclusion to the Clinical Frame — 219

Conclusion — 227

Notes — 249

Bibliography — 259

Index — 269

About the Author — 275

Acknowledgements

Firstly, I would like to express my especial gratitude for the support and input of Jocelyn Dunphy-Blomfield and Ross Kalucy, who have both contributed a wealth of experience and insight to guide me through the preparation of this work.

I would also like to thank a range of mentors, peers and colleagues for their input and support over this time as well: Robin Chester, Graeme Smith, Leonardo Rodriguez, Tra'ill Dowie, Theo Turpin, James Hundertmark, Rick Curnow, Malcolm Battersby, Michael Baigent, Tarun Bastiampillai, Matthew Ritson, Maria Tomasic, Jackie Amos, Sue Shannon, Jenny Curran and Shanthi Saha. And I am very grateful for the support of Jon Mills in endorsing this project for the New Imago series, as well as excellent editorial guidance from Alison Pavan, Kasey Beduhn, Molly White (Rowman & Littlefield) and Anita Singh (Deanta).

Most importantly, though, I would like to thank my wife Jackie and my beautiful children Bridie, Lloyd, Zara and Piper for the love and care they have given to me over this period of work, and also more broadly in the life we share together.

Introduction

Within the clinical disciplines that seek to understand psychopathology and the action of psychotherapy, the conceptualization of disorders of the self, character disorders or so-called personality disorders remains problematic. The "borderline" concept, in particular, has a rich and complex history in psychodynamic, psychoanalytic and psychiatric theory over the past 70 years or so, especially when consideration is given to the concept's prehistory, extended back to the types of hysterical problems Charcot, Freud, Breuer and Janet treated and wrote about. The term "hysteria" was a broad-ranging, far-reaching term, the designated cases of which, today, would resemble an admixture of what psychiatrists might term posttraumatic stress disorder, conversion disorder, somatoform dissociation, dissociative disorder, so-called complex posttraumatic stress disorder (Herman, 1997), as well as borderline and histrionic personality disorders. It is interesting to contemplate how the borderline concept itself may have supplanted this earlier concept of hysteria both, perhaps, sharing analogous forms of culturally laden and historically specific complexity. The borderline concept now is over-represented in clinical research and practice in comparison to other so-called personality disorders, and it has many more complex affinities than these other personality disorders within debates and controversies in fields as diverse as gender studies, developmental research, forensic science and cultural studies exploring phenomena such as self-harm, sexualisation, sexual abuse and other complex or prolonged forms of trauma.

THE HISTORY OF THE "BORDERLINE" CONCEPT AND ITS OVERDETERMINED NATURE

The borderline concept itself is commonly recognized to have first arisen in the psychoanalytic work of Adolph Stern in 1938 (in his discussions of the "borderline group," 1938) and then Robert Knight in the late 1940s and 1950s (in his work with "borderline states"—Knight, 1953, for example). Since that time, the borderline concept has had a range of applications in many of the schools of psychoanalysis or affinities with related concepts beginning with Deutsch's notion of the as-if personality (1934, 1942), and other notable contributions such as Winnicott's interest in the false self and borderline states and Khan's notion of cumulative trauma (1960, 1974, 1983). Perhaps the most major and systematized contribution in the field was made by Kernberg in the 1960s and 1970s when he developed a system of three distinct personality organizations—psychotic, neurotic and borderline—and proposed a modified form of psychoanalytic therapy for some patients with borderline personality disorder (for example, 1975). There have been other systematic approaches to borderline pathology in psychoanalytic theory (Bergeret, 1975, for example) and the borderline concept has been incorporated into or related to numerous other schools of thought and fits within a broader trend of approaches to so-called disorders of the self, or personality and character disorders. If the "borderline" concept was initially used to designate a state, a pathological entity, an organization or simply a group of patients established by exclusion from strict alignment with neurosis or psychosis, this "excluded middle" term would expand to fill a field of ever increasing centrality and dominance. This field would be aligned with a greater interest in personality organization and disorders of the self, exemplified by two central North American figures in psychoanalytic thinking and practice: Kernberg, with his fusion of the object relations, structural and ego psychology approaches underpinning a central interest with "personality organization," and Kohut, with his own school of thinking, Self Psychology, focussing upon pathological narcissism and self-cohesion (1971, for example).

Simultaneously with this trend in psychoanalytic theory beginning with Stern, clinical psychiatry during the 1940s and 1950s developed a variety of other terms which were used for this group of patients, such as "ambulatory schizophrenia" (Zilboorg), "preschizophrenia" (Rapaport), "latent schizophrenia" (Federn), "pseudoneurotic schizophrenia" (Hoch and Polatin), "schizotypal disorder" (Rado) and "borderline states" (Knight). In 1968, Grinker's group operationalized the borderline term to permit the first empirical research conducted on patients, who were referred to as presenting with the "borderline syndrome." The next major advance in the field occurred in 1975 when Gunderson and Singer (1975) published a widely acclaimed article that synthesized the relevant published information on borderline disorder, and defined its major characteristics. Gunderson and colleagues then published a specific research instrument to enhance the accurate diagnosis of borderline disorder (1981). This instrument would permit researchers over the world to approach borderline disorder as a diagnostic entity that had its own content validity, verifiability and structural integrity. Subsequently, "borderline personality disorder" first appeared in the DSM III as a bona fide diagnosis in 1980.

Within modern orthodox psychiatry, the borderline concept now sits uncomfortably when it is used to describe, in the "categorical" terms of the DSM IV (American Psychiatric Association, 2000), a form of personality disorder that is not seen as a primary psychiatric disorder (or "Axis One" disorder) in its own right, but rather a form of personality disturbance on a secondary diagnostic axis (or "Axis Two"), where many primary psychiatric disorders are commonly, if not universally, seen to co-associate with the personality disorder. The disorder is defined as "a pervasive pattern of instability of interpersonal relationships, self-image, and affects, and marked impulsivity beginning by early adulthood and present in a variety of contexts." Here, the affective instability and impulsivity (and difficulties with anger, feelings of emptiness and recurrent suicidal and self-harm gestures) that are seen to be intrinsic to borderline personality disorder can also associate with Axis One mood and anxiety disorders. Similarly, the stress induced psychotic and dissociative symptoms that are seen to be intrinsic to borderline personality disorder can also associate with "Axis One" psychotic and dissociative disorders. This all means that borderline personality disorder forms part of a rich array of dissociative, anxiety, substance use, mood, and somatoform disorders not to mention eating disorders and other syndromes which commonly co-associate (see Zanarini, 1998, for example).

In all of this, the borderline personality disorder diagnosis is overrepresented in clinical presentations and in clinical research, much moreso than other forms of personality disorder or many of the primary (or "Axis One") psychiatric disorders. In many ways, then, the "borderline" concept simultaneously holds a privileged and denigrated position in orthodox psychiatric research and treatment, somewhat analogous to the form of splitting that is linked to the clinical presentation of the disorder itself in so many of the theories that describe it. This position of interest has led to a rich array of formalized, empirically validated treatment approaches that began to develop as recently as the early 1990s, when Linehan's group introduced a modified form of cognitive behavioural psychotherapy, "Dialectical Behaviour Therapy," for the identifiable group of patients with borderline personality disorder who present frequently to public hospitals with self-harm and suicide attempts (Linehan et al., 2006).

Since then, other "manualized," empirically validated forms of psychotherapy have been developed, many of which seem to suggest the requirement or the pressure for a rapprochement of the psychoanalytic and empirico-scientific paradigms such as Fonagy, Bateman and Target's "Mentalization-based Treatment," "Transference-Focussed Psychotherapy" which is a modified form of Kernberg's original approach (Clarkin, Yeomans and Kernberg, 2006), Ryle's Cognitive Analytic Therapy (Ryle, 1997), Meares's Conversational Model (2000), Supportive Psychoanalytic Psychotherapy (Appelbaum, 2006), Schema-Focused Therapy (Giesen-Bloo et al., 2009) and Systems Training for Emotional Predictability and Problem Solving (or "STEPPS," Blum et al., 2008). This rapprochement has developed further in the field of formal research-based diagnostic systems, where psychoanalytic schools in North America have developed their own independent diagnostic manual, the *Psychodynamic Diagnostic Manual* (PDM Taskforce, 2006) while simultaneously the organization and parties developing the newest version of the DSM (the DSM V), indicated tendencies, subsequently abandoned, to introduce more elaborate psychoanalytically or psychodynamically based diagnostic formulations (see Clarkin et al., 2010, for example).

Arguably, some of the most rich and productive developments in this field of research and clinical practice, in which psychoanalytic and psychodynamic approaches begin to enter into fruitful exchange with empirical psychiatric approaches, have been hybrid approaches which meld research in scientific domains as diverse as ethology, developmental neuroscience, functional neuroimaging and empirical psychology with clinical models of the development and treatment of problems designated as "borderline." Liotti (1992, 1995, et al., 2000), for example, has advanced Bowlby's attachment paradigm, and more recent ethological and developmental research, to develop a Cognitive Evolutionary model of understanding disorders such as borderline personality disorder and dissociative disorders, which he would view as intrinsically developmental, attachment-based disorders. Fonagy, Bateman, Jurist, Gergely and Target have linked similar attachment research to develop their theory of mentalization to explain borderline disturbances and a model of therapy (Fonagy et al., 2002; Jurist 2005; Jurist, 2010). Schore (1994, 2003) has reviewed developmental neuroscientific research to formulate a model of psychotherapy which addresses developmental deficits in affect regulation and interpersonal relatedness.

Psychoanalytic and psychodynamic schools have also sought to re-incorporate the concept of dissociation and this concept has become of crucial interest in relation to borderline pathology (see Howell, 2005; Bromberg, 1995; or Meares, 2000 for example). In doing this, the empirical issue which becomes implicated relates to the nature and significance of trauma as an aetiological or intrinsic factor in borderline and, by association, dissociative disturbances.

Many schools and thinkers, in particular those of the North American Relational traditions, have shown renewed interest in understanding the action of dissociation, denial, disavowal and repression in trauma responses, exploring the intersubjective field of trauma re-enactments in the analytic setting. In the current psychodynamic and psychoanalytic literature, debates around this issue of trauma, and the significance of abuse as an aetiological factor, often return to the historical antecedents to the borderline conceptualization, in particular the history of debates around hysteria, dissociation and seduction (the equivalent of abuse in late Victorian clinical parlance). Here we return to the critical period when the two primary followers of Charcot, Janet and Freud, diverged in their approaches to hysteria: Janet maintaining a core interest in dissociation following trauma as a central pathological feature in hysteria, and Freud, in his renunciation or suppression of his own Seduction Theory, going on to develop his own topographic model which situated many elements of trauma within intrapsychic conflict rather than real trauma.

More broadly, clinicians such as (van der Hart et al., 2006) and Herman (1997) have championed developmental trauma and abuse as primary determinants of borderline disturbance, their ideas encapsulated within concepts such as *structural dissociation* and *complex posttraumatic stress disorder*. It is interesting to note in this context the co-appearance of posttraumatic stress disorder and borderline personality disorder in the DSM III (1980). Modern debates around the veracity and verifiability of real trauma, such as the debates around *False Memory Syndrome*, are perhaps a more pronounced or polarized manifestation of a broader dilemma that the complex and ambiguous notion of "trauma" introduces: can trauma easily be considered as a specific empirical event or series of events (abuse, seduction), or as a type of psychic impact (acute stress, shock, breach, disintegration of defences), or does the nature and impact of trauma begin to become confused and complicated once it is elaborated or elucidated as a pattern of experiences or relationships with others that are aberrant or pathogenic in some way, but, perhaps, not understood as simply as an "abuse" event, or series of "abuse events" in which a defenceless, vulnerable child without any form of agency has the abuse imposed in a situation of fear, threat and control? This simple understanding does not permit adequate consideration of a child's agency (for example the motivation to please an adult, capacity to repress or deny occurrences, incapacity to comprehend or understand what has occurred, the impact of extreme stress and fear responses on memory formation, and the variable developmental trajectories of memory systems, sexualisation and social understanding) and relational determinants (for example deceit, control, manipulation, collusion, seduction, sadistic treatment). These dilemmas have arisen in recent controversy around Harvard psychologist Clancy's (2010) study of "sexual abuse survivors" which suggests many elements of the conventional clinical understanding of childhood and adult responses to sexual abuse are incorrect and therapeutically imposed upon the patients with histories of abuse. Her argument and research differs to the approach of False Memory advocates—she acknowledges the occurrence of sexual abuse but minimizes or at the very least qualifies the nature of the pursuant traumatisation—but nevertheless has roused the ire of many advocates and therapists of "abuse survivors."

As such, contemporary theoretical and clinical developments in the field of understanding "borderline personality disorder" include a range of complex multidisciplinary, integrative approaches. One can see here, that the apparently unified and homogenous quality of the concept belies a complex and overdetermined history of involvement from numerous disciplines, theories and clinical approaches. Even as early as the 1980s prominent "borderline personality disorder" theorists were already fearing that the research and literature had "gotten out of hand": "the borderline literature has swollen to a size too vast to be digested by one anthologist" (Stone, 1986 in Fromm, 1995). Given this, I would argue that an interpretative model is required to elucidate this field, and overcome some of the ambiguity that has arisen.

"BORDERLINE": A PROBLEMATIC "LIMIT CONCEPT"

In reviewing all of these historical, theoretical and clinical elements related to the borderline concept I have sought to describe its emergent dominance and centrality as a clinical concept, in all of its heterogeneity and complexity. I would suggest that the borderline concept now paradoxically occupies a *central* place in what is a *decentred*, discontinuous and mobile field of ideas and clinical movements in psychoanalysis, psychology, psychodynamic theory and orthodox psychiatry. It seems to be a unified, homogenous concept that is nevertheless overdetermined by a diverse array of heterogeneous antecedents in the history of conceptual developments in psychoanalysis, psychology, psychodynamic theory and orthodox psychiatry. This prompts questions. Empirically, can the borderline concept easily represent a distinct category amenable to objective scientific understanding? Clinically, does the borderline concept represent a meta-category or a sub-category of problems? Conceptually, can borderline pathology easily be situated in an individual seen as separate to the field of relationships in their lives—not to mention the clinical context of the assessment and treatment of such a disorder and the broader cultural situation of theories and practices from which notions of borderline pathology emerge? These could be seen to be but a few of the questions that could be raised concerning the coherence of the borderline concept as it is currently adopted.

Here, one can also introduce the idea of the borderline concept as a *limit concept*, aggregating many of the elements that psychological, psychiatric and psychoanalytic systems grapple with or have failed to incorporate elsewhere. I would argue that this dominance and centrality relates to the concept's designated capacity to capture, incorporate or enfold many of the clinical phenomena, or conceptualizations in psychopathological theory, which do not fit anywhere else due to limitations or restrictions in these systems. I would argue that this relates to many of these systems being dominated by, while at the same time often attempting to overcome, tendencies towards *categorical*, *individualistic*, *synchronic* (non-temporal) and *intrapsychic* approaches to understanding, favouring these over the *dimensional*, *relational*, *diachronic* (temporal) and *interpersonal* approaches to understanding. The implications of this are broad for scientific orientations that aim to study individual "selves" in categorical, objective, temporally constant terms. The latter, excluded approaches will inevitably return whenever attempts are made to preserve or incorporate an interest in the shifting and dynamic tendencies in individuals and their responses to relational events seen in the context of broader developmental trajectories that are understood both in terms of normative sequences and specifically individual sequences over time. Even broader questions can also be raised about the nature of knowledge and interpretation in these clinical fields when questions are raised about the intermediary or compositional role of language in clinical encounters and theoretical approaches.

This project, then, is an undertaking to develop an interpretative approach to understanding the borderline concept by taking into account the fundamentally relational, language-based and temporal nature of individual selfhood. It will attempt to analyse "borderline experience" from this perspective, both as it pertains to an individual's subjectivity as well as a clinician's understanding. In fact, I would argue that the two co-exist and are always already embedded within a whole series of historically derived clinical and cultural practices. As such, borderline "experience" will be treated as a form of "found object" that is analysed and related to in this work, not theorized or derived in a foundational sense. It will be seen as a form of self-experience and clinical experience that occurs within a particular historical and socio-culturally determined context. This context arises both for the suffering individual and the treating clinician together, and could not exit without either party participating.

To undertake this analysis, it will be important to formulate an orientation or approach to interpreting the field of borderline experience. There is a long history of approaching such issues in the discipline of philosophy. In the context of this work, then, I will have recourse to philosophical conceptualizations and frames to understand and approach an analysis of the borderline concept. I would argue that it would be especially beneficial to apply philosophical analysis to the borderline concept and the clinical field in which it has arisen. Some clinical theorists have already undertaken this form of analysis (for example Bromberg, 1998; Fonagy et al., 2002; Meares, 2000 refer to philosophical concepts and theories) but it has never occurred in a *systematic* form. Undertaking this may be beneficial in providing a frame from which to understand many of the complexities and ambiguities that emerge around concepts such as trauma, abuse, self ("selfhood," "self-states," "multiple selves" and so forth), repression, dissociation, and numerous others that coalesce around the borderline concept.

The primary philosophical orientation, here, will be that of *hermeneutics*, which is the study of interpretation. *Hermeneutics* is especially relevant to our topic because interpretation permeates all of the layers and elements of the topic: interpretation can refer to a clinical technique (in psychoanalysis and psychotherapy in general); or a method of understanding the relevance and import of scientific findings in other disciplines in their relevance to clinical work (for example ethology, cognitive psychology and developmental neuroscience); or to a broader philosophical orientation to knowledge and our understanding of subjectivity and selfhood, time, language and relatedness. It is with this discipline of hermeneutics in mind, that the project has been entitled "Reinterpreting the Borderline," to capture the idea of hermeneutic analysis and understanding in all of its complexity.

THE PHILOSOPHICAL APPLICATION OF HERMENEUTICS AND FRAMES

I would argue that interpretation is a fundamental element to this task. To introduce the type of philosophical analysis I will undertake, I would like to adopt the key concept of the *frame* to characterize the hermeneutic nature of the undertaking. Etymologically, the term "frame" has a complex array or origins and uses. In Old English, *framian* was used as a verb meaning "to profit, be helpful, make progress"; *fram* was used as an adjective meaning to be "vigorous, bold, going forward, progressing"; and *fremman* as a verb to "help forward, promote, further, perform, accomplish." In all of these meanings there is a sense of projection into the future, structuring or ordering a field. These meanings are extended progressively in Middle English, where *fremia* meant to "make ready," "to prepare timber for building"; and *framen* was used to refer to the human body (the skeletal "frame") or the "border or case for a picture," as well as, more broadly, any "established order or plan."

Over time, then, there appears to have been a trend from movement towards structure in the uses to which "frame" is put. When one thinks of the uses the term "frame" is put to today, it can refer to any of these older meanings, with the general sense of progression and movement (to advance, promote, perform, execute, commit, do) as well as a wide array of designations referring to structures, positions or orientations (skeletal frames, picture frames, frames of mind, frames of reference, frames as containers). "Frame" can refer to progression over the course of time, or an orientation or structure at a particular moment in time. In film, it can refer to an isolated instant within a progression; in photography, a frozen composition that is captured from a temporal environment. There are a multitude of other uses, such as the criminal context of *framing* another. This involves deception and manipulation of a situation based upon the limits of the perspectives of the participants in the situation. In the realm of experimental psychology, Tversky and Kahneman (1981) have shown that *framing* can affect the outcome of decision making in experimental paradigms where judgments about perceptions of reality can vary dramatically based upon how these perceptions are *framed*. This formalizes the notion that frames are a limited or contingent perspective of reality that affects or biases decisions, attitudes and beliefs. In political science, Kuypers (2009) has advanced "framing analysis" as a form of rhetorical analysis (primarily in political media narratives) to explore the manipulation of public perceptions and opinions by political groups.

Perhaps the most relevant use of the frame concept to our subject is found in the work of Erving Goffman (1959, 1961, 1963, 1974) whose approach to the sociological analysis of social relations led to important foundational work in the understanding of total institutions such as psychiatric asylums as well as forms of social function such as stigma which are seen to operate in the field of psychiatry. Later Goffman (1974) developed his own paradigm within sociology that he called *frame analysis*. This approach, broadly fitted within approaches to social constructivism which saw experience (self-experience, cultural experience) being ordered by frames involving conventions of acting (roles, performance, speech acts) and interpreting the self as it manifests in the context of interpersonal situations. Frames, here, become constructs through which *experience* is organized. Without delving deeply into Goffman's (1974) approach one can see the relevance of considering a *frame of experience* which simultaneously encapsulates self-experience (and self-interpretation) as well as broader contexts and systems of cultural experience which may include perspectives as diverse as the scientific, the aesthetic and the moral or ethical. Interestingly, a distantly related social thinker, Michel Foucault (1961) had also earlier in his career addressed the question of the modern evolution of psychiatric practices (asylums, modern clinical approaches to the understanding of mental illness) and how these formed a part of the "experience of madness" insofar as modern rationality and institutional practices came to terms with the aberrant presentation of madness in culture by means of isolation (the asylum) and *clinicalization* (modern psychiatry). Later he became more concerned with broader questions to do with the history of the modern evolution of many forms of scientific and institutional practices in a range of disciplines and how these could be understood in terms of forms of what he termed *power/knowledge* which he saw, in loose terms, as framing experience and practice in the individual and social fields as well as, in fact, serving to constitute forms of subjectivity or selfhood. Indeed he would conceptualize this by drawing reference to something analogous to *frames*, what he would call *dispositifs* (translated loosely as apparatuses, plans or schema). Of course it is problematic to make such broad and tentative comparisons between thinkers such as Goffman and Foucault, suffice it to say this is done merely to demonstrate an orientation to experience (individual and clinical experience) which looks at underlying social construction, the mediating influence of historical context and pragmatic or socio-political influences. Indeed, Goffman and Foucault may have shared a certain goals of contextualizing (sociologizing or historicizing) aspects of psychiatry, although their projects certainly had methodological and conceptual elements that were quite divergent to one another.

For our field of investigation, here, this form of social constructivist understanding of a *frame* is relevant. To this point, I have already alluded to many elements of the context in which the borderline conceptualization emerged: its possible supplanting of the Victorian notion of hystericism; the convergence of psychoanalytic and orthodox psychiatric theory and research to focus on personality organization and pathologies of selfhood leading to the concept of "personality disorder" which in turn comes to fall within a scientific realm of empirico-objective study; borderline personality disorder then becoming an object of study within evidence-based clinical medicine, and specifically with regard to effective treatments in the form of manualized, protocol-based models of psychotherapy. I have also described that along with this has arisen a group of related integrative theoretical models of borderline personality disorder which refer to developmental neuroscience, attachment disorder (attachment being operationalized and objectified in research protocols), and developmental psychopathology particularly in relation to variants of abuse and trauma. Now, if the focus is broadened to consider the social and historical context of the appearance of the borderline concept there are other factors that can be introduced into my frame of consideration. Considering these factors may permit a certain critical outlook towards the seemingly objective, innocuous, scientific or taken-for-granted approaches of understanding borderline personality disorder. It may further destabilize them. What I have in mind here is to bring to attention a specific form of discordant relationship between elements in latter twentieth-century Western culture which have enabled or required the borderline to appear. In the age of hysteria, the hysteric may have appeared out of the dynamics of the inability to express the unthinkable, the will to implicit silencing, the action of taboo, privacy and secret. In the borderline era, the borderline may be a fragmented, chaotic expression of the limits of our permissivism, the after-effects of our openness to explicitness (sexual, violent, graphic) and the collision of our high ambitions for individualism (individual rights and responsibilities) with frank problems of neglect, omission and maltreatment seen in the formative course of individuals' lives. The borderline's experience is constructed within a symbiotic relationship between the clinical and cultural elements of the organization of self-experience. These individual and cultural elements reflect the terrain of the failed reach or grasp of our civility in terms of the purported control of the law and human services. This is the terrain of the brutal, the savage, the rough, the bad and inhumane ways we treat each other, our children, a terrain which is then related to by means of *clinical sterilization, clinicalization, medicalization* or *technologization*. Here, therapies could be seen as technological forms of (substitutive) care and factors such as "abuse" and "trauma" could come to be seen as discrete and aberrant causative events that can potentially be prevented or repaired.[1]

I would emphasize at this point, though, that I do not intend to pursue a purely socio-historical critique of the borderline concept, nor do I intend to explicitly question whether there is a legitimate position for a psychotherapist to hold. Here, I speak as a practising psychotherapist with the intent not of defending my position but rather, describing an interpretive position or frame that does, at the same time, take some of these factors into consideration. In this way, I am analysing and questioning my practice from within my frame of work at the same time as if I were on the outside of it.

With these denotations and connotations in mind, one can also look at the clinical notion of the "psychotherapeutic frame." Traditionally (see Langs, 1979, for example), it has referred to both the temporal and the structural elements of the psychotherapeutic setting (the site of the psychotherapeutic work, the contract around which session times and payments occur) as well as a broader interpersonal context within which the psychotherapeutic work will occur (the degree of anonymity or neutrality or physicianly manner of the therapist, their interest or free-floating attention, their orientation to listening and reflection or interpretation). Typically, borderline patients are considered to be some of the more difficult patients to hold within a psychotherapeutic frame. This is a more concrete manifestation of the commonly identified difficulties or dilemmas regarding the treatability of these patients. Interestingly, psychotherapeutic treatment of borderline patients often becomes very focussed on defending and maintaining the integrity of the frame, more than what actually occurs *within* the frame. To develop a new term, this could be referred to as *frame-work*, a form of simultaneously working within a frame at the same time as working to establish, maintain or describe the frame as if from the outside.

THE STUDY'S METHODOLOGY: THE FRAMEWORK OF HERMENEUTIC ONTOLOGY DEVELOPED FROM THE PHILOSOPHY OF MARTIN HEIDEGGER

Through philosophical analysis one can extend the context of the frame in psychotherapy to a broader notion from which to consider the borderline concept as it is applied in theories of developmental psychopathology and clinical work. This use of the notion of the frame, a "framework" or "frame of consideration," begins to evoke all of those meanings (modern and earlier) around progressing, moving forward, structure, encapsulation, orientation and perspective. I am using "frame" here in a holophrastic sense: intimating or alluding to a path to thinking in developmental theories and in the clinic around the issue of borderline pathology or what I would call "the borderline experience." I use holophrastic here to imply that one is trying to progress or move forward in an understanding: to encapsulate, structure and elucidate one's perspective. Here, there may already be an inchoate, implicit or tacit understanding which moves towards a more explicit, structured understanding. It is a metaphorical usage, extending the developmental metaphor of a holophrastic expression from infant to mother to the utterances occurring in the psychotherapeutic milieu from patient to therapist, and further to the therapists' and theorists' own position in relation to the work they undertake and the world horizon they live within. Thought from within this frame, which may be called a *hermeneutic circle*, may seek to extend itself beyond itself, to encapsulate itself. In both philosophy and psychotherapy there are similar dilemmas or problems that arise when one attempts to simultaneously think from the inside and the outside. At their worst, both philosophy and psychotherapy can be accused of spuriousness, being outside of life; philosophy being an obscure, alienated form of contemplation devoid of practical meaning and engagement; psychotherapy engendering a form of "non-relationship," outside of a person's actual life and real relationships. Both, though, have the capacity to change thinking, change perspectives, and individuals' *frames* of meaning, living and experiencing. This requires a simultaneous thinking from the outside and from the inside that is specialized but hopefully applicable to other domains of life.

A particular endeavour in this work, then, will be to articulate a framework where the work of the frame is operationalized—*frame-work* so to speak. It is an endeavour to articulate *and* practice, simultaneously, a hermeneutic framework of understanding science in developmental psychopathology to inform psychotherapeutic treatment of borderline cases. Implied, here, is an erosion of traditional distinctions between theory and practice, content and form, with the orientation that one can't "articulate what it is" without simultaneously "undertaking what it is." This, here, is a writing endeavour but it is perhaps analogous to a certain type of "interpretive stance" I will come to articulate for psychotherapy, a therapeutic posture of open-mindedness in which one maintains a free-floating attentiveness, an elaborative stance in which thoughts and ideas are permitted to develop sometimes of their own accord. Here, there is a sense in which the psychotherapeutic relationship is not a relationship that achieves specific ends in terms of the intentions of the therapist: there will be a certain type of absence on the part of the therapist. Anything else, certain kinds of presence on the part of the therapist in terms of motivations, intentions and so forth, can constitute violations of the *frame*, not even having to be as explicit as sexual or other such overtly exploitative violations. Subtle violations can be the foreclosing of meaning, the imposition of too much theoretical or clinical certainty or attitudes of omniscience or omnipotence. A certain negative posture of the therapist, that is passive but elaborative, receptive and attentive, will be described. I say this is analogous to the philosophical framework that will be elaborated to dismantle modes of thinking (objectivist, reductionistic, pseudoscientific) that can lead to problematic orientations to the understanding of borderline experiences—orientations that I have already referred to as categorical, individualistic, synchronic and intrapsychic approaches. Here, these orientations can be dismantled or deconstructed (in a loose sense) by being explored through a hermeneutic frame where there is an analogous orientation of receptive attentiveness, negativism and interpretive stance. Here, there is an underlying appreciation of the limits of understanding, the sense that there is a contingently limited hermeneutic frame from which understanding and interpretations can be articulated.

The work will be divided into three parts or *frames*: the *Philosophical, Developmental* and *Clinical Frames*. In the *Philosophical Frame*, a central theme will be the elaboration of a hermeneutic orientation that emerged from the work of Martin Heidegger in the first half of the twentieth century but was then elaborated by some of his followers and subsequent philosophers influenced by him. In Heidegger's principle early work *Sein und Zeit* (*Being and Time*, 1928^2), he transformed the discipline of hermeneutics to extend it beyond the study of interpretation as it is applied to written texts or forms of methodology in the human sciences (philology and historiography, for example). For Heidegger (1928) it became an *ontological* undertaking, now concerned with the interpretation and understanding of Being in general, and the conditions of man's being in the world in particular. The hermeneutic frame of reference, here, involves considering man as intrinsically self-interpreting, and any movement towards the understanding or interpretation of the world or Being in general beginning with the fact that man is always already in the world, moving towards an interpretation and understanding of it from a position of already being there. This means the mode of interpretation is already enfolded within a *frame* or *hermeneutic circle*. The relevance of this type of approach will be elaborated upon in the philosophical part of this work, drawing reference to numerous parts of Heidegger's work, and works of philosophical thinkers explicitly or implicitly influenced by it, and with varying degrees of affiliation with or criticism of it, including Hans-Georg Gadamer, Paul Ricoeur, Emmanuel Levinas, Jacques Derrida as well as Gilles Deleuze and Felix Guattari. It is important to articulate, at the outset, that this undertaking will be selective and broad in its approach, skirting over some of the complexity and detail that is intrinsic to each thinker and differentiates one thinker from another. The challenge will be to render a line of thought emerging from this tradition, what I call *hermeneutic ontology*, in order to adapt and apply it to the developmental and clinical fields of interest, the terrain of *borderline experience*. This is, in itself, a novel project, although there are related clinical theorists that will be referred to and drawn upon, who have previously engaged with Heidegger's work in a translational way for the clinical domain.

Heidegger's work has many affinities and relations with psychodynamic theory, psychotherapy and psychoanalysis. All of these relationships will be referred to in this work in a process of mapping out or elucidating a philosophical orientation to the clinical terrain of borderline experience. Firstly, his ideas were separately developed by Ludwig Binswanger, Medard Boss and Gion Condrau into schools of existential psychoanalysis (Binswanger, 1963; Boss, 1963 and 1979). Secondly, various analysts originally trained in Heideggerian philosophy subsequently developed psychoanalytic theories which were either explicitly or implicitly influenced by the analysts' philosophical training: Herman Lang (1997), for example, trained under Gadamer (one of Heidegger's principle followers) and wrote about Heideggerian and Lacanian conceptualizations of language and the unconscious; and Loewald (1980), a student of Heidegger in the 1930s, subsequently wrote prolifically in what is commonly described as an orthodox Freudian style which nevertheless somehow inhabits Freudian conceptualizations and implicitly or subtly develops them with arguably obvious influences from his hermeneutic and phenomenological training. Thirdly, Heidegger's work has been engaged by a modern movement of Intersubjective psychoanalysts Robert Stolorow, Lewis Aron, George Atwood, Donna Orange and Roger Frie. This has occurred within a broader engagement with a range of philosophical projects of thinkers who were either contemporaries of or influenced by Heidegger, such as Maurice Merleau-Ponty, Emmanuel Levinas, Paul Ricoeur and Hans-Georg Gadamer. William Richardson and Louis Sass (1989, 1992) have also advanced the engagement of Heideggerian hermeneutic philosophy with psychoanalysis, particularly in relation to Lacanian theory (Richardson) and the understanding of schizophrenia (Sass). One North American psychoanalyst and philosopher, Jon Mills (1997, 2005, 2014), has explored the affinities of Heideggerian and other philosophies with contemporary schools of psychoanalysis to establish his own model of Process Psychology. Another North American psychoanalyst and academic, Alan Bass (2000, 2006) has also advanced a sophisticated elaboration of Freudian theory seen through the lens of Nietzschean, Heideggerian and Derridiean philosophy. And finally Heidegger (1959–1969) himself held the Zollikon Seminar regularly for over ten years with a group of psychiatrists and analysts in Switzerland.

All of these developments and applications of Heideggerian thought, both in the philosophical tradition and in the domain of clinical theory within the fields of psychiatry and psychoanalysis, will be drawn upon in the process of elaborating the three frames of the study, which I will now briefly summarise in terms of their structures and thematics.

PART I OF THE STUDY: THE PHILOSOPHICAL FRAME

The *Philosophical Frame* will begin with some foundational descriptions of Heidegger's (1928) approach to hermeneutic ontology and will explore concepts of selfhood, interpersonal relatedness, temporality, moodfulness and language within a broader hermeneutic orientation that will subsequently be related to theories of developmental psychopathology and psychotherapeutic action. This will involve a hermeneutic approach to understanding being, living, and action that will overcome some of the individualizing, non-temporal, categorical, intrapsychic approaches to understanding, compensating for these with the dimensional, relational, diachronic, embodied and technical approaches to understanding. A further chapter will critically explore, in some depth, the work of psychiatrist Ludwig Binswanger, who attempted to apply and develop Heidegger's thought to the clinic. I will attempt to elaborate some of the difficulties and tensions that arise when Heidegger's philosophical approach to hermeneutic ontology is brought into engagement with a clinical realm of understanding. This will involve an appreciation and analysis of what Heidegger termed *Ontological Difference*. *Ontological Difference*, loosely, refers to the difference between an "Ontic" approach to the consideration of beings or entities in the world, understood empirically, theoretically or scientifically, and an "Ontological" approach to considering Being in general, and the unique worldhood of human Being in particular. If we take the latter "Ontological" approach as primary or originary, and the "Ontic" approach as secondary, we can potentially develop an understanding of human experience that avoids the types of reductionism, objectification, scientism and other biases that I have described as pervading the clinical field of study in this work. Heidegger's *Hermeneutic Ontological* approach, then, grounds an understanding of Being, and, in turn, of selfhood, interpersonal relatedness, temporality, moodfulness and language, in a manner that avoids scientific or objectivist reductionism. This analysis should, in turn, prepare a more critical and qualified approach to applying Heidegger's thought in the later frames of this work, where four hermeneutic ontological themes will be developed as a framework to approach the theoretical field of developmental and clinical approaches of borderline personality disorder.

Subsequently, in the *Philosophical Frame*, I will develop further ideas from the perspective of *hermeneutic ontology* under four thematic headings where Being and experience are understood in terms of *relationality, embodied affectivity, temporality* and *technicity*. Some of this discussion will incorporate the hermeneutic philosophy of Heidegger, and subsequent hermeneutic philosophers Hans-Georg Gadamer and Paul Ricoeur, as well as further developments of philosophy in this tradition that can fruitfully engage with psychotherapy, such as aspects of the work of Jacques Derrida, Emmanuel Levinas, Gilles Deleuze and Felix Guattari as well as Bernard Stiegler, who all wrote repeatedly on psychoanalysis and certain clinical issues. An attempt will be made to understand a unique hermeneutic domain for developmental understanding and "clinical knowledge" generated within psychotherapeutic practice. As alluded to above, part of this *Philosophical Frame* will hopefully not only articulate such an orientation (from the outside) but hopefully also begin to frame it in such a way that the reader's own perspective becomes influenced so that the following parts are approached from this perspective as if it were internalized, in a sense.

While I am developing and adapting the conceptualisations and work of an array of post-Heideggerian thinkers, who all acknowledge their influence and points of departure from Heidegger, the overall intent and import is the establishment of a *hermeneutic ontological* orientation that is coherent and true to Heidegger's (1928) original project, but also extends it considerably both in terms of Heidegger's own subsequent developments as well as the developments and departures of those post-Heideggerian thinkers. Here, I will focus upon originary or foundational notions of temporality, relationality, embodied affectivity and technicity. An awareness will be cultivated of the existential horizon within which understanding and interpretation occur, encapsulated in Heideggarian concepts such as "worldhood," "care" and "thrownness."

In terms of the *relational* theme, I will develop ideas around dialogicality, difference and alterity; in terms of *temporality*, I will develop ideas around care and heterochronicity; in terms of *embodied affectivity* I will develop ideas around the sub- and supra-individual processes of desiring, becoming and differentiation; and in terms of *technology* and science, I will re-situate understanding within becoming (at an individual and cultural level), related to processes of individuation, exteriorization and interiorization. What I aim to achieve in this approach, is a novel *hermeneutic ontological* orientation which is developed as an interpretative framework that I will then apply in the subsequent developmental and clinical parts of the work. In terms of a philosophical approach, I would emphasize that I am not attempting, in a rigorous way, to integrate the different philosophers I engage with within a closed philosophical system, so much as engage them within a more open, interpretative system that is established along the lines of the four thematics I develop (*relationality, temporality, embodied affectivity* and *technicity*) and that is readily applicable to the developmental and clinical domains I go on to explore.

PART II OF THE STUDY: THE DEVELOPMENTAL FRAME

Now if one considers *developmental origins*, one becomes aware of limits and horizons in the understanding of the infant's world. In the second part, the *Developmental Frame*, I want to explore concepts established by developmental theorists that are consistent with my hermeneutic ontological perspective that refer to notions of limits, horizons, backgrounds and facticity. I will discuss a developmental orientation from which one can begin to understand clinical problems such as "borderline phenomena," "traumatization" and "dissociative symptoms." This discussion will make reference to developmental theories derived from infant and attachment research (Daniel Stern, 1985; Liotti, 1992, 1995; Schore, 1994, 2003; Fonagy et al., 2002; for example), and psychoanalytic psychotherapy (Kernberg, Winnicott, for example) but would also seek to relate these phenomena and theories to the hermeneutic ontological concepts of relationality, temporality, embodied affectivity and technicity developed in the *Philosophical Frame* of the project. I will attempt to define developmental origins and sequences in terms of their relationality, temporality, embodied affectivity and technicity in such a way that a respect for complexity and interpretive limits is maintained. Developmentally, this is relevant when one approaches infantile and childhood experience and the processes of individuation or subjectification that occur in development. This complexity, in a developmental sense, relates to the elaborate and sophisticated passage of progressive formation we undergo: there are phases of prolonged dependence beginning with maternalization but extending into all manner of familial, educational and other social or cultural contexts that permit the potentiation of complex forms of emotional relatedness, linguistic capacity, technical ability, and complex embodied affectivity. In all of this, we tend to firstly envisage an endpoint, the modern, adult individual, and then attempt to conceptualize this developmental complexity from the perspective of the endpoint. We conceptualize an individual with sophisticated intrinsic capacities (representational, linguistic, social and emotional) that constitute us and are fixed and enduring. This loses the sense of ourselves as situated and thrown, always continuing to develop, form, evolve and *become*, with continuing transitions between potentiation and degradation where the complexity and ineffability of our horizon of existence forbids us from getting outside ourselves to attain the objectivity we seek. Theories and ideas that are consistent with this type of hermeneutic ontological outlook, that focus on the types of temporality, relationality, embodied affectivity and technicity I have described, will be explored. To this end, I will explore the affinity that the hermeneutic ontological outlook has with certain developmental ideas emerging from theorists such as Donald Winnicott, Hans Loewald, Christopher Bollas, Jacques Lacan, Jean Laplanche, Julie Kristeva and André Green.

As such, in the *Developmental Frame*, there will be a critical outlook towards theoretical models that adultomorphize infantile subjectivity, or portray it as individualistic, or adopt descriptions that rely on modes of objective presence such as representational theories of consciousness or neurobiological models that correlate to developing neurocognitive capacities. In the developmental part or "frame" of this work such a critical outlook will be applied to the attachment (e.g., Allan Schore), cognitive-evolutionary (e.g., Giovanni Liotti) and mentalisation (Peter Fonagy and Anthony Bateman) models of development of borderline pathology. I will also explore the psychoanalytic developmental theories of Borderline Personality Organization advanced by Otto Kernberg and the trauma models of borderline disturbance advanced by thinkers such as Bessel van der Kolk, Onno van der Hart and Ellert Nijenhuis.

In a broader discussion, I will attempt to relate a hermeneutic ontological *framework* to some of the biases I see in theoretical conceptualizations of borderline pathology which, are, no doubt self-serving biases which favour certain kinds of therapeutic intervention: models of borderline pathology which focus on forms of early development (pre-oedipal, mother–infant, attachment-based) often favour forms of dyadic therapy which see the therapy metaphorically as a form of reparation of developmental deficit; models of borderline pathology which focus on forms of abuse and trauma often favour models psychotherapy which rely on traumatic integration and catharsis (e.g., Bessel van der Kolk, Ellert Nijenhuis, Onno van der Hart); models of personality deficit which focus on pragmatic psychotherapies which rely on the acquisition of ego or self-functions (Peter Fonagy and Anthony Bateman's mentalization based psychotherapy, Otto Kernberg, John Clarkin and Frank Yeomans's transference-focused psychotherapy and Marsha Linehan's dialectical behaviour therapy). Ultimately, I will attempt to contextualize or situate these approaches within a broader technological and socio-cultural context from which "borderline experience" has emerged, a context that the clinician is also embedded within and must come to terms with.

PART III OF THE STUDY: THE CLINICAL FRAME

In the third and final part, the *Clinical Frame*, I will develop the hermeneutic orientation already established in the *Philosophical* and *Developmental Frames*, using it to describe a therapeutic stance that can be adopted in the treatment of an array of problems or disturbances that fall under what I have described as the field of borderline experience. As alluded to above, the borderline concept could be seen to be a limit concept where many paradoxical ideas and issues coalesce in the clinical fields of psychiatry, psychotherapy and psychoanalysis: for example, relational phenomena or experiences described in terms of "projective identification"; temporal phenomena encapsulated by terms such as *Nachträglichkeit* as it is manifest in deferred action and recovered memory that is experienced in the context of histories of "trauma" and "abuse"; complex disturbances of embodiment and identity encapsulated in concepts such as somatoform dissociation, stimulus entrapment and multiple personalities; and finally, disturbances of subjective agency and control, identified in concepts such as conversion and disavowal. Many other complex phenomena also aggregate here: for example, the behaviour of self-mutilation that can enact or symbolize the boundaries between body and affect, control and dyscontrol, privacy and communication, dissociation and grounding; or, the phenomenology of overwhelming affective states, which form dynamic clusters where the affects of shame and anger influence the dynamics of internal discipline and external hostility.

In the *Clinical Frame* I will attempt to elaborate upon a more complex model of therapeutic action, which will attempt to understand, incorporate or critically engage elements of other clinical approaches within a broader hermeneutic frame of understanding. I will describe how much of the literature on borderline experience idealizes, through notions of stability, cohesion, integration and regulation, the idea of an individualized, functional self, ego, "I" or subjectivity that is unified and somewhat separated from its relational, temporal, embodied, affective, technical and cultural contexts. I will demonstrate how objectivist, reductionistic modes of thought (such as representational models of consciousness, Cartesian dualities) and categorical, synchronic, individualistic models of psychopathology are favoured and how these lose the depth and complexity of clinical experience. In all of this, the ultimate endeavour will be to defining a clinical outlook to borderline experience that emerges out of, and encapsulates, as much as it can of a horizon of understanding that is mindful of the complexity of our experience in terms of its relatedness, temporality, embodiment, affectivity, technicity and, ultimately, its otherness to itself.

This clinical section, then, will elaborate how an interpretive process can be adopted clinically where the patient and therapist dwell together more openly and attempt to describe and explore the alterity and difference in what is experienced without a reliance upon the inference of scientific causal mechanisms, definitive explanation or recourse to forms of objective presence. This process uses doubling or empathy but in a manner in which one could consider the work occurring in a transitional or transformational space (after Winnicott and Bollas) with a differential relational dynamic (after Loewald) but is also dialogical (after Intersubjective and Relational theorists such as Aron, Stolorow, Orange, Atwood, Frie, Mitchell, Bromberg and Donnel Stern). It entails an open understanding of the operation of time, its heterochronicity and bidirectional nature and its focus on project and potentiation (after Green and Laplanche). It also entails an awareness of embodied affectivity and desire founded in processes of alterity, difference and lack (after Lacan and Kristeva).

A number of central, classical clinical issues will be explored in this approach. It will pay particular attention to issues around the conceptualization of *dissociation, splitting* and *disavowal*, as these have arisen from the work of Janet and Freud, and how tensions here relate to current clinical approaches to borderline experience that adopt models of dissociation (the traumatology movement with thinkers such as Bessel van der Kolk, Onno van der Hart, Ellert Nijenhjuis and Judith Herman, relational thinkers such as Philip Bromberg, and attachment-based theorists such as Giovanni Liotti). It will also review terms such as *abuse* and *trauma* in the context of earlier and historical usage, current research in traumatology, and a more complex analysis of how the therapist and patient work together "in time." It will also explore the ethical and interpretive agency of the therapist from a hermeneutic perspective (evoking concepts of fallibilism, prejudice, embeddedness and the sensibility to two-person dynamics). It will also explore clinical interpretative perspectives in light of preceding discussions about dialogue, conversation, narrative, differentiality and otherness.

Most broadly, it will be seen that the hermeneutic perspective can simultaneously permeate one's clinical approach to psychotherapy, one's orientation to theoretical thought within psychotherapy and developmental psychopathology, and offer a broader, personal interpretive orientation towards the situation of psychotherapy for the psychotherapist. Questions will be posed regarding the role of otherness and differentiality in the dialogue that unfolds in treatment: what role the authority of the therapist has, compared with the authority of the individual entering into therapy; and what ethical issues are pursued and what limits and boundaries are maintained. In this context, I will relate my hermeneutic ontological orientation to other clinical schools that attempt to be mindful of these issues when they pursue more a focus on dialogical, perspectival and co-constructivist approaches that attempt to eschew authoritarian, medicalizing, objectifying or, indeed, *subjectifying* stances.

Such schools include the Intersubjective School (with the work of Stolorow, Atwood, Orange, Aron and Frie focused upon in particular) and the school adhering to Russell Meares's Conversational model.

Part of what I will describe will be an attitude of openness and respect for complexity founded in the hermeneutic outlook that I have described. Much of this relates to an awareness of context, not just in terms of the situation of referral and the origins of the treatment for the individual, but also the situation of the practitioner and the treatment that the practitioner offers. This situatedness is complex for both parties, in terms of personal, familial, cultural and historical origins for the patients, and personal, professional and institutional origins for the practitioner, and influences the form of frame that is established. Part of this involves the clinician developing an ethico-critical stance with which to approach the treatment context. It requires empathy, relating, hospitality, a dialogical focus, a respect for complexity and difference as well as an awareness of the differentiality of the context.

Many of these elements are very germane to the "borderline" presentation. I would argue, as many have done in the past (e.g., Fromm, 1995) that the borderline designation is often more readily adopted by the clinician than the patient, is often alienating, and can reflect a reductionism in the clinician's perspective in order to project, isolate or externalize the clinician's confusion or anxiety about their orientation to an individual that presents to them. This confusion and anxiety can relate to senses of urgency, being too involved or implicated, losing a sense of boundaries and controls. An ethico-critical stance may look towards sharing, empathy and kinship. It may engage in dialogue with a respect and acceptance of otherness, an attempt at hospitality and adjustment for the sake of the other. The practitioner may need to submit to experiences of helplessness and hopelessness in the face of the other individual, where the capacity to sit with and attempt to relate may be all that can be shared. At other times, the practitioner may have to overcome roles into which they did not expect or accept to be cast, more aware that the differential nature of the relationship and their authority has to be handled more actively and carefully so as to not be destructive. This can also be understood in terms of a broader ethico-critical stance and awareness of context, where there are a range of clinical, cultural and technical factors that are relevant to the presentation of the "borderline individual." This stance must be aware of the underlying social construction and historical context of the borderline field, in terms of its "technological" constitution and culture-boundedness. As I have already said, I do not intend to develop a primarily *sociocultural* critique of the "borderline personality disorder" concept. However I would argue that this contextualist and social constructivist understanding can be important to frame the ethical and critical orientation of the practitioner within their clinical work. Indeed it may motivate them to be more politically active or socially engaged in a broader way in domains such as health economics, social services and political advocacy. In the *Clinical Frame*, though, I will focus primarily upon the clinical issues I have described, developing these under the existing headings already adopted in the previous frames: the relational themes, temporal themes, themes of embodiment and affectivity, and, finally, technical themes.

FINAL COMMENTS

The central purpose of this project, then, will be to elaborate an interpretative framework originating from Heideggerian philosophy and referred to as a *hermeneutic ontological orientation* that I will apply to the understanding of the developmental and clinical issues of individuals presenting within the context of *borderline experience*. The orientation of *hermeneutic ontology* that I develop will serve to explore and elucidate not only the "borderline concept," which I argue has become a problematic limit concept, but also other commonly adopted notions in this field such as "trauma," "dissociation," "abuse" and "personality disorder." Not only will I attempt to historicise and critically appraise the borderline concept and these other implicated concepts, but I will also attempt to contextualise them within a more open and complex field of understanding that favours approaches to interpretation that focus upon the fundamentally relational, temporal, embodied, affective and technical aspects of our existence. I have used the concept of *frames, framing* and *frame-work* to introduce the notion that this type of analysis is simultaneously a form of theoretical contemplation outside the clinical field and a mode of intervention within the field, something analogous to the action of psychotherapy outside the field of everyday relations, or the action of philosophical contemplation outside the field of everyday thought and experience. The ultimate goal will be the achievement of a systematized philosophical, developmental and clinical orientation that demonstrates the utility and productivity of the engagement of philosophical thought with a clinical domain that has become overburdened by ethical ambiguity and a lack of conceptual clarity. It is with this goal in mind, in all of its complexity, that I have entitled the project "Reinterpreting the Borderline." The "borderline," here, refers simultaneously to a domain of theory that has become increasingly ambiguous and overdetermined while at the same time reliant upon that reductive and condensed limit concept; as well as the context of an individual and their clinician meeting and grappling with this designation, sharing it as a motif or label that needs to be understood and in some way overcome. The goal of this project is to engage this field of thought and experience, and open it up to greater understanding and ethical clarity. In doing this, we will attempt to understand how a term originally used to identify a marginal territory in the theory and practice of psychiatry, psychotherapy and psychoanalysis has now become such an overused and pervasive label applied to several generations of suffering individuals, with all of the connotations of scientific clarity and objectivity that this label now implies. The project will then simultaneously attempt to reinterpret this "borderline" term, both to reintroduce clinical, ethical and cultural elements that are overlooked, and to reemphasize personal and experiential elements that are undervalued.

Part I

PHILOSOPHICAL FRAME

INTRODUCTION

In the philosophical part of this work a central theme will be the elaboration of a *hermeneutic* orientation emerging in the work of Martin Heidegger but elaborated by some of his followers and subsequent philosophers influenced by him. One notable aspect of Heidegger's philosophical career is that he had attempted to build a grand system of thought in his project *Sein und Zeit* (*Being and Time,* 1928). Subsequently, though, he abandoned this project although his thought and writing continued, the change or transition becoming known as the *Kehre* (or "turning"). Following the *Kehre*, Heidegger became fascinated by his philosophical predecessor, Friedrich Nietzsche, who had famously stated that: "The philosopher believes that the value of his philosophy lies in the whole, in the building: posterity discovers it in the bricks with which he built it and which are then often used again for better building: in fact, that is to say, that that building can be destroyed and nonetheless possess value as material" (1886, 201). It is interesting to note that Heidegger himself demolished his project and rebuilt ideas from it, and many others have continued in this activity thereafter.

Following this, my approach will not be to construct a systematic description of Heidegger's philosophy so much as to adapt an approach, or an *orientation* that can influence the subsequent discussion of scientific and clinical work relevant to an understanding of borderline experience. As such, I have adopted the notion of the "frame" and "framework" to describe what I will undertake. The elaboration of a philosophical frame based upon hermeneutic ontology will hopefully see a movement and structure, an approach, crystallize to orientate and influence the subsequent parts of the work. This approach will focus on core elements of Heidegger's hermeneutic philosophy which characterize our being in the world as relational, temporal, embodied and technical in a manner that radically influences our thinking about ethics, dialogue, meaning and otherness (as this relates to other people and the exterior world). I will show that Heidegger's thought addressed some of these issues well, but in certain domains was incomplete or subsequently revised or developed by post-Heideggerian thinkers. The goal will be to lay the philosophical foundations, a hermeneutic *frame*, from which the subsequent developmental and clinical frames of analysing borderline experience can be developed.

Why pursue Martin Heidegger's work, which is often described as esoteric and forbidding in spite of Heidegger repeatedly being acknowledged as one of the most influential thinkers of the twentieth century? To begin with, Heidegger's work has been increasingly noted to have many affinities and relations with psychodynamic theory, psychotherapy and psychoanalysis. Heidegger (1959–1969) himself held the Zollikon Seminar regularly for over ten years with a group of psychiatrists and psychoanalysts in Switzerland. In these seminars he approached the task of elaborating the implications of his thought (the ontological, phenomenological and hermeneutic standpoints) for clinicians. In spite of the fragmented and patchy nature of these seminars (based upon, as they were, incomplete and provisional transcriptions by the attendees), one sees kernels of insight, elaborations of ideas, which inspire the task of further thought in this direction. For example, at points, Heidegger (1959–1969, 59–69) addresses philosophical problems about interpersonal relatedness and the relationship between "internal states and representations" and interpersonal interaction, as these appear in object relations concepts such as introjection, projection and projective identification. It is helpful to philosophically analyse the problems around the ambiguity and incoherence of such concepts as projection and introjection, as they appear in the Kleinian and other object relations traditions.

Also, in the middle of the twentieth century while Heidegger continued to work philosophically, albeit from a somewhat reclusive position outside of institutional academe, his ideas were separately developed by Ludwig Binswanger and Medard Boss into schools of existential psychoanalysis (Binswanger, 1963; Boss, 1963 and 1979). Heidegger (1959–1969) himself critically responded to this and elaborated what are some of the philosophical difficulties in building a systematic clinical approach (in a clinical-scientific domain) from his own philosophical approach, which is concerned with different questions to do with broader philosophical domains such as ontology, phenomenology and hermeneutics. The question then becomes how a broad philosophical approach can be brought into dialogue with, or influence, thinking in a different though related clinical domain. This issue will be addressed in passing by looking at some of the problems or difficulties raised with regard to Binswanger's and Boss's work, on the way to developing my own approach or orientation.

One can seek guidance, here, from the various analysts who were originally trained in Heideggerian philosophy but who subsequently developed psychoanalytic theories which were either explicitly or implicitly influenced by the analysts' philosophical training: Herman Lang (1997), for example, trained under Gadamer (one of Heidegger's principle followers) and wrote about Heideggerian and Lacanian conceptualizations of language and the unconscious; and Loewald (1980), a student of Heidegger in the 1930s, subsequently wrote prolifically in what is commonly described as an orthodox Freudian style which nevertheless somehow inhabits Freudian conceptualizations and implicitly or subtly develops them with arguably obvious influences from his hermeneutic and phenomenological training. In both of these thinkers one can see the subtle influences that Heidegger's form of hermeneutic stance can have in its application to a clinical field. Lang's (1997) and Loewald's (1980) work will be described at different points in this project. There are also representatives of the intersubjective, interpersonal and relational schools, such as Orange, Stolorow, Aron, Atwood and Frie as well as other analytic thinkers with philosophical training or interests, such as Alan Bass and Andre Green, who have drawn reference to Heidegger's work and other thinkers of the hermeneutic tradition that I will uncover.

And finally, there are those philosophers who have either advanced a hermeneutic orientation and then engaged with the fields of psychoanalysis, psychotherapy and psychiatry, or have developed their own orientation that has then been related to these fields at the same time as being related to but distinguished from Heidegger's work. From all of these vantage points, the discussion below will attempt to elucidate a hermeneutic frame or perspective from which to approach the theoretical and clinical domain of borderline experience.

Chapter 1

Heidegger's Project of *Being and Time* (1928)

Heidegger's own methodology was developed from two disciplines: the first being *hermeneutics* (loosely, the study of methods of interpretation, originally of scripture and other texts, but broadened to any form of human actions, utterances or practices amenable to understanding); and the second being *phenomenology* (loosely the study of one's immediate perceptions and experiences). His early principle work *Being and Time* (1928[1]) was the beginning part of an enormous project aimed at a general theory of Being (*ontology*) which began with an exploration of the specific nature of the existence of human beings. What is significant for us, here, is that Heidegger, along with other eminent contemporaries such as Merleau-Ponty and Wittgenstein, elaborated a type of conceptual framework that undermines any decontextualized, individualistic notion of the self seen as a discrete autonomous agent, who divorced from the world processes the data of experience (perception, interaction with others) in a representational, algorithmic way. Heidegger's notion of *Dasein* (literally "being-there") and being-in-the-world indicates our irreducible and unsurpassable "embeddedness" in a concrete and contingent "life world"—we are always already in the world, practically immersed in the necessities and activities of life as an existential project into which we are thrown as finite beings. It is an inescapable context in which our being is already shared with others, housed in language, immersed in time within the horizon of death. In this context, our being, our self, is always an issue for us. But it is only from within this context that as selves we may begin to attempt to understand or explain who or what we are. This context is a background we can never fully think about or master as we are always already a part of it. Heidegger holds that we exist within this context or horizon of being with an implicit understanding or what he might call a *pre-understanding* of how to go about things, with at the same time the possibility of explaining or explicitly understanding the nature of our being something which is furthest away from us.

Heidegger's exploration (with Nietzsche before him) of this notion of an existential limit, and the idea of self-estrangement and an opaque background to our being, I believe, is significant for our understanding of selfhood as psychotherapists. The philosophical part, or "frame," of this work is an exploration of the philosophical conditions of this understanding. It will be seen to have a bearing upon how we think about dimensions of the self indicated in notions like the Unconscious. It also has a bearing upon how we can think about all of these concrete and very real elements of existence such as our development, and the rich spectrum of our affective, interpersonal, embodied experiences. If we think about it, these elements seem so immediate to us—going about life day to day with our thoughts, in our bodies; sharing emotions and exchanges in our relations with others. We negotiate the phases of life: bringing our children into the world, nurturing them; our own growth, our relationships; and ultimately our losses and own death. By far the majority of people today and in history wouldn't feel they need a philosopher or a psychotherapist to tell them how to go about all of this. We go about our lives where any explanation of these things, be it theoretical, scientific or technical is always secondary and derivative. These forms of explanation may have a practical use: when things break down or go wrong we need to conceptualize what the problem is in order to fix it. An analogy would be our daily immersion in driving a car, using our computer or riding a bike, things we do happily until something goes wrong and we need to rely on technical knowledge (much of which we often don't have ourselves) then to explain and fix what is going on. This form of thinking is secondary to the usual and habitual immersion in activity. Now in the natural world, we are not the designers, engineers or technicians. There may be all sorts of reasons why it is problematic to use this form of thinking about the world and ourselves. Heidegger explored how this form of thinking can lead to problems in our dealings with ourselves and nature, leading to a whole system of thinking about forms of alienation and inauthenticity in our modern subjectivity, and forms of technocracy and abuse of the environment in our relationship with nature.

Heidegger opens his foundational work *Being and Time* (1928) by referring to the entire history of philosophy as a "forgetting" of the "question of Being." One needs to be reminded here that Heidegger, like many German and French thinkers, privileges philosophy as the most central or pure domain of thought which may be representative or typical of broader historical movements and epochs of thought. As such in talking about this "forgetting" he is referring to philosophical thought from Plato and Aristotle onwards but is also including the modern scientific disciplines that emerged out of metaphysics in the seventeenth century and subsequent humanistic disciplines such as psychology and anthropology. Heidegger's project begins with an attempt to recover this "question of Being"—find an opening or a clearing in which to think about Being again. This will require a methodology of interpretation, a hermeneutic method, which will involve partly reading what has become omitted or hidden in philosophical discourse (but somehow remained implicit to it) in order to reveal it and allow it to be openly apprehended. The other element of his method of approaching the "question of Being" for Heidegger will be *phenomenological* insofar as it concentrates on what is experientially immediate and apparently self-evident to all of us. It is governed by phenomenology's principle of principles—the principle of presence and of the presence in self-presence, such as it is manifested in the Being that we ourselves are (our experience of what seems self-evident including our self-awareness or self-consciousness). It is this proximity of Being to itself, and our questioning of Being to our own Being, that intervenes in Heidegger's choice or deduction of the exemplary form of Being for his analysis—what he calls *Dasein*. Heidegger's point is that we who are close to ourselves, we interrogate ourselves about the meaning of Being. This interrogation, as a process of interpretation, occurs within this "hermeneutic circle of Being."

To explain what is important about this notion of a "hermeneutic circle" I could refer to moments when Heidegger (1929) links this starting point for interpreting Being with the Kantian origins of an attempt to instigate a "Copernican Revolution" in metaphysics. This revolution relates to a reversal of the common-sense view of the subject–object distinction, specifically regarding the knowing subject and the object known. Just because it locates the ground of any knowledge of any object within the knowing subject, Kant's revolution represents, as Heidegger recognized, the first serious attack on the traditional Platonic-Aristotelian approach to insight into the nature of things by focussing on that which needs to be known (the objects themselves or "things in themselves"). For Kant, in contrast to the Aristotelian tradition, thought does not know the thing itself without any intermediary: thought merely interprets what sense-intuition "reports." The concept is not "necessarily in conformity with its object"; in fact, the Copernican Revolution proclaims the reverse: it is the object that, to be known, must conform to the knowing requirements of the knower—for Kant, the transcendental categories. These transcendental conditions govern the synthesizing operation of our immediate apprehensions and our pure concepts—they, in a way, permit existent things to be recognized. The "beyond" of this knowing, the *noumenal*, is unknowable. Kant thus brought us to the point where the ground of the presence or absence of an object in knowledge is to be seen within the nature of the knower. He has thus created the possibility of a new form of enquiry—namely, "the metaphysics of the subject." Heidegger's approach would be, then, that the invocation of transcendental laws regarding the how-and-what we can know concerns precisely the condition and nature of being—and moreover, the meaning of "Being" and the copula "is" in themselves. This, of course, is precisely the original motivation and orientation for Heidegger's "fundamental ontology" (the hermeneutic and phenomenological enquiry into the Question of Being). It is not the place to explore the relationship between Kant's transcendental philosophy and Heidegger's fundamental ontology any further so much as to point out that for Heidegger the hermeneutic circle simultaneously refers to self-understanding (the phenomenology of self-interpretation) and philosophical understanding (interpreting Being evolving through the history of philosophy). Both relate to thinking about Being through interpretation and approaching this through what is present phenomenologically and not objectively. For Heidegger, phenomenological interpretation is descriptive and opens a space to make thinking possible: it is about *potentiality*.

Heidegger's own revolution, then, is to re-situate and broaden out our notions of understanding and interpretation beyond them being, simply, methods of reading or procedures of critical reflection. Understanding and interpretation *become* modes of being: the universal, pre-reflective mode in which we conduct ourselves in the world is itself of a *hermeneutic* nature. The world is familiar to us through basic, intuitive ways of going about things, where tacit and intuitive approaches, pragmatic forms of know-how, predominate. Most originally, Heidegger argues, we do not begin by understanding the world simply through the acquisition of objective facts, algorithms or representational knowledge from which we can establish or derive universal propositions, laws, or judgments that, to a greater or lesser extent, correspond to the world. The world is already implicitly intelligible to us, familiar to us, something with which we are at home. Explicit understanding and interpretation follow this, or co-exist with this. The hermeneutic circle of interpretation, then, refers to the interplay between our self-understanding and our understanding the world. Hermeneutics now deals with the meaning, or limits and lack of meaning in our own lives. This begins with individuals and their own situation, or situatedness.

Consider, for example, how Heidegger (1928) conceptualizes emotional states or affects in a theory of affects that steers away from any notion of "pure" or discrete affects, where affects fall within a complex process of the doubling or synthesizing of the self which is not divorced from the existential situation involving other modes of being such as interpersonal exchange (relatedness and language), memory (temporality) and embodiment (corporeity). Affect becomes the tone, atmosphere of this binding, or failure to bind. In this context, Heidegger uses the term *Befindlichkeit* which is Heidegger's own neologism developed from the German colloquial verb *befinden*. This verb is used in the everyday question "Wie befinden Sie sich?," which broadly translates as "How are you?." There is no literal translation of this question into English as the verb refers to, at once, *feeling* and *finding oneself*, such that "Wie befinden Sie sich?" literally means "How are you feeling?" at the same time as "How do you find yourself?." In adapting this verb, Heidegger wants to capture an expression that embodies states of mind, mood states, as a type of *feeling* and *finding oneself situated*. By describing moods as a kind of *situatedness*, he is attempting to overcome a sense of inwardness or depth (moods being *intrapsychic*, if you will). *Befindlichkeit* refers to a state that is both inward and outward looking. Moreover, such states are self-referential: one *finds oneself* in this state; it is self-interpreted actively and is an issue for oneself. This self-understanding is not cognitive so much as an implicit, lived-in awareness: this is how I am. Thus *Dasein* always has the potential for an implicit understanding (*Verstehen*) of its state. And moreover, this understanding is articulated through *Dasein*'s discourse (*Rede*). It is in this manner that the three *Existenziale* interact. One exists with mood states: we feel a moodful situatedness of which we may have an implicit understanding that can be articulated in our discourse with others and ourselves. Thus the situatedness of *Befindlichkeit* is interactional, interpersonal and implicitly self-reflective: *Befindlichkeit* embodies the wholeness of *Dasein*'s situatedness and is prior to an explicit understanding that would distinguish inner and outer, self and other, feeling and cognition, or speech and action. Understanding and discourse always belie a state of *Befindlichkeit*.

Another significant element of his existential analysis relates to the embeddedness of any form of behaviour or action within the situatedness of worldhood involving time and temporality. Importantly, *Dasein* is formally characterized by Heidegger as having that fundamental self-relation—that "comporting itself to its own Being"—which, above being directed towards and absorbed in any specific worldly activity or goal in the way I have discussed, is ruled by an inherent and intrinsic "directedness" of its own. This manifests itself in any the specific activities we engage in. Although I cannot really elaborate upon this in detail, put loosely this unifying "directedness" in *Dasein* is referred to by Heidegger as the "Care Structure": the fact that *Dasein* intrinsically has "concern" in its existence, no matter what this concern may be for, in its dealings and comportments. At the heart of this is the notion of "Temporality" Heidegger later introduces in *Being and Time*, as well as that of "Ontological Difference" which Heidegger introduces in *The Basic Problems of Phenomenology* (1982) around that concept of Temporality.

Through these notions, Heidegger wants to assert that *Dasein* is not "in time" like other things in its world are. For we are not simply in a "present" which is as a function of its "past," on the way to a "future" which will come to be as a function of that "past and present." Rather, our existence is uniquely led by its "future"—a "future" which is, in effect, guiding, pulling or directing the present in a particular direction out of its past. Specifically, when we are absorbedly coping with a particular task this "future-driven" quality, or "future-directedness," manifests itself in an ability of *Entwurf* (Projection) which allows a form of *Umsicht* (practical circumspection) to lead it through specific tasks and more broadly how it goes about anything. This overall directedness is seen by Heidegger to be the unifying aspect of all of our concerns in the world. In this way, *Dasein*'s Being has a unifying "Care Structure" which makes it a "perpetual coming to be" at any possible level. Such capacities as *Entwurf* and *Umsicht* are ineliminable and intuitive and not able to be nomologically understood. They cannot be built up from component abilities in some incremental way. They are not programmatic— understood in terms of explicit rules, algorithms, prototypes, formulae. It is general, global, presiding, primordial. It is a base intuition. To understand that this is not just a simple assertion on Heidegger's behalf we must also carry through the formal structure that this concept exists within and in terms of. Heidegger has disclosed it through his hermeneutic phenomenological analysis of *Dasein's* way of Being within a greater ontological framework driven by a fundamental "Question of Being." This means that Heidegger is in no way making assertions about a type of traditional subjectivity conceived of as a "conscious subject" or "transcendental ego" or "human being or soul." *Entwurf* and *Umsicht*, here, only have an import insofar as they are ontological, within Heidegger's own analytic of the ontology of *Dasein*. This analytic, ultimately, was alluded to as extending to the notion of "Care" which offers a unifying structure to the being that is *Dasein*, understood within that horizon of Temporality that separates *Dasein* off, purportedly, from other beings by virtue of an "Ontological Difference" that resides in Being as a whole.

HEIDEGGER AND THE CENTRALITY OF HERMENEUTIC ONTOLOGY

The first division of the first part of Heidegger's grand project *Being and Time*, appeared in 1928 with a hurriedly put together version of the proposed second division of Part 1. Although Heidegger never published the other three proposed divisions of the project—two would form a Part 2, enough of the project can be established from those divisions published, now considered autonomously as *Being and Time* (1928), as well as from the text of a 1928 lecture course assembled under the title *The Basic Problems of Phenomenology* (1982), to get an idea of what Heidegger called his "preparatory ontological analysis of *Dasein* in the averageness of its everyday existence." These two texts, then, will be considered with regard to how they present such an analysis within Heidegger's wider formal approach to phenomenology which he comes to call "fundamental ontology," all of which he wanted to establish within what he referred to as the horizon of a problematic of "Temporality." All of this begins with the two introductory sections of Being and Time (1928) where Heidegger asks the "Question of Being."

DASEIN AND THE "QUESTION OF BEING"

The two introductory sections of the project of *Being and Time* (pp. 2–39, 1928), begin with Heidegger making a call for a radical reformulation and reconception of the task of philosophy, based around our understanding of being—particularly our understanding of the word "being" and the copula form "is." Any general philosophical approach to this understanding has been lacking in modern philosophy, thus requiring Heidegger to restate a "Question of Being" that may penetrate this problem. I can now turn to that point in the first introductory section at which the "Question of Being" is asked, in all of its formal structure.

Heidegger, here, first comments that our "vague average" understanding of the word "being" or "is" finds itself acknowledged as a Fact: "Inquiry, as a kind of seeking, must be guided by what is sought. So the meaning of Being must already be available to us in some way. As I have intimated, we always already conduct our activities within an understanding of Being. Out of this understanding arise both the explicit question of the meaning of Being and the tendency that leads us towards its conception. We do not know what "Being" means. But even if we ask "What is 'Being'?", we keep within an understanding of the "is," though we are unable to fix conceptually what that "is" signifies. We do not even know the horizon in terms of which that meaning is to be grasped and fixed. But this vague average understanding of Being is still a fact" (1928, 5). I have stressed the "we/us" and "always already" in this. For they are determined in correspondence with this understanding of "Being" or of the "is." In the absence of every other determination or presupposition, the "we" at least is that which is open to such an understanding, what is always already accessible to it, and the means by which such a factum can be recognized as such. It automatically follows that this "we"—however simple, discreet and erased or undisclosed it might be—inscribes the so-called formal structure of the "Question of Being" within the horizon of metaphysics.

Given this "formal structure of the Question of Being," the issue, then, is to acknowledge the exemplary being that will constitute the privileged analysand for an analysis of the meaning of Being. And I recall that the formal structure of this question, of any question in fact, must be composed of three instances: what Heidegger calls the *Gefragte*, or that which is asked about—here the meaning of Being; the *Erfragte*, that which is to be found out insofar as it is properly targeted by the question; and finally the *Befragte*, that which is initially interrogated, the being that will be interrogated, to which will be put the meaning of Being. Heidegger, then, asks: "In which entities is the meaning of Being to be discerned? From which entities is the disclosure of Being to takes its departure? Is the starting point optional, or does some particular entity have priority when we come to work out the Question of Being? Which entity shall we take for our example, and in what sense does it have priority?" (1928, 7).

What essentially dictates the answer to this question, though I cannot go into great detail, is Heidegger's own brand of phenomenological approach or heuristic. It is governed by phenomenology's principle of principles—the principle of presence and of the presence in self-presence, such as it is manifested to the being and in the being that we ourselves are. It is in this proximity of being to itself, and our questioning of being to our own being—this familiarity with itself of the being ready to understand Being—that intervenes in Heidegger's choice or deduction of the exemplary being. It is the proximity to itself of the questioning being that leads it to be chosen as the exemplary being. The proximity to itself of the inquirer of this question authorizes the identity of the inquirer and the interrogated. Heidegger's deduction is that we who are close to ourselves, we interrogate ourselves about the meaning of Being: "Thus to work out the question of Being adequately, we must make an entity—the inquirer—transparent in his own Being. The very asking of this question is an entities mode of Being; and as such it gets its essential character from what is enquired about (the *gefragte*)—namely, Being. This entity which each of us is himself and which includes inquiring as one of the possibilities of its Being, we shall denote by the term "*Dasein*." If we are to formulate our question explicitly and transparently, we must first give a proper explication of an entity (*Dasein*) with regard to its Being" (1928, 7).

Ultimately, then, when Heidegger (1928) says he wants to perform a new fundamental ontology of Being, he is talking of what he calls a "hermeneutic phenomenology": a phenomenologico-ontological analysis of the being of *Dasein* that we ourselves are, and by its definition, that leads us to be able to perform the analysis in the first place. It is hermeneutic because it can only ever be a kind of interpretation—a self-interpretation of that being of ours which gives us, uniquely, a complicated presence and self-presence which Heidegger often refers to as our "hermeneutic circle."

I have taken this route to show how Heidegger's construction of his radical notion of human "being" begins with a uniquely ontological "Question of Being" which establishes *Dasein*—literally "that being which is present to/for itself"—as the exemplary being of his fundamental ontology which has as its primary object the very meaning of Being in general. We, as *Dasein*, have the proximity, identity or "self-presence" of the "entity that we ourselves are"—of inquirer and interrogated at once—that allows this unique Question of Being to be put of and to ourselves. *Dasein*, then, does not have the form of some subjective consciousness, as in a transcendent philosophy or transcendental phenomenology. It is also prior to any metaphysical predicate such as "ego," "human" or "soul." For the grounding of this fundamental ontological analytic in *Dasein*, means that *Dasein* is something originary, primordial—it will lay bare "the horizon for an Interpretation of the meaning of Being in general."

It is only with this albeit limited conception of Heidegger's formal approach to *Dasein* in mind, that we can go on to consider the preparatory ontological analysis of *Dasein* that Heidegger presents in the first division of Being and Time (1928), without looking at it as some novel but traditional approach to a characterisation of the subjectivity of the human subject. For it is based in a hermeneutic phenomenological approach to the characterisation of the ontology of Being in general. With this constantly in mind, I will now try to extract some aspects of this analysis that are useful to the import of this overall project.

THE ANALYSIS OF *DASEIN* IN ITS EVERYDAY EXISTENCE

Early in the first division (sections 9 & 12, 1928), Heidegger characterizes the formal aspects of *Dasein* which are fundamental to any ontological understanding of its mode of being, which is the object of the whole of his ensuing analysis. These aspects are "formal indications" of what will both guide that ensuing analysis as well as become more evident through that very analysis. These kinds of "indications," though I cannot really elaborate here, are what are unique to a Heideggerian hermeneutic approach to phenomenological reflection. What is crucial here, before I go on, is Heidegger's distinction between the "ontic" and "ontological" approaches to any knowledge of being. "Ontic" knowledge, briefly, is any kind of theoretical, scientific, naturalistic or empirical knowledge which arises out of contemplation which is somehow detached from, or derivative to, our everyday way of going about in the world. Ontic knowledge is concerned with the "thinghood" of entities or beings. More fundamental to ontic knowledge, then, is the "ontological" knowledge that comes before this. In *Dasein*'s average, everyday existence, any thought or activity it engages in takes the form of a deep embeddedness in what Heidegger calls the "world." This "world," at once, exists through *Dasein*'s activity—its being is determined by *Dasein*'s own mode of being; while it also determines *Dasein*'s mode of being, as a "being-in-the-world." Any ontological knowledge of *Dasein*, then, must be seen in terms of its worldhood—while any knowledge of the world must be seen through the

Dasein for whom the world is the basis for its own mode of being. If this is unclear, all we have to realize is that, of our own being as *Dasein*, while this is defined as having a proximity and presence that is the essential orientation of the ontological analytic of *Dasein*, this proximity, in itself, is ontic. Section 5 of the introduction, in effect, seems not to contradict but rather to limit and contain what was already gained earlier in the introduction, to wit that the *Dasein* "which we are" constitutes the exemplary being for the hermeneutic of the meaning of Being by virtue of its proximity to itself, of our proximity to ourselves, our proximity to the being that we are.

At this point in section 5, Heidegger marks that this proximity is ontic. Ontologically, that is, as concerns the Being of that being which we are, the distance, on the contrary, is as great as possible: "Ontically, of course, *Dasein* is not only close to us—even that which is closest: we are it, each of us, we ourselves. In spite of this, or rather for just this reason, it is ontologically that which is farthest" (1928, 16). In other words, we have a very interesting opposition here. While the ontic proximity of our being to ourselves gives rise to ontic interpretations of our being, these are, in effect detached and derivative, hypothesizing theoretical, scientific . . . ontic subjects of being— "consciousness," the "ego," the "soul" and so on. Conversely, the ontological distance of our being requires a unique and penetrative phenomenological analysis—or Interpretation—to bring it out as explicit.

The ontological analytic of *Dasein*, then, will maintain itself in the space that separates and relates to one another such a proximity and such a distance. This space, in effect, is the interaction of the being of the world of *Dasein*'s worldhood, and the being-in-the-world of *Dasein* itself. It can only be penetrated phenomenologically in a hermeneutic way—our ontological understanding of *Dasein*'s way of Being, that precedes ontic reflection into subjectivity, can only ever give an Interpretation, and not a definitive realisation, of Being. As vague or underdeveloped as this point may be, its relevance will be more clear when it comes to serve us in our understanding of Heidegger's ontological analytic which I will now begin to describe first in terms of those "formal indications" which will structure it.

Heidegger formally terms *Dasein*'s mode of being *Existenz*, or existence. This *Existenz* is alternatively titled the formal "essence" of *Dasein*. In section 12 he characterizes this existence as, firstly, being of an entity which "in its very Being comports itself understandingly towards that Being" (1928, 53). This "formal concept of existence" refers to the way in which *Dasein*, by definition, relates to itself in terms of trying to interpret, understand and define its own Being. This is a self-relation which is ongoing and self-regulating. Heidegger discusses this fundamental self-relation at many different levels.

At the broadest level, this self-relation of *Dasein* to its own being can be understood in terms of a "*Jemeinigkeit*"—a being which is in each case "mine." This means that every way *Dasein* understands itself—in terms of any properties or attributes, roles or identities—is accompanied by a residual notion of "mineness" in that interpretation. This gives these understandings of *Dasein*'s own Being a sense of being unique and unrepeatable in their contexts in the world for *Dasein* (1928, section 9, 41–3).

At another level, this self-relation deals with the way *Dasein* can be seen to be delivered up to its being. Because *Dasein* is a "being-in-the-world," it is constantly bound to various roles and identities which are, in turn, bound to a worldly context—as defined by some location and activity—in such a way that *Dasein* can never predetermine its worldhood in any way. *Dasein* must deal with, adapt and cope with those contexts as they arise—it must deal with whatever the world "throws at it." It is in this way, that though *Dasein*'s worldhood results from the type of being it views itself as at any one point in time (roles, identities, etc.), it is still the type of context, situation or environment that this world delivers up to it that it has to react to at this level. In other words, to deliver up to its being, *Dasein*, as a being-in-the-world, must "cope" with that world which is first delivered up to it.

This self-relation, or "comportment," of *Dasein* to its own Being, then, can be viewed in terms of two notions of "one's own Being." Firstly, there is the sense of the self-relation referring to *Dasein*'s own intimate understanding of its being as a form of role, identity or kind. *Dasein*, for example, can see itself as being a student, a motor mechanic, a male, a lesbian, an *animale rationale* or a human being. And secondly, there is the sense of *Dasein* seeing its being as relating to more context-bound and contingent properties, attributes and relations. *Dasein*, for example, can see itself as a being which is in desperate need of a break from study, is requiring a special type of spanner to finish the job, is running late to a meeting, is happy with the way her relationships are going, is in need of better word processing software, is anxious because it is mortal. In other words, one's self-relation—one's comportment to one's own being—can operate at both levels.

And it is clearly the second sense of comportment which is entailed by the first sense. For the second sense deals with any current context or activity in which *Dasein* finds itself in the world. Its current location and activity—its current "predicament"—is only due to, and is only seen in terms of, that more general first sense of being which "presides" over it. This first sense of comportment as general understanding of role, identity or kind allows *Dasein*'s further understanding of its "predicament" to be specifically due to that general understanding which put it there in the first place; and, more importantly, it allows *Dasein* to apply that understanding to that predicament, in the sense that it will then know how to act (or how it should), what to do, how to interpret its behaviour in the specific activity and location that defines the context of that predicament.

In other words, we can see that in each context or predicament *Dasein* finds itself, where it sees itself as having a particular role or identity, an essential feature of its intelligent behaviour there—its coping with, adapting to, or interpreting of that situation—will be its ability to constantly gauge and negotiate the specific constitution of that situation at any one time, and, moreover, especially in the way that this constitution may change across time (Christensen, 1995, 19–21). When I comport to myself an identity as a student, for example, this entails a whole infinitude of specific, context- and predicament-bound comportments that allow me to engage with the world in that unique and unrepeatable way that is my own activity as a being-in-the-world, one of whose attributes is a *jemeinigkeit* in that general identity or role I am operating with, in a very specific context or situation delivered up to me by the world, which will change both expectedly and unexpectedly across time.

This all lends itself to *Dasein* exhibiting intelligent behaviour in its activity because this comportment is an ongoing and self-correcting process of presiding over its activities, judging their success. It is flexible and adaptive—*Dasein* seeing the appropriateness and relevance of adopting more specific comportments as the need arises. And most importantly, this can only ever be viewed as some kind of intuitive or judgemental skill. For, as is so introspectively (or phenomenologically) clear to ourselves, the predicaments and situations—the world—into which *Dasein* finds itself thrown, will always be different across the contexts, and will vary across time within any one context, that *Dasein* delivers up to itself. This means that *Dasein* can never simply rely on any kind of programmatic rules of how to act in a situation—either given or inferred from past experience. Indeed, at best, these could only ever be rules of thumb, which *Dasein*, itself, would have to judge as being relevant or applicable to its current novel situation or context. And this, to be sure, would be just another aspect of that intuitive kind of skill *Dasein* needs to cope with the world into which it is thrown and up to which it delivers itself.

In this way, the manner in which *Dasein* comports itself up to its own Being is ongoing and self-regulating. The roles and identities it comports to itself are not programmatic in explicitly stipulating the ways *Dasein* should act in any given context—*Dasein* has an idea of the comportment, but it requires a lot of judgemental and intuitive skill to initiate it—bring it about—in the novel contexts that arise. Of course, a lot of this will be ad hoc for *Dasein*—working a lot of specific actions out as new situations arise across time. Indeed, as is phenomenologically clear, the more novel or unexpected the situation, the more ad hoc the comportment may be. This is why *Dasein*'s intuitive skills need to be especially adaptive and open-endedly flexible—for as commonplace and familiar a predicament or context in the world may be, there will always be something novel about it which requires a "coping with."

Dasein does not need to be unambiguously successful—only flexible and able to adapt to the unexpected, as well as its own initial failures and crises in attempting this. Of course, this requirement cannot always be fulfilled by *Dasein*—for just as there is an element of experimentation and adaptation in *Dasein*'s actions, there must be elements of both trial and error—as well as, ultimately, unrecoverable failure. . . .

It only really needs to be noted here, that Heidegger attributes to *Dasein*'s understanding of the roles and identities to which it comports itself, a deep notion of evolution and historicity. Not only are they embedded within the ongoing complexity of *Dasein*'s own existence, but also the evolving history of the culture of *Dasein*. That is, their fluidity—their being adapted, changed, improved—is not only continuing throughout *Dasein*'s own ongoing existence, but has been evolving hitherto over the entire history of the culture of which *Dasein* is a part.

In much the same way, it only needs to be noted that much of Heidegger's analysis of *Dasein* in its everyday existence deals with activities which are discrete and very well defined—dealing with metaphors such as "workshops," being the location of activities such as "hammering," where *Dasein* has a very explicit, though not completely formal, goal, or "towards-which," that it is aiming at. Given that the world is not full of earthy artisans doing such well-defined activities at such well-defined sites, I will try to deal more with the general abilities and comportment of *Dasein* that Heidegger, himself, extracts from these analyses; though it is important to recognize that many important things arise out of them, such as Heidegger's famous distinction between the ontological understanding of objects as interconnected *zeug* ("equipment") having *zuhandensein* ("Being at hand or ready to hand") that commands our undisturbed activity, and the derivative ontic understanding of objects as individual, even theoretical, entities having *vorhandensein* ("Being on hand or present at hand") that arise when creative adjustment fails and there is some kind of breakdown in the activity, requiring some explicit contemplation outside of it to remedy the situation. Avoiding this will help us to get the fullest sense of the intelligent skills of *Dasein* as being intuitive, creative and judgemental in a way that is not programmatic or dealing with explicit rule-based learning.

Therefore, despite the appeal of Heidegger's formal approach to *Dasein*'s existence at such macro- and micro-scopic levels, I will limit the following discussion to an attempt to get a better understanding of the way Heidegger (sections 31–32, 39, 41–42, 1928) characterizes this intuitive ability of *Dasein* to comport itself to its own Being within the everyday, local, indiscrete and changing contexts into which it is thrown in the world. In this way, I will be, in a sense, occupying the general space that resides between those two levels.

PROJECTION AND SIGHT IN *DASEIN'S* UNDERSTANDING

I have sought to establish that *Dasein*, in "comporting to itself its own Being," comports to itself roles and identities that impact upon the way that it interprets itself and its predicament in specific contexts, environments and activities. This self-relation of interpretation in how to act and read situations was described as intuitive and judgemental because it is *Dasein*'s ability to judge what is relevant in the world presently delivered up to it, especially in its relevance for acting effectively or appropriately. Inasmuch as any programmatic rules of action or explicit learned inferences can be used by *Dasein* to cope with current novel situations, they too are all dependent on this ability, for all situations delivered up to *Dasein* will inherently have some forms of unique and unrepeatable qualities not only in how *Dasein* delivers the world up to itself, but in how this world is delivered up to *Dasein*—in the sense that *Dasein* is always "thrown" into a world which is novel, unique and full of unexpected elements.

This ability is at the heart of what Heidegger calls *Dasein*'s "absorbed coping" with the world. Heidegger, invariably, gives it the formal name *Verstandnis*, or "Understanding," in the sense of the German verb *verstehen*—"to be competently able to," "to understand how to" (and not in the sense of an explicit "awareness" or "comprehension"). In this way, Heidegger is referring to this ability as an ability of insight—rather than an expert knowledge or a trained expertise. Furthermore, it must not be confused with any specific aptitude, competence or skill—a kind of "know-how" ability, such as being talented at shearing or motorcycle repair. Though Verstandnis certainly intervenes in any such activity, it is not, in any way, the specific skill, competence or capability itself. This is why, in some ways, Heidegger's constant discussions of artisan activities, such as "hammering," may have been a poorly chosen metaphor to link to *Verstandnis*. For it is only something that allows any possible activity to be performed in a flexible, adaptive and, most importantly, intelligent way.

Across sections 31–32, Heidegger links this general, abstract ability of Verstandnis with the abilities of *Sicht* ("sight") and *Entwurf* ("projection"). At my level of discussion, sight is identifiable with Umsicht ("practical circumspection"), the ability which presides over any activity and allows creative adjustments to be made—a flexible and open-ended approach to the activity that allows *Dasein* to adapt to any changes and novel circumstances that may arise—so that the activity may always be brought to completion—to fruition and the fulfilment of its goal. In terms of Umsicht being characteristic of Verstandnis, it involves no will towards a concrete conceptualisation of the end product or end point of the activity—vis-à-vis a formal "blueprint," image or discursive plan of the completed activity; but, rather, it involves an intuitive "working understanding" of the way the activity is "progressing" towards a completeness—and the way this progression can be further aided, or left unhampered and uninhibited, as opportunities knock or obstacles present themselves.

In other words, in *Dasein*'s everyday absorbed activity, Heidegger is asserting that this intuitive *Umsicht* allows it to flexibly and adaptively "work through" the changing circumstances and novel situations that arise, without ever needing any explicit rules of operation or action, or a concrete conception of the goal of the activity. This *Umsicht* allows *Dasein* to judge how it is progressing precisely in terms of what further things need to be done—this *Umsicht*, furthermore, will see when the activity is complete.

And it is the process that operates when this intuitive Umsicht works its way through activities that Heidegger entitles *Entwurf*. This *Entwurf*, ultimately, is what *Dasein* is conscious of as its overall goal—it is what allows *Dasein* to see in its current situation and circumstances a manifestation of what is progressing towards that goal. In this way, the goal is only ever explicitly known as a "rough sketch" or "intuitive notion" of what is otherwise just appropriately "seen" as something which must be projected towards—something that must be achieved through acting upon what is currently given. When *Dasein* judges that nothing else needs to be done, then the activity has been completed—the goal, previously nothing more than a "towards which," has been attained. Any consciousness or declaration of an explicit goal is only derivative to the underlying "projection" of the "towards which" upon the current circumstances, situation and "predicament" manifesting themselves to *Dasein* in the environment of the activity. They, in a sense, are only ever ontically derived from the preontological "absorbed coping" that is already active.

This ontic level of conscious reflection, however, does become active when the creative and adaptive coping comes across such difficulties that *Dasein* needs to stop in its activity and detachedly reflect on how to go about rectifying the situation so it can go about completing what it was doing.

There are two types of such "breakdown." The first is, in a sense, "temporary breakdown," for it only requires a detached reflection upon the way the activity is being performed and the problems that are arising in it, for it to be recovered again, whereby *Dasein* goes back into a mode of "absorbed coping" in the activity. The second is more a "total breakdown," for it requires an ontic reflection on the nature of the task—its goals and how they are to be achieved, in order for it to be continued. The obstinate problem is analysed individually along with other aspects of the task in a more detached, theoretical way. *Dasein*, here, is said to think of its activity in terms of discrete, theoretical entities—or beings that are *vorhanden*, in order to try and re-establish the progression of the task (see Dreyfus, 1991, 72–83). It must be understood, here, that in both situations detached, ontic reflection is only ever engaged in as a last resort, in order to bring about, again, that effective absorbed coping with the activity over which the *Verstandnis* of *Dasein*'s mode of being presides.

EXISTENZ AND HERMENEUTIC ONTOLOGY

Although we get a very deep sense of the way in which these characteristics of *Dasein*'s *Verstandnis*—these abilities of *Umsicht* and *Entwurf*—are somehow primordial, preontological or ineliminable, it is Heidegger's phenomenological attempt to render these in a discursive way—to give an Interpretation of them—that makes his ontological analysis of *Dasein*'s existence unique. This phenomenological Interpretation can only ever be that—it is *hermeneutic*; but through this, we at least have an explicit sense of aspects of that primordial, fundamental, preontological level of the existing *Dasein* that we ourselves are.

This ontological approach to *Dasein*'s mode of being—*Existenz*—then, offers us a new way of looking at traditional concepts such as "subject" and "object," "consciousness," "ego," "soul" as well as, ultimately, "being." Importantly, *Dasein* is formally characterized by Heidegger as having that fundamental self-relation—that "comporting itself to its own Being"—which, above being directed towards and absorbed in any specific worldly activity or goal in the way I have discussed, is ruled by an inherent and intrinsic "directedness" of its own. This manifests itself in any more specific directedness *Dasein* comports itself towards, whether in the world, to other *Dasein*s in the world, or to itself. Although I cannot really elaborate upon this any more, this unifying "directedness" in *Dasein* is known simply by Heidegger as the "Care Structure": the fact that *Dasein* intrinsically has "concern" in its existence, no matter what this concern may be for, in its dealings and comportments.

At the heart of this is the notion of "Temporality" Heidegger later introduces in Being and Time (sections 61–71, 1928), as well as that of "Ontological Difference" which Heidegger introduces in *The Basic Problems of Phenomenology* (sections 20–21, 1982) around that concept of Temporality. Through these notions, Heidegger wants to assert that *Dasein* is not "in time" like other things in its world—entities other than *Dasein*—are. For *Dasein* is not simply in a "present" which is as a function of its "past," on the way to a "future" which will come to be as a function of that "past and present." Rather, *Dasein*'s existence is uniquely led by its "future"—a "future" which is, in effect, guiding, pulling or directing the present in a particular direction out of its past. Specifically, when *Dasein* is absorbedly coping with a particular task, as I have focussed on, this "future-driven" quality, or "future-directedness," manifests itself in *Dasein*'s ability of *Entwurf* which allows its *Umsicht* to lead it through the task. This overall directedness is seen by Heidegger to be the unifying aspect of all of *Dasein*'s concerns in the world. In this way, *Dasein*'s Being has a unifying "Care Structure" which makes it a "perpetual coming to be" at any possible level. One may be able to see from this, then, just how the *Umsicht* and *Entwurf* that operate in *Dasein*'s *Verstandnis* can be assimilated into these greater unifying notions of "Temporality" and the "Care Structure."

The analysis I have described is one in which Heidegger was Interpreting through his hermeneutic phenomenological approach to *Dasein*'s mode of Being as *Existenz*. It is that Verstandnis whose special ineliminable properties of *Umsicht* and *Entwurf* allow *Dasein*—and we, as *Dasein*—to act in the world in our uniquely intelligent, concerned way. This action, furthermore, must be contained within that formal characteristic of "comportment to one's own Being," that self-relation which, ultimately, is the basis of the *Verhandsin* found in *Dasein*'s mode of Being. It is something which cannot be nomologically understood—something which is ineliminable, intuitive and abstract. It is something that cannot be built up from component abilities in some incremental way. It is not programmatic—understood in terms of explicit rules, algorithms, prototypes, formulae. It is general, global, presiding, primordial. It is a base intuition. It is something that can only ever be Interpreted.

To understand that this is not just a simple assertion on Heidegger's behalf I sought to introduce this in some depth through the formal structure that this concept exists within and in terms of. Heidegger has disclosed it through his hermeneutic phenomenological analysis of *Dasein*'s way of Being within a greater ontological framework driven by a fundamental "Question of Being." I will refer to this as the *hermeneutic ontological* orientation. This means that Heidegger is in no way making assertions about a type of traditional subjectivity conceived of as a "conscious subject" or "transcendental ego" or "human being" or "soul." "Intelligence," here, only has an import as something ontological, within Heidegger's own analytic of the ontology of *Dasein*. This analytic, ultimately, was alluded to as extending to the notion of "Care" which offers a unifying structure to the being that is *Dasein*, understood within that horizon of Temporality that separates *Dasein* off, purportedly, from other beings by virtue of an "Ontological Difference" that resides in Being as a whole.

Having undertaken this relatively detailed exposition to introduce Heidegger's hermeneutic ontological approach, I will now turn to developing this towards the analytical topic of this work. To do this, I intend to cover three themes or domains simultaneously: firstly to map out how Heidegger's project of Being and Time, which remained incomplete, developed and was deviated from in his later, so-call post-*Kehre* works; secondly, how along with this, there were many attempts by other thinkers to explicitly or implicitly transpose his thinking into other philosophical domains and also clinical domains in psychiatry and psychoanalysis; and thirdly, how subsequent philosophers explicitly or implicitly developed or deviated from his ideas but also, in the process, drew reference to psychoanalytic and psychiatric concepts as a part of elucidating their own approaches. In a sense, all of this relates to how Heidegger's hermeneutic ontology came to be understood and interpreted, both by himself in subsequent works, and by other thinkers (philosophers and clinicians). The tensions that arise here, involve the boundaries between hermeneutic approaches as they relate to ontological study, as opposed to related scientific and humanistic disciplines such as historiography, psychology, psychiatry, psychoanalysis, anthropology and so forth which can be seen as ontical. This also relates to the challenge of maintaining the integrity of a hermeneutic ontological standpoint with reference to ontological difference: how much of the richness of existence can be incorporated into this, into understanding the thrownness, finitude, temporality, relationality, facticity and otherness of Being as it relates to *Dasein*.

As such, the following parts of the philosophical part of this work will elaborate further on the Heideggerian project and in each part show how it can potentially be related to the realms of developmental and clinical theory in psychotherapy: firstly in how a psychiatrist attempted to do this (Binswanger) and secondly how various subsequent philosophers have attempted to enrichen Heidegger's thought by way of reference to clinical (psychiatric, psychoanalytic) domains. I will develop a range of ideas and conceptualisations from subsequent philosophers, making this cohesive and systematic by establishing four principle themes that can be applied in the subsequent *Developmental* and *Clinical Frames*: those of *relationality, embodied affectivity, temporality* and *technicity*. This will be a method of developing thought and relating it to our clinical topic without straying too far: this is important given the extraordinary influence Heidegger has had on many fields and thinkers.

Chapter 2

Ludwig Binswanger
Dilemmas Relating Heideggerian Thought to the Human Sciences

Ludwig Binswanger was a Swiss Psychiatrist who maintained a correspondence both with Freud and Heidegger, as he developed his own school of existential psychotherapy based upon Heideggerian thought. It will be useful to analyse Binswanger's project as it is a direct attempt to apply Heideggerian thought to the clinic. Much of Binswanger's work remains untranslated into English so a focus will be on this work as well as the interpretations made of his broader writings by philosopher and analyst Roger Frie. Frie (2003) argues that Binswanger's mature works depart radically from their Heideggerian origins but it will be useful to explore these origins and departures for the purpose of this project.[1]

Let us begin by making reference to Foucault's incisive but nevertheless problematic introductory remarks at the beginning of Binswanger's *"Dream and Existence"*:

> Nothing could be more mistaken than to see in Binswanger's analyses an "application" of the concepts and methods of the philosophy of existence to the "data" of clinical experience. It is a matter, for him, of bringing to light, by returning to the concrete individual, the place where the forms and conditions of existence articulate. Just as anthropology resists any attempt to divide it into philosophy and psychology, so the existential analysis of Binswanger avoids any a priori distinction between ontology and anthropology. One avoids the distinction without eliminating it or rendering it impossible: it is relocated at the terminus of an enquiry whose point of departure is characterized not by a line of division, but by an encounter with concrete existence. . . . To be sure, this encounter, and no less surely, the status that is finally to be assigned to the ontological conditions, pose problems. *But we leave that issue to another time.* We only want to show that one can enter straightway into the analyses of Binswanger and get to what they signify by an approach no less primordial, no less basic, than that by which

> he himself reaches the concrete existence of his patients. Detouring through a more or less Heidegerrian philosophy is not some initiatory rite which might open a door to the esotericism of the analysis of *Dasein*. The philosophical problems are there; but they are not preconditions. (Michel Foucault, 1984–1985, Introduction to *Rêve et Existence*, 32–3)

As already elaborated, at the beginning of *Being and Time* (1928) Martin Heidegger recalls an Ancient and forgotten "Question of Being," and laments the path that modern science and metaphysics have taken in eschewing this fundamental Question. He accords to his ontology of human existence a priority which makes it, at once, so esoteric and so separate from the anthropological and psychological understanding of selfhood and human being of modern times that they are seemingly rendered mutually exclusive. Heidegger (1928) states that the most concrete and, if you will, *primordial*, elements of human existence, represented by *Dasein* and its *being-in-the-world*, are those that are most distant and enigmatic to our understanding. There is a sense, then, in which his "existential analytic of *Dasein* comes *before* any psychology or anthropology, and certainly before any biology" (1928, 71). We *exist* implicitly or tacitly with our Being, but fail to understand it or acknowledge it: we are, thus, *pre-Ontological*.

As already discussed, for Heidegger it is always more practical and obvious for us to conceptualize ourselves *ontically*. Ontical enquiry concerns physical, factual entities that are understood theoretically and the facts discovered about them. We have a tendency to this form of enquiry: we remove ourselves from our everyday environments in order to theorize the selves and the world we perceive, contemplate each empirically or naturalistically as separate, objective *entities*. An ontological analytic of our existence, conversely, captures something deeper and *existentially prior*. It is purported to be foundational, to do with the very question of the nature of Being *per se*, and not beings *as* entities in a natural world (and man *qua homo natura*).[2] It requires a deeper hermeneutic-phenomenological analytic to arrive at this *ontological* understanding, overcoming our tendency to objectify and theorize. This ontological enquiry is foundational because it follows from the unique and basic characteristic of human *Being*: we are beings for whom our own *Being* is an issue.

The question remains as to the import and meaning of what is achieved by this analytic. Heidegger refers to the enmeshment of ontical enquiry and practical application: ontical enquiry emerges from and services the exigencies and demands of practical activity (viz. the symbiotic relation of science and technology). He endorses the positive findings of ontical enquiry, its utility and applicability, but undermines any pretensions it may have to ontological *truth* on the part of its practitioners. When we consider the practical domain of the *Geistwissenschaften*, fields of application such as psychiatry, law and penal practice, particular conflicts arise for this Heideggerian distinction between the ontological and the ontic. The ontical enquiry behind these fields (psychology, jurisprudence, criminology correspondingly) is what is most proximate to Heidegger's ontological analytic: *Dasein* as Being for whom its own existence is an issue, takes its first steps of self-understanding ontically through such fields. Heidegger's analytic is purported to plumb an understanding that is more primordial and primary. And yet fields such as psychology and anthropology may share the methods of enquiry Heidegger's analytic adopts: they can engage in hermeneutic and phenomenological investigations and not be purely naturalistic or scientifically objective; they may confront phenomenological questions, questions of selfhood and authenticity, that are not altogether removed from Heidegger's own analytic. Questions of method and foundation thus arise when one attempts to differentiate an ontological analytic from an anthropological or psychological one. These questions, of necessity, make one want to ask whether the ontological analytic is, *a priori*, always removed from, or beyond, or irrelevant to, those practical fields, such as psychiatry, to which a psychological or anthropological analytic may apply itself. And this is our principal interest, here: *whether Heidegger's ontological analytic is germane to a clinician's work with concrete individuals and putative "mental" illnesses.*

The Swiss psychiatrist Ludwig Binswanger, claimed to pursue his own clinical work from a Heideggerian inspiration. He identifies his approach, *Daseinsanalyse*, as a clinical correlate of Heidegger's ontology of *Dasein*. Most simply and obviously, this is seen in each of Binswanger's case studies in which he eruditely reflects upon the circumstances and history of a concrete, individual *Dasein*. What is most curious about this "manifestation" of Heideggerian thought is the seeming contradictoriness of particularizing and objectifying Heidegger's ontological concepts within a clinical domain which characteristically underpins its work ontically. How does one begin to approach this contradiction without knee-jerk appeals to bastardization and pretentiousness?

Our attention is drawn to the opening quotation, taken from Foucault's extended introduction to Binswanger's existential analysis of dreams. It encapsulates the pith and heart of our exploration here.[3] Foucault is very apt to point out the fallacy of criticizing Binswanger's work as merely an applied Heideggerianism. Indeed, there would be something fallacious and self-defeating about this kind of clinical approach. The crucial issue, here, is the notion of *anthropology*, a notion that Binswanger uses himself to characterize his work (it being an "existential anthropology"). For Heidegger, the term "anthropology" represents an exponent of the *Geistwissenschaften*: he links it to the Helleno-Christian and Modern theological and hermeneutic traditions.[4] For Binswanger, however, it can be used to describe an existential analytic which bears a direct relation to the *Daseinanalytik* of *Being and Time*. This relation Foucault characterizes well when he describes the nature of Binswanger's existential anthropology:

> Nothing could be more mistaken than to see in Binswanger's analyses an "application" of the concepts and methods of the philosophy of existence to the "data" of clinical experience. It is a matter, for him, of bringing to light, by returning to the concrete individual, the place where the forms and conditions of existence articulate. Just as anthropology resists any attempt to divide it into philosophy and psychology, so the existential analysis of Binswanger avoids any a priori distinction between ontology and anthropology. (1984–1985, 32)

The very issue, then, is the impact that the avoidance of a distinction between ontology and anthropology has for Binswanger's work and its relationship to Heidegger's own *analytik*. If Binswanger unqualifyingly adopts Heidegger's ontological formulations of *being-in-the-world*, he is, in a sense, suspending the issue of their appropriateness to an existential analysis levelled directly at concrete individuals and case histories. Foucault describes this headstrong ignorance of the distinction between the anthropological and ontological by way of entering into the clinical milieu thus:

> One avoids the distinction without eliminating it or rendering it impossible: it is relocated at the terminus of an enquiry whose point of departure is characterized not by a line of division, but by an encounter with concrete existence.... To be sure, this encounter, and no less surely, the status that is finally to be assigned to the ontological conditions, pose problems. *But we leave that issue to another time.* (1984–1985, 33)

Indeed, Foucault never returned to this issue of the adequacy of Binswanger's analytic to its ontological conditions. This is the very issue that will be explored here: the appropriateness and adequacy of Binswanger's existential-clinical analytic seen in relation to Heideggerian ontological conditions. Whilst one can agree with Foucault that "Heidegerrian philosophy is not some initiatory rite which might open a door to the esotericism of the analysis of *Dasein*" as, for example, Binswanger conducts this clinically. And one can, with Foucault, acknowledge that this essentially "philosophical" problem is not a precondition to the legitimacy of all that Binswanger did. However, the residual philosophical problem is of interest insofar as it relates back to the correct understanding of what is *ontological* for Heidegger, and whether this ontology can inform notions of illness, difference, embodiment and sexuality (to name a few concepts that are largely absent from the *Daseinanalytik*) in some kind of clinical-anthropological domain. Furthermore, given the

Heideggerian criticism of traditional forms psychological and anthropological enquiry, one is entitled to ask if a closer reading of *Being and Time*, can in some way inform a psychotherapist's work—help the psychotherapist avoid or overcome traditional or habitual errors of understanding.

I will begin by extending further some notions from Heidegger's (1928) analytic—to allow us to frame our exposition of Binswanger's *Daseinsanalyse*. It will present an ontological thematic from the *Daseinsanalytik*: the thematic of the authenticity of moodfulness (*Befindlichkeit*). I will then attempt to offer an exegesis of certain aspects of Binswanger's mature works of *Daseinsanalyse*. This will establish Binswanger's project as an existential analysis of "structures" or "modes" of being-in-the-world—what Binswanger calls *world-designs* (*Welt-entwerfen*). Binswanger wanted this form of existential *Daseinsanalyse* to precede or frame the work of clinical psychopathology. I will conclude our discussion by exploring the tensions and conflicts of this tripartite relation of *Daseinsanalytik–Daseinsanalyse–Clinical Psychopathology*. Particular attention will be paid to this intermediary form of existential analysis sitting, as it does, between a formal analytic of Being and a clinical engagement with concrete individuals. I will attempt to make some conclusions about such an existential analysis based upon our own Heideggerian exposition and our critical analysis of Binswanger's work....

HEIDEGGER: *BEFINDLICHKEIT* AND AUTHENTICITY

Heidegger describes the ontic givenness of empirical psychology and other human sciences as a form of *Vorhnanden-sein* (presence-to-hand). For these ontic approaches, it seems obvious to describe human existence as a self-encapsulated entity, a theoretical object, with notions such as "ego," "psyche," "mind," "consciousness" and "subject." These notions possess a dualistic complementarity with notions such as "the physical world," "the body" and "the other." Heidegger's ontological analytic begins with the notion of *Da-Sein*, literally *being-there*. This notion refers to a *being-in-the-world* in which primacy is given to the phenomena of worldhood, of the meaning that is disclosed in an existence which already finds itself thrown into its worldhood. In other words, Being is always situational and relational: here, worldliness, embodiment and human interaction are always already ready-to-hand (*zuhanden*). *Dasein* only understands itself theoretically in terms of *Vorhnanden-sein* when it takes pause from this everyday immersion in the *Zuhnanden-sein* of worldhood. This removal may be for different reasons to do with contemplation, breakdown or crisis.

In its immediate, worldly existence, *Dasein* is described as having three fundamental modes (*Existenziale*) of existence which interact and combine:

those of *Befindlichkeit* (state of mind, moodfulness), *Verstehen* (understanding) and *Rede* (discourse or speech). The former of these three is of most interest to our enquiry here insofar as it establishes the ontological basis of mood and affect for Heidegger.

Befindlichkeit is Heidegger's own neologism developed from the German colloquial verb *befinden*. This verb is used in the everyday question "Wie befinden Sie sich?," which broadly translates as "How are you?." There is no literal translation of this question into English as the verb refers to, at once, *feeling* and *finding oneself*, such that "Wie befinden Sie sich?" literally means "How are you feeling?" at the same time as "How do you find yourself?." In adapting this verb, Heidegger wants to capture an expression that embodies states of mind, mood states, as a type of *feeling* and *finding oneself situated*. By describing moods as a kind of *situatedness*, he is attempting to overcome a sense of inwardness or depth (moods being *intrapsychic*, if you will). *Befindlichkeit* refers to a state that is both inward and outward looking. Moreover, such states are self-referential: one *finds oneself* in this state; it is self-interpreted actively and is an issue for oneself. This self-understanding is not cognitive so much as an implicit, lived-in awareness: it is interpreted by *Dasein*. Thus *Dasein* always has the potential for an implicit understanding (*Verstehen*) of its state. And moreover, this understanding is articulated through *Dasein*'s discourse (*Rede*). It is in this manner that the three *Existenziale* interact. One exists with mood states: we feel a moodful situatedness of which we may have an implicit understanding that can be articulated in our discourse with others and ourselves. Thus the situatedness of *Befindlichkeit* is interactional, interpersonal and implicitly self-reflective: *Befindlichkeit* embodies the wholeness of *Dasein*'s situatedness and is prior to an explicit understanding that would distinguish inner and outer, self and other, feeling and cognition, or speech and action. Understanding and discourse always belie a state of *Befindlichkeit*.

And so, how is this ontological notion of *Befindlichkeit* something different to, more primordial and essential than, the ontic conceptualizations of mood states we find in psychological theories, which refer to affects, moods and emotions? These conceptualizations are, indeed, linked back to *vorhanden* concepts like "self," ego," "subject": they are, in fact, *attributes* of these thing-like concepts. Yet they do nevertheless refer to the Being of *Befindlichkeit* and arise out of our own theoretical contemplation of *Befindlichkeit*. Heidegger would hold that he attempts, through his ontological reflection, to illuminate something different in his analytic of primordial *Befindlichkeit*.

Much of the formal ontology of *befindlichkeit* relates to its temporality. Heidegger describes the temporality of *Dasein* in terms of its thrownness. The German word for this is *entwerfen*, which refers to, at once, "sketching," "throwing out," and "projecting." By using such a term to characterize the temporal nature of *Dasein*, Heidegger wants to highlight the fact that *Dasein* is always already situated in a context that has a coming-to-be (a past) and a going-to-be (a future): it is simultaneously future-oriented and past-oriented. That's to say, it is always an implicitly goal-oriented, futural process, that is nevertheless always grounded and contextualized in a past "having-been." *Dasein* does not exist as an "I-thing" prior to this temporal, goal-driven, *thrown* process that is *entwerfen*. This temporal *entwerfen*, this ecstatic horizon of Being, is fundamental to *Dasein's* worldhood.

And so, when Heidegger describes the thrownness of *Dasein*, one element is that of *Befindlichkeit*: *Dasein* finds itself thrown in a particular state of *Befindlichkeit*. Indeed, *Befindlichkeit* and thrownness are mutually dependent[5]:

> My mood represents whatever may be the way in which I am primarily the entity that has been thrown.... One's mood discloses in the manner of turning thither or turning away from one's own *Dasein*. Bringing *Dasein* face to face with the "that-it-is" of its own thrownness—whether authentically revealing it or inauthentically covering it up—becomes existentially possible only if *Dasein's* Being, by its very meaning, constantly *is* as having been. The "been" is not what brings one face to face with the thrown entity that one is oneself; but the ecstasis of the "been" is what first makes it possible to find oneself in the way of having *Befindlichkeit*. (1928, 340)

It is interesting to note, here, the notion of *authenticity* that Heidegger inserts into his discussion of a temporal *Befindlichkeit*. Authenticity requires that one bring oneself before how one already is, one's *having-been*. *Dasein* is, in a sense, already disclosed in its mood... *Befindlichkeit* is primarily past-oriented. One is *authentic* by going after, projecting towards, what the mood discloses. Here, *Verstehen* is the futural exponent of *Befindlichkeit*: one understands one's *Befindlichkeit* by authentically projecting one's being futurally in a manner that is consistent with it, reveals it; or inauthentically in a manner that is inconsistent with it and masks it. Formally, this is quite abstract and elusive. What is most interesting for our exploration here is that Heidegger begins to elaborate all of this by discussing specific mood states. This is relevant to us because it may be the part of Heidegger's analytic that is most proximate to an ontology of what we understand ontically as psychic illness. To go into this I begin by exploring Heidegger's analysis of the fundamental mood states of fear and anxiety.

Heidegger makes the simple distinction that fear is an *inauthentic* and anxiety an *authentic* form of *Befindlichkeit*. Authenticity, here, relates to *Befindlichkeit* because *Befindlichkeit* represents potentiality for Being, a form of relation to one's *having-been* that opens up futural potentialities. One *understands* how one is disclosed in one's *Befindlichkeit* by understanding how one *has been* up until now. This understanding implicitly leads to the way in which one projects oneself into future possibilities in the world: *Verstehen* affects the manner in which we relate to our world and our being futurally. *Befindlichkeit* and *Verstehen* are thus interlocked and form the potential for a kind of self-consistency or self-constancy that is temporal in nature. But this temporal interlocking of past-oriented *Befindlichkeit* and future-oriented *Verstehen* can also enveil *Dasein* in an inauthentic form of self-deceit which loses sight of self-constancy and potentiality.

Heidegger, here, first demonstrates the inauthenticity of fear. Fear, as a form of *Befindlichkeit*, shows *Dasein* backing away from its potentiality-for-being: one feels threatened from without, is bewildered, and loses a sense of oneself as *having-been*. By fearfully forgetting oneself, one *understands* the world inauthentically by clinging on to notions such as self-preservation, or a bewilderment. Heidegger analyses this state of *Befindlichkeit* in some detail but illustrates one facet of it quite brilliantly by discussing the fearful behaviour of inhabitants in a burning house: some will be stunned and bewildered and not know what to do; some will act purely in the interests of self-preservation and the preservation of others; while some will seek to preserve the most indifferent things that *merely represent* one's *having-been* that are close to hand, such as treasured objects or photographs (1928, 140–2 ;340–6). Heidegger's analysis does not attempt to in some way negatively valorize *fear* (its exigency and terror) so much as characterize *Dasein's* relation to the potentiality of its Being when it finds itself in this state, in comparison to other states of *Befindlichkeit*. Fear is inauthentic simply because it is a state in which *Dasein forgets* its potentiality-for-being. The initial comparison, here, is with a more *authentic* state of Being that emerges in the state of anxiety: "Fear is occasioned by entities with which we concern ourselves environmentally. Anxiety, however, springs from *Dasein* itself. When fear assails us, it does so from what is within-the-world. Anxiety arises out of Being-in-the-world. As thrown Being-towards-death (1928, 344)."

Anxiety, for Heidegger, represents a resolute state of *Befindlichkeit* that is the antithesis of fear: "he who is resolute knows no fear; but he understands the possibility of anxiety as the possibility of the very mood which neither inhibits nor bewilders him. Anxiety liberates him *from* possibilities which 'count for nothing', and lets him become free *for* those which are authentic" (1928, 344). Thus, anxiety is a *clearing* of worldly concern, an openness to the possibility of one's world and one's thrownness.

> The forgetting which is constitutive for fear, bewilders *Dasein* and lets it drift back and forth between 'worldly' possibilities which it has not seized upon. In contrast to this making-present which is not held on to, the Present of anxiety

is such that it cannot lose itself in something with which it might be concerned. If anything like this happens in a similar state-of-mind, this is fear, which the everyday understanding confuses with anxiety. . . . Anxiety merely brings one into the mood for a *possible* resolution. (1928, 344)

The fact that this state is linked to the primary horizon of *Dasein*'s thrownness, its Being-towards-death, does not mean that death, as the ultimate clearing, is the foremost or only authentic action. Rather, death, as *Dasein*'s horizon, is *understood* in a manner that influences the past-oriented *Befindlichkeit* of anxiety, which in turn, comes to further influence one's understanding and futural concern for one's world: "Anxiety discloses an insignificance of the world; and this insignificance reveals the nullity of that which one can concern oneself—or, in other words, the impossibility of projecting oneself upon a potentiality-for-Being which belongs to existence and which is founded primarily upon one's objects of concern. The revealing of this impossibility, however, signifies that one is letting the possibility of an authentic potentiality-for-Being be lit up (1928, 343)."

In other words, the authenticity of anxiety lies in the forgetting of objects of concern, their insignificance being disclosed in the face of Being-towards-death. This creates the potentiality for authentic Being. This potentiality requires an *understanding* that projects an attempt at the realization of what is disclosed in *Befindlichkeit*. This linking of *Verstehen*, *Befindlichkeit* (and *Rede*) has, in a sense, the potential to be a constantly evolving temporal process of self-realization. It also establishes the freedom of authenticity.

Heidegger's broader analysis of authenticity is not important to us here.[6] We have understood that *Dasein*'s *Jemeinigkeit*, its "mineness" or "own self-sameness," can be pursued authentically or withdrawn from inauthentically as *Dasein* negotiates its being in the world. This relates primarily to *Dasein*'s temporal relationship to its thrownness. Heidegger describes this relationship as the basic ontological structure of self-constancy in *Dasein*. This very temporal process of self-constancy in *Dasein*'s worldhood is what he calls *Dasein*'s *Care*. It would be understood ontically as the continuity and constancy of *selfhood*, what constitutes a subject's individuality or personality as self-same diachronically. Just as Heidegger does not explore the specific experiential causes of fear or anxiety (an *ontic* analysis) so much as the primordial structures of these states (an *ontological* analysis), he does not describe Care in such a manner that an ontic analysis of selfhood, or psyche, is achieved (whereby a schema of personality, or a depth psychology is mapped to describe human selfhood). As an ontological structure, *Care* simply represents *Dasein*'s temporal relation to its worldhood. Nor does he go on to refer to other states of *Befindlichkeit* except fleetingly:

> How is a temporal meaning to be found in a pallid lack of mood which dominates the 'grey everyday' through and through? And how about the temporality of such moods and affects as hope, joy, enthusiasm, gaiety? Not only fear and anxiety, but other moods, are founded existentially upon one's having been; this becomes plain if we merely mention such phenomena as satiety, sadness, melancholy, and desperation. Of course these must be Interpreted on the broader basis of an existential analytic of *Dasein* that has been well worked out. (1928, 345)

What Heidegger has offered us here is the structure of an *ontological* analytic of mood. The temporal process of *Dasein*'s Being, in its manifold structure of *Care*, is the basis of *Dasein*'s self-constancy. *Befindlichkeit*, one's *having-been*, is related to in the thrownness of the present and affords the opportunity for either an *inauthentic* abandonment or an *authentic* resoluteness in relation to futural projection as being-towards-death.[7] Authenticity is the realization of the potential to realize what is disclosed in one's *Befindlichkeit*, to become "what one is."

This analytic is the most that Heidegger offers in the first two divisions of *Being and Time* a propos of the ontological basis of what may be understood ontically as psychic illness. This analytic of *authenticity*, as it is understood within the self-constancy of *Care*, may provide the basis of an exploration of other mood states ontologically but Heidegger does not entertain this. And I am not necessarily interested in this, either, as I am not intending to establish the possibility of a mere "Heideggerian application" here. Because I am clinically motivated, I must now tackle the problem from the other side, entertain a psycho-anthropological approach, confront the "data" of clinical experience and concrete individuals, "the place where the forms and conditions of existence articulate." I will now confront the clinical work of Ludwig Binswanger, whose existential analysis "avoids any a priori distinction between ontology and anthropology." I enter this in good faith, believing with Foucault that one can avoid "the distinction without eliminating it or rendering it impossible: it is relocated at the terminus of an enquiry whose point of departure is characterized not by a line of division, but by an encounter with concrete existence. . . ."

BINSWANGER: *DASEINSANALYSE* AND WORLD DESIGN

When Binswanger specifies the relationship between his *Daseinsanalyse* and the psychopathology of psychiatry, he states that the former engages in a form of analysis prior to distinctions between health and illness, and prior to objectivist or inductivist approaches: "*Daseinsanalyse* distinguishes itself from psychopathology not only in that it does not proceed with objective–discursive and inductive methods to examine an ensouled organism, but rather seeks a phenomenological interpretation of existential forms and structures. It also differs in that it assiduously ignores the biologically oriented distinction between sick and healthy (1963, 110)."

Daseinsanalyse is thus prior to scientific psychopathology because it is *existential*. And yet, Binswanger is always careful to delineate between his *Daseinsanalytic* approach and Heidegger's own *Daseinanalytik*:

> Existential analysis (*Daseinsanalyse*, as we speak of it) must not be confused with Heidegger's analytic of existence (*Daseinsanalytik*). The first is a hermeneutic exegesis on the ontic-anthropological level, a phenomenological analysis of actual human existence. The second is a phenomenological hermeneutic of Being understood as existence, and moves on an ontological level. The similarity of the expressions is justified by the fact that the anthropological or existential analysis relies throughout on that structure of existence as being-in-the-world which was first worked out by the analytic of existence. (1958, 270)

At this point, here, Binswanger is situating his work in between the strictly ontic domain of objectivist–inductivist psychopathology and the strictly ontological domain of Heidegger's *Daseinsanalytik*. *Daseinsanalyse* seems to share something with each: with the former it shares a practical and empirical engagement with concrete individuals in a clinical setting; and with the latter it shares an engagement with human existence through hermeneutic/phenomenological analysis. Combining these two forms of engagement we have what Binswanger calls a form of "hermeneutic exegesis on the ontic-anthropological level, a phenomenological analysis of actual human existence." It is not ontological because it is concerned with actual human existence, concrete individuals, and not Being *per se*. And by eschewing "objective–discursive and inductive methods" to favour a "phenomenological interpretation of existential forms and structures," it finds itself in a unique ontic-anthropological domain.

Of interest, here, is the nature of this domain—what Binswanger confronts in human existence and draws out clinically from concrete individuals through hermeneutic-phenomenological analysis. Foucault aptly pointed out that Binswanger's work suspends the distinction between the ontological and anthropological. We see above, and I can verify elsewhere, that Binswanger never claims to be analysing at an *ontological level*. But, as I will show, the existential forms and structures he claims to draw out and interpret at the *ontic level* are mostly described as *ontological*. These axes—the ontic-ontological and the ontological–anthropological—will be of primary interest. What could it mean to have a clinical analysis that is a form of "regional ontology" performed at the *ontic level*? To reflect upon these ambivalences, we must first immerse ourselves in *Daseinsanalyse*, its concrete case studies and the "existential forms and structures" it elucidates, in order to arrive at a point when I can begin to make these assessments. . . .

Daseinsanalyse's central construct is that of the *Welt-Entwurf* or "World-Design" of each individual. Binswanger states that this concept is of a Heideggerian derivation and seems to be a synthesis of *Dasein*'s *worldhood* (*Weltlichkeit*) as thrownness and *entwerfen*:

> *Dasein*, although it exists essentially for its own sake (*umwillen seiner*), has nevertheless not itself laid the ground of its *being*. And also, as a creature "come into existence," it is, and remains, *thrown*, determined, i.e., enclosed, possessed, and compelled by beings in general. Consequently it is not "completely free" in its world-design either. The "powerlessness" of *Dasein* here shows itself in that certain of its possibilities of being-in-the-world are *withdrawn* because of commitment to and by beings, because of its facticity. But it is also just this withdrawal that lends the *Dasein* its *power*: for it is this that first brings *before Dasein* the "real," graspable possibilities of world-design. (1963, 212)

Binswanger seems to capture, here, the conflict between facticity and freedom that underpins the idea of authenticity as I elucidated it earlier. The fact that Heidegger did not use this term, *Welt-Enwurf,* as a description of worldhood will be of much interest after I have established the centrality of the notion for Binswanger's analyses. He characterizes this centrality thus:

> We know that we have to ascertain the kind of spatialization and temporalization, of lighting and coloring; the texture, or materiality and motility, of the world-design toward which the given form of existence or its individual configuration casts itself. Such a methodical clue can be furnished only by the structure of *being-in-the-world* because that structure places a norm at our disposal and so enables us to determine deviations from this norm in the manner of the exact sciences. (1958, 201)

Thus Binswanger's analyses are somehow a weighing up of specific, individual *world-designs*, against a normative or universal *being-in-the-world*. These analyses are best exemplified in the case histories of his *Schizophrenie*, and I will look at "The Case of Lola Voss" in some detail here. They are all exercises in characterizing and analysing the limitedness and self-restrictedness of individual *World-Designs*: the outcome when *Dasein* flees into a static, restricted, narrowed *World-Design*. To continue the quotation above, we follow Binswanger's own description of the achievement of these analyses:

> Much to our surprise it has turned out that, in the psychoses which were so far investigated, such deviations could not be understood merely negatively as

abnormalities, but that they, in turn, represent a new norm, a new *form* of being-in-the world. . . . To explore and ascertain the world of these patients means, here as everywhere, to explore and ascertain in what way everything that is—men as well as things—is accessible to these forms of existence. For we know well enough that that-which-is as such never becomes accessible to man, except in and through a certain world-design. (1958, 201)

This relationship between *world-design* and *being-in-the-world* is of crucial importance as it represents, at the same time, the locus of clinical explanation for Binswanger, and the locus of correspondence between Binswanger's ontic-anthropological *Daseinanalyse* and Heideggerian ontology. I will treat these analyses of *world-designs* as purely *descriptive*, as Binswanger seems to. The clinical imperatives of therapy and cure, that Binswanger introduces, will be discussed only briefly afterward.

In "The Case of Lola Voss," Binswanger recounts the history of a woman who becomes obsessed with the notion that people and events in the world represent "signs" to be read and interpreted, all seeming to indicate, for her, a doomed existence. Lola fatalistically reads these signs as the threats of exterior, alien forces, signs that portend for her a singular meaning and destiny in her life. Binswanger describes the phenomenology of Lola's constant interrogation of the world for the meaning of fate in terms of *mundanization*: "In the case of Lola, we could observe in an extreme degree the phenomenon of what we call mundanization (*Verweltichung*), a process in which the *Dasein* is abandoning itself in its actual, free potentiality of being-itself, and is giving itself over to a specific world-design (1963, 284)."

In *Schizophrenie*, Binswanger wants to describe all cases of psychosis as the formation of an ideal world-design, which he describes elsewhere as a form of *extravagance*. At the root of this ideal-formation is the abandonment of potentiality-for-being. He thus goes on to say that:

> Far from widening or deepening the ability of being-oneself, the Extravagant ideal restricts the possibilities of being-oneself, so much so that the existence is only able to be itself within quite specific, ever narrower limits; outside these limits it becomes more and more dependent and bonded, that is, squeezed in a vice of a single world-design or world-model . . . What all such cases have in common is that, to express it in everyday language, they are not able to harmonize ideal and reality . . . Becoming overwhelmed in this sense finds its extreme expression in the phenomenon of delusion. (1963, 285)

Lola is commanded by strange voices to do certain things to protect herself against the uncertainty of existence and the potentiality of her own being. Lola constructs a "system of verbal symbols," *signs*, by which she is able to interpret the single "meaning" of her existence, the fate to which it is driven through this language of signs she lives through and interprets. This "fate," for Lola, is never altogether clear: it is not a single event or catastrophe so much as a doomed, threatened fearful *holding-chaos-at-bay*, a *warding-off* of chaos with a constant interrogation of signs, constantly fearful and cautious about this so as to avoid the nameless unspeakable doom of not doing so. Her world becomes a self-enclosed, self-referential "homogeneity of symbolic reference."

Her engagement in reading this idealistic, homogenous, self-referential system of signs represents, for Binswanger, the *fleeing* from or *abandonment* of *Dasein*'s own capacity to realize its potentiality authentically *in* the world. Alluding to our narrative of authenticity above, the *anxiety* of authentic becoming has been avoided and supplanted by the most inauthentic, idealistic becoming of *fear*. In this sense, one attains an inauthentic control over authentic anxiety. The extremity of the dissonance of maintaining this self-referential, closed system *qua World-Design*, in the face of one's being-in-the-world, is at the heart of the extreme phenomena of psychosis.

The other cases in *Schizophrenie*, of Ellen West and Jürg Zünd, are phenomenologically quite different but thematically or structurally identical. Thus in a phenomenological interpretation of existential forms and structures a uniformity is understood. Once this uniformity is understood: "the task of psychopathology is therefore to assimilate the material offered to it by *Daseinsanalyse*, to categorize it, to test it and to articulate it" (1963, 110).

By elucidating Binswanger's approach to *Daseinsanalyse* in this manner, I acknowledge that I have robbed it of much of its colour. Each analysis is tripartite, composed of the *Case History*, *Existential Analysis* (my primary concern) and a *Psychopathological-Clinical Analysis*. My parsimony has overlooked the narrativity of his *Case Histories*, which have extensive explorations of interviews with the patients, analyses of their writings, anecdotal descriptions of incidents in the sanitoria and outside, and the involvement of other, often famous, clinicians (Bleuler, Minkowski, Jung, Janet). And my description of the *Existential Analysis* of Lola Voss ignores the very eclectic and peripatetic musings that cross multiple themes and the writings of many clinicians and theorists. And, I have overlooked questions of therapy and cure which inevitably arise in the third and final part of the analysis, when the *Psychopathological-Clinical Analysis* is performed. The fact that questions of treatment emerge here is interesting because it invariably involves a retreat into conventional psychopathological descriptions and therapies, and often a very fatalistic or pacifistic clinical outlook (at least in relation to psychosis). It would seem that existential analysis becomes involved descriptively as an anamnetic, and not a therapeutic, method—Binswanger engaging in *Daseinsanalyse* with the relish of a philosopher or descriptive psychologist. The structural unity he determines in his phenomenological investigation of the case histories, through a form of existential-anthropological analysis, purportedly has an instructive or even heuristic value in the psycho-pathological clinical domain. One recalls that Binswanger says "the task of psychopathology is therefore to assimilate the material offered to it by *Daseinsanalyse*, to categorize it, to test it and to articulate it" (1963, 110). I should conclude this section with an attempt to describe this heuristic value. . . .

Towards the end of "The Case of Lola Voss," Binswanger makes the following summary of the fundamental existential finding or motif of his *Schizophrenie* studies and its treatment of delusions:" . . . we can approach the scientific understanding of the delusions only if we recognize that we are dealing with a certain mode of decapacitation or, to use a synonym, with a certain mode of mundanization. We say expressly, "a certain mode!" Therefore, it is our task to demonstrate and describe precisely each stage of this process of decapacitation while considering all possible structural links in the structure of the existence of the being-in-the-world (1963, 336–7)."

Binswanger establishes this interpretation of *decapacitation* or *mundanization* as the existential structure behind not only psychotic phenomena but also neurotic phenomena. It is, in fact, a structure or schema with which one can begin to understand any of the phenomena that come to be characterized as *psychopathological*. Existential analysis becomes an analysis of structure and structural links of world-designs within being-in-the-world. And for the clinic, what is most pertinent to this structure for us relates to the universal existential thematic of anxiety:

> I have shown that, like the genuine phobias, delusions can only be understood in terms of existential anxiety . . . World no longer means the totality of conditions that the existence has taken in its stride, but a condition definitely determined by the being as something frightful, a condition of hostility, of something that is, once and for all, hostile or threatening. It is a world design that is no longer carried by nor bears any traces of love and trust, or of the closeness to humans and things that results from these feelings. (1963, 337)

When Binswanger counterpoises fear, fright and hostility with love, faith and trust it would seem that he has the Heideggerian analytic of authenticity in mind. Here, the decapacitation or mundanization of being-in-the-world is an inauthentic *abandonment* of the world: "It was existential anxiety that drained this existence . . . that forced all its resources into the service of the war against anxiety. It threw the existence into misery and placed it under compulsion, the compulsion to ward off anxiety at any cost . . . this means that existential anxiety has cut off the existence from its deepest roots" (1963, 322–3). Thus, the structures Binswanger focuses upon in his existential analyses, these *world-designs*, present themselves within a Heideggerian analytic of authenticity and anxiety. *World-designs* perform a function of inauthentic abandonment and *mundanization* in the face of an authentic anxiety that becomes overpowering. The intricacies of the relationship between the maintenance of these *world-designs* and everyday being-in-the-world is the basis of phenomena that are of interest to ontic psychopathology. These phenomena represent the slippage between the norm of being-in-the-world and an extreme form of inauthenticity. Binswanger elucidates all of these phenomena (delusions, phobias, hallucinations, obsessions, flights of ideas, *inter alia*) from this basic structure.

To explain the heuristic value of Binswanger's existential-phenomenological analysis any further, one would need to ask very specific questions to do with method. Indeed, at this juncture of the exposition I have arrived at that terminus where I can finally begin to ask and answer questions that concern the distinction between the ontological and the anthropological that Binswanger has, in a sense, suspended when he has turned to "the concrete individual, the place where the forms and conditions of existence articulate." These questions, in particular, relate to the ontological status of Binswanger's notion of "world design" as it is applied to his existential-phenomenological investigations; and, more broadly, to the position of these investigations with regard to the Heideggerian distinction between the ontic and the ontological.

FINAL COMMENTS: DILEMMAS AND POSSIBILITIES ARISING FROM BINSWANGER'S ADOPTION OF HEIDEGGERIAN PHILOSOPHY

As stated from the outset, it is not at all accurate or appropriate to look at Binswanger's *Daseinsanalyse* as the application of Heideggerian ontology to the ontic level. The issue of ontic-ontological difference relates to Binswanger's work because it is a clinico-anthropological study of human individuals in their concrete existence that nevertheless wishes to contextualize itself within Heidegger's own analytic of Being. Binswanger refers to ontological concepts when he explores the existential *structure* of the lived experience of a concrete human *being* as a variant or modification of a universal *Being*. *Daseinsanalyse* thus suspends the distinction between an anthropological and ontological analysis, something which poses philosophical problems.

One can draw reference to Heidegger's own opinions about Binswanger's work and the relationship between ontology and medical psychiatry. From 1959–1969 he delivered a series of seminars, the *Zollikon Seminare* (1959–1969), to medical psychiatrists, organized by Swiss psychiatrist Medard Boss.[8] The opinions are very cursory but nevertheless indicate Heidegger's general orientation towards Binswanger's early work. The errors he identifies in Binswanger's work are important and have been overlooked in our discussion to date. Heidegger refers to Binswanger's consistent misrepresentation of a continuity of the transcendental analytics of Kantian critical philosophy and Husserlian phenomenology with Heideggerian ontology, in spite of the extended tracts of *Being and Time* which outline a rupture or break. Heidegger demonstrates the impact of this confusion with Binswanger's application of ontological concepts to concrete "existential" phenomena. Binswanger, for example, refers to *Care* as a self-centred, resolute disposition which is counterpoised by the more ethereal, flighty disposition of *love*. Elsewhere, Binswanger describes *love* as pertaining to a particular *being-beyond-the-world* in contrast to *being-in-the-world* (1963, 193–4). This kind of existential description clearly conflates Heidegerrian ontological conceptualization with ontical description. Admittedly, these kinds of errors of Heideggerian application are found more in Binswanger's earlier texts before the unique position of a specific domain of *Daseinsanalyse* is well established. But it may belie a problem that would continue to exist in the later work in a more complex or masked form. This confusion about the transcendental is well demonstrated in earlier passages such as this:

> Heidegger, in his concept of being-in-the-world as transcendence, has not only returned to a point prior to the subject-object dichotomy of knowledge and eliminated the gap between self and world, but has also elucidated the structure of subjectivity as transcendence. Thus he has opened a new horizon of understanding for, and given a new impulse to, the scientific exploration of human existence and its specific modes of being. . . . If for a moment we remember the definition of being-in-the-world as transcendence and view from this point our psychiatric analysis of existence, we realize that by investigating the structure of being-in-the-world we can also explore psychoses; and realize furthermore that we have to understand them as specific modes of transcending. (1963, 193)

There is a lot to this passage: it is interesting to note that Binswanger, here, is making a direct link between psychiatry and Heideggerian ontology by way of a *transcendental* notion of being-in-the world. In this early text, he is not establishing the intermediary status of a *Daseinsanalyse*. He is stating that one can look at specific modes of transcendental structure to understand existential phenomena such as psychosis. This resolution or undertaking is a linking of specific modes or modifications of universal structure to concrete phenomena. Despite Heidegger's complaints about this misrepresentation of his work as "transcendental ontology," he does, in the *Seminare*, distinguish between different meanings of *Daseinsanalytik* and *Daseinsanalyse* that invite legitimate analysis (1959–1969, 150–156[9]). For Heidegger, the *Daseinsanalytik* is the ontological analytic of Being found in *Being and Time*.

And as a part of this analytic there are concrete illustrations or exemplifications of this structure (quasi-ontological *Daseinsanalyse*—refer, for example, to our discussion above of fear and the occupants of a burning house). And finally, there is a more formal *Daseinsanalyse* which describes concrete existential experiences within an ontic anthropology. Heidegger describes this latter form of *Daseinsanalyse* as an existential anthropology that could be applied to the clinic and to psychopathology. However he makes no effort whatsoever to describe just how this form of *Daseinsanalyse* would actually relate to the *Daseinsanalytik*. In the concluding sessions of the *Seminare* he does, however, attempt to outline some parameters of an existential psychiatry *qua Daseinsanalyse* by referring to a contemporary report on the notion of "stress." Extricating "stress" from the Skinnerian conception outlined in the report, Heidegger discusses "stress" as a demand or claim directed at *Dasein*. At such a level, "stress" is impacting upon *being-in-the-world* and is an aspect of *Dasein*'s thrownness. Stress in this sense, is universal and does not relate to some extrinsic element imposed upon a world-less ego. It can be seen to be part of the basic constitution of *Dasein*, linked to the structure of its three *Existenziale*—*Befindlichkeit, Verstehen* and *Rede*—unified under *Dasein*'s *Care* (1959–1969, 180–185). Unfortunately, Heidegger does not substantiate such a link between the *Daseinsanalytik* and a *Daseinsanalyse* of stress any further. Yet this small attempt at a linking between the *Daseinanalytik* and a notion such as "stress" does suggest certain things.

I have suggested that Binswanger's more mature writings substantiate a link between the *Daseinsanalytik* and a clinical anthropology by way of the *Daseinsanalyse* of *world designs*. World-designs are never purported to be a purely Heideggerian (ontological) concept, and Binswanger's definitions of the concept show the manner in which it is intended to represent a specific existential structure, a modification or variant within universal *being-in-the-world*. The issue, here, is the possibility of constructing an ontic-anthropological analysis of concrete existence that somehow relies upon, or exists within a universal ontological "domain." If we accept that there is much in the concrete existence of beings that the Heideggerian ontological analytic of *Dasein* omits, why can this not be explained in terms of an existential structure such as *world-design*. If Heidegger's analytic does not capture the full breadth of human concrete existence— sexuality, embodiment, the symptomatology of what are conceptualized ontically as psychosis and neurosis—are there not existential structures which are, in a sense, not formally ontological but nevertheless somehow *fit* the analytic of *Dasein*[10]?

I have attempted to draw out a possible relationship, here, by *fitting* Heidegger's analytic of authenticity and *Befindlichkeit* with Binswanger's *Daseinsanalyse* of world-design. The link emerged when we saw in Binswanger's existential analyses the general notion of *mundanization* or *decapacitation.* This notion represents an existential structure or schema with which one can begin to understand any of the phenomena that come to be characterized ontically as *psychopathological*. Existential analysis becomes an analysis of structure and structural links of *world-designs within being-in-the-world.* And for the clinic, what is most pertinent to this analysis of structure relates to the universal ontological thematic of anxiety. Psychopathology is thus represented existentially as the dominance of a *world-design* as an idealistic, homogenous, self-referential system of signs. Ontologically, this dominance is a *fleeing* from or *abandonment* of *Dasein*'s own capacity to realize its potentiality authentically *in* the world: the *anxiety* of authentic becoming has been avoided and supplanted by the most inauthentic, idealistic becoming of *fear*. And the extremity of the dissonance of maintaining this self-referential, closed system, this *World-Design*, in the face of one's being-in-the-world, is at the heart of the extreme phenomena of psychopathologies. Thus, we can understand psychopathology *Daseinsanalytically* as a decapacitation or mundanization, and, as such, an inauthentic *abandonment* of the world.

This type of *Daseinsanalytic* understanding of what we confront psychopathologically is not *merely* ontic. In developing an existential understanding of the structures behind psychopathological phenomena, so many of the aporia and antinomies of man's ontic understanding of his existence may be overcome. Heidegger seems to have encouraged a notion of ontological difference that does not represent a complete divide. It would seem, then, that ontological understanding can potentially influence or permeate a practical activity such as psychiatry or psychotherapy. And this would not be a purely critical influence, seeking to undermine so many of the dominant biologistic, cognitivist or humanistic approaches within psychiatry, all of which ontically interpret human being. Psychiatry, understood in the broadest of terms, is a practical field concerned with individuals whose Being is *especially* at issue for itself or others—Being that is problematized. When a psychiatrist or psychotherapist is enlisted to assist another individual in orienting himself towards his own Being, the psychiatrist, of necessity, is called upon to operationalize and apply an understanding of normativity in selfhood. In this field, Heideggerian authenticity may constitute the goal of treatment as a form of health. Hermeneutic ontology may assist in determining the extent but also the limits of understanding in treatment, and the horizon within which ontical concepts operate in the practically driven therapeutic activity.

This ongoing tension around the space, or borderline if you will, between the ontic and the ontological, will be taken further now by exploring some of the key philosophical themes that can be extracted from Heidegger's (1928) project that have been taken on, developed and deviated from in subsequent philosophical thinkers who all have, importantly, adopted psychoanalytic or psychiatric clinical concepts to assist in the development of their thought.

This makes us aware of how germane the clinical is, or can become, to the Heideggerian project, when issues emerge about the tensions raised by the concept of Ontological Difference.[11] Such tensions include the extent to which various elaborations of Dasein's ontology incorporate elements of existence such as a broader, deeper and more complex forms of affectivity, memorality, relationality as well as embodiment and ethical concern than was envisaged by Heidegger himself in his early project. The later Heidegger, who became increasingly focussed upon language and thought as the foci of the understanding of Being, distanced himself further from affinities with humanistic approaches or philosophical anthropology. However, later philosophers influenced by Heidegger engaged with the early Heideggerian project to develop hermeneutic ontology further in this direction, while others explored the progression of Heidegger's thought and analysed the sustainability or complexity of ontological difference. I have chosen to elaborate upon this orientation further in relation to four thematic headings where Being and existence are understood in terms of *relationality*, *embodied affectivity*, *temporality* and *technicity*. In doing this, I plan to develop a framework of philosophical concepts that are described as primary or originary and fall under the rubric of *hermeneutic ontology*. This framework will be described now in the next chapters, before it will then be applied to the developmental and clinical consideration of the borderline concept.

Chapter 3

Relationality

Individuation, Dialogue, Alterity, and Ethical Care

We can recall that the early Heidegger's (1928) articulation of the thrownness and finitiude of *Dasein* included fundamentally relational notions: *Dasein* incorporated *Mitsein* (being-with) and *Mitwelt* (being-in-the-world-with) as primary elements of existence. The existential ground of affectivity is *Befindlichkeit*, a complex neologism ("how-one-finds-oneself-ness") which encapsulates the notion of primary self-referentiality ("how I find myself") and discourse ("how I articulate this to another"), as if the other is always already present to be spoken to in an analogous discourse with oneself. More broadly, this reminds us of the fundamentally self-referential nature of existence (*jemeinigkeit*) and the role of language as a primordial mediating structure (*Rede*).

In the Zollikon Seminars, Heidegger (1959–1969) on occasions sought to differentiate how he thought about this *originary relationality* in contrast to clinical thinkers such as Ludwig Binswanger and Harry Stack Sullivan. One particular issue Heidegger took up was Binswanger's extension of his concept of *Mitsein* to what Binswanger saw as a broader notion of reciprocal human relationship. What is at issue here is whether Heidegger's own conception of originary relationality remains poorly elaborated or whether, in fact, there is an inherent individualism to it. Part of this relates to some of Heidegger's conceptualizations of relationality that he elaborated upon in the latter parts of *Being and Time* (1928). In the second division of *Being and Time* (1928) Heidegger does establish a notion of the Care structure around *Dasein* reaching its potentiality-for-being in terms of authenticity and inauthenticity not only in relation to finite origins of thrownness but also in relation to the unsurpassable possibility or horizon of death. Heidegger characterizes death as non-relational, and being-towards-death as, thus, seeming to represent an individual, non-relational existential horizon. Dasein can inauthentically flee from this horizon by an immersion in public anonymity, what he refers to as *das Man* or "the They." At the same time, Heidegger does also characterize an authentic form of Care of others, or being-with-others when he describes solicitude: Dasein's capacity to leap ahead (*vorspringen*) of the Other and assist in a return to authentic being in the world, a return to a realisation of potentiality-for-being.

Now, with Heideggerian terms such as solicitude, authenticity and being towards death, Binswanger joined others in criticizing an inherent individualism in these conceptualisations which is at odds with his broader ontology and the originary relationality he articulates in the earlier, foundational parts of *Being and Time* (1928).[1] This forms part of Binswanger's own arguments to advance Heidegger's fundamental ontology and *Mitsein* along the lines of a theory of reciprocal love. Interestingly, Heidegger evokes the primary or originary relationality of *Dasein* as an ontological fact when he distances himself from Binswanger's work in the Zollikon Seminars:

> What was Binswanger expressing in his endeavour to develop a supplement? What is lacking in reference to the thinking in *Being and* Time, when Binswanger attempts to make such a supplement? In *Being and Time* it is said that *Dasein* is essentially an issue for itself. At the same time, this *Dasein* is defined as originary Being-with-another. Therefore *Dasein* is always concerned with others. Thus, the analytic of *Dasein* has nothing whatsoever to do with solipsism or subjectivism. But Binswanger's misunderstanding consists not so much of the fact that he wants to supplement "care" with love, but that he does not see that care has an existential, that is, ontological sense. Therefore, the analytic of *Dasein* asks for *Dasein's* basic ontological (existential) constitution and does not wish to give a mere description of the ontic phenomena of *Dasein*. (1959–1969, 116)

And elsewhere in the seminar he levels a related critique on emerging intersubjective or relational thinkers in psychology such as Harry Stack Sullivan:

> When they assert that a human being is determined as a being [who stands] in a relationship to other humans, the American [psychologist] Harry Stack Sullivan and his similarly oriented colleagues make an essential assertion [*Wesensaussage*] about the human being, the foundations of which are not even questioned. (Essential means a projection, an a priori determination made in advance). They take human comportment toward other human beings as a statement [*Feststellung*] of something *about* the human being and not as an essential assertion determining the human being as a human being in the first place.
>
> Relationship to . . . the being-in-relation-to . . . characterizes the unfolding essence of the human being. "Characterize" [*kennzeichnen*] is the correct word here and not "constitute" [*ausmachen*] because this would imply that being-in-relation-to . . . is already a complete determination of the human being, while the

relationship to the understanding of being refers to a yet "deeper" determination of the human being's unfolding essence. (1959–1969, 153)

As such, the limited nature of Heidegger's expansion of originary relationality in the latter parts of *Being and Time* (1928) when he addresses issues of death, solicitude and authenticity has led Binswanger to make his departure, and Heidegger himself to distance himself from such departures when he reaches his own *Kehre*, as exemplified by his *Letter on Humanism* and subsequent works which will be covered below.[2]

What remains for us, then, is to explore more systematically some further philosophical elaborations of originary relationality that have followed and either explicitly or implicitly been influenced by Heidegger, and take a philosophical form that is more commensurate with or acceptable to the Heideggerian project. In the following section of this chapter, I will explore some of these developments which also relatedly situate subjectivism and individualism in more of a constructivist way: subjectification and individuation becoming processes secondary to and mediated by more fundamental (pre-) ontological processes.

RELATIONALITY AND PROCESSES OF INDIVIDUATION, DIALOGUE AND THE DIALECTIC WITH OTHERNESS

Originary relationality implies that relational processes are ontologically prior, and notions of self, subject or individuality are secondary and ontical. The derivation or genesis of the "individual" or "subject," then, may emerge from something ontologically prior. I have already articulated that Heidegger's *Kehre*, which can be seen as a movement away from the ontology of *Dasein* (which could too easily slip from ontology into anthropology due to the ambiguity or tensions maintained in the notion of Ontological Difference) to more of an interest in language and thought as the sites of the enunciation of Being. This coincided with philosophical trends in which concepts such as self, individual and subject were seen not so much as ontical entities so much as derivatives of processes mediated by ontologically prior actions or forces: these could be seen as sub- (linguistic, biological or psychic) or supra- individual (socio-cultural, historical). Gilbert Simondon (1958, 1989), for example, developed a theory of individual and collective individuation, in which the individual subject is considered as an effect of psychic and collective individuation, rather than as a cause.[3] Michel Foucault, in the many phases of his writing, also articulated the many linguistic, social, historical and political determinants of subjectivity, coining the expression *subjectification* which was also adopted by Deleuze.

If I seek to articulate, further, *relational* determinants to processes akin to subjectification or individuation I can begin by seeing them emerge out of Heideggerian concepts such as *jemeinigkeit* and *befindlichkeit* which are individuating or subjectifying processes that are reflective and dialogical. Two hermeneutic philosophers, Hans-Georg Gadamer and Paul Ricoeur extended these conceptualizations much further in their own projects.

Gadamer, a student of Heidegger, developed a dialogical approach to hermeneutics that in line with Heidegger's thought rejects subjectivism. Understanding is a dialogical process from the beginning, and there is an emphasis, taken up from Aristotle's *Nichomachean Ethics*, on the concept of phronesis (or "practical wisdom") related to our practical "being-in-the-world," where understanding is constituted by dialogue and relates immediately to our practical situation and more broadly to our existential situatedness, as opposed to a more theoretical, subjectivist apprehension. This orientation, and its Heideggerian roots, is developed by Gadamer to establish a philosophical hermeneutics that provides an account of understanding in its universality (that is hermeneutic ontology referring to the hermeneutic situation of existence) which can then be applied to all manner of fields such as aesthetics, theology, politics and so forth. In addition to overcoming subjectivism, it also seeks to avoid attempting to, whether in relation to the *Geisteswissenschaften* (human sciences such as psychology) or other fields, found a set of theoretical rules or approaches to understanding which take it beyond being a dialogical, practical, situated activity. Thus in Gadamer's most important work, *Truth and Method* (1960), our hermeneutic situatedness, especially in how it is enunciated in *Being and Time* (1928), is referred to as an horizon (*Horizont*) from which understanding emerges. Gadamer refers to this horizon as a form of prejudice, but in a positive sense, as prejudice involves forestructures of understanding, or pre-judgements out of which understanding emerges both dialogically and practically: that is, understanding always emerges through dialogue and has a practical concern or interest. Gadamer, also, historicizes understanding, as situatedness which is historically determined. Thus, if we look to the manner in which Gadamer advances the notion of originary relationality, it is through articulating the horizon or historical embeddedness out of which dialogical, practical understanding emerges. Gadamer, below, articulates the points of continuity between *Being and Time* (1928), Heidegger's *Kehre*, and Gadamer's own project in terms of the importance of dialogical understanding and originary relationality:

> Even in *Being and Time* the real question is not in what way being can be understood but in what way understanding *is* being, for the understanding of being represents the existential distinction of Dasein . . . The question of being, as

Heidegger poses it, breaks into an entirely different dimension by focussing on the being of Dasein that understands itself. . . .

The role that the mystery of language plays in Heidegger's later thought is sufficient indication that his concentration on the historicity of self-understanding banished not only the concept of consciousness from its central position, but also the concept of selfhood as such. For what is more unconscious and "selfless" than that mysterious realm of language in which we stand and which allows what is to come to expression so that being is "temporalized" (*sich zeitigt*)? But if this is valid for the mystery of language, it is also valid for the concept of understanding. Understanding too cannot be grasped as a simple activity of the consciousness that understands, but is itself a mode of the event of being. To put it in purely formal terms, the primacy that language and understanding have in Heidegger's thought indicates the priority of the "relation" over and against its relational member—the I who understands and that which is understood. Nevertheless it seems to me that it is possible to bring to expression within the hermeneutical consciousness itself Heidegger's statements concerning "being" and the line of enquiry he developed out of the experience of the turn (*kehre*). I have carried out this attempt in *Truth and Method*. Just as the relation between the speaker and what is spoken points to a dynamic process that does not have a firm basis in either member of the relation, so the relation between the understanding and what is understood has a priority over its relational terms. (1976, 49–50)

In this, we can see that just as the later Heidegger would hold to the primacy of thought and language, Gadamer here holds to understanding and relationality as primary, within a historically embedded field of dialogue and activity. Understanding is always a process of negotiation (with oneself or with an other) in dialogue, a matter of coming to agreement and establishing an horizon or fusing horizons (*Horizontverschmelzung*) where any horizon is a larger context or situation of pre-Understanding out of which understanding emerges. Here, understanding is an ongoing process, and is not a means to arriving at objective truth or accessing an inner realm of determined subjective meaning. Gadamer argues against there being a technical method for the *Geisteswissenschaften* that would place them alongside the natural sciences (*Naturwissenschaften*) in terms of objective knowledge, and indeed, he holds that there is no such methodology for the natural sciences themselves in this regard. What is primary is understanding as a continuing process that is historical, situated, and dialogical. The basic model of dialogical understanding that Gadamer finally develops in *Truth and Method* (1960) is that of conversation. It involves a linguistic exchange with the good will to reach a mutual understanding or shared meaning. Just as Heidegger asserted language as the house of Being, Gadamer asserts that language is the medium of dialogical engagement, or conversational praxis. Language is worldly and relational, and as such, Gadamer like other philosophers such as Ludwig Wittgenstein and Donald Davidson, reject the idea of a "private language." Language is the medium of relational existence. However Gadamer has been criticized by other philosophers, particularly Derrida, for overstating the primacy of understanding and the importance of good will to arrive at agreement in conversation. This will be explored further below.

Another hermeneutic philosopher who develops Heidegger's ideas around originary relationality is Paul Ricoeur. In his mature, hermeneutic writings, Ricoeur's focus is on the study of man, anthropology, from a hermeneutic perspective. Ricoeur often acknowledges Heidegger's earlier ontology as an influence or point of departure, but goes on to explore the constitution of selfhood, man, human being, from this perspective with particular attention paid to discourse, action, temporal agency, historicity and narrative identity. In *Oneself as Another* (1992) Ricoeur's conception of selfhood or self stands opposed to both Cartesian dualism (and the self-transparent cogito) and anti-Cartesian conceptions which see the self as illusory and a product of sub- or supra-individual processes (especially Nietzschean will to power). Ricoeur (1992) seeks to develop a *hermeneutics of the self*, which he ultimately seeks to ground ontologically in the final study of the work. For Ricoeur the self is embodied, historically and culturally constituted, but creative and agentic. It has a dual identity: an *idem*-identity of spatio-temporal sameness; and an *ipse*-identity allowing it to initiate activity imputable to it. Importantly, Ricoeur claims that this grounding of the self in two modes of identity will never be empirically verifiable but only be understood by means of *attestation*. Attestation is the lived assurance, or precondition of understanding, that the self has of existing and acting in both of these orders of causality. Ricoeur (1992, 308–317) does ontologically ground these ideas about selfhood with reference to early Heideggerian hermeneutic ontology (worldhood, the Care structure and so forth). Importantly, though, he does critique and extend some of the Heideggerian limitations around relationality described above. In particular, Ricoeur develops an analysis of selfhood as always existing in dialectical tension with *otherness*: the otherness of the body, the otherness of other people, the otherness of death, the otherness of conscience. These elements of otherness which coexist with or dialectically constitute selfhood are those that are sometimes limited or neglected by Heidegger, as described in preceding sections above: Heidegger's prioritisation of temporality over spatiality in the second division of *Being and Time* (1928) precludes the inclusion of a fuller analysis of the "ontology of the flesh" (and embodiment, as such); and Heidegger's analysis of the non-relationality of death and the limitations of his conceptualizations of authenticity, conscience and solicitude omit a fuller conceptualisation of relatedness in the ethical and socio-cultural spheres.

As such, the two elements of relationality to be drawn out from this brief discussion of Gadamer's and Ricoeur's thought would be the forms of the self, subject or individual that are constituted by or secondary to relational processes: in particular, dialogue or conversation as well as the dialectic with otherness (the otherness of embodiment, of the other, of death, of conscience and so forth). Nevertheless both thinkers remain committed to Heidegger's hermeneutic ontological orientation in articulating these elements of selfhood as historically, linguistically and factically embedded or situated. Other thinkers following Heidegger, however, have taken these trends further to challenge or depart from the Heideggerian project.

OTHERNESS AND ETHICS

Questions of otherness and dialogicality have been explored by Jacques Derrida and Emmanuel Levinas, two philosophers who have made radical deconstructive and ethical departures from their Heideggerian roots. When these thinkers mount a philosophical critique of "logocentrism" or the "ontology of Sameness" both argue that the Western metaphysical tradition since the time of Greco-Roman thought has discriminated against Otherness in favour of Sameness insofar as this is represented by Logos, Being, Substance, Reason or Ego. Both thinkers acknowledge a profound influence from Heidegger but nevertheless include him in this tradition, even if he is, in either of their perspectives, the last or final metaphysician. For both thinkers, it could be said that Otherness represents anything that surpasses our capacity to understand, interpret or represent, and differs or is alien. It is beyond the metaphysical, and this includes ontology and, ultimately, thought. In both thinkers, then, dominant, traditionally metaphysical forms of thinking can do violence to otherness. In a similar way dialogue needs to be cautious, non-invasive or non-violent, and appreciative of otherness.

Put loosely, Derrida's deconstruction is a discursive, rhetorical approach to undermine this violence by inhabiting and destabilizing texts in which dominant or oppressive forms of meaning, representation or categorization are at play. Derrida's concept of *différance* encapsulates the idea that all meaning, in a sense, is contextual, intertextual and ultimately textual (in an expanded meaning of text):

> This concept can be called *gram* or *difference*. The play of differences supposes in effect, syntheses and referrals which forbid at any moment, or in any sense, that a simple element be *present* in and of itself, referring only to itself ... This interweaving results in each "element" ... being constituted on the basis of the trace within it of the other elements of the chain or system. This interweaving, this textile, is the *text* produced. (1981, 26)

Différance is a neologism which simultaneously refers to "differing" and "deferral." It can describe the production of meaning through signs and metaphors: firstly (relating to deferral) there is the notion that signs and metaphors will never fully summon forth what they mean, but can only be defined through appeal to additional signs, words or metaphors, from which they differ. Thus, meaning is forever "deferred" or postponed through an endless chain of signification. In Derrida's work, this broad form of textuality (chains and traces of interrelated, contextual meaning) is in some way primary but also ineffable, we cannot get outside it or behind it to fully understand it. Derrida's deconstructive method is used to destabilize oppressive and repressive regimes of signs and meanings which name, categorize and alter something different. Another significant concept, here, is the concept of the supplement and supplementarity: in loose Derridean terms, a supplement is something that, allegedly secondarily, comes to serve as an aid to something "original" or "natural." "Supplement" has a double meaning here: it is not only secondary as a stand-in, a signifier or a representative; it also adds to and modifies. If what is originary or natural is also other, it cannot in a sense ever be represented other than supplementarily, and within the textual.

In the ethical and political spheres, Levinas and Derrida have both argued that justice demands a respect and appreciation of otherness. What is alien before us cannot always be encapsulated by our own language or categories projected upon it, and this may be a form of oppression or violence. This can be an ethical orientation for deconstructive practice, preserving or protecting otherness, and for Derrida justice calls for hospitality of otherness or the other, welcoming in, accommodating without changing or domesticating or oppressing. For Levinas, this relation to otherness establishes an infinite responsibility in the face of the Other. In both cases, the otherness is revered and respected. In the case of Levinas (1961, 1974), otherness and the role of ethics is given primary status in philosophy, where ethics becomes first philosophy and otherness is accorded priority and something for which the thinker holds infinite responsibility. This call is represented in the "face of the Other," which defies representation, categorization or totalizing understanding. Instead the Face, ethically, should evoke a form of passive, reactive humility and responsibility to the other, a *subjection* to the other and to otherness, beyond voluntary individual agency. This has been argued to be in some ways an excessive compensation for the perceived excessive violence of dominant or traditional regimes they criticize (e.g., in Critchley and Bernasconi, 2002).[4]

In loose terms, then, the Derridean deconstructive orientation, which can sometimes be seen to be beguiling and abstruse in its polemicism and subversiveness and the Levinasian radical ethics which can be seen to be sometimes excessive and even paranoid and masochistic in its stance of subjection to the face of the Other, are challenges to the hermeneutic orientation exemplified by Heidegger, Gadamer and Ricoeur because they reinforce the limits of thought in the face of alterity, leading to more negative, critical, radical or subversive stances within ethics and philosophizing.[5] A paradigmatic example would be Derrida's encounter with Gadamer at a 1981 Paris Symposium. In the spirit of dialogic and mutual understanding, Gadamer prepared a text comparing the manner in which the two of them interpreted Nietzsche (in Michelfelder and Palmer, 1989). Derrida's response was only delivered after the conference in the form of three indirect but incisive questions which were seen as a form of polemical engagement with Gadamer "from the outside." Significantly one of these questions related to Gadamer's claims about general or universal hermeneutics and the possibility of including psychoanalysis within this. If the possibility of shared understanding and good will, as encapsulated in the idea of *Horizontvershmelzung* ("fusion of horizons") has its limits then psychoanalysis could represent an interpretative discipline in which other dynamics of suspicion, resistance, and so forth operate. Gadamer subsequently conceded this but upheld the desirability of his hermeneutic principles. Whilst the detail of the ensuing debate and correspondence cannot be covered here, the complexity, points of difference, and movements between criticism, concession, dialogue and impasse, could be seen to represent a dialectical tension between the Gadamerian movement of good will and *Horizontvershmelzung* as opposed to the Derridean action of deconstruction and openness to alterity.

In subsequent chapters, the thought of Derrida will be returned to, as it has engaged directly with the field of psychoanalysis and psychotherapy on a number of occasions, and the stances I refer to can be seen to yield important and constructive outcomes in the debates they participated in. Moreover, the ethical principles they uphold, within the field of interpretation but in tension with the hermeneutic principles I have developed, can be translated into the clinical interpretive realm. What I shall turn to now, is the extent to which conceptions of difference and alterity that arise but depart from Heideggerian ontological foundations can influence conceptions of embodied affectivity.

Chapter 4

Embodied Affectivity
Body, Affect, Impulse, and Alterity

Following on from our discussion of the extension of originary relationality in Heideggerian hermeneutic ontology by post-Heideggerian philosophers, I now turn to the issue of embodied affectivity. We have already seen that *Being and Time* (1928) includes an analysis of affectivity as *befindlichkeit*, and agency as it appears in concepts such as the care structure, being-in-the-world, *Entwurfen* and *Sicht* which capture the temporal, purposive immersion in projects. But there is a more limited conceptualization of embodiment which as alluded to above Ricoeur (1992) points out is influenced by a limited focus on spatiality. Though Heidegger develops few ideas around embodiment we are aware that his understanding of the body explicitly confronts Cartesian mind/body dualism:

> Ultimately we dare not split the matter in such a way, as though there were a bodily state housed in the basement with feelings dwelling upstairs. Feeling, as feeling oneself to be, is precisely the way we are corporeally. Bodily being does not mean that the soul [consciousness/mind?] is burdened by a hulk we call the body. In feeling oneself to be, the body is already contained in advance in that self, in such a way that the body in its bodily states permeates the self. We do not 'have' a body in the way we carry a knife in a sheath. Neither is the body [*Leib*] a body [*Korper*] that merely accompanies us and which we can establish, expressly or not, as also present-at-hand. We do not 'have' a body [*Leib*] rather, we 'are' bodily [*leiblich*]. (*Nietzsche, Volume 1,* 98–9)

This idea of being-embodied suggests that as beings-in-the-world we are bodily, and that embodiment mediates our existence.[1] In his "Geschlecht" series of essays on Heidegger, Derrida (1983) focuses upon a deconstructive analysis of the concept of "Geschlecht" in Heidegger's work, and how this pertains to numerous tensions and problems in his work. The German word

Geschlecht refers to a family of terms in English including gender, sex, race, lineage and family. In the first essay, Derrida turns to whether Heidegger totally omits any question of sexual difference or gender from the thinking of Being. In Derrida's analysis, he intends to uncover that the neutrality of *Dasein* does not so much represent a negative resistance to sexual differentiation (rendering it secondary, ontic) so much as a primal source of every sexuality, a form of elusive potency and multiplicity. As such, this type of deconstructive argument confirms the idea that the relative impoverishment of Heidegger's own ontological development of embodied affectivity belies a potentially fertile ontological foundation.

Arriving at this point after having explored the impact of difference and otherness (alterity) on the Heidegerrian foundations of originary relationality, gives us occasion to look at the extension of this foundation in another radical post-Heideggerian philosopher, Gilles Deleuze, who addressed issues of embodied affectivity in his work.

Deleuze's thought was committed to ontology but unlike Heidegger's call to the end of metaphysics, Deleuze held to perpetuating but subverting metaphysics where metaphysics becomes an endless, creative production of concepts. Deleuze's thought is difficult to access: not only was he prolific, and a philosopher's philosopher who immersed himself in the complexity of other thinkers' work and the history of philosophy with a radically revisionist perspective, we see, unlike Heidegger's often closed system of neologisms and novel concepts, a prolific and mobile series of references taken from diverse fields including mathematical calculus, thermodynamics, geology, psychoanalysis, biology and numerous others (inspiring, to a degree, aspects of my approach in this project). In the core work which was the principle articulation of his ideas, *Difference and Repetition* (1968), we see the establishment of a metaphysics of difference as opposed to identity: philosophy becomes an ontology of difference, where identity follows or is encapsulated by difference, captured in paradoxical statements such as "pluralism equals monism." Deleuze, here, refers to ontology as univocity (from Duns Scotus), an endless and open play of relationships of differentials. He subverts the Kantian transcendental turn to refer to his project as *transcendental empiricism*: experience and existence exceed our concepts by presenting novelty and this raw experience of difference actualizes thought. In this approach, Being is difference, an always differentiating process of becoming. These central ideas are articulated in many of his other works addressing key philosophers and the history of philosophy, with an endless array of concepts produced in open systems of philosophical articulation. Importantly for us, though, is that Deleuze also collaborated with a psychoanalyst, Felix Guattari, in the production of two key works which create a critical system of concepts around a theory of desire, *Anti-Oedipus* (1972) and *A Thousand Plateaus* (1980). Desire, here, refers to an ontological field that encapsulates the embodied, affective and impulsive. I intend to describe their approach here, to reveal a radical ontology of desire that could be seen loosely to depart from a Heideggerian ontological origin. Because their system is so complex and laden with both psychoanalytic and philosophical references, I have chosen to elaborate it in some depth. For the clinician and philosopher alike, it requires a tolerance of the creative and subversive use of what appear to be familiar philosophical and clinical concepts. I believe this elaboration is also especially relevant because it provides a bridging trajectory to issues and topics of relevance to the subsequent *developmental* and *clinical* parts of this work.[2]

In *Anti-Oedipus*, Deleuze and Guattari (1972) are seeking to develop a theory of desire that elevates the social over the familial, where the best model for social desire is the "schizophrenic unconscious." This model, which underpins their approach of schizoanalysis as an overcoming of psychoanalysis, avoids the familial constitution of a unified self by focussing upon a sub-individual realm of body parts, or "libidinal intensities," and their supra-individual interconnections in the social, thus providing a single system of configurations of "desiring-production," a system which can be analysed with the critical aim of, at once, overcoming both the Freudian approach to subjectivity and the Marxist approach to sociality. To understand further Deleuze and Guattari's (1972) analysis of the modern repression of desire through Oedipalization, I need to first elaborate upon their theory of desiring-production based upon the model of schizophrenia. This theory of desiring-production will be elaborated upon briefly in order to explain what Deleuze and Guattari (1972, 68–130) refer to as the five paralogisms of psychoanalysis. Importantly for us, the paralogisms can be applied to both psychoanalysis and transcendental theories of representational consciousness alike. The paralogisms will be explored at this broad level and invoked in subsequent parts of this work in the broader discussion of the hermeneutic engagement with psychoanalysis and clinical psychiatry and its rendering or "treatment" of "borderline personality disorder." This will be with a view to exploring and understanding the manner in which the conceptualization of schizoanalytic unconscious work may be relevant to understanding and responding to borderline phenomena and experiences in psychotherapy.

L'Anti-Oedipe (1972) is by no means an anti- or post-psychoanalytic text—it still very much endorses and advances a concept of the unconscious and of desire. Nor could it be said to be comprehensively anti-Lacanian since it adopts many of the concepts of the Lacanian sphere, admittedly often with a view to undermining, re-positioning or parasitically inhabiting them. Ultimately, Deleuze and Guattari (1972) are seeking to develop a theory of desire that elevates the social over the familial, where the best model for social desire is the schizophrenic unconscious. This model, which underpins their approach of *schizoanalysis* as an overcoming of psychoanalysis, avoids the familial constitution of a unified self by focussing upon a sub-individual realm of body parts, or "libidinal intensities," and their supra-individual interconnections in the social, thus providing a single system of configurations of "desiring-production," a system which can be analysed with the critical aim of, at once, overcoming both the Freudian approach to subjectivity and the Marxist approach to sociality. This critical approach, which is fundamentally Nietzschean in character (the text purportedly corresponding to Nietzsche's *The Antichrist* in its confrontation with these two modern forms of "piety"), attempts to provide a history and politics of socio-libidinal activity, locating the control and inhibition of desiring-production today within the *capitalist* system, a system which is, ironically, advanced by the Freudian and the traditional Marxist alike. Reality, insofar as it is a system of "desiring-production" which incorporates flows of psychic desire and social labour, does not have its origins in either Freudian or Marxist thought: "We maintain that the social field is immediately invested by desire, that it is the historically determined product of desire, and that libido has no need of any mediation or sublimation, any psychic operation, any transformation, in order to invade and invest the productive forces and relations of production (1972, 29)."

The Freudian, Deleuze and Guattari (1972) will hold, subordinates desire to a reality principle formed on the basis of Oedipus; and this subordination actually serves the system of psychic repression utilized by capitalism. The seeming contradiction in this—an exaggeration of the significance of psychoanalysis in culture along the way to rejecting it as a theory—will be at the heart of the discussion here.

It is important to frame their adoption of this clinical category, *schizophrenia*, which they use to define and elaborate their model of desiring-production. In doing this they are in no way aligning themselves with the politics and moralism of the anti-psychiatry movement that was so prevalent at the time in Anglo-American discourses (in the work of Laing, for example). This movement, very much founded on an existential humanism, is in many ways diametrically opposed to Deleuze and Guattari's approach. For Deleuze and Guattari (1972) do not propose that the *schizophrenic* is labelled so by a socially repressive political apparatus, *capitalism*, because of its social deviance. Nor do they claim that *schizophrenia* represents a form of alienation created by the family system, a system which is subservient to this socially repressive apparatus of capitalism. And they do not see, then, that schizophrenia is a type of subjectivity that will ultimately disappear when the capitalist apparatus and its familial exponent is overcome. In opposition to the anti-psychiatric approach, Deleuze and Guattari (1972) recognize *schizophrenia* as a fundamental process of being, a possibility, something which is *not* simply manufactured by socio-cultural conditions such as the family (thus being curable or erasable by the upheaval of these conditions). Rather, it precedes these conditions, and is currently controlled or subjugated by the capitalist-familial conditions that prevail currently: it is pathologized, institutionalized, rendered silent and crippled.

What follows will be an exposition of those parts of *L'Anti-Oedipe* (1972) which deal with the critique of psychoanalysis, what the authors call the familialism of psychoanalysis, referring to its overemphasis of the Oedipal Complex. An attempt will then be made to locate this critique in relation to their positive conception of *schizoanalysis*. This will involve a discussion of the differences between the psychoanalytic and the *schizoanalytic* notions of *desire*. This section will then conclude with an attempt to extract their positive conception of *desire* as a radical description of embodied affectivity that is always, in a sense, socialized and contextualized within and constructed by supraindividual processes.

DESIRING-PRODUCTION AND REPRESSION: THE PARALOGISMS OF PSYCHOANALYSIS

Deleuze and Guattari's (1972) thesis about psychoanalysis's overemphasis of the Oedipal Complex is not in any way a claim that the complex is an invention of Freud's so much as a discovery. It recognizes that the complex exists and is one of the primary modes of restricting desire in contemporary society. Deleuze and Guattari (1972) would hold that the way this discovery is treated by psychoanalysts makes them complicit with a modern form of social "repression" particular to capitalism.

Capitalism functions by reducing all socio-libidinal relations to commodity relations of universal equivalency. Historically, the rise of capitalism, then, has seen a "deterritorialization"[3] of desire, whereby traditional social relations that once structured and codified desiring production have been undermined—kinship systems, class structures, religious customs have all lost their relevance and currency. In this context, desire is "reterritorialized" into the nuclear family, where it is individualized, essentially a process of *commoditization* which allows it to be regulated within the wider capitalistic system of socio-economic relations. The prominence of psychoanalysis, in this context, has arisen due to its focus upon the nuclear family (the Oedipal triangle that the authors derisively refer to as "Daddy-Mommy-Me") which has substituted the traditional role of the family which has been deterritorialized. Deleuze and Guattari refer to this deterritorialization as a *schizophrenization* of desire—desire set adrift as fluxes of intensities (words, drives, things, meanings, etc.) which are then reterritorialized in a process of Oedipalization.

In other words, Deleuze and Guattari (1972) are not entering a psychoanalytic debate on the importance of the Oedipal Complex; instead they are acknowledging this complex as a foundational structure of contemporary subjectivity as it exists within the capitalist regime. This structure serves to repress desire. They agree that the complex exists for the normal individual within this regime, but, interestingly, limit its role in schizophrenia, where it is the absence of Oedipalization that is present. To understand further Deleuze and Guattari's (1972) analysis of the modern repression of desire through Oedipalization, I need to first elaborate upon their theory of desiring-production based upon the model of schizophrenia. This theory of desiring-production will be elaborated upon here to explain what Deleuze and Guattari (1972, 68–130) refer to as the "paralogisms" of psychoanalysis. Strangely, the paralogisms can be applied to both psychoanalysis and transcendental theories of representational consciousness alike. The paralogisms will be summarized at this broad level here.[4]

Deleuze and Guattari (1972) conceptualize desiring-production using concepts based upon psychotic phenomena: *desiring-machines* (based upon a type of body fragmentation or somatic delusion that can be experienced in psychosis); the *body without organs* (based upon a type of body emptiness/deadness or somatic/nihilistic delusion that can be experienced in psychosis, the term taken from Antonin Artaud); and the *nomadic subject* (based upon the movement, multiplicity or invention of identities in the delusional thinking of psychotics). These terms embody the ontology of desiring-production.

We begin with *desiring-machines*: "Everywhere it is machines—real ones, not figurative ones: machines driving other machines, machines being driven by other machines, with all the necessary couplings and connections" (1972, 1). These machines represent at once the unconscious, the bodily, the natural and the social fields.[5] They are diverse and heterogonous, forming chains through which pass flows or fluxes of matter, energy, information; coupling in binary, *connective syntheses*, one to another to another. These machines and their combinations never function smoothly and are not *technical* in the sense of machines with separate, dependent parts unifying to operate as a structural whole; the functionalism of assemblages of desiring-machines is based upon moments of production, followed by breaking down, followed by recombining.

The moment of or tendency towards antiproduction that exists within (or immanent to) production has a limit. This limit refers to a regression to the pure, full *body without organs*, which constantly re-initiates desiring-production. This body without organs is one of the most elusive concepts in *Anti-Oedipus*. Loosely, Deleuze and Guattari (1972) refer to it as a *plane of immanence*, resembling Spinoza's immanent substance, whose attributes would be the desiring-machines. Desiring-machines are the functioning intensities for which the *body without organs* represents the capacity for a uniform, pure, zero-intensity:

> Where do these pure intensities come from? They come from two preceding forces, repulsion and attraction, and from the opposition of these two forces. It must not be thought that the intensities themselves are in opposition to one another, arriving at a balance around a neutral state. On the contrary, they are all positive in relationship to the zero intensity that designates the full body without organs. And they undergo relative rises or falls depending on the complex relationship between them and the variations in the relative strength of attraction and repulsion as determining factors. In a word, the opposition of the forces of attraction and repulsion produces an open series of intensive elements, all of them positive, that are never an expression of the final equilibrium of a system, but consist, rather, of an unlimited number of stationary, metastable states through which a subject passes. (1972, 19)

Thus, all intensities are positive, and must be considered according to their positive processes of production, connective synthesis, even when processes produce diminishing intensities. The relationship between desiring-machines and the body without organs is an ontological relationship of immanence which serves to supplant or precede transcendental principles which found dichotomies such as words/things, meaning/matter, natural/artificial, social/physical, mind/body, interior/exterior. This relationship, based upon a Spinozist ontology, is complex and variable in the role it has for desiring-production—the elements of which cannot be summarized here other than to highlight the notion of *disjunctive synthesis* central to the relationship. The body without organs has the capacity to perform a disjunctive synthesis whereby all desiring machines—all chains of connective syntheses—are libidinally invested at once.[6] What does this mean? For subjectivity, this is the opportunity for *nomadism*. The *nomadic subject* is a locus of becoming, migrating from machine to machine in a process of *becoming other* affecting conjunctive syntheses.

Deleuze and Guattari (1972) take the "schizophrenic experience of unbearable intensities," as the primary level of existence. Here, the nomadic subject achieves an *identity* through its *immanence* to the totality—an inclusiveness within the totality as a disjunctive synthesis. Deleuze and Guattari (1972) cannot offer a phenomenology of this nomadic experience, an experience without an interior, without a representational, transcendental subjectivity, so much as repeat it. This nomadic, schizophrenic subjectivity is a delirium that may seem "irrational," non-sensical, because it jumps across all of those dichotomous fields of words/things, meaning/matter, natural/artificial, social/physical, mind/body, interior/exterior, etc. Being immanent to the processes of desiring-production, the schizophrenic/nomadic subject experiences these processes and relations passing through him: when he tries to name them, he cannot speak as an individuated ego extracting himself from the social field; rather he speaks as a nomad from within a collective assemblage of enunciation, naming whatever relates to him or passes through him. This process of extraction from the field, the process of an attempt to render the experience as perceptions (*qua* hallucinations) or thoughts (*qua* delusions), is secondary to (*transcendental* to) that pure, unbearable experience of (*immanent*) intensities.[7]

Any explanation of repression should be elaborated in this context. Desire represses itself because of the unbearable effects and intensities it produces in its most immanent, most pure state. Just as there is the potentiality for *nomadism* and *schizophrenia* in this system, there is also a protection against this—*repression*. And just as a form of *disjunctive synthesis* produces nomadism in subjectivity, so there are other psychic *syntheses* which produce repression.[8] These syntheses are transcendental syntheses which pre-empt or protect against the inclusive disjunctive synthesis of schizophrenia.[9]

Repression occurs when desire becomes fixed to a transcendent manifestation of the social field. It leads to a *segregation* of desire, a formation of intensities that cannot be influenced, paired or invested in by other systems of desiring-production, other machines. Once this segregation of a desiring machine or formation of machines has occurred, a version of *disjunctive synthesis* occurs (different to the type that occurs in nomadism). Differential positions such as male/female, parent/child, black/white, dead/alive, which would be *inclusive* for the nomad, are *exclusive* in repression. This is the agency of the law in repression, law as a product of this antiproductive form of desire. The law creates boundaries, principles, order as a defence against the chaos of undifferentiated desiring-production. This defence of repression through *exclusive disjunction* permits the perception of this undifferentiated, immanent desiring from a transcendental, unproductive position: it is seen as something on the other side of the boundary, the side beyond the law. Instead of being inexplicably, unbearably chaotic, desire is perceived through the law as a transgression, a sin, a suffering, an opposition. Repressed desire is then perceived as a choice: either one experiences desire by identifying with something separated by the law in relation to which any production or movement will be represented as a *transgression*; or one "internalizes" the law by identifying with it in order to repress the desire of others.

In this process of the exclusive disjunction of repressed desire through the law, complete objects—"persons" or "subjects"—are formed or perceived. Prohibition of the law serves to constitute whole objects, individuated persons, a transcendental "I" separated from "others."[10] This is our normal mode of consciousness as *representational thought*. Thus objects and others which are desired are segregated by the law as objects of lack. They are elusive because they are representational, they lack an immediacy and an *immanence* for the individuated ego: they are transcendental objects of lack. This immanence has been repressed from desire; it refers to the intensity of the inclusiveness of nomadism, something which cannot be represented, or understood from within the field of repressed desire of the individuated ego. It is only perceived as a "lack" in the objects of repressed desire: the formation of the whole subject, the ego, occurs at the same time as this lack is introduced into desire. This ego is alienated within the eternal deferral of desire as a cycle of prohibition by the law and transgression to overcome lack.

Now, the modern version of this process of indoctrination of the law as lack, the exclusive disjunctive synthesis, the process of primal repression, is the Oedipal Complex. Insofar as "oedipalization" represents the modern and pervasive form of transcendental subjectivity, of desire as lack, psychoanalysis has thus not only discovered but has also served to advance this social repression of the psyche. This will now be analysed in more detail in order to establish Deleuze and Guattari's positive conception of *schizoanalysis* as a militant analysis that may overcome this repressive role of psychoanalysis.

OEDIPALIZATION AND FAMILIALISM: CAPITALISM VERSUS SCHIZOPHRENIA

Deleuze and Guattari (1972) have established that contemporary human consciousness is founded upon a repression of desire through "transcendent," exclusive, fixed uses of syntheses. These syntheses produce *representations* of a biunivocal nature: principles, laws and boundaries divide up the field of representations relating complete or detached objects and persons by rules of exclusion. The fundamental relational representation which acts to repress desire in our modernity is that of *familialisation*. This process can be explained in terms of syntheses. A conjunctive synthesis between individuated persons ("mother" and "father"), in which desire is subordinated to the law of reproduction/procreation, leads to the filiation of a new individual by an exclusive disjunction: gestation, birth and growth are the segregation of the child from the mother's body by means of socially imposed prohibitions which serve to ground their identities as separate, whole, individuated subjects. The same set of prohibitions then determines the possible alliances which can be made between these individuated subjects. Deleuze and Guattari (1972) characterize these transcendent uses of syntheses as *the law*, *lack* and *the signifier*, the three instances in which desire is subjected to repression through *familialisation*.

Deleuze and Guattari (1972) are stating their Nietzschean quest quite openly, here.

The transcendent uses of syntheses underpin the paralogisms of psychoanalysis broadly discussed above. These transcendent uses of the syntheses in the *law*, *lack* and the *signifier* all interrelate: desire cannot exist as lack until its object has been prohibited by the law; desire cannot be subjected to this law until it is founded upon a signifying structure enabling the representation of objects separate from the ego. The structure of the signifier, then, is at the foundation of the repression of desire. This structure is of lack: in the Oedipal triangle the phallic signifier is defined in terms of castration (the male) and envy (the female). The possessor of this phallus, the father, founds the symbolic laws of lack. Desire through the law will always seeks a pleasure which transcends it and can never become present. And so the authors are stating that this structural signification cannot be separated from the piety of a religiosity. The transcendental signifier becomes internal to desire; desire is now defined negatively as the limiting *structure* of consciousness, intrinsic to it, not confluent with the extrinsic, machinic socius. The psychic and social dimensions of repression become inseparable—the psychic subject is formed through the oedipal signifying structure originating in the family, and the social formation of the subject leads to substitutions of meaning or "signifieds" that fit within this structure. Insofar as desire is structured by the phallic signifier arising in familial formation, it is forced to invest itself in a social signification of lack. Thus, in the capitalist regime of socio-libidinal activity, the subject's Oedipalized desire is structured to desire its own social repression. This desire as lack is an acceptance that desire will always lack something because it is a search for a transcendental signified.[11] What does this mean? The Oedipalized subject invests itself in society with the family as its model, society substituting the original signified (the object of adjusted Oedipal love defined as *lack* through the *law*) with other transcendental signifieds, servicing the original familial *structure of signifying*.

Psychoanalysis functions to repair this structural desire when it is impaired in the neurotic. For those subjects for whom it never took root, psychotics, desiring is no longer possible because society will not service a desire that is not oedipalized. Psychoanalysis, according to the authors, deems that these subjects suffer from a "loss-of-reality": "an Oedipal "organization" is imposed on the psychotic, though for the sole purpose of assigning the *lack* of this organization in the psychotic . . . The psychotic reacts with autism and the loss of reality. Could it be that the loss of reality is not the effect of the schizophrenic process, but the effect of its forced oedipalization, that is to say, its interruption?" (1972, 123). Thus, the psychotic, the schizophrenic, is rendered silent by a *regime* of oedipalization to which it cannot submit and which it cannot avoid.

In this way, normal (*qua* modern/bourgeois) consciousness, neurosis and psychosis can all be traced back to the fundamental field of desiring-production. Each can be defined in terms of a *reaction* to this field's repression through oedipalization. This tracing back to desiring-production, the socio-libidinal activity of desire, which contains, and has the potential to subvert, the Oedipal complex, is at the heart of the critical activity of *schizoanalysis*: schizoanalysis will analogously contain and subvert psychoanalysis and its concept of the Oedipus complex. Where psychoanalysis affirms the transcendent use of syntheses that occurs in oedipalisation, schizoanalysis will affirm the *immanent* use of syntheses, the use that reflects an unmediated, unrepressed unconscious, the schizophrenic unconscious: "Schizoanalysis sets out to undo the expressive Oedipal unconscious, always artificial, repressive and repressed, mediated by the family, in order to attain the immediate productive unconscious (1972, 98)."

This concept of undoing an Oedipalized consciousness, to arrive at a schizophrenic unconscious, is then, a freeing-up in the name of productivity, fluidity, of overcoming repression. Schizoanalysis would be attacking conscious, individuated investment in the social in the name of an unconscious, social desiring-production: "It is a militant analysis, on the contrary, because it proposes to demonstrate the existence of an unconscious libidinal investment of sociohistorical production, distinct from the conscious investments coexisting with it (1972, 98)."

Schizoanalysis, then, will incorporate a psychoanalytic account of psychic repression alongside a Marxist account of social repression.[12] This derives from the fact that desire in its purity, for Deleuze and Guattari (1972), is social desiring-production. The unconscious is not fundamentally a transcendent source of energy, of instinctual drives, which necessitates its own repression through ego individuation in order to adjust to the "reality" of the social. It is, rather, a "factory" of machines immanent to the socius: sexual desire and labour, power and productivity, forming a nexus of relations, of machines linking up. The schizophrenic nomad experiences this by being immanent to the field without recourse to a transcendental signification: he traverses the field of relations, the intensities pass through him, a subjectivity of inclusive disjunctive synthesis. His unconscious is most open to, most consistent with and immanent to the field of desiring-production. The extremity of this is protected against through the Oedipalization of the unconscious—the repression of desire through familialisation producing an unproductive, representational consciousness, removed from the immanent field of desiring-production; an unconscious subordinated to a deferral of desire by the mediation of law, lack and the signifier. The ultimate error of psychoanalysis is to have understood this theoretically not as being historically contingent under the regime of capitalism; but as being the fundamental, universal state of desiring-production. In doing so psychoanalysis has reinforced it within that universalizing regime.

FINAL COMMENTS: DELEUZE AND GUATTARI'S ONTOLOGY OF DESIRE

Let us try to recount Deleuze and Guattari's (1972, 1980) version of *schizophrenic desire* in *Anti-Oedipus* and *Mille Plateaux*. The first of these texts offers an "ontology" of schizophrenic desire in terms of the abstract concepts of *desiring-machines*, the *body-without-organs*, and the immanent energy of *desiring-production*. The goal of expressing this ontology is to analyse modes of desiring, and *being* ultimately, in light of psychosis. Ignoring the overriding narrative of psychoanalysis's archaic and repressive role in modern Capitalism, the emphasis on psychosis in *Anti-Oedipus* derives from a combination of Deleuze's prior melding of Nietzschean and Spinozist ontology with Guattari's Lacanian clinical background.

In *Anti-Oedipus*, the psyche does not experience desire as an interpretive consciousness generating a representation of experience through the presuppositions of a phenomenological subject. In the machinic model of desiring, machines (libidinal intensities of bodies, relations, productions, events) are pre-psychical and pre-social—they interact forming machinic processes of flows and outputs. In these processes, "society" or the "psyche" can be produced as a constellation of experience, a product, but neither has any primacy. Machines are processes of composition and function which are productive but also contain an element of anti-production, the *body-without-organs*. The event of *production* is at one and the same time a process of producing and one of the products of this "producing." In other words, the "event of production" can be considered alongside the process, a separate but immanent element of it. And such an event can progress towards a moment of antiproduction immanent to production. These events are contrasted to the field of differences in which desiring-machines come together and function by connecting themselves as assemblages. They are the field that embodies the machinic process all at once as an identity.

Now, Deleuze and Guattari (1972) make this identity that is the body-without-organs a correlate of the death drive of the unconscious insofar as it encompasses the whole of production sufficiently to be able to make the whole process stop for a moment before functioning again. Thus the body-without-organs represents a principle of repetition for Deleuze and Guattari (1972) which conditions machinic desiring-production to eventually produce an empty, unproductive body. Desiring-machines are thus haunted by a desire for their own abolition. The drive to continually produce production is merely an indirect means to produce antiproduction: the drive to continually produce actually represses production—a cycle emerges where the endless repetition of desiring passes via an empty state of non-production. Deleuze and Guattari (1972) expand upon this abstract ontological formulation of the body-without-organs by equating it with the functioning of the death drive in the unconscious: desiring fluctuates between a repetitive process of desiring based upon a "model of death" and the anti-productive limit of this process as an "experience of death." The unconscious always desires a process of becoming which culminates in an "experience of death": "The experience of death is the most common of occurrences in the unconscious, precisely because it occurs in life and for life, in every passage or becoming, in every intensity as a passage or becoming... (1972, 330)."

The authors refer to this antiproductive moment or culmination of desiring as a *schizophrenic* experience of intensive qualities in their pure state, "an intense feeling of transition, states of pure, naked intensity stripped of all shape and form" (1972, 18). Later, they (1980, 1992) would refer to it as *chaos*. And it is important to emphasize that for all their abstract ontologizing of desire in this system of machines and intensities and events, the fundamental emphasis is placed upon exteriorizing desire, not offering a phenomenology of the schizophrenic unconscious so much as expressing it, producing it in their text. The words of the schizophrenic are the curious expression of the experience of relations and forces at the transcendental level. They may seem irrational when they jump across the entire fields of nature and history, the psychic and the social, the virtual and the actual.[13] The almost unbearable experience of these intensities leads desire to be repressed, hence Deleuze and Guattari's (1972) analysis of the repression of desire, something explored in the second section of our text above. Fundamentally, they theorize this as an inversion or reversal of the death drive: instead of the model of death repetitively culminating in desire as an experience of death as *becoming*, the experience of death is converted back into the model to make the dead and abstract body its goal—a sheltering from the suffering and intensity of this *becoming* of a live, unconscious body in a fixed and constant abstraction of desire.

And so, with this model of desire as *machinic heterogenesis*, desire emerges as a complexity of intensities that cannot be comprehended in terms of the organization of bodily components, in terms of the linguistic structures of signification, nor through the interpretation of subjective intentions. In *Mille Plateaux*, Deleuze and Guattari (1980) explore the implications of the broadness of this heterogenesis, where there are relations between the most disparate things: "a semiotic fragment rubs shoulders with a chemical interaction, an electron crashes into a language, a black hole captures a genetic message, a crystallization produces a passion, the wasp and the orchid cross a letter" (1980, 69). The fields of application are open and seemingly endless.

For the purposes of our analysis here, it is interesting to look at the implications Deleuze and Guattari draw for machinic heterogenesis as desire being a *universalized sexuality*. Deleuze and Guattari (1980) want to define sexuality as perversion. In oedipalized sexuality the object of desire is always missing from its place in reality because it is symbolic, governed by the phantasm of a signification of lack. There is a hylomorphic relation in this desire between the phantasm as a form of expression and the content of the actual person/object that partially embodies it for the subject, with the result that the phantasm is unchanged but intensified by the encounter, interpersonal/object relations being governed by the form of the phantasm. And so, because this phantasm is shaped by the desire of the Other, it only has *one* sex defined by the missing phallic signifier. This is in contrast to Deleuze and Guattari's (1980) perverse, machinic sexuality, in which multiple sexualities or *assemblages* emerge, defined by symbiotic relations of machinic heterogenesis. Libidinal intensities or "thresholds" interact and combine to form a very contingent, specific multiplicity that is the assemblage of all of its elements. These constitute an event or episode of desiring as *becoming*. Deleuze and Guattari (1980) analyse two such episodes: the "becoming-horse" of Little Hans in Freud's classic analysis, and the "becoming-whale" of Captain Ahab in Melville's *Moby Dick*.

In these analyses, the authors look at the assemblage of multiplicities to see what capacity or power it has to produce a becoming. The horse for Little Hans, for example, is composed of active and passive affects: "having eyes blocked by blinders, having a bit and bridle, being proud, having a big peepee maker, pulling heavy loads, being whipped, falling, making a din with its legs, biting, etc." (1980, 257). And Little Hans's life is composed of an assemblage of elements onto which the horse may be mapped: "his mother's bed, the paternal element, the house, the café across the street, the right to go out onto the street, the pride of winning it, but also the dangers of winning it, the fall, shame . . ." (1980, 257–258). Now the problem for Little Hans' becoming-horse is whether he can form a symbiotic play with it: "an assemblage . . . in which the horse would bare its teeth and Hans might show something else, his feet, his legs, his peepee-maker, whatever" (1980, 258). Each affect is a possible exterior relation, a potential assemblage of bit and bridle, pride and shame, the penis, blinders and heavy loads, the street, and so forth. Little Hans is not so much imitating the horse as incorporating *becoming-horse* into this episode of his life: "Being expresses them both in a single meaning in a language that is no longer that of words, in a matter that is no longer that of forms, in an affectability that is no longer that of subjects" (1980, 258). And while it may be easy to describe such an assemblage of multiplicities or affects in a subjective *episode*, the importance lies in just how they come to constitute a desire or becoming. Why should Little Hans wish to play with the horse, make the horse a desiring-machine? This has to do with an exercise of power, an effectuation of affects through the assemblage. Becoming-horse is like a performative statement, what the authors call an *assemblage of enunciation* of desire.

The importance of this conceptualization of desire for us, here, relates to its emphasis upon firstly the positivity, the productivity, the *exercise* of power in desire; and secondly, the multiplicity, the specificity, the perversity of the assemblage of enunciation that is desire. This type of desire as *becoming*, a desire of "multiple sexualities" or "transsexualism" favours *difference*. For Deleuze and Guattari (1980), "multiple sexualities," perversity and sexual difference, are the key productive elements of sexual desire.

Deleuze and Guattari (1972) in referring to the "experience of death" as the repetitive culmination of desiring-production, the moment of stasis in the system in which the body-without-organs perfects itself, seem to be invoking a limit state similar to that of Lacanian *jouissance*. They refer to it as a schizophrenic experience of intensive qualities in their pure state, "an intense feeling of transition, states of pure, naked intensity stripped of all shape and form" (1972, 18). The almost unbearable experience of these intensities leads desire to be repressed. Later, they (1980) refer to this moment of culmination as *chaos*, but they also establish a theory of desire in which machinic assemblages of desiring form to exercise desire as an *enunciation*, a specific and discrete type of *becoming*. In distinguishing between *chaos* and *becoming*, they seem to be distinguishing between a transitory psychotic limit of desire which resembles *jouissance*, and a more enduring form of desire defined in terms of *becoming* and *enunciation*. These later concepts are the basis of a general theory of the expression or exercise of desire which celebrates schizophrenic desire, like any other desire, under the ethics of *difference*.[14] This ethics encourages the *exercise* of desire as power but, it seems, fails to analyse the degree to which psychotic states are an active *exercise* of desire, a *productive, creative desire*, or merely an *enunciation* of a *disempowered experience*. In abandoning an individuated conception of selfhood we are often unsure as to where the *exercise* of power lies. The psychotic's desire, here, may not be exercised by an empowered agent, and is perhaps only a suffering experienced and enunciated under the gaze of clinicians and theorists.

We can see that the rich conceptualization of desire, in Deleuze and Guattari's (1972, 1980) work, does depart from a neutral and somewhat ill-defined potentiality in Heidegger's ontology. This emphasizes those elements of ontology that relate to becoming, potentiality and differentiation, as well as productivity and creativity in the enunciation and differentiation of desire as process. Loosely, Deleuze held subjectification, individuation (and familialisation) as secondary processes that emerge from these supra and sub individual processes, within an organic and socio-political field of articulation. Part of our project may be inspired by an attempt to extend Deleuze and Guattari's (1972, 1980) critical analysis of oedipalized subjectivity (and by extension hysteria, neurosis, and the subjugated "schizophrenic unconscious") in our contemporary age of "borderline experience," the project devoting itself to the critical analysis of the role the "borderline" construct plays in the subjectification of desiring processes and experience.

It is now important to turn to two remaining domains, those of temporality and technicity, both of which entail processes of individuation and subjectification as they occur *in time* and *in the world*.

Chapter 5

Temporality

The Timeless Unconscious, Nachträglichkeit, *and the Shattering of Time*

Heidegger and Freud share a philosophical heritage in which Kant's "metaphysics of the subject" and the subsequent developments of neo-Kantian and Hegelian thought were met by Nietzsche's nihilistic ideas about the various challenges posed to self-interpretation by unconscious motivations and forms of illusion and self-deception. Both Heidegger and Freud developed approaches to interpretation which paid close attention to reading or interpreting symptomatically what is omitted, hidden, implicit, forgotten or repressed. After Nietzsche, this sensitivity to what is absent, what needs to be revealed, disclosed or brought to light, is also an "historical" sensitivity: for Heidegger, as I alluded to above, there is an historical narrative of the forgetting of the question of Being and this narrative within the history of philosophy correlates with his hermeneutic exploration of *Dasein's* own tendencies to immerse or become purposefully absorbed in its environment (*Umwelt*) working towards various goals and projects (*Entwurfen*), often not mindful of the existential context into which we have been thrown (our "thrownness" or *Geworfenheit*) and its horizons (death, our own facticity or what Heidegger would term our *historicity*). Heidegger would hold that this mode of being in the world conceals or omits a sense of the Being which is immanent and implicit to our going about things but not understood in any explicit way. Furthermore Heidegger would refer to the initial tendency for ourselves (*qua Dasein*) to understand ourselves and the world as falling into the terms of objective presence (what he calls "ontical" understanding), seeing ourselves as the objective entities that we are in the objective world in which we exist. This form of "ontical" understanding entails all of the possible technical and scientific elaborations of understanding self and the world as objective entities and is aligned with the philosophical tradition of Platonic-Aristotelian metaphysics which understands the world in terms of objective presence.

Part of Heidegger's project in *Being and Time* was to elucidate that this forgetting of Being philosophically also entails a distortion in the understanding of time. Put simply time may be officially and scientifically understood as an unfolding of successive objectively present moments in a linear sequence of past, present and future, something that is different, Heidegger will hold, to his phenomenological description of time he will attempt to arrive at in *Being and Time*. This is representative of the forgetting of the temporal nature of Being. A primary role of interpretation in Heidegger's ontology will be to open up a space in which this Being can be thought, revealing the hidden and undisclosed nature of the temporality of Being. As I have shown, fundamental to this understanding is a conception of the phenomenological or existential structure of temporality, Care (*Sorge*) which is based in *Dasein*'s *thrownness* (historicity, factual context), *projection* (being towards) and how this is involved in its present concern for its *Umwelt* (environment) and *Mitwelt* (being-with-others).

We can think of an analogous type of understanding of what is hidden and what becomes disclosed or revealed when we think of Freud's approach to the interpretation of neurotic symptoms. Neurotic symptoms have an historical nature understood in terms of a theory of infantile sexuality and modes of fixation, repression and regression occurring within the delayed action of unconscious memory. This historical nature is akin to thrownness insofar as it acts on the present and projects itself (and I mean this both in a temporal sense and a Freudian sense) into current activity including the transferential enactments and the remembering, repeating and working through in the analytic session. This hidden form of temporality (unconscious memory, conflict, transference) is counterpoised with the more regulated, official, objective time of the analytic session in the analytic work and an objective sense of what is the past and what is the present. The analytic work, interpretive work, makes historical links and the nature of this interpretive work, *working in time*, and working with the *historical unconscious*, is what is of interest here.

This idea of an historical Unconscious is problematic because, for Freud, the unconscious is also often referred to as timeless. We may be familiar with many moments in which Freud refers to the unconscious as "timeless." For example, in his (1915) article "The Unconscious" which appears in his papers on metapsychology, he states: "The processes of the system *Ucs.* are *timeless*; i.e. they are not ordered temporally, are not altered by the passage of time; they have no reference to time at all. Reference to time is bound up, once again, with the work of the system *Cs* (*SE, 14,* 186)."

Elsewhere in the paper he does refer to the relational and temporal aspects of the unconscious: "It is a very remarkable thing that the *UCs.* of one human being can react upon that of another, without passing through the *Cs.* . . . descriptively speaking the fact is incontestable (*SE, 14,* 193); and ". . . the greater part of what we call conscious knowledge must in any case be for very considerable periods of time in a state of latency, that is to say, of being psychically unconscious. When all our latent memories are taken into consideration it becomes totally incomprehensible how the existence of the unconscious can be denied. (*SE, 14,* 171)." Here, we are looking at a particular site in Freud's topographical writings where an issue appears that re-emerges in many situations in Freud's work: how atemporal unconscious elements (drives, motivations, conflicts) are influenced by memory; how the Unconscious acts as a system of memory; and how the Unconscious operates relationally as opposed to intrapsychically. One further implication of this relates to how, after Freud renounces his own Seduction Theory, within his conceptualizations of the intrapsychic and unconscious basis of neurotic conflict, any conflict or impact introduced by *actual* or *real* past traumatic events operates psychopathologically.

At this level, we need to elucidate the ways in which memory *acts upon* the present, and how, simultaneously, the present (interpretation, working through) acts upon the past via memory. Memory, here, can become a bidirectional constructive or representative process.

If we place these issues in the context of an attempt to understand the manner in which the Freudian analyst understands the historicity of the analysand and the unconscious work they undertake, we can begin to see how tensions arise when we attempt to understand the temporal or historical nature of the interpretations made: do the interpretations make causative links which relate different forms of objective presence (worldly or intrapsychic events), or do they uncomfortably cross a boundary between the objective presence of worldly objective events and an atemporal intrapsychic realm which is either understood in itself as an objectively present "psychic apparatus" (of drives, instincts) or simply a realm of interpretation (of symbolic primary processes).

The hermeneutic exercise of interpreting the exploration and use of temporal concepts in Freud's works, ultimately, is a difficult and complex one: there is no single work which elaborates upon a theoretical formulation of time, and Freud adopts varying and sometimes contradictory elaborations of notions of history, memory and temporality as his project developed over thirty to forty years, and arguably as an open, transforming and sometimes unresolved set of theoretical, clinical ideas within psychoanalysis and beyond in realms such as anthropology, theology and aesthetics. Fortunately, a psychoanalytic theorist, with some philosophical literacy, André Green, conducted this form of hermeneutic project to enable us to make further links between Freud's thinking of time, and Heidegger's hermeneutic ontology. I will now explore this as a means of establishing some of these links which will become useful when I come to contemplate developmental and clinical time in subsequent parts of this work.

GREEN, *NACHTRÄGLICHKEIT*, AND FRAGMENTED TIME

In the work *Time in Psychoanalysis* (2002) and related papers, Green attempts to extract Freud's thinking about time, memory and working through across the course of Freud's works (pre-psychoanalytic, Structural, Topographic) to extract and map out a psychoanalytic theory of time steeped in Freudian origins. A central concept of Freud's that he focuses upon is *Nachträglichkeit* which is often translated into English as "deferred action" and into French as *après-coup*. Green emphasizes that these translations do not emphasize the bidirectional nature of time that is captured in this concept: memory or past experience can remain suspended in conflict, fixation, repression or disavowal, so that any action on psychic life can be re-appear at a later time with a form of deferred action; but, conversely, a current experience can trigger a movement backwards in time, a regression which returns retroactively to the past state, reintroducing the necessity of its action and the possibility of working through by another means. And so, the bidirectional nature always refers to both a delayed effect and the related reconstruction, or working through of it . . . to this, Green (2002, p41) adopts a pun around the word *re-presentation*, capturing the idea of a deferred return, and a new reconstruction. I will emphasize this notion of *re-presentation* to capture Green's rediscovery of the bidirectional action of *Nachträglichkeit* as an active and constructive form of memory.

Green (2002, pp. 9–21) shows how this bidirectional action of time, appeared from the beginning and throughout Freud's writings but that this manifests in different renderings of temporality which seem to co-exist, whereby he concludes that time for Freud is *heterochronic* or *fragmented*. Freud's psychosexual theories, for example in *The Three Essays on the Theory of Sexuality* (1905), uphold a theory of sexual development that is sequential, linear and progressive, but that elements of time in this theory are bidirectional: it involves sexual diphasism where unresolved elements of infantile sexuality are repressed and *re-present* in puberty and adulthood to be worked through, entailing bidirectional elements of fixation and deferred action as well as regression. *The Interpretation of Dreams* (1910) refers to the pure present of the unconscious psychic dream space and the manner in which primary processes work upon unconscious memory traces, *re-present* them, where the dream is a form of phantastic memory construction, analogous to screen memory: the bidirectional nature of psychic life is the move. In the landmark paper *Remembering, Repeating and Working Through* (1914) Freud introduces a focus upon repetition and enactment: what cannot be represented (or remembered in the sense of a conscious, constructive act), continues to repeat itself (re-present, in the sense of enactment as a more primitive form of action memory), and this process manifests in the psychoanalytic setting with transferential enactment. This is extended when Freud, in *Beyond the Pleasure Principle* (1920) develops the concept of repetition compulsion as a manifestation of the death instinct, and Green argues, of all drives or instincts. In fact, with the Id supplanting the unconscious in this latter phase of Freud's writings (not replacing it, for the structural and topographic models by no means intertranslate or substitute for one another), both unconscious atemporal drives, and traces of experience, somehow exist within non-psychic space through which ego function has as its role to bind and represent these aspects of the Id.[1]

I would add that Freud (in *Beyond the Pleasure Principle*) uses the term *Bindung* (translated as binding) to explain these ego processes and the phenomenon of repetition compulsion. *Bindung* also refers to a process in which psychic trauma, seen as an extensive breach of the ego's boundaries, is compulsively repeated in symbolic activity (one recalls his discussion of the *Fort-Da* game). And finally, there is a later notion of Binding (such as it appears in *An Outline of Psychoanalysis*) as one of the major characteristics of Eros and the life instincts—the move to self-preservation, ego integrity and self-unity, as opposed to the destructive, degenerative, fragmentation of the death instinct (*Entbindung*). I introduce these versions of Freudian *Bindung* because they refer to movements towards consciousness formation, ego integrity, self unity and later the self-preserving instinct to compulsively work through trauma via unconsciously driven symbolic relational enactments to re-establish integrity and unity. These forms of *Bindung* are forms of *re-presentation*, action and integration that are temporal, in Green's sense of bidirectional time, and link to self-function or ego function. Interestingly, when using these later conceptualizations of *Bindung* Freud does not return to explore the question of unconscious time. For example, in *Beyond the Pleasure Principle* he states:

> At this point I shall venture to touch for a moment upon a subject which would merit the most exhaustive treatment. As a result of certain psycho-analytic discoveries, we are to-day in a position to embark on a discussion of the Kantian theorem that time and space are 'necessary forms of thought'. We have learnt that unconscious mental processes are in themselves 'timeless'. This means in the first place that they are not ordered temporally, that time does not change them in any way and that the idea of time cannot be applied to them. These are negative characteristics which can only be clearly understood if a comparison is made with *conscious* mental processes. (1920, *SE 18*, 28)

We see here that in this re-assertion of a timeless unconscious Freud simultaneously turns to the requirement of directing more attention towards an understanding of conscious mental processes, the integrity and functioning of the ego. Here we have something of a critical juncture in Freud's elaboration of his metapsychology which I will not develop too much here: there is one movement in Freud's later work which focuses on the centrality of ego function and would no doubt be later adopted by the Ego Psychology schools; the other movement focussing on the death instinct[2] (*entbindung*) in its necessary relationship with the life instincts.

In all of this, Green (2002) uses *Nachträglichkeit* as a bridging concept for what he sees as a heterochronous, fragmented temporality, with an analogous history in the analysand:

> Freud's heritage leaves us with an uncompleted task and we know only too well that he was constantly re-working history in all its forms. For history, he believed, could not be reduced to what is left behind in the form of visible traces (accessible to consciousness) nor to that of which traumas conserve the memory. There is not one history (great or small), but *several* histories within the spheres of the individual, culture and the species, which are interrelated, interwoven, overlapping and sometimes opposed—each living according to its own rhythm and its own time. . . . And rather than giving up and opting for the simplest solution—a strictly ontogenetic point of view—we should have the courage to do justice to this complexity, attempting to gather in the scattered threads of this web in order to bring together the multiple figures of time. (2002, 27)

This analysis has been pursued to extend notions of temporality from the foundations of Heideggerian hermeneutic ontology to a point that we can begin to think about developmental and clinical time beyond the beginnings of conceptualizations of thrownness, Care, *Sicht*, *Entwurfen* and being-towards-death. Green's (2002) analysis shows us that in the complex and open system of Freud's works, memory processes, as *re-presentations*, are complex and heterogonous (enactment, narrative memory, screen memory, dream work, intrapsychic object relations, primal fantasy and myth) due to the heterochronicity of time. What underpins this is a complex, heterogonous, and to Freud, timeless, field of unconscious traces, drives, instincts, processes or, relatedly, *Id*. This could be considered, in Heideggerian terms, to be an ontological field never separable from a *hermeneutic* horizon. Freud goes so far as to elaborate ego and binding processes that relate to memory work and *re-presentation* and Green states that although experience, finally, is heterochronous and heterogonous, ego or self-function pursues cohesion, binding and meaning to constitute itself. This is work *in time*, although there is a double forgetting of time: "The unconscious is unaware of time *but consciousness does not know that the unconscious is unaware of time*" (2002, 37).[3]

For Heidegger, the Freudian *Id* and unconscious would be incoherent or aporetic concepts with metaphysical underpinnings, if not thought of in terms of forgetting, a pre-Ontological background, a limit or a horizon. It is not inconsistent with a hermeneutic ontological orientation to think of personal time (and then developmental and clinical time) in terms of traces and *re-presentations*, within a broader perspective of Care, projection, futurity and *being-towards-death*. In this way, both the past and the future collapse within bidirectionality, where Being is a process of *becoming*, and the past is seen in terms of elements of potentiation and *Nachträglichkeit* as *re-presentation*. The self, as a secondary process of individuation is posited alongside the ego binding processes within a hermeneutic perspective of the *jemeinigkeit* of Being. In subsequent parts of this work, these elements will be developed in conceptualisations of both developmental and clinical time.

DERRIDA, *NACHTRÄGLICHKEIT*, AND *DIFFÉRANCE*

Freudian *Nachträglichkeit* (and along with it *Verspätung* or delay/deferral) played a significant role in the development of Derrida's ideas, appearing in a lecture entitled "Freud and the Scene of Writing" at a time where Derrida is introducing a key deconstructive analysis of the suppression of writing in the metaphysical tradition which favours a metaphysics of presence, immediacy and speech, such as he had taken it up in the essays published in *De la Grammatologie* in 1967.

Derrida is interested in the fact that with the Freudian concepts of *Nachträglichkeit* and *Verspätung* there is an apprehension of time which is characterized by belatedness and that there is consequently no pure and simple present. Derrida questions the notion of presence and self-presence and looks subsequently into the opposition between the conscious and the unconscious in Freud, showing how Freud subverts it. According to Derrida, there does not exist in Freud an unconscious which would be situated in a precise place and would belong to a definite time, an unconscious which would have to be retranscribed in another place and another time (the conscious). The past is contained in the present. And Derrida makes reference to this Freudian basis in *Writing and Difference*: "That the present in general is not primal but, rather, reconstituted, that it is not the absolute, wholly living form which constitutes experience, that there is no purity of the living present – such is the theme, formidable for metaphysics, which Freud, in a conceptual scheme unequal to the thing itself, would have us pursue. (1978, 266)."

All these considerations will open the way to Derrida's concept of *différance*, in that, Derrida writes, "the Freudian concept of trace must be radicalized and extracted from the metaphysics of presence which still retains it."

In the context of his deconstructive analysis, Derrida is interested in the fact that Freud relies upon the metaphor of a writing machine to represent the functioning of the psyche. In the 1925 text "Note on the Mystic Writing-Pad" Freud seizes upon the metaphor of a children's toy writing machine, the *Wunderblock* (the Mystic Writing-Pad) to describe the functioning of the psychic apparatus in terms of the production of a permanent trace in memory whilst maintaining ongoing, indefinite capacity to receive new stimulation or percepts. In practical terms, the Mystic Writing-Pad is a device constituted of a slab of wax covered with a transparent sheet made of two layers: a transparent celluloid sheet (used as a protection) and a sheet of thin translucent waxed paper. To write, one uses a pointed stylus with which one scratches the surface and which forms grooves, which with the sheet in contact, form visible traces. To wipe off or erase these traces, one lifts the transparent sheet and the contact is interrupted. The traces remain in the slab, but the paper and celluloid sheet are again clear to be re-inscribed. Freud saw this as an ideal metaphor for the limitless reception of conscious perception, and the capacity of indefinite preservation in the unconscious that can be inscribed behind perception with indelible memory traces.

In the essay "Freud and the Scene of Writing," Derrida (1972a) notes Freud's reliance upon technological writing metaphors when he attempts to describe the action of unconscious memory. Derrida (1972a) analyses Freud's use of the "mystic writing-pad" as a means of explaining unconscious memory as trace/inscription. Derrida (1972a) points to Freud's failure to recognize the existence of more sophisticated archiving technologies to use metaphorically, as well as Freud's lack of awareness of and reliance upon such technological metaphors of description. Derrida (1972a) argues that this device is used metaphorically as a *supplementary machine*. In loose Derridean terms, a supplement is something that, allegedly secondarily, comes to serve as an aid to something "original" or "natural." Supplement has a double meaning here: it is not only secondary as a stand-in, a signifier or a representative; it also adds to and modifies.

In Derrida's deconstructive terms, the originary form that is favoured (presence, speech, essence, the natural) may indeed always be dependent upon, or altered by, the supplement. In the various pieces where Derrida (1978, 1987, 1998) analyses Freud's work, a core theme is the supplementary representation of the unconscious, and unconscious memory in particular, where all manner of technological metaphors are adopted. As described earlier, a central theme in Derrida's analysis will always relate to a key Derridean concept: that of *différance*. *Différance* is a neologism which simultaneously refers to "differing" and "deferral." It can describe the production of meaning through such metaphors: firstly (relating to deferral) there is the notion that metaphors will never fully summon forth what they mean, but can only be defined through appeal to additional signs, words or metaphors, from which they differ. Thus, meaning is forever "deferred" or postponed through an endless chain of signification.

In a lecture subsequent to "Freud and the Scene of Writing," "La différance," Derrida (1972b) makes links between *Nachträglichkeit* and his own concept of *différance*, which has two meanings; the first refers to the determining functions of *Nachträglichkeit*, namely, time and deferral, the second, to difference as differentiality. Now, Derrida here recognizes that the notion of *Nachträglichkeit* has enabled him to unfold a philosophy of the future and not of the past, dialectics or synthesis. He writes: "This structure of deferral (*Nachträglichkeit*) forbids us . . . to consider temporalisation (temporisation) as a simple dialectical complication of the living present, an original and unceasing synthesis (constantly returned to itself, assembled on itself, assembling) of retentional traces and protentional openings" (1972b, 3). Deferral is adding, supplementing meaning, constituting the present as a form of delay beyond or different to apparently immediate temporal present that is illusory. Derrida argues that this demonstrates that writing unfolds in a discontinuous time where unconscious traces remain and can have a deferred action or presence at any time, but the originary nature of those traces, and of temporal presence, is only ever understood supplementarily, in the play of *différance*.

In all of this, we have arrived at a thinking of time, via Freud's oeuvre, in which *Nachträglichkeit*, *re-presentation*, heterochronicity and, finally, *différance*, can be seen to relate to a hermeneutic ontological orientation, extending Heideggerian concepts of Care, *Geworfenheit*, *Entwurfen* and being-towards-death, to permit a fuller understanding of historicity and potentiality that will be extended in subsequent parts of this work when we consider developmental and clinical time.

Having explored the fields of relationality (with a subsequent exploration of dialogue, care and otherness), embodied affectivity (with a subsequent exploration of desire, potentiation and multiplicity) and now temporality (with a subsequent exploration of *Nachträglichkeit*, *re-presentation* and *différance*), what remains is a return to a fuller understanding of *Umwelt* and a re-thinking of the place of ontic thinking, technical and scientific thinking. It is apt that the discussion of Derrida's analysis of the Mystic Writing-Pad brings us to this point, as it highlights the role of *thinking technologically* and the role this plays within the frame of hermeneutic ontology.

Chapter 6

Technology and Science
Exteriorization, Interiorization, and Becoming

On first inspection, the theme of technology and its relationship to psychotherapy appears to be somewhat abstruse. These two terms initially appear to have a discordant relationship, if we think of technology evoking the mechanical, inhuman and industrial, and psychotherapy evoking some form of caring, empathic, human relationship in a clinical setting. The common ground, though, relates to both being forms of human activity that apply skills, crafts or methods that are productive. Technology is etymologically derived from the Greek word τέχνη (*techné*) which is often translated as *craftsmanship*, *craft*, or *art*. It is the rational approach to producing an object or accomplishing a goal or objective. *Techné* resembles *epistēmē* in the implication of knowledge of principles, although *techné* differs in that its intent is making or doing, as opposed to disinterested understanding. Psychotherapy relates to therapy which is etymologically derived from the Greek word θεραπεία which is the activity of curing and healing a disease, or taking care of or attending to a sick person. Perhaps the two terms have their closest affinities when we think of the term "technique" which is readily adopted by psychotherapists to describe an approach or method in therapy; while in even more general terms it can refer to any method or approach adopted in a technological endeavor to produce an outcome or endpoint. In this, there is always a creative or productive endpoint. It is interesting to highlight some other Aristotelian concepts (for these concepts were elaborated on in depth by Aristotle in works such as *Nichomachean Ethics*): *Techné*, for example, can be compared with *phronesis* which refers to know-how or practical wisdom, where the mode of action is considered in order to deliver change, especially to enhance the quality of life but may not rely on any formal or explicit knowledge (*techné* or *epistēmē*) to bring this about.

There are many relevant issues here for the psychotherapist: how explicitly or scientifically are we able to understand our practice? What recourse to technical or scientific knowledge do we have? How scientifically do we understand the objects of our treatment? In contemporary times, these questions are transposed into the era of evidence-based medicine and managed care that has fuelled psychotherapy outcomes research to become a competition between different manualized, brand-name psychotherapies. In resisting this, it might not simply be a matter of upholding a more idiographic, hermeneutic orientation to therapy (perhaps in relation to some specific humanistic, psychoanalytic or psychodynamic school or approach). It might require a deeper analysis of how the technical and scientific domains relate to therapeutic practice.

Part of this analysis involves an exploration of technology and how it might relate to our understanding of ourselves insofar as this might become operational in psychotherapeutic practice. To bring us to a point where we can explore and understand this a bit better, I will now outline some aspects of Heidegger's orientation and thinking around technology, and then explore how this has been amended and elaborated upon by a more contemporary thinker, Bernard Stiegler, before I give some examples of how this might be applied to psychotherapeutic understanding as this will be developed in the developmental and clinical parts of my project which is, in the broadest sense, a critical exploration of the borderline concept.

HEIDEGGER ON TECHNOLOGY

We are reminded of preceding discussions of Heidegger's notion of Ontological Difference (which refers to the differences between beings *qua* entities and Being *per se*). Understanding beings is what Heidegger refers to as an *ontical* process, to do with the factuality, the concreteness, the naturalistic qualities of entities. This is something in contradistinction to the Ontological (pre-) understanding of Being which forms a part of Dasein's existence. As we have seen, Ontological Difference, in itself, is a highly complex concept, particularly in how it assists or confuses the delineation between hermeneutic ontology and related fields such as anthropology, psychology and so forth.

In the "Letter on Humanism," Heidegger (1947) argued that Jean-Paul Sartre had misconstrued this kind of difference in Sartre's inversion of the traditional metaphysical difference between essence and existence (the inversion being Sartre's favouring of existence over essence). In doing this, Sartre continued to uphold these metaphysical categories on the way to maintaining a humanistic orientation (prioritizing existence in philosophical study as a way of restoring the "dignity of man"). Now Heidegger (1947) in this essay reminds the reader that Being, the thinking of Being through language, somehow takes priority over this humanistic priority of existence. One of the implications of this is that our thought becomes challenged again by this call to thinking Being, rather than residing comfortably in our pre-reflective, immediate existence, or a dichotomous approach to reflecting on our existence as something separate to and prioritized over the world of entities outside of us. We are reminded that Heidegger's notions of worldhood, care and thrownness destabilize such dichotomies as "self and other," "mind and body," "inner and outer," "mental and physical" and so forth. The tension to explore, then, concerns how such dichotomies are dissolved while a concept such as Ontological Difference remains. Interestingly, in other writings shortly after the *Letter on Humanism*, Heidegger elaborates on some of this with regard to what he entitles *The Question Concerning Technology* (1954).

In the 1954 essay "The Question Concerning Technology" Heidegger approaches the question of modern technology as a pervasive fact of modern human life. Drawing on Rousseau he captures the problem in his opening statement: "everywhere we remain free and chained to technology (1954, 311)." Heidegger goes on to famously raise a suspicion of our modern techological culture, claiming it conceales truth and poses an ethical risk to our way of life. The objectivity, reductionism and operationalism of technologcal culture would conceal or enframe a true understanding of Being. Heidegger's answer to the question concerning technology was *poesis* or art. Art is essentially poetical and therefore contains the potential for "the bringing forth of the true into the beautiful" (1954, 339). In this, we must find a way of living in a "free relationship" with technology (1954, 311). The question is not "Do we accept or reject technology?" but rather "How do we live with it?" Heidegger does not say that art will poetically reveal the truth of Being; only that it is possible (1954, 340). But art is a way of coming closer to the dangerous power of modern technology so that its saving power may emerge. The question remains for Heidegger whether this appcal is a form or romanticism or nostalgia, a form of anachronistic limit Heidegger cannot pass beyond, and whether Heidegger has not truly understood the role of technology in our existence.

STIEGLER ON TECHNOLOGY

Bernard Stiegler thinks this is the case. Bernard Stiegler has reframed the question concerning technology around the concept of human *becoming* in his project *Technics and Time (Volume 1)*. Stiegler (1994) sees an intrinsic relationship between the evolution of human beings (anthropogenesis) and technology (technogenesis). Stiegler (1994) asserts that human beings are inherently technological and develop through the evolution of technology. His claim rests on the connection between technics and time and a revision of Heidegger's (1928) project of *Being and Time* placing technics in a central role in human becoming. Technics, here, is linked to the process of exteriorization:

> There is today a conjunction between the question of technics and the question of time, one made evident by the speed of technical evolution, by the ruptures in temporalization (event-ization) that this evolution provokes, and by the processes of deterritorialization accompanying it. It is a conjunction that calls for a new consideration of technicity. . . . Life is the conquest of mobility. As a "process of exteriorization," technics is the pursuit of life by means other than life. (Stiegler, 1994, 17)

While Stiegler agrees with Heidegger's claim that *Dasein* is a temporal being, who is *thrown* into existence and worldhood, he questions whether this temporality is still *too interior and individualistic* and criticizes Heidegger for overlooking the fact that human temporality is externalized in technics. As such, *Dasein* is essentially "prosthetic," that is, *Dasein* is always seeking to temporalize itself externally through artifacts and technical activity. The temporality of *Dasein* is constituted prosthetically which also means that time is constituted through technology or what Stiegler prefers to call "technics." Time is therefore inscribed in technics which leads Stiegler to conclude that human becoming, that is its temporality, develops through technology. He calls the mode of human becoming "epiphylogenesis" which involves "the evolution of the living by other means than life (1994, 135)." Whereas, Heidegger saw being and time as constitutive of *Dasein's* facticity, Stiegler argues that it is constituted in an "epigenetic layer of life" which is an "epigenetic sedimentation, a memorization of what has come to pass, is what is called the past, what we shall name the *epiphylogenesis* of man, meaning the conservation, accumulation, and sedimentation of successive epigeneses, mutually articulated (1994, 140)." At a very primordial level, language can be seen as an epigenetic layer and therefore a technic through which human beings temporalize themselves. If we now return to Heidegger's notion of technology as a mode of disclosure we can see the implications of Stiegler's claim. If *Dasein* is temporal, and time is constituted through technics as Stiegler claims, then technology becomes the mode of human becoming.

Stiegler's anthropology gets its metaphysical bearings by returning to the myth of Prometheus retold by Plato in the *Protagoras*. In Plato's retelling of this myth the gods assigned Prometheus (forethought) and his brother Epimetheus (afterthought) the task of assigning powers and abilities to mortals. Epimetheus begged Prometheus to let him have the exclusive responsibility of assigning powers and abilities to the mortals. Prometheus agreed, and Epimetheus began assigning powers and abilities in such a way as to bring harmony and balance to the natural world. But, by the time Epimetheus came to the human being he was out of powers and abilities and Prometheus had to steal the art of fire (*empuron technen*) in order for the human being to have a power and ability. Stiegler (1994) sees this myth as pointing to a fundamental "lack" or "de-fault" (*défaut*) in the metaphysical origins of the human being which is overcome through technics; that is to say the art of fire compensates for the human being's lack of power and ability. Human beings are metaphysically undetermined and contingent; that is, human beings are finite. This leads Stiegler to claim that "discovery, insight, invention, imagination are all, according to the narrative of the myth, characteristic of a *default*." The origins of human technology are therefore bound up with the origins and finitude of humanity. Thus, for Stiegler, the question concerning technology is not "How shall we act?" or "How shall we live?" but rather "What shall we become?" Stiegler views technics as "the horizon of all possibility to come and of all possibility of a future" which philosophy has "repressed as an object of thought" (Stiegler, 1994, ix.). In response to this repressive approach Stiegler has argued that "the *modern* age is essentially that of *modern* technics" (1994, 7).

So, in a sense, Stiegler (1994) may be overcoming a Heideggerian bias, realizing a potential of Heidegger's radical ideas about worldhood that had become, possibly, too interior and individualized when brought into alignment with his demarcation asserted by the ontological difference (the distinction between Being in general and beings). The contrast between Heidegger and Stiegler could not be more stark. Whereas Heidegger sees an ontological distinction between *Dasein* and the tools it takes up, Stiegler sees both as intertwined. This intertwining is a process of exteriorization which he refers to as *instrumental maieutics*. Instrumental maieutics is the process whereby human temporality is externalized through the use of instruments and simultaneously given back to the human being. Stiegler puts it this way, "the cortex is determined by the tool just as much as that of the tool by the cortex: a mirror effect whereby one, looking at itself in the other, is both deformed and formed in the process (1994, 158)."

One further extension of Stiegler's (1994) perspective, then, is the notion of the re-interiorization that may occur through the technical processes of exteriorization. That is, our existence, insofar as we relate to ourselves and comport ourselves towards our own Being, may involve the manner in which we conceive of ourselves technologically, or the manner in which our exteriorized existence is re-interiorized as self-conceptualization. In Stiegler's (1994) terms, this would not be a form of understanding simply as we are, so much as understanding that arises through our becoming . . . it is contingent, factical and technologically biased. Human becoming remains projective and futural in the manner Heidegger envisioned in concepts such as *Sorge*, *Entwurfen* and *Umsicht* but it is now a more technically driven world of becoming. In terms of the evolution of behavioural modernity, Stiegler articulates it this way:

> This co-evolution is not piloted by biological evolution that would overdetermine or condition technical evolution: it is a co-determination, a reciprocal determination . . . In other words, the conditions of the brain's evolution are more and more intricately correlated to the conditions of evolution of tools, which are themselves artificial organs up to the point when, cortical evolution finally stabilized, the co-evolution between the technical system and the other social systems is modified. This is the moment of emergence of the socio-demographic group and, along with it, the typical idiomisation of psychic and collective individuation, which must be intricately correlated with the explosion of the organological evolution of artefactual technical prostheses. (Stiegler, 2009)

Technology is a fundamental element of self-understanding, epistemology and becoming, so that interiorisation and exteriorisation co-exist as worldhood. Examples here may be techniques and practices that facilitate symbolic or representational art (from the most primitive forms), language itself (in its spoken and written forms) not to mention how these may interact in such sophisticated modern technologies as film and digital media. The artefactual technological world is an ineliminable part of temporality, not only as dead history but a living form of memory, as well as an instrumental aspect of our becoming. *Individuation*, for Stiegler, is a psychic, collective and technical *process*, the result of which is the hypothetical individual. This is the opposite of the humanistic doctrine and aligns with but considerably extends Heidegger's concerns about technology: a suspicion around technology now reflects a suspicion of the kind of individual that is produced.

Now this is as far as I want to go, here, in terms of exegesis. I will now proceed to explore the relevance of what I've covered, particularly with these philosophical ideas of exteriorisation, re-interiorisation and individuation in mind, to the field of study.

THE METAPHOR OF THE MIRROR

To begin with, let us consider the tool of the mirror: the first mirrors used by people were most likely pools of dark, still water or water collected in a primitive vessel of some sort. The earliest artefacts of manufactured mirrors were pieces of polished stone such as obsidian, examples having been found in numerous cultures as far back as 6000 BC such as Anatolia, ancient Egypt, and cultures of Central and South America (such as the Mayan, Aztec and

Inca cultures). Metal-coated glass mirrors are said to have been invented in the first century AD, and forms of curved mirrors were described and studied in classical antiquity by the thinkers such as Diocles and Ptolemy. We can be led to contemplate, in Stiegler's terms, how such a primordial technology as that of the mirror has effected human individuation. Richard Rorty (1979) in *Philosophy and the Mirror of Nature* mounts an original and sustained attack on the Western philosophical tradition based on it having been seduced by the metaphor of the mirror as it is adopted in conceptualizations of the mind as representational, as an organ that mirrors the world through its representations of it, proceeding to make arguments about the modern philosophical tradition which in some ways draw support from and confirm many of Heidegger's positions (though I won't elaborate on this). The mirror, then, can be seen to be at the origins of our notions of the reflective, representational mind.

Alongside this, I can allude to the mythical status of the mirror, which Freud of course attributed such significance to in his analysis of the Myth of Narcissus and his adoption of the term *narcissism* linked to his ideas around primary and secondary Narcissism, the ego ideal and eventually the super ego. Another important link is to any modern psychological theories which refer to a representational mind in terms of the metaphors of the specular image and reflection. In the subsequent sections we will explore in depth, the more specific modern use of the mirror metaphor in theories of mirroring and attunement in attachment relationships that are seen to lead to the development of reflective ego capacities the deficits of which are seen to permeate theoretical conceptualizations of borderline pathology. In the mentalization school (Fonagy et al., 2002), the development of the self is explained in terms of a social biofeedback theory. Fundamental early attachment experiences permit the infant to move from a mode of psychic equivalence through intense engagement in attachment relationships (through forms of mirroring and feedback) to more reflexively understand intentional engagement with the environment and others. This manner of engagement implies that the young child begins to internalize and represent their engagement, initially in a pretend mode (the mode of daydream, fantasy, imagination, play) but eventually in a metarepresentational stance that the group call mentalization (Jurist, 2005, 2010). There are analogies with Schore's (1994, 2003) "right hemispheric frontal cortical basis of affect regulation" which is seen to develop in such an attachment context; as well as the models of other attachment and cognitive-evolutionary theorists, where developmental experience involves forms of cognitive-representational modelling, for example the "inner working models" and "schema" (e.g., the work of Giovanni Liotti). What is common in all of these schools is a conceptualization of borderline pathology as a failure of the acquisition of mirroring abilities which limit reflective capacity which would otherwise permit greater self-governance (seen in terms of affect regulation, integration, impulse control) and greater relational stability (seen in terms of integrated and stable relations with the other without the characteristic difficulties of splitting, heightened insecurity and reactivity and so forth).

In referring to all of this I simply want to emphasize, in terms of the philosophical discussion above, the pervasive utility of technological metaphors, such as that of the mirror, in theories of psychology and psychopathology (and their related models of psychotherapy). Without expanding on this greatly here, I can briefly refer to other pervasive metaphors that I will elaborate upon in subsequent sections: the role that computational science and the artificial intelligence paradigm have had in the parallel development of cognitive science and cognitive therapies; the role that the development of film and digital media in conceptualizing forms of information processing and representation as these are understood in disorders such as post-traumatic stress disorder.

In exploring what I think is wrong with this, in the terms of the discussion above, I would first remind us of Heidegger's (1954) caution in *The Question Concerning Technology* about the ubiquity of technology and the utility of technological metaphors in understanding while having their (existential) limits in terms of understanding Being *per se*. I would then remind us of how this was further developed by Stiegler (1994) who argues that it can be more useful to understand how technologies form a part of human becoming situated within existence, rather than assisting in the establishment of objective knowledge or understanding situated outside of existence (which is aporetic). From these perspectives we have to remind ourselves of these inherent limits of *thinking technologically* and the role that technological thinking can play in affecting or limiting *individuation*. In Stiegler's terms, there is a technological context in which forms of individuation have arisen which we may do better to try to understand; at the same time as being suspicious of the more *post hoc* (or supplementary) technological metaphors used to explain an originary or natural form of existence as if it were an object of scientific study.

In conclusion, let me make some final comments about the impact of the technology of the mirror as it may have been portrayed in the Myth of Narcissus. In the familiar versions of the myth recounted by Ovid and Pausanias the beautiful youth Narcissus was loved by the nymph Echo, who is punished by being deprived of her capacity for speech, no longer being able to converse except by echoing speech. As a result, Narcissus rejects her and she withers away until only her voice remains. After this, Narcissus discovers his own image in a pool and falls in love with the beautiful youth he sees until he recognizes himself and grieves at being unable to capture the beautiful image as another. In the thrall of this image he too withers away, or alternatively takes his own life. One theme here is that both the faculties of speech and vision become isolated and forced to repeat themselves until they die away: speech becomes a mere echo and vision a mere reflected image. They lose their function as communication and representation, there is a loss of meaning. So it is that this myth is a foundation myth for a toxic flower that represents frozen beauty and deadness. And so each individual, Narcissus and Echo, withers and perishes. What then, makes an individual? It is a process of individuation, which is simultaneously sub- and supra-individual: there must be the voice and the listener; there must be the other who the seer appreciates. These will always form part of the realms of understanding and meaning that fall within the technological process of becoming.

FINAL COMMENTS TO CONCLUDE THE PHILOSOPHICAL FRAME (PART I)

What I have pursued, in the philosophical frame, are the foundations of a hermeneutic ontological orientation which departs from Heidegger's foundational work *Being and Time* (1928) but loosely encapsulates philosophical advances made both subsequently by Heidegger's writings after his *Kehre*, as well as by some subsequent philosophers that I have labelled post-Heideggerian, who have variably taken up issues developed in Heidegger's thought, and developed them in directions that I have seen to be useful for the developmental and clinical analyses of the borderline concept and field of borderline experience I intend to undertake below.

The hermeneutic ontological orientation situates thought, meaning and understanding within the existential embeddedness and situatedness of Being in general. This situatedness is temporal insofar as it is historically mediated and constantly evolving as a process of becoming. This situatedness is also relational insofar as understanding and reflection always involve dialogue and discourse either with an other or with oneself as another, where this relationality is also embedded within a limited horizon beyond which otherness also intervenes and needs to be come to terms with, both in terms of an appreciation and respect for our limits and then in terms of ethical standpoints. This situatedness is also embodied and affective: it relates to processes of becoming, potentiality and differentiation, where subjectification and individuation are secondary processes that emerge from supra and sub individual processes, within organic and socio-political fields of articulation. And finally, this situatedness is always practically engaged and concerned, and we articulate ourselves and come to understand ourselves through our technological engagement, such that technology and science are embedded within our field of existence as becoming.

The critical standpoint of this hermeneutic ontological orientation thus seeks to undermine, overcome or contextualize approaches to thinking that assert numerous traditional errors or aporias that were seen to be encompassed by "traditional metaphysics": the representational model of consciousness, Cartesian dualism, as well as the favouring of modes of objective presence (objectivism, reductionism, essentialism, scientism and so forth) when approaching the understanding of existence and the world.

Developmentally, this is relevant when we approach infantile and childhood experience and the processes of individuation or subjectification that occur in development. In the proceeding part of this work, "the Developmental Frame," there will be a critical outlook towards theoretical models that adultomorphize infantile subjectivity, or portray it as individualistic, or adopt descriptions that rely on modes of objective presence such as representational theories of consciousness or neurobiological models that correlate to developing neurocognitive capacities. This will include a critical outlook being applied to the attachment (e.g., Allan Schore), cognitive-evolutionary (e.g., Giovanni Liotti) and mentalisation (Peter Fonagy and Anthony Bateman) models of development of borderline pathology. In comparison to these, theories and ideas that are consistent with a hermeneutic ontological outlook, that focus on the types of temporality, relationality, embodied affectivity and technicity I have described, will be explored. To this end, I will explore the affinity that the hermeneutic ontological outlook has with certain developmental ideas emerging from theorists such as Donald Winnicott, Hans Loewald, Christopher Bollas, Jacques Lacan, Jean Laplanche, Julia Kristeva and André Green.

And clinically, this hermeneutic orientation is relevant when we approach the psychotherapeutic situation as a relational context of interaction, discourse and dialogue (both linguistically and practically mediated vis-à-vis actions, enactment and non-verbal expression) influenced by limits, horizons, differentiality and otherness. In the final part of this work, the "Clinical Frame," there will be a critical outlook towards clinical models that focus upon individualistic pathology outside of the relational contexts that ethically, socially and culturally embed the treatment situation. This critical outlook will be reflected in discussion of modalities of psychotherapy such as Linehan's Dialectical Behaviour Therapy, Kernberg, Clarkin and Yeomans's Transference-focused Psychotherapy and Fonagy, Bateman and Target's Mentalization-based Therapy. An emphasis on ethical, social and cultural embeddedness can serve to focus on the respect or hospitality of otherness, as well as the violence that can occur when individuals are medicalized or subjectified in the treatment context. The preceding analyses of temporality and embodied affectivity will be utilized in a critical analysis of the fields of traumatology (e.g., Judith Herman, Bessel van der Kolk) and structural models of dissociation (Onno van der Hart and Ellert Nijenhuis) as they are applied to borderline phenomena, and commonly used terms such as abuse, trauma and dissociation. References will also be made to a number of the North

American Intersubjective and Relational thinkers (Stolorow, Aron, Atwood, Orange, Bromberg, Donnel Stern) who attempt to be mindful of these issues when they pursue more a focus on humanistic, dialogical, perspectival and co-constructivist approaches that attempt to eschew authoritarian, medicalizing, objectifying or, indeed, *subjectifying* stances. Questions will be posed regarding the role of otherness and differentiality in the dialogue that unfolds in treatment: what role the authority of the therapist has, compared with the authority of the individual entering into therapy; and what ethical issues are pursued and what limits and boundaries are maintained.

In all of this, the ultimate endeavour will be to defining a clinical outlook to borderline experience that emerges out of, and encapsulates, as much as it can of a horizon of understanding that is mindful of the complexity of our experience in terms of its relatedness, temporality, embodiment, affectivity, technicity and, ultimately, its otherness to itself.

Part II

DEVELOPMENTAL FRAME

INTRODUCTION

In the preceding part of this work, an interpretive or hermeneutic orientation was developed with reference to the work of Martin Heidegger and some philosophical thinkers that followed him. One of the principal philosophical themes that was developed there with regard to hermeneutic ontology is the idea that self-experience, self-understanding and selfhood are all inextricably linked to our temporal, relational and linguistic situatedness or embeddedness in the world, all encapsulated conceptually in Heideggerian ideas such as thrownness and worldhood (complex concepts which also include our relations to the physical environment and our own embodiment). Importantly, it was emphasized that any interpretive stance which seeks to look at this situatedness from the outside, so to speak (that's to say from a naturalistic, scientific standpoint), will inevitably resort to modes of thinking that will be flawed insofar as they rely on implicit assumptions about the ways things are, which necessarily omit or reduce other elements of experience or existence. Another principle theme that develops from the idea that our situatedness or thrownness is an horizon or frame without an "outside," and one that is fundamentally temporal, is the notion that our way of being is dynamic and constantly evolving or projecting forth, comporting itself towards itself, involving forms of self-interpretation that evolve over time in a structure involving the binding of past, present and future.

There are a series of complex issues I explored there relating to the relationship between philosophy, science and technology, and I explored how this relationship can influence interpretation in the field of scientific or naturalistic approaches to thinking, selfhood and experience in research fields such as cognitive science and artificial intelligence but also, more relevantly to my study, in experimental and clinical fields such as psychology, psychiatry and psychotherapy. One of the fundamental themes is that human being and selfhood often defy naturalistic-scientific understanding, conceptualization that is categorical, individualistic, synchronic and intrapsychic. I argue that these should not be favoured over the dimensional, relational, diachronic and interpersonal approaches to understanding that may be important to focus on in an understanding of borderline experience. I also emphasized that scientific and technological understanding operates within a frame or horizon that has an opaque background, elements of ineffability and unknowability.

In this second part, *the developmental frame*, these ideas will be further elaborated in the field of theoretical and scientific consideration of early development, where there has been increasing understanding of the necessary relational, linguistic and time-cued aspects of the development of selfhood. Clinical theorists have sought to integrate the many scientific fields in which development is studied such as ethology, developmental neuroscience, developmental psychopathology and attachment research to understand disorders such as dissociative disorders and borderline personality disorder. In the field of scientific consideration of early development, there has been increasing understanding of the necessary relational, linguistic and time-cued aspects of the development of "the self." Clinical theorists have sought to integrate the many scientific fields in which development is studied such as ethology, developmental neuroscience, developmental psychopathology and attachment research to understand disorders such as dissociative disorders and borderline personality disorder.

The attachment paradigm arising out of Bowlby's work and advanced by such researchers and clinicians as Ainsworth, Main, Lyons-Ruth, Crittenden and Holmes, is perhaps the most well elaborated of these naturalistic-scientific approaches. There are several theorists or groups of theorists that have focussed their models on borderline pathology. Liotti (1992, 1995, et al., 2000), for example, has advanced Bowlby's attachment paradigm, and more recent ethological and developmental research, to develop a Cognitive Evolutionary model of understanding disorders such as borderline personality disorder and dissociative disorders, which he would view as intrinsically developmental, attachment-based disorders. Fonagy, Bateman, Jurist, Gergely and Target have linked similar attachment research to develop their theory of mentalization to explain borderline disturbances and a model of therapy (Fonagy et al., 2002). They explore a range of research around parental affect mirroring and early development of interpersonal interpretative capacity to develop a social biofeedback theory of early development which leads to mature capacity to mentalize, core disturbances of which underpin borderline disturbances. Schore (1994, 2003) has reviewed developmental neuroscientific research to formulate a model of psychotherapy which addresses developmental deficits in affect regulation and interpersonal relatedness associated with borderline disturbance.

Now all of these theorists refer to and integrate a lot of groundbreaking and fascinating empirical research, but one can rightly question the use to which this research is put, in establishing broad or foundational theoretical constructs about selfhood and subjectivity. In all of this work there is a favouring or privileging of the centrality of the formative influence of foundational dyadic attachment relationships in the achievement of selfhood. There is often, in a sense, a considerable extrapolation of the research used to derive these central theoretical constructs which, as a result, I feel are potentially reductionistic and oversimplified. In particular, I will refer to these approaches as having an over-reliance upon what I will term the "attachment metaphor." What I want to show is that in favouring such notions there is a loss of complexity in how we understand the evolution of development, the complexity of self-experience in later development, and ultimately in what occurs in psychotherapy (and in particular the psychotherapy of individuals with borderline problems).

In this part of the work, I intend to critically review these theories but will first elaborate upon the themes I developed in the philosophical part, the "Philosophical Frame," applying these to developmental realm. In the Philosophical Frame, I focussed upon originary or foundational notions of temporality, relationality, embodied affectivity and technicity. From a hermeneutic ontological standpoint, we became aware of the existential horizon within which understanding and interpretation occur, encapsulated in concepts such as worldhood, care and thrownness. Now if we consider *developmental origins*, we become aware of limits and horizons in our understanding of the infant's world. In this part, I want to explore concepts established by developmental theorists that are consistent with this hermeneutic ontological perspective that refers to notions of limits, horizons, backgrounds, and facticity. In terms of the relational theme, I will develop ideas around dialogicality, difference and alterity; in terms of temporality, I will develop ideas around care, bidirectional time and heterochronicity; in terms of embodied affectivity I will develop ideas around the sub- and supra-individual processes of becoming and differentiation; and in terms of technology and science, I will re-situate understanding within the becoming (at an individual and cultural level), related to processes of individuation, exteriorization and interiorization. Developmentally, this is relevant when we approach infantile and childhood experience and the processes of individuation or subjectification that occur in development. This complexity, in a developmental sense, relates to the elaborate and sophisticated passage of progressive formation we undergo: there are phases of prolonged dependence beginning with maternalization but extending into all manner of familial, educational and other social or cultural contexts that permit the potentiation of complex forms of emotional relatedness, linguistic capacity, technical ability and complex embodied affectivity. In all of this, we tend to firstly envisage an endpoint, the modern, adult individual, and then attempt to conceptualize this developmental complexity from the perspective of the endpoint. We conceptualize an individual with sophisticated intrinsic capacities (representational, linguistic, social and emotional) that constitute us and are fixed and enduring. This loses the sense of ourselves as situated and thrown, always continuing to develop, form, evolve and *become*, with continuing transitions between potentiation and degradation where the complexity and ineffability of our horizon of existence forbids us from getting outside ourselves to attain the objectivity we seek.

As such, in this "Developmental Frame" there will be a critical outlook towards theoretical models that adultomorphize infantile subjectivity, or portray it as individualistic, or adopt descriptions that rely on modes of objective presence such as representational theories of consciousness or neurobiological models that correlate to developing neurocognitive capacities. A critical outlook will eventually be applied to the attachment (e.g., Allan Schore), cognitive-evolutionary (e.g., Giovanni Liotti) and mentalisation (Peter Fonagy and Anthony Bateman) models of development of borderline pathology. I will also explore the psychoanalytic developmental theories of Borderline Personality Organization advanced by Otto Kernberg and the trauma models of borderline disturbance advanced by thinkers such as Bessel van der Kolk, Onno van der Hart and Ellert Nijenhuis. In comparison to all of these approaches, theories and ideas that are consistent with a hermeneutic ontological outlook, that focus on the types of temporality, relationality, embodied affectivity and technicity I have described, will be explored. To this end, I will explore the affinity that the hermeneutic ontological outlook has with certain developmental ideas emerging from theorists such as Donald Winnicott, Hans Loewald, Christopher Bollas, Jacques Lacan, Jean Laplanche and André Green.

Part of this part of the work will involve an attempt to evoke the unknowability of infant "experience," its alterity, and its inextricability from the relational, temporal, embodied, affective and technical contexts. I want to suggest that there is no originary form of infant "experience" to be understood outside these contexts.

In this part, then, it will be argued that many of the more modern, empirically based approaches to borderline experience implicitly rely upon unexplored assumptions or folk psychological concepts of "self," "consciousness," "representation" and so forth when interpreting scientific research and synthesizing it into a developmental theory of psychopathology. It will also be argued further on in this part of the work that more traditional psychoanalytic models, especially those of the ego psychology and object relations school, have a tendency to adultomorphize infant and early childhood experience leading to inferential errors in clinical work and paralogisms in theoretical constructions. This will all be with a view to destabilizing those models of self-development that have integrated scientific research (ethology, developmental neuroscience, developmental psychopathology and attachment research) into models of borderline pathology where there is a naturalistic-scientific orientation.

Chapter 7

Relationality

Transition, Transformation, and Differentiality

In the philosophical part of this work, I discussed the notion of originary relationality that can be seen to be derived from Heidegger's project insofar as human being is always already situated in a relational context, with concepts such as *Mitwelt*, *Mitsein*, *jemeinigkeit*, *Befindlichkeit* referring to being that is always already with others, where moodfulness is always seen dialogically in how one interprets oneself both to oneself (as another) and to others. This relationality was also seen to be embedded within a limited horizon beyond which otherness or alterity also intervenes and needs to be come to terms with, both in terms of an appreciation and respect for our limits and then in terms of ethical standpoints. I derived from Gadamer's and Ricoeur's thought that forms of the self, subject or individual are constituted by or secondary to relational processes: in particular, dialogue or conversation as well as the dialectic with otherness (the otherness of embodiment, of the other, of death, of conscience and so forth). Nevertheless both thinkers were seen to remain committed to Heidegger's hermeneutic ontological orientation in articulating these elements of selfhood as historically, linguistically and factically embedded or situated. We also saw that thinkers such as Levinas and Derrida emphasized notions of otherness and differentiality in order to limit or curtail our understanding and avoid metaphysical standpoints that oppress or alter the complexity and finitude of meaning or understanding, and that interpretation is always necessarily ethical in nature.

All of these notions translate into considering development, where development can be seen to be an intrinsically temporal concept (development referring to change, becoming, acquisition and so forth), but also an intrinsically relational one, where it is scaffolded, cued and embedded in relationality. It is apodictic that psychodynamic and psychoanalytic theories of development and developmental psychopathology all explore temporal and relational issues in understanding the development of the self, the ego, consciousness, adult object relations or whatever the model of maturation entails. Now it is inconceivable to offer a complex comparative analysis of different psychodynamic developmental models, but what is of interest here will be primarily exploring the notion of developmental *origins* that are primarily relational. Many theorisations focus upon the earliest phases of development and describe the infant's relation to the world and care givers in terms of fusion, states of undifferentiatedness and so forth. In this chapter, I would like to explore ideas that are most consistent with the concept of *originary* relationality I have developed: I will elaborate upon the originary relational nature of development as it appears in three thinkers, Donald Winnicott, Christopher Bollas and Hans Loewald who look at the earliest phases of development psychodynamically, exploring the dynamic progression from an infantile state of primary narcissism and dependence, a progression which explores the founding of selfhood and consciousness in terms that are by definition relational in a sense that overcomes any conceptual reference to causal objective presence in terms of either intrapsychic or environmental concepts. Here, the emergence of selfhood, or the process of individuation, is seen to be secondary to originary relationality, the horizon of which fits within our frame of hermeneutic ontology. I have chosen these three thinkers because they elucidate core concepts that can carry though to my subsequent clinical analysis, earliest relational elements of development that carry through in subsequent development, before processes of individuation lead to a sense of self that differentiates self and other, inner and outer, self and world, or any sense of representational or cognitive understanding. In doing this, I hope to found an understanding of unconscious processes, unconscious communication, in radically relational terms that are consistent with the hermeneutic ontological orientation I have advanced.

WINNICOTT: TRANSITIONAL EXPERIENCE

Across Winnicott's works in the 1950s and 1960s there is a focus, even idealization, of the mother–infant relationship which initially emerged from his attempts to reconcile with or differentiate himself from the dominant Kleinian psychoanalytic culture he was a part of, but then became more independent and well established in its own right. His descriptions and valorisation of good-enough parenting, the value of the holding environment of the mother or carer's hands-on nurturance, technical care and security-giving warmth, were transferred into conceptualisations of empathic, therapeutic care, and the sense of self one develops as an adult, having an implicit or innate sense of being, and comfort within one's own skin. Like Heidegger, Winnicott emphasizes the importance of an immersion in practical activity, dwelling in one's purposeful activity, to give a sense of being in the world, engaged and occupied. Importantly, Winnicott articulated the developmental origins of these capacities as inextricably or originally relational and developed this in arguably his most important work, *Playing and Reality* (1971) through the development of his concepts of the *transitional object*, the *facilitating environment* and, most broadly, *transitional phenomena*.

Winnicott first coined the term *transitional object* as a designation for any physical object (typically something soft like a cloth or toy) to which an infant or child attributes a special value and through the use of which the child is able to make the shift from the earliest oral relationship (feeding with the mother) to genuine object-relationships. In his observation of infants, Winnicott noted that between the ages of four and twelve months children would often become attached to a particular object that they invested with a primordial significance. This object would be manipulated, sucked, or stroked, and often became an indispensable aid for falling asleep. Parents recognized its value, and would facilitate its use by the infant. What interested Winnicott (1951) was this "first not-me possession" and the zone it occupied between the sucked thumb and the teddy bear, between early oral eroticism and a true object-relationship. In *Playing and Reality* (1971), Winnicott developed his thinking around the transitional object into a much more elaborate theory of play and transitional experience.

To explain the origin of the transitional object, Winnicott (1971) went back to the first connection with the mother's breast. The mother, he argued, puts the actual breast in a place where the infant is ready to "create" it thus experiencing an illusory omnipotence. The inevitable frustrations of this not being a perfect accommodation by the mother will come to be tolerated through the use of the transitional object, which allows the child to exercise its feelings of omnipotence in a playful manner. In playful activity with the object, the child arrogates rights over it, which, though loved passionately, is also expected to resist and triumph over hate. In libidinal terms, the activity involved here is of an oral kind: the object is just as highly cathected with narcissistic libido as with object-libido. It is not recognized as part of either external or inner reality. There is thus an essential paradox at the heart of this conceptual framework: the infant creates the object, yet the object was already there, waiting to be created and cathected. This paradox will never be resolved: in the course of normal development, the object is destined to be gradually decathected, losing its significance as diffuse transitional phenomena spread over the entire intermediate realm between subjective inner reality and common external reality, until the whole sphere of culture is included (art, religion, imaginative life, scientific invention and so on). For Winnicott, observation of young children's abnormal use of transitional objects could be used to infer abnormal development and become associated with different types of psychopathology.

What is of interest here is Winnicott's (1971) notion of the *transitional space* emerging out of primary narcissism. The capacity for a sense of agency and play in the world emerges from a primary narcissistic state in which the infant does not apprehend the influence of the mother as something other than an extension of itself. Here, in what Winnicott called the *facilitating environment*, the infant fluctuates between states of primitive anxiety and feelings of omnipotence where there is no sense of inner or outer. Impingements or failures of the environment which the infant may experience as milder primitive anxiety (if gentle enough), lead to an engagement with the world in which transitional states emerge with the development of a sense of projective intentionality and subjective objecthood (the classical example being self-soothing with the transitional object). Progressively, play in the transitional space culminates in mature object relating (a mature sense of unitary self and world, self and others) but where there is still, for Winnicott, a privileging of play and transitional phenomena as being at the heart of mature health, creativity and vitality (aesthetic sensibility, intellectual endeavours, religious faith, other mature forms of pleasure and transcendence). As such, two notions of developmental time operate here: linear, progressive developmental time and regressive, unconscious time insofar as the self has a capacity to progress through different self-states—mature objecthood, play/creativity in the transitional space, primary narcissistic states (e.g., narcosis) and profound impingement and environmental failure creating primitive anxieties. These Winnicottian conceptualizations illustrate a developmental component to the bidirectional temporality I described in the philosophical part above[1] and describes a form of originary relationality which avoids the delimiting of inner and outer or subject and object at the same time as privileging a space or phenomenology that is transitional in a way that is analogous to Heidegger's notion of relational worldhood and also evokes the processes of exteriorization and interiorization discussed in relation to Stiegler's work. At the broadest level, the transitional object and transitional phenomena may be conceived of in three ways: firstly, as typifying a phase in the child's normal emotional development in which processes of individuation are acted out in the process of play; secondly, where this play is used as a defense against separation anxiety (analogous with but considerably developing Freud's discussions of the *Fort-Da* game, for example); and, lastly, as an articulation of a more universal sphere of agency and creativity that is intrinsic to our sense of engagement, dwelling and agency in the world.

If there is a dialectical relationship between omnipotence and primitive anxiety, in Winnicott's terms, a sense of cohesion of the self (well-being, security) is gained by internalizing or capturing a sense of the object (*qua* mother[2]). We remember Winnicott talking about the hallucinated breast not relieving the hunger of the infant, and acknowledge that this internalization does not reinforce a sense of omnipotence. This internalization does, rather, affirm a sense of being secure or being held (by the mother, by the facilitating environment). It is commonly observed (e.g., Luepnitz, 2009) that in considering self-development within the transitional space Winnicott conspicuously overlooks adequate consideration of the constitutive role of language whereby mirroring in the maternal relationship occurs more at an affective, gestural, empathic level, where transitional relating in the equipmental object world of play leads to an eventual cohesive self in which play and symbolism develop again without a strongly linguistic component[3]. The linguistic, here, can refer to the dialogical, and this, in turn, can be the manner in which the mother, or any other interlocutor, can work on, or engage with the child, even if the infant cannot accommodate whatever dialogical element is offered, uttered or implanted. Nevertheless Winnicott's theorization of the infant world of transitional experience does include consideration of active impingements, inclusions or intrusions from the relational space that are beyond the infant but are nevertheless experienced or retained at some level, and this will be developed in a subsequent part below in our discussion of originary temporality in development.

BOLLAS: TRANSFORMATION AND THE "UNTHOUGHT KNOWN"

The most influential of Christopher Bollas's works, *The Shadow of the Object* (1987), articulates a theory of unconscious processes and self-experience that could be argued to have Heideggerian tones to it: Bollas emphasizes the immediacy of non-reflective being in the world, but also goes on to emphasize that objects and interactions with others in the relational world are invested with unconscious significance related to developmental experience and self-states which exist as remnants of relational contexts in early development. For Bollas, these early experiences are highly unique and specific to each person in their process of individuation but Bollas (1987) certainly articulates that these origins for the individual are primarily relational.

Bollas (1987) develops these ideas by referring to an even more fused or symbiotic space prior to Winnicott's transitional space—what he calls the infant's *transformational object*. In early mother–infant or carer–infant relating an implicit, non-representational aesthetic of relatedness is constitutive for the infant's self-development and modes of self-experiencing as an "ontogenetic process." It remains as a constitutive remnant that Bollas (1987) refers to as "never cognitively apprehended but existentially known," what he characteristically refers to as the "unthought known." What is significant about this conceptualization is that it refers to the constitutive process of mother–infant relating and then self-relating as an implicit, mnemic, non-representational (and therefore simultaneously non-subjective and non-objective) form of existential presence:

> In the relation to the self as an object the person re-creates elements of the mother's facilitation of his existence. The structure of the ego is a form of deep constitutive memory, a recollection of the person's ontogenesis, and, although it may have little to do with the mother as the patient knows her in the whole object sense (as a person), in some respects it informs us of how she mothered this particular baby. It is her active presence, her deep instruction, her activities as a transformational object, that the baby integrates into that psychic structure that constitutes the ego; in this grammar of the ego are stored the rules for the handling of the self and the objects. When that structure coheres, if even marginally, the baby will begin to express his knowing of his being through fantasy, thought and object relating. This Unthought Known constitutes the core of one's being and will serve as the basis of subsequent infantile and child fantasy life. (1987, 60)

Just as Winnicott's conceptualization of the transitional space evokes the developmental progression of worldhood (in the Heideggerian sense), this conceptualization of the *Unthought Known* permits an understanding of primitive mood states as they relate to a form of worldhood. As we saw in the preceding philosophical part of this work, Heidegger (1928) himself conceptualizes emotional states or moods in a theory of affects that steers away from any notion of "pure" or discrete affects, where affects fall within a complex process of the doubling or synthesizing of the self which is not divorced from the existential situation involving other modes of being such as interpersonal exchange (relatedness and language), memory (temporality) and embodiment (corporeity). Affect becomes the tone, atmosphere of this binding, or failure to bind. In this context, we saw that Heidegger uses the term *Befindlichkeit* which is Heidegger's own neologism developed from the German colloquial verb *befinden*. This verb is used in the everyday question "Wie befinden Sie sich?," which broadly translates as "How are you?." There is no literal translation of this question into English as the verb refers to, at once, *feeling* and *finding oneself*, such that "Wie befinden Sie sich?" literally means "How are you feeling?" at the same time as "How do you find yourself?." In adapting this verb, Heidegger wants to capture an expression that embodies states of mind, mood states, as a type of *feeling* and *finding oneself situated*. By describing moods as a kind of *situatedness*, he is attempting to overcome a sense of inwardness or depth (moods being *intrapsychic*, if you will). *Befindlichkeit* refers to a state that is both inward and outward looking.

Moreover, such states are self-referential: one *finds oneself* in this state; it is self-interpreted actively and is an issue for oneself. This self-understanding is not cognitive so much as an implicit, lived-in awareness: this is how I am. Thus *Dasein* always has the potential for an implicit understanding (*Verstehen*) of its state. And moreover, this understanding is articulated through *Dasein*'s discourse (*Rede*). It is in this manner that the three *Existenziale* interact. One exists with mood states: we feel a moodful situatedness of which we may have an implicit understanding that can be articulated in our discourse with others and ourselves. Thus the situatedness of *Befindlichkeit* is interactional, interpersonal and implicitly self-reflective: *Befindlichkeit* embodies the wholeness of *Dasein*'s situatedness and is prior to an explicit understanding that would distinguish inner and outer, self and other, feeling and cognition, or speech and action. Understanding and discourse always belie a state of *Befindlichkeit*.

Now the further step Bollas (1987) makes here is to elaborate upon the manner in which moodfulness, universally and in psychopathology, can be constituted by forms of unconscious memory, elements of what he calls the *Unthought Known*:

> Moods are complex self states that may establish a mnemic environment in which the individual re-experiences and recreates former infant-child experiences and states of being . . . Who is it that emerges from within the mood? Since a special being state is established, what is the total self's relation to this part of the self? In what way may we be able to learn something of the person's relation to himself as an object through mood experience? (1987, 102)

Bollas (1987) effectively evokes moods as forms of self-states, dissociative elements of self, which may be more or less integrated in terms of ego function. His exploration of malignant and conservative moods is relevant to a clinical understanding of borderline phenomena and I will discuss this in the clinical part of this work below when I look at dissociative models of the self such as Howell's notion of the dissociative mind and Bromberg's notion of selfhood as "standing in the spaces" and the alignment such notions of selfhood has with ideas about traumatization (e.g., Donnel Stern's notions of "unformulated experience" and some of Russell Meares's conceptualizations in his "Conversational Model").

In many situations Bollas (1987) demonstrates inconsistency and uncertainty about how to articulate or interpret elements of the Unthought Known in the clinical context, and interestingly sometimes relies upon linguistic representational modes to describe it (referring to it as "an ego grammar" or the "private language of the self"). The paradoxical issue, here, pertains to how one articulates the inarticulable. And for Bollas (1987) there is always the risk of applying concrete or oversimplistic interpretations of psychopathology in terms of dysfunctional maternal care patterns, seeming to miss the point that psychopathology may involve a complex layering of hierarchical developmental experience and unconscious constitution and that play, symbolism, metaphor and other sophisticated elements of exchange permeate self-relationship and the transference relationship. Bollas (1987) does manage to maintain an appreciation of and respect for the complexity of the *Unthought Known* when he emphasizes the role of unconscious communication in treatment, and ultimately all relationships, with elements that will remain inarticulable, or ineffable, or never objectifiable even if the analyst can attempt to elaborate upon, receive or work on the unconscious communication as it manifests in analytic work.[4]

LOEWALD: DIFFERENTIAL RELATING, DIFFERENTIATION, AND INTERNALIZATION

Loewald (1980), a student of Heidegger in the 1930s, subsequently trained as an analyst and wrote prolifically in what is commonly described as an orthodox Freudian style which nevertheless somehow inhabits Freudian conceptualizations and implicitly or subtly develops them with arguably obvious influences from his hermeneutic and phenomenological training. As such, on initial inspection, much of Loewald's writing offers seemingly traditional formulations of Freudian libido theory and structural and topographical theories. In all of his writings, there are few references to Heidegger, although in a Yale lecture in 1978 he describes individual development as a "continuous appropriation of the unconscious levels of functioning, an owning up to them as potentially *me*, ego" and links this to an existential framework, referring to Heidegger: "I believe that Heidegger's concepts of *Geworfenheit*—man is thrown into the world, unplanned and unintended by himself—and *Entwerfen*—the taking over and actively developing the potentialities of this fact—have grown in the same soil" as Loewald's own ideas about human development (1978, 19). And so, upon closer inspection we can perhaps begin to see how notions such as throwness and project inhabit Loewald's re-workings of Freudian ideas.

In terms of thrownness, and originary relationality for that matter, Loewald (1980) does describe the infantile world of primary narcissism, as an undifferentiated world which is primarily relational. He describes this in terms of subject–object unity, where the mother's unconsciously regresses to unify with the child in a mother–child unity that to the infant is pre-differentiated. Loewald (1980) talks about the progression out of primary narcissism in the mother–infant relationship through the notion of the "internalization of a differential." Differentiality, for Loewald, refers to an immanent sense of the bigness, the unknowability of this object (the maternally mediated world, this having affinities with Winnicott's transitional space and Bollas's transformational Object), but somehow a sense of the security and cohesion it has afforded in its responsiveness (compare this with Winnicott's *facilitation* or Bion's *containment*). Loewald (1980) relates the movement of "internalization of the differential" to the drive and ego development in classical early Freudian terms. The mother's relational anticipation (the attunement, responsiveness and mirroring in her care, nurturing and expressivity) induces a sense of agency in the infant, in terms of the formation of drives, verbal expression, corporeal intentionality and so forth. Here, internalization and differentiation is linked to binding (*Bindung*) as a secondary process that leads to ego formation and consciousness formation. This differentiality, and the action of fusing, accommodating, inducing, mirroring, is internalized as an organizing agency. In articulating this, Loewald (1980) emphasizes that it is always already relational and this is well exemplified by his description of verbal acquisition. Here, the mother: "speaks with or to the infant, not with the expectation that he will grasp the words, but as if the speaking to herself with the infant included . . . he is immersed, embedded in a flow of speech that is part and parcel of a global experience within the mother-child field (1980, 185)."

So all forms of relationality, are always already present in an immanent sense, but in an undifferentiated, uninternalized form. In terms of *Entwurf* (project), then, Loewald (1980) states that differentiality is constantly sought to be overcome, such that becoming, is a process of internalization and ego formation (as *individuation*). The relational world into which the infant is thrown provokes this process of differentiation, as does the dependence of the infant. Ego formation, in this sense of *project* or becoming, entails the formation of a sense of an internal, integrated, agentic ego or self, and along with this a sense of a coherent, differentiated, external world of objects and others. This process of becoming, to Loewald, is hierarchical, progressive, and never completed. As such, Loewald reconciled or was able to maintain a focus upon both pre-oedipal and oedipal developmental approaches, referring to a progression through these as processes of increasingly complex differentiation. What are important to us, here, are the relational origins of these processes of differentiation and internalization, their consistency with notions of projection and thrownness, and the novel idea, in psychoanalytic developmental theory, of the persistence of *differentiality* as an ongoing impetus for the project of development as becoming. We can also see that there is no "pre-relational" infant or subject, and no pre-linguistic infant.[5]

This adds a specifically developmental orientation to notions of care, worldhood and horizon, in terms of the notion of bidirectional time I elucidated earlier. If the most primary or originary remains with us (in the capacity to regression), we can think in terms of differential horizons: one can think of the most regressive elements we continue to entertain as adults and in our modern cultures, in our awe and apprehension of the ineffable, the bigger than us. This can induce infantile states that at once can seem nostalgic (because they reflect the regressive core of us, resonating an originary primary narcissism within a differential horizon) but at the same time painfully present and future oriented: think of the infantile paranoia evoked in our fears of Armageddon and apocalypse (global warming, nuclear annihilation, cosmic disasters) or our awe and idealization inspired by religious and scientific zeal. These are not merely regressive, infantile projections, and the underlying regression to *undifferentiated* infantile states are still relevant to the world we are thrown into and concerned with, in spite of our increasing sophistication and differentiation individually and culturally. That is, the world, in spite of our ongoing individual and cultural becoming and differentiation, continues to remain beyond us, bigger than us, *differential to us*, evoking an ongoing process of becoming that challenges us to continue to differentiate.[6]

FINAL COMMENTS

I have discussed Winnicott, Bollas and Loewald in order to explore notions of originary, differential relationship which involve a dynamic progression from an infantile state of primary narcissism, a progression which explores the founding of consciousness, ego in terms that are by definition relational and overcomes any conceptual reference to causal objective presence (avoiding models that adultomorphize infantile subjectivity, or portray it as individualistic, or adopt descriptions that rely on modes of objective presence such as representational theories of consciousness or neurobiological models that correlate to developing neurocognitive capacities). All of these conceptualizations carry through developmentally to adult relations and are consistent with the notion of bidirectional time I described earlier. Winnicott's explication of transitional phenomena, for example, carries through to adult life and exemplifies creative, agentic existence where engagement in the world and relations with others involves the reciprocity and simultaneity of the subject's work on the object and the object's work on the subject, what Winnicott called subjective objecthood. Bollas's notion of the transformational object describes the non-representational, immanent presence of the earliest relational systems which are maintained in one's relation to oneself and others, and are the source of complex, relationally based mood states and experiences throughout life. And Loewald describes the infantile origins of individuation (as agency, drive and so forth) as being immersed in differential relationships with the mother, language and the world all of which propel or drive development as a process of differentiation and internalization.

All of these conceptualizations uphold the importance of originary relationality where individuation, the development of the sense of an agentic self, and a differentiated sense of self and other, inner and outer, mind and body and so forth, are products of early relational processes which endure insofar as there always remain elements of differentiality, alterity, the implicit and immanent, the ineffable or the unrepresentable, that are more primary and originary and operate behind, within or outside the individual. There relational origins are in many ways enigmatic and ineffable. This extends the sense of ourselves as situated and thrown, always continuing to develop, form, evolve and *become*, but with a factical, contingent and finite developmental origins that are relationally based, and a differential horizon and a sense of alterity both within ourselves and without. I have wanted to emphasize these origins, and concepts that assist in describing the dynamics of originary relationality, because I will want to contrast them with other relational concepts that are adopted in developmental psychopathological theories of borderline pathology: theories that refer to intrapsychic object relations (and primitive defences), cognitive and dialogical models, internal working models (and motivational systems), and developmentally acquired capacities such as "mentalization." I will hold that these models do not account for the aspects of relationality I am beginning to describe here, and this will become relevant to the clinical work I pursue and articulate in the following "clinical" part of the work.

I would now like to move to an exploration of other elements of embodiment and affectivity that fit this hermeneutic ontological perspective where the models of two thinkers, Jacques Lacan and Julie Kristeva, involve attempts to derive an understanding of embodied affectivity in terms that are arguably consistent with our understanding of originary temporality and originary relationality.

Chapter 8

Embodied Affectivity
Desire and Becoming

In the philosophical part of this work I explored *L'Anti-Oedipe* and *Mille Plateaux*, where Deleuze and Guattari (1972, 1980) develop a theory of desire that elevates the social over the familial, where the best model for social desire is seen to be the schizophrenic unconscious. This model, which underpins their approach of schizoanalysis as an overcoming of psychoanalysis, avoids the familial constitution of a unified self by focussing upon a sub-individual realm of body parts, or "libidinal intensities," and their supra-individual interconnections in the social, thus providing a single system of configurations of "desiring-production," a system which can be analysed with the critical aim of, at once, overcoming both the Freudian approach to subjectivity and the Marxist approach to sociality (making schizoanalysis, in a sense, a critical fusion of historical materialism and semiotic psychoanalysis). We saw that the rich conceptualization of desire, in Deleuze and Guattari's (1972, 1980) work, can be seen to depart from a neutral and somewhat ill-defined potentiality in Heidegger's ontology. This emphasizes those elements of ontology that relate to becoming, potentiality and differentiation, as well as productivity and creativity in the enunciation and differentiation of *desire* as process. Loosely, Deleuze held subjectification and individuation (and familialisation) as secondary processes that emerge from these supra and sub individual processes, within an organic and socio-political field of articulation. The critical, *schizoanalytic* orientation sought to historicize and polemically engage current manifestations of subjectivity.

These works, and especially *L'Anti-Oedipe*, often critically engaged but sometimes aligned themselves with the thought of French psychoanalyst Jacques Lacan, and it is often difficult to determine whether any criticism on Deleuze and Guattari's part is directed at Lacan's work itself, or a prevailing, dogmatic *Lacanisme* that was pervasive at the time Deleuze and

Guattari produced their work. For Lacan's work, which spans four decades, is a complex and evolving system of ideas mostly composed of transcribed seminars he delivered (but was ambivalent about publishing) alongside more formal published texts many of which would appear in his *Ecrits* (1977[1]). This system is amenable to misinterpretation and simplification, but is also rich in its exploration of embodied affectivity, with a mobile and shifting set of conceptualizations that are highly relevant to this project.

In the broadest and loosest sense, Lacan sought to decentre subjectivity throughout his works by situating processes of individuation or subjectification "outside": developmentally the reflective process occurs when the infant identifies itself as whole firstly through the reflection outside of itself in a mirror, the so-called "mirror phase" of imaginary identification, the *Imaginary Order*, in which the ego and the imaginary relationship with one's body is constituted. The infant or child is also subject to the dialogical process that occurs when the child is initiated as a speaking subject and is dependent upon language, in the *Symbolic Order*, where the "I" of speech is situated. As such, individuation or subjectification is seen as decentred, a form of lack or alienation in which the ego, subject or self is produced without, or from the exterior reference of the image and the word. This alienation is seen as originary, insofar as there is no pure or non-alienated origin prior to this. The third or other Order or register, *the Real*, may represent this origin but only as the unknowable pre-Symbolic, pre-Imaginary reality, which can drive need, anxiety, dread, but remain ineffable or non-representable, only understood in terms of any experiential residue or secondary effect. We will see that the manner in which Lacan describes embodied affectivity, in the concepts of *desire* and *jouissance* with reference to these three Orders or Registers, will be of interest to our hermeneutic ontological thematic and our developmental orientation. It will be an involved exercise to map this out, but Lacan's conceptualizations can be seen to capture notions of alterity, becoming, and difference that will become highly relevant to our subsequent clinical study.

What is of especial interest, here, will be Lacan's later developmental formulation of *desire*, as the primary and originary form of embodied affectivity, and how this links to his later formulation of psychosis. Lacan's later ideas around psychosis can potentially be related to the borderline concept (although Lacan and Lacanians mostly reject the latter concept[2]). To arrive at this point, we need to traverse the development of Lacan's ideas about desire and psychosis, and explore how they come to merge in his later ideas about psychotic structure and psychotic desire. What is significant to note, here, is that Lacan remains committed to a deficit model of psychosis, in fundamental distinction to Deleuze and Guattari's formulations of schizophrenia as a form of creative potentiality. Also, Lacan's latter ideas about psychotic desire become more originary and radical, involving developments of his theories of the Real, *jouissance*, the Thing and extimacy into pre-Symbolic concepts of meaning such as *lalangue*. Because of the density and complexity of these ideas, but their utility to my interest in embodied affectivity as originary desire, I intend to map this out in some depth, as well as, at the end, describe Lacan's latter ideas in comparison to the development of the ideas of one of his followers, Julie Kristeva, whose own critical ideas focussing upon originary desire and pre-Symbolic development are directed more explicitly to borderline pathology as well.

LACAN'S FORMULATION OF PSYCHOSIS, DESIRE, AND PSYCHOTIC DESIRE

In his 1955–1956 Seminar on psychosis, Lacan (1993) develops a series of concepts specific to the clinical phenomena of the psychoses. Like many of Lacan's conceptualizations, this series departs from a Freudian origin: after Freud, psychosis is defined in relation to that other fundamental category of psychopathology, neurosis. Psychosis involves a radical rejection (*Verwerfung*) of a fundamental or grounding element of the Symbolic order, the paternal signifier *qua* "the Name-of-the-Father." *Foreclosure* (translated so via Lacan's own adaptation of Freud's concept of *Verwerfung* as *forclusion*) differs from neurotic *repression* (*Verdrangung*) because it precedes it: what is foreclosed is irredeemably lost to the subject, abolished from the symbolic; whereas the repressed is already symbolic. In this way, psychoses develop around a *lack* in the symbolic structuration of subjectivity whereas neuroses develop from a *repression* within it. Indeed, Lacan develops Freud's conception of repression into a primary, universal function in the development of the subject: *foreclosure*, in this sense, is a rejection of a primal repression of key signifiers into the Symbolic register which would re-emerge at crucial stages in development. This fundamental lack from the Symbolic register, then, impacts upon the two other registers, the Imaginary and the Real, and will be exhibited throughout the subject's life in subsequent development and object relations.

Understanding Lacan's (1993, 1977) approach to psychosis, then, pivots around an understanding of the Symbolic register. The basis of this approach lies in the fact that psychotic phenomena (observed in the history and symptoms expressed and exhibited by the psychotic) are fundamentally interpretable and understandable for the analyst: composed of language and speech they constitute a discourse which is meaningful insofar as it interpretable back to the Symbolic register, making analysis a *Symbolic* analysis so to speak. Importantly, this Symbolic register must be seen as a *structure* of signifiers. And this structure must also permeate language and speech.

The analyst can, then, interpret and direct the manner in which speech is directed to a symbolic Other, the Unconscious being the discourse of this Other which is so fundamental to the identity of the Subject. The foreclosure of such a fundamental signifier as "the Name-of-the-Father" in psychosis will be seen to affect the structure of the register enough to effect the loss of this Other, leading to substitutive relations within the Imaginary and the Real which underpin psychotic phenomena. The genesis of this *foreclosure* (and of psychosis) is primarily an outcome of the Oedipal Complex (though not in a strictly Freudian sense), but this loss of the Other may be latent for a long time before any psychosis eventuates, if, indeed, it ever eventuates. By the same token, this *foreclosure*, according to Lacan, is irreversible (though not untreatable . . .) and will always be manifest in clinically identifiable latent, pre-psychotic, psychotic or post-psychotic states.

What follows below, then, is an elaboration of this Lacanian concept of the speaking subject as grounded in a correspondence with the Symbolic register, and the nature of the circumstances which lead to psychosis when the loss of this correspondence has already been latent due to the foreclosure of the primal signifier of the Name-of-the-Father. Leading on from this will be an explanation of the symptomatology of the psychoses from the onset of psychosis with regard to the compensations which occur in the registers of the Imaginary and the Real. And concluding this chapter will be a discussion of the basic or fundamental field of explanation of psychosis, and any subjectivity for that matter, which is *signification* which refers to both meaning *per se* and the structural relation of signifiers to the signified in the speaking subject.

THE OEDIPAL COMPLEX AND THE OTHER

For Lacan (1977, 1993), it is the absence of the paternal signifier, *le Nom-du-Père*, not the absence or rupture created by an actual parent, that is at the origin of psychosis—psychosis originates in the symbolic, not the concretely, historically familial. For Lacan, the Oedipus complex too, is symbolic: the pre-Oedipal/pre-Symbolic child begins as situated in an imaginary, dyadic relationship with the mother:

> A mother's requirement is to equip herself with an imaginary phallus, and it's very clearly explained to us how she uses her child as a quite adequate real support for this imaginary prolongation. As to the child, there's not a shadow of doubt—whether male or female, it locates the phallus very early on and, we're told, generously grants it to the mother, whether or not in a mirror image. The couple should harmonize symmetrically very well around this common illusion of reciprocal phallicization. Everything should take place at the level of the mediating function of the phallus. (1993, 319)

The Oedipal complex, then, as Lacan adapts it from the Freudian formulation, operates around a *lack* introduced to this imaginary, reciprocal relation by the symbolic nature of the phallus:

> Now, the couple finds itself on the contrary in a situation of conflict, even of respective internal alienation. Why? Because the phallus is, as it were, a wanderer. It is elsewhere. Everyone knows where analytic theory places it - it's the father who is supposed to be its vehicle. It's around him that in the child the fear of the loss of the phallus and, in the mother, the claim for, the privation of, or the worry over, the nostalgia for, the phallus is established. (1993, 319)

The father's role in the Oedipal complex is marked, for Lacan, by his absence which is engendered by his possession of *the phallus*. That's to say, the lack of the phallus in the mother–child dyad is introduced symbolically (as the *phallic signifier*) via the father: "The father has no function in the trio, except to represent the vehicle, the holder of the phallus. . . . So fundamental is this that if we try to situate on a schema what it is that makes the Freudian conception of the Oedipus complex cohere, it is not a question of a father-mother-child triangle, but of a triangle (father)-phallus-mother-child (1993, 319)."

Thus what begins as an imaginary dialectic relationship between mother and child has, through a relationship of lack or absence, a third, symbolic element, the primordial signifier of the *phallus*, introduced. This is, as it were, the primary, the initial moment at which subjectivity begins for the child. It is a symbolic process of phallicization of the subject—a symbolic structuring of the unconscious initially in terms of this primordial signifier, which allows a subject to enter into the symbolic world of language and speech: "If the Oedipus complex isn't the introduction of the signifier then I ask to be shown any conception of it whatever. The level of its elaboration is so essential to sexual normalization uniquely because it introduces the functioning of the signifier as such into the conquest of the said man or woman (1993, 189)."

In other words, the functioning of the signifier, here, in the symbolic and the sexual, is what Lacan will refer to as the Law: "the Law is there precisely from the beginning, it has always been there, and human sexuality must realize itself through it and by means of it. This fundamental law is simply a law of symbolization. This is what the Oedipal complex means" (1993, 83).[3]

Before we reckon with the genesis of psychosis in this context, several points of clarification need to be made. Firstly, this Oedipal complex, this *moment* of primordial signification or symbolization, is not "*temporal but logical*" (1993, 81) or, one could alternatively say, not *chronological but topographical*. What does this mean exactly? It means that the Oedipus complex is not to be situated in a contingent, historical moment within a child's concrete, interpersonal environment so much as in a universal, structural condition within a child's intrapersonal make-up. That's to say, the necessity of the Complex pertains to a fixed structural relation the child has with the world from the outset, in how the child inevitably positions itself in relation to the desire of the adult other/Other (*qua* Mother and Father). This positioning occurs regardless of the stimuli the child receives in his/her relations with concrete adults.[4] In terms of the Oedipus complex, then, the child is forced to situate itself in relation to the desire of the Other, initially at the imaginary level of the fantasy of the maternal other, then at the symbolic level when the absence of the phallus possessed by the paternal Other implicates itself. The child's sexuality, here, is a duality: it is at once, child-centred and auto-erotic (perceiving its own position in relation to the phallic *signifier*) and at the same time Other-centred (insofar as the phallic signifier is introduced and mediated by the Father who possesses it and the Mother who lacks/envies it).

Through the Oedipal Complex, then, the child becomes a Subject inextricably linked to dialogue with the Other in what has opened up as the Symbolic Order. Insofar as the phallic signifier, the *symbolic* object that the Father introduces, is the keystone of the Oedipal complex, Lacan establishes the Name-of-the-Father as the primordial signifier of the Subject's symbolic relation to the Other in all its elements and dimensions:

> The Oedipus complex means that the imaginary, in itself incestuous and conflictual relation, is doomed to conflict and ruin. In order for the human being to be able to establish the most natural of relations . . . a third party has to intervene, one that is the image of something successful, the model of some harmony. This does not go far enough—there has to be a law, a chain, a symbolic order, the intervention of the order of speech, that is of the father. Not the natural father but what is *called* the father. The order that prevents the collision and explosion of the situation as a whole is founded on the existence of the name of this father. (1993, 96, ital. added)

Thus subjectivity becomes inculcated with symbolic relations, speech relations: the Oedipal complex is the necessary, structural moment when speech and the Symbolic are founded through the meaning, *the signification,* imposed by the Father on a pre-Oedipal, imaginary relation to the Mother. This *signification*, via the signifier Le-Nom-du-Père, is multifarious in the bearing it has on that pre-Oedipal relationship: it represents both its prohibition (le "Non"); at the same time as the intrusion, the determination of the Name (le "Nom") *qua* the symbolic in irrevocably changing and structuring it (the impact the phallus has as a *signifier*). The realization of the Oedipal complex is thus structurally determinative in all future object relations: at this broader level, the elusive Nom-du-Père represents the impact of the Law (le Non) and the structure of signifiers themselves (le Nom) on all that is related to.

The Name-of-the-Father is thus at the origin of the Subject's symbolic relation to the Other through language.[5] The Other becomes an absolute that the Subject addresses through his symbolic "speech" acts and in doing so constitutes himself because the structure of meaning predetermines these acts.[6] This obscure formulation refers to nothing other than a split, a rift that symbolic relations bring to the subjectivity of the speaking subject: *"the Other is, therefore, the locus in which is constituted the I who is speaking with him who hears"* (1993, 273). This Other to whom the Subject *speaks* is beyond him, is beyond the imaginary, beyond "all concrete dialogue, all interpsychological play" (1993, 273). And so when Lacan is emphasizing these subjective relations of speech and language (insofar as the symbolic and the unconscious are structured as languages), the Other will always speak to and be spoken to by a Subject in a reciprocity. This reciprocity is the locus of the signifier, of *signification*, and ultimately serves to structure and constitute one's subjectivity as a subject who speaks:

> In true speech the Other is that before which you make yourself recognized. But you can make yourself recognized by it only because it recognizes you first. It has to be recognized for you to be able to make yourself recognized. This supplementary dimension—the reciprocity—is necessary for their to be any value in this speech . . . aimed at beyond all you can know, for whom recognition is to be valued only because it is beyond the known. It is through recognizing it that you institute it, and not as a pure and simple element of reality, a pawn, a puppet, but as an irreducible absolute, on whose existence as subject the very value of the speech in which you get yourself recognized depends. Something gets born there. (1993, 51)

Thus the structure of this relation is a tenuous play of meaning, beyond the apparent immediacy of the imaginary or the apparent groundedness of the real: the structure is to be found at the level of *signification* in the symbolic register, typified by this primal, fundamental signifier, le Nom-du-Père. Elsewhere, Lacan will say that this relation defines the unconscious as "the discourse of the Other" (1977, 193).

This description of the Name-of-the-Father, and the status of the symbolic Other, is at best provisional[7] but will suffice for an elaboration of what *foreclosure* implies for the subjectivity of the psychotic: that is, how the absence of the imposition of structural *signification* in the unconscious and a loss of the dialogue with the symbolic Other leads to compensatory relations in the orders of the Imaginary and the Real which constitute all of the positive phenomena that plague, haunt and inspire this psychotic subject.

PSYCHOTIC DESIRE AND *JOUISSANCE*

From the seminar of 1958 Lacan began to substantiate his notion of the *jouissance* of desiring. If desire is a metaphorical process defined by lack, it will ultimately *lack* an object to completely satisfy it. The pursuit of desire, however, affords an enjoyment or *jouissance* that sustains it. This *jouissance* is also the limit of desire, the barrier reached for in pursuing an object of lack without attaining it, the pleasure and suffering thereof. This barrier and limit of desire is a fundamental advance from a desire limited by the Law and a principle of pleasure/unpleasure. In the seminar on *The Ethics of Psychoanalysis* Lacan (1992) substantiates this notion of *jouissance* as the limit of desiring by defining it in relation to the Real. The object of desire as lack becomes the elusive *Thing*, a concept which links the symbolic Subject's alienation from his drives to the desiring of symbolic objects of lack, drives and objects linked by the elusive relation of *extimacy*. And so, desire, which was hitherto seen as limited by or permeated by the Law, is now seen as attainable at the limits or boundaries of the Law, *jouissance* becoming the transgression of the Law. This type of desire is now *beyond the pleasure principle*, beyond simple pleasure and well-being, and somehow continuous with a *jouissance* of pain/pleasure.[8] Lacan (1992) shows here in his ethical analysis that this kind of desiring that transgresses the Law to reach for *jouissance* is nothing less than reaching for a being-for-death, the ethics of desire thus being something beyond the Law and beyond the pleasure principle. Pursuing this form of *desire/jouissance* for Lacan (1992), is the only true ethical imperative beyond the seeming social imperatives of the "service of goods," sundry codified appeals to the ethics of Virtue, Duty and Utility that subordinate desire. This encounter with an authentic being-for-death through *jouissance*, as a transgression of the ethics of the Law as the service of goods, is analysed by Lacan (1992) in its relation to the function of evil: the extimacy of the Thing (the subject's intimacy to, but alienation from, the Thing of desire) draws the subject towards *jouissance* but may also make him/her flee from its intensity, the thwarted encounter producing a primal aggressivity. Both the transgression and fleeing of *jouissance* as being-for-death are Lacan's (1992) own version of Freud's death drive. It invokes a productive desire beyond the simple pleasure of object relations, genital objecthood, contained by the signifying Law of lack and banalized within an ethical code of the service of goods.

By 1960, Lacan (1977) traces this notion of *jouissance* back to the structural oedipal setting of the Subject's entry into the Symbolic.[9] In this setting, the signifier forbids the *jouissance* of the body of the Other, insofar as the phallic signifier of lack represents a denial or loss of original *jouissance* from the body of the mother. Of course, this original *jouissance* (a primary, direct experience of satisfaction of the drive) is an illusion, but a necessary one that is perpetuated in the sense of a *loss* of the *jouissance* of the Other. Thus, the signifier acts to repress the Thing where the Subject feels *jouissance* should be—that's to say, the signifier enables the expenditure of *jouissance*, but only insofar as it is felt to be the remainder of what has otherwise been lost to or denied from the Subject. This remainder or surplus *jouissance* is searched for in the *objet petit a*, the lost object of *jouissance*. In a desire of objects of lack, objects representing a loss of an illusory, original *jouissance*, the pursuit paradoxically produces *jouissance* itself.[10]

Interestingly, both of the texts advance a notion of *jouissance* as the most authentic, necessary aspect of Subjectivity. But this authentic limit is beyond a simple desire as the search for pleasure codified by traditional ethics and their socio-historical correlates; and it is a desire which is enveiled by an illusory nostalgia for the pre-Symbolic/pre-Oedipal satisfaction of the drive. This is certainly a considerable substantial development of the concept of desire as it stood in the earlier seminar on the psychoses. The nature of desire/*jouissance* as an ethical limit seems to be separate from that earlier sense of desire as identification with a Name-of-the-Father that evokes an authoritative, constant, patriarchal signifier central to and exemplary for the Symbolic Order. And the illusory nostalgia which is the impetus behind a *plus-jouir*, seems to differ from that earlier desire falling within a discourse of the Other that reaches beyond the wall of language, the veil of the imaginary relation, to a purer Symbolic relation of metaphorical substitutes for the desire of the mother as other. These advancements seem to make the Subject all the more fallible and enveiled in a form of self-deceit. Desire/*jouissance* seems to embody the Subject's orgiastic flight to the truth of himself, his "excluded interior," only to confront a limit. This seems to be the function of the Real in relation to the Symbolic. The *jouissance of the Thing* is the reaching beyond the endless repetition of the Symbolic into the Real—the Real becoming *that which the Symbolic lacks*—even if this is only a limit, a chimera for the Subject.[11]

As brief and caricatural as this description is, it is adequate as a reference for us to discuss the manner in which Lacan's understanding of psychosis developed after the earlier seminar on psychosis. For although the psychotic's desire remains pathological amidst these remappings of the conceptualization of desire, it seems to change or advance. Whereas the *desire* to pursue *jouissance* for the normal Subject is directed towards a Thing when it was originally denied from the place of the Other, for the psychotic's desire this *jouissance* emerges in the place of the Other, it is the *jouissance* of the Other. Thus for the psychotic all manner of patterns of *jouissance* emerge that relate to the original, pre-Oedipal/pre-Symbolic imaginary relationship: the psychotic Subject becomes the object of the Other's *jouissance*. This Subject's *jouissance* is sacrificed to the Other because its body was never emptied of the (m)other's *jouissance* via the oedipalizing effect of the phallic *signifier*. In other words, the mediation of the Symbolic in the psychotic Subject's *jouissance* has been foreclosed. *Jouissance* has not been exteriorized to the world of signification, the Symbolic Order, at the limit of which, in turn, is the Real, the endless domain of Things reached for in the act of *jouissance*. In foreclosure this function of the Real as the "excluded interior," the domain of extimate Things, is absent: the psychotic's *jouissance* remains interior to the imaginary, narcissistic self-relation. When this psychotic Subject encounters the interpellation of *Un-Père* from the outside world, it has summoned its own uncontrolled, unSymbolic death drive from within. And without recourse to the Symbolic, which mediates or links drive and object, this *appel* can only take the form of an appearance in the Real of the horrifying action of the *jouissance* of the Other.

In other words, in this formulation the desire of the psychotic functions at the level of the Imaginary without recourse to the Symbolic. The function of the Real is reversed: the psychotic Subject is subjected to a *jouissance* of the Other that emerges from the Real, he is a passive witness to or is subjected to the strangeness of a *jouissance* that is not his, to which he is either a victim, a martyr, a disembodied, dead captive or a chosen one. This differs radically to the normal Subject's repetitive Symbolic search for *jouissance* that affords him only transitory glimpses of the Real in the elusive extimacy of the Thing. We are compelled to ask to what extent is this normal act of *desiring* an *alienation* from the Real, governed by this mediation of the Symbolic, characterized by the relation of *extimacy*; and to what extent is the psychotic's desire—illusory, passive and victimized as it may be—a more profound and enduring experience of the *immanent* subjectivity of the Real? In what position would Lacan (1992) have put this desire of the psychotic within his formulation of an ethics of desire? It may not have the will and courage of the *hero* of desire, but is it courageous for what it continues to suffer? And is this desire foreclosed from Symbolic mediation something more than simply unformed, imaginary and pathological? If all desire is illusory or phantastic how much does Lacan want to favour the Symbolization of desire as the necessary, healthy, ultimate grounding of subjectivity?

Lacan (1992) postulates desire as an authentic being-for-death through *jouissance*: the extimacy of the Thing (the subject's intimacy to, but alienation from, the Thing of desire) draws the subject towards *jouissance* but may also make him/her flee from its intensity, the thwarted encounter producing a primal aggressivity. Both the trangression and fleeing of *jouissance* as being-for-death are Lacan's (1992) version of Freud's death drive. This desire allows for an endless array of *difference* in the metonymic relations of *Things of desire*, even if they are metaphorically unified by the phallic signifier of lack. Lacan (1977, 1992) comes to see this unified *plus-jouir* as an illusory nostalgia for a pre-Symbolic/pre-Oedipal satisfaction of the drive. Desire/*jouissance* comes to represent the Subject's orgiastic flight to the truth of himself, his "excluded interior," only to confront a limit. The *jouissance of the Thing* is the reaching beyond the endless repetition of the Symbolic into the Real—the Real becoming *that which the Symbolic lacks*—even if this is only a limit, a chimera for the Subject. And most importantly for our analysis, the psychotic's *lack* in the Symbolic does *not*, in some way, give him greater access to this nostalgic, illusory Real; it merely subjects him to a regressive, Imaginary type of desire in which he/she is completely disempowered by the phenomena of the Real that emanate from the *jouissance* of the Other. Thus, in terms of Lacan's (1992) ethics of desire, the psychotic is by no means a hero in the desire he experiences.

We seem to have arrived at a fundamental point of divergence for Lacan compared with Deleuze and Guattari. For Lacan during this time, the ethics of desire is limited by the Real, and even from this point of view, in which the phantasy of desire is always illusory but at least yields a creative and productive *jouissance*, psychotic desire remains a pathology of lack and disempowerment. For Deleuze and Guattari (1972), in *L'Anti-Oedipe*, psychosis represents the limit of desire as the *experience of death*; but in the second work, psychotic desire may represent one of many enduring sources of becoming and enunciation reinforced by an ethics of *difference*—and yet it does not exist as a clinical entity. Their failure in mapping out this ethics for a clinician lies in the absence of an attempt to differentiate the extent to which the desire of the psychotic as *becoming* is a productive, creative exercise, or is more a type of subjection, a suffering.

LACAN WITH DELEUZE AND GUATTARI: DESIRE, PSYCHOSIS, AND BECOMING

I need to conclude, now, by analysing a final trend in Lacan's work in the 1970's in which the privilege accorded to the Symbolic mediation of reality, and the centrality of the Name-of-the-Father in this Order, begin to erode. This will enable us to think about the extent to which Lacan's ethics of desire may edge towards a Deleuze and Guattari's (1972, 1980) ethics of difference, and how this may be relevant to our clinical orientation to psychosis (before this is extended to the realm of borderline pathology).

Lacan's notion of foreclosure was radically broadened in the topological period within a general theory of the symptom, or *sinthome*. As we saw above, initially for Lacan (1993) the foreclosure of the Name-of-the-Father designated the specific pathological lack of the psychotic Subject, the lack of the Symbolic Other. Then we saw that Lacan's later introduction of a theory of the Real demonstrated a universal lack in the Symbolic itself: the *jouissance* of the *objet a/Thing* being empty, surplus, nostalgic but nevertheless organized and arranged by the Symbolic register, with the paternal metaphor still arguably at its heart. By the 1970's though, Lacan's topographical period, a more general theory of the *sinthome* emerged to account for a diversity of symptomatic forms of *suppléance* (suppletion or adjustment) to the lack in the Symbolic Order/Other, this *suppléance* serving to constitute specific types of *jouissance*. The universal lack in the Symbolic Order/Other that Lacan would talk of, here, would involve a broader concept of foreclosure than that which was applied in the seminar on the psychoses. And Lacan would become even more preoccupied with the impossibility of the Real, with a theoretical system that could encapsulate or account for it. This is not the place to expand upon all of these trends, which revolved around the development of a topology of the "Borromean knot" in the seminars of 1972–1973 (Seminaire XX, *Encore*) and 1974–1975 (Seminaire XXII, *R.S.I.*) to explain the interdependence of the three Orders of subjectivity. This topology would be the focus of a great number of theoretical developments and new conceptualizations which would destabilize Lacan's earlier work.

What needs to be looked at briefly, here, is the de-stablilization of the privileged position of the Symbolic as ensuring coherence of the Subject that Lacan would enact by introducing a fourth, central term—the *sinthome*—to the topographic knot by the time of the seminar of 1975–1976 (Seminaire XXIII, *Le Sinthome*). The introduction of this fourth term was a fundamental rupture in Lacan's theories. Each subject's *jouissance* would now be seen to be organized by the symptom/*sinthome*, and not the primary metaphor of the Name-of-the-Father which would signify the Things of *jouissance* as objects of lack. This general concept of the *sinthome* would delimit the *Bejahung* of the paternal metaphor as a specific exponent of the *sinthome* like many others—no different to the delusional metaphor of the psychotic, for example. The Name-of-the-Father may be central to the Symbolic Order, but it is no longer necessary as a means of stabilizing or harmonizing (the three registers of) subjectivity. What is primary is the *sinthome* enabling an access to *jouissance*, organizing it. In the absence of the *sinthome* performing this function, the Subject effectively becomes "unknotted"—the unbinding of the three Orders being the basis of psychosis. Thus, the *sinthome* is the fundamental form of *suppléance*. Its knotting of the three orders is an organization of *jouissance*. Thus language and signifiers are no longer seen as necessarily separate from *jouissance* for Lacan. Lacan describes the manner in which both language (*langage*) and *jouissance* are constituted by the unconscious as *lalangue*, an unconnected flux of meaningless signifiers permeated by *jouissance*. Thus, meaning (*sens*) can now be charged with *jouissance* as *jouis-sens*. In a 1974 topographical paper, just before the formulation of the *sinthome*, Lacan refers to three types of *jouissance* in terms of his Borromean knot: *jouis-sens* forming at the intersection of the Imaginary and the Symbolic; the *jouissance* of the Other forming at the intersection of the Imaginary and the Real; and phallic *jouissance* at that of the Symbolic and the Real. Within these descriptions Lacan gives primacy to the *objet a* as holding a central place binding the three orders. Thus the *objet a* is seemingly maintained as a universal component of all types of *jouissance*.

Importantly for this analysis, Lacan (1976), in *Le Sinthome*, demonstrates that the potentially or latently psychotic James Joyce, whose writing of "epiphanies" is a *sinthome* that binds the Orders, enables him to circumvent psychotic collapse. These "epiphanies" of writing are a transformation of psychotic potential into creative potential. The description of the *jouissance* Joyce achieves through his writing is exemplary in Lacan's derivation of a theory of the *sinthome*. It is not the time to explore the analysis undertaken in *Le Sinthome* (1976) in any detail so much as to identify some of the implications it might have for the earlier notion of psychosis.

When Lacan (1976) introduces a theory of the *sinthome* the most important notion for us is that something is generally foreclosed from all Subjects, the *suppléance* of which is the *sinthome*, which has the potential to organize a multiplicity of types of *jouissance* around it. In theorizing this, Lacan analyses the exemplary case of a psychotic Subject whose *sinthome*, whose *jouissance*, is a form of writing. This analysis, thus, allows for an enduring and non-pathological *suppléance* for the psychotic, something different from the latent/prodromal state of the psychotic theorized in the earlier seminar, a state which was still defined by a *lack* of access to the Symbolic Other. This form of *suppléance* does not carry the threat of an interpellation of what has been foreclosed, something specific to the earlier definition of psychosis for Lacan (1993). And moreover, Lacan (1976) makes it an exemplary form of *suppléance* amongst all the forms of *jouissance* of Subjects.

Thus, our analysis of the developments and ruptures in Lacan's conceptualizations around the Symbolic and the Real, around the Other, desire and *jouissance*, and around foreclosure and lack, has taken us along a meandering path of conceptual shifts and ruptures. I began this discussion by highlighting the historicism that arguably pervades Lacan's (1977, 1993) earlier conception of the nature of the acculturation of the child—the historical specificity of the authority of the Law of the Name-of-the-Father. I pointed out that Lacan's (1993) earlier Symbolic version of the Oedipal Complex does not necessarily entail any particular familial system or even a father, but what is universal to it is *Un-père* who represents for Lacan the disciplining of the child in terms of identification with the Law. It was pointed out that a type of Catholic or Biblical symbolism may permeate these formulations arising at a time of legal and social disenfranchisement of the father in French history, as well as the cultural decline of Catholicism. This was brought out in order to identify the issue of historicism for all the influence it might have upon our acceptance of Lacan's (1993) formulation of the Symbolic Order as a whole, and particularly as it pertains to any foreclosure behind psychosis. The notion of a more historical understanding of the Symbolic Order was seen to permit the clinician to be more open to the types of foreclosure that emerge in psychosis.

And subsequently, Lacan's (1992, 1977) theory of desire/*jouissance* was explored to see the ways in which it allows for an endless array of *difference* in the metonymic relations of *Things of desire*, even if they are always metaphorically unified by the phallic signifier of lack. The *jouissance of the Thing* is the reaching beyond the endless repetition of the Symbolic into the Real—the Real becoming *that which the Symbolic lacks*. And viewed in these terms it was seen that the psychotic's *lack* in the Symbolic does *not*, in some way, give him greater access to this nostalgic, illusory Real; it merely subjects him to a regressive, Imaginary type of desire in which he/she is completely disempowered by the phenomena of the Real that emanate from the *jouissance* of the Other. For Lacan during this time, the ethics of desire is limited by the Real, and even from this point of view, in which the phantasy of desire is always illusory but at least yields a creative and productive *jouissance*, psychotic desire remains a pathology of lack and disempowerment.

And so we arrive at this final stage of Lacanian theory in which psychosis remains as a pathology of lack, but one which is susceptible to a creative *suppléance*, a *sinthome*, as enduring and viable as that which organizes the *jouissance* of the phallic signifier. In other words, the lack of the Symbolic, the need for the three registers of subjectivity to be bound in a *sinthomic* organization of *jouissance*, is a universal characteristic of subjectivity. The emphasis, here, is upon an access to the multiplicity of types of *jouissance*, a creative and productive access to which the psychotic can purportedly have now. We have not undertaken to analyse the case of the psychotic James Joyce in any detail at all here.[12] What is most important is the position this later formulation takes in a trend we have come to recognize: a trend in which Lacan's earliest conception of psychosis as a pathology of Symbolic lack co-exists with a "universalizing bias" in the formulation of the Symbolic; which then gives way to an acknowledgement of a fundamental lack in the Symbolic itself, allowing for the Real to be given a primacy it didn't previously have; whence this acknowledgement culminates in the point of view that a universal lack or foreclosure itself is the basis of a multiplicity of *jouissances*, one of which is the exemplary *jouissance* of a psychotic. This includes psychosis in the multiplicitous field of creative *jouissances*. The *breakdown*, the unravelling of psychosis still exists though as a pathology, even if it can be overcome, organized by the cohesion brought about by a *sinthome* of *jouissance*.

And so, for the topological Lacan, *desire/jouissance* is still dependent upon organization, cohesion, structure—even if this is no longer fundamentally a symbolic structure. Any Lacanian ethics of desire that would persist at this late stage would be an ethics of difference—the call to servicing the multiplicitous *jouissances* structured by the *sinthome*. But this would still be a call to an enduring, structural arrangement of a *sinthomic* Subject. For Deleuze and Guattari (1980), conversely, *desire as becoming* always involves a loss of structure, a breakdown or deterritorialization of structure or *stratification* which will achieve *becoming* as a *line of flight*. These becomings are inconceivable to stratified, representational thought[13]: "their semiotic is nonsignifying, nonsubjective, essentially collective, polyvocal and corporeal, playing on very diverse forms and substances. This polyvocality operates through bodies, their volumes, their internal cavities, their variable exterior connections and coordinates (territorialities)" (1980, 175). They are strange perversions, deterritorializations that fracture and dissipate lines of representation and structure, machinic functioning, that would continue to exclude, repress and compartmentalize desire. Desire becomes a shifting process, constantly transforming itself, machinic functioning breaking down and recommencing. It is neither active nor passive, internal nor external, imaginary nor real, signified nor said. It is an exchange of affects, a multiplicity of meaning, a *possible world* of becoming. Like Lacan with Joyce, Deleuze and Guattari (1980) take on a writer, in their case Franz Kafka, to illustrate this mode of desiring. Becoming is a process that submits signification and subjectivity to deterritorialization-reterritorialization in order to bring about expression or *enunciation*. This "expression of territories," the formation of "assemblages of enunciation," is a mode of expression inseparable from its content—it thus adopts signification from within rhythms, sounds, colours, smells, emotions . . . all manner of *affects*. It is also a reactionary "line of flight" that departs from established or dominant codifications in any field of references: it can take place through the act of writing itself for a writer such as Kafka, but only if it is an experimental writing, a "minor literature." In this minoritarian approach, the form of the language is adopted, inhabited, but with a view to destabilizing it, heterogenizing it in a process of becoming:

> One must find the minor language, the dialect or rather idiolect, on the basis of which one can make one's own language minor. That is the strength of authors termed "minor," who are in fact the greatest, the only great: having to conquer one's own language, in other words, to attain that sobriety in the use of the major language, in order to place it in a state of continuous variation . . . Conquer the major language in order to delineate in it as yet unknown minor languages. . . .
> The notion of minority is very complex, with musical, literary, linguistic, as well as juridicial and political references. The opposition between minority and majority is not simply quantitative. Majority implies a constant, of expression

or content, serving as a standard measure by which to evaluate it . . . majority assumes a state of power or domination. . . . It assumes the standard measure. . . . A determination different from that of the constant will therefore be considered minoritarian, by nature a subsystem or an outsystem . . . For the majority, insofar as it is analytically included in the abstract standard, is never anybody, it is always Nobody—Ulysses—whereas the minority is the becoming of everybody, one's potential becoming to the extent that one deviates from the model. . . . That is why we must distinguish between: the majoritarian as a constant and homogenous system; minorities as subsystems; and the minoritarian as a potential, creative and created, becoming. . . . All becoming is minoritarian. . . . Minorities, of course, are objectively definable states, states of language, ethnicity, or sex with their own ghetto territorialities, but they must also be thought of as seeds, crystals of becoming whose value is to trigger uncontrollable movements and deterritorializations of the mean or majority. (1980, 105–6)

Again, this is not the place to embark upon an analysis of such a *literary form*, the literary form of minoritarianism, very involved and arguably of little clinical relevance. It only needs to be pointed out that what is conjured up in this minor literature, what makes it creative in the minoritarian sense, is independent of intentionality or *subjective agency*—the *becoming* unfolds, emerges, forms through the writing with little deliberation as to its import as a *becoming*. Moreover, it is revolutionary and reactive by its very nature despite this lack of intentionality and agency: Kafka does not set out to produce something that is minoritarian, it is an outcome independent of intention.

It only remains to be reiterated, then, that Deleuze and Guattari's (1980) notions of desire, enunciation and becoming are based upon a theory of expression which favours minoritarian, machinic heterogenesis and which relies upon an ethics of *difference*. This ethics endorses the *exercise* of power away from homogeneity and hegemony, a power that *produces difference*; but ignores the degree to which this is an active *exercise, creative* and *intentional,* or merely a more *passive experience, a subjection to heterogenesis* in which expression or enunciation result as a by-product. We are never unsure as to whether the authors favour difference, heterogeneity, the minority or whatever, but it would seem that in abandoning an individuated conception of "subject," Deleuze and Guattari (1980) avoid any theory of agency, of active organization or structure in subjectivity, in the name of selfless heterogenesis and machinic multiplicity. Ultimately, *Mille Plateaux* (1980) achieves a further formalization of the ontology of concepts begun in *L'Anti-Oedipe* (1972), and separates it from the reductive historical metanarrative of that first text. It applies this ontology in a manner which is consistent with its own theory of expression: the mode of its expression, its exposition of plateaus of analysis in fields as diverse as literature, anthropology, music, economics, hermeneutics and art is inseparable from its content, a theory of expression as machinic heterogenesis. The concepts are mixed and combined in those fields, applied to the established systems of problematics and conceptualizations in those fields in order to destabilize them. In this way old concepts are reworked and new connections are forged among the distinctive features composing them, the system permeated by the ontological apparatus that has been introduced. This process of application serves an ethics of difference, a pragmatics which advocates the overcoming of sedimentation, stratification, enduring structure. Thus, when it is applied to the problematic of desire the notion of *becoming* itself *becomes* the manifestation of their ontological system in this problematic. However, here there seems to be little role for a *clinic* of becoming. Deleuze and Guattari (1980) only give scant *clinical* references to how becoming may be a positive phenomenon, and only when this has been misunderstood or repressed in the clinic by psychoanalysts (Freud's analyses of the Wolf-Man and Little Hans). And by linking psychosis to *becoming* as a polymorphous, pre-Oedipal origin of multiplicity, fragmentation and perversity, this approach may indeed represent, to the Lacanian, a nostalgia for an illusory original satisfaction of the pre-Oedipal drive, but also may, in actuality, derive from a state of potential even topologically prior to the imaginary setting of this nostalgia (the mirror stage). Desire here is a *universalized sexuality* of perversion: multiple sexualities or *assemblages* are encouraged to emerge, defined by symbiotic relations of machinic heterogenesis where libidinal intensities or "thresholds" interact and combine to form unique and specific assemblages. In endorsing such a free-play of the becoming of desiring there is little room for a clinical pathologizing of desire. This is in fundamental opposition to the references Lacan makes throughout his work to a *lack* of structure, formation and volition to the psychotic's desiring whether this be Schreber's transsexuality, a passive disempowered *jouissance* of the Other that the psychotic suffers or the *sinthome-less, jouissance-less* unravelling of the psychotic. There is no role for a clinic of *desire* where desire is *exemplified* by the psychotic for Deleuze and Guattari. Any intervention Deleuze and Guattari (1972, 1980) propose for *desiring* or *becoming* never manifests as a form of treatment—it is always displaced into their broader politico-discursive narrative of a revolution of desire, or the more abstract notion of the minoritarian becoming of machinic assemblages of enunciation. And yet it is not inappropriate to ask whether Deleuze and Guattari (1972, 1980) may have overlooked the kind of clinic Lacan's (1992) ethics of desire would endorse, a clinic in which the analyst had the one primary calling to advocate the subject's pursuit of his own desire . . . set in the context of Lacan's later developments of a desire/ *jouissance* structured by multiplicitous *sinthomes*, this ethics of desire would only be removed from Deleuze and Guattari's ethics of difference at certain critical points. . . .

I have already mapped the ways in which desire itself can be interpreted as a sublation of the Freudian death drive, culminating in a limit or antiproductive moment, for both Lacan (the *jouissance* of the Real *Thing*) as well as Deleuze and Guattari (*schizophrenia, chaos*). And I have illustrated the different forms that an enduring form of multiplicitous desiring may take for the subject: for Lacan, it becomes the variable structures of the *sinthome*, a form of binding *suppléance* of a lack; and for Deleuze and Guattari it is the expression of *machinic assemblages* of becoming. I have described the ways in which Deleuze and Guattari's (1972, 1980) conceptualization is based upon perverse, fragmentary machinic assemblages of affects, a *becoming* the Lacanian may arguably feel is harking nostalgically back to a pre-structural, psychotic unconscious as illusory origin. If becoming is a melding of form and content for Deleuze and Guattari, then psychosis remains an exemplary and self-consistent form of becoming. Lacan's conceptualizations are different at this level: they involve a fallibilization of man, the structuring or organization of *jouissance*, by the signifier or the *sinthome*, which is necessary for desire to be accessed and articulated but at the same time defines man to be necessarily alienated from the Real, even if it is held by man to be the ultimately desirable origin, however illusory or unobtainable. For Deleuze and Guattari, this formulation is just another neurotic repression of the most self-consistent form of becoming. Lacan's orientation was always to hold that this is the most that desiring can be, the goal being to at least have access to this limit as a creative, volitional, directive pursuit, and not a subjection, a victimization, or something leading to an unravelling.

Thus, there is a fundamental incommensurability in the relation between these theorists' conceptualizations of psychosis: for Deleuze and Guattari it is an exemplary form of *breakthrough*— it is creative, productive, self-consistent, expressive; whereas for Lacan it is a pathological form of *breakdown*— unformed, passive, subjected, lacking. Hence Deleuze and Guattari would say that Lacan's conceptualizations are unified by a neurotic attempt to reterritorialize or repress the exemplary type of becoming that is psychosis; while Lacan would say that Deleuze and Guattari are reactionaries that naïvely celebrate a psychotic pathology that doesn't yield a creative *jouissance* or a stable, meaningful subjectivity because it alternatively lacks a discourse with the Other, does not search out a Thing of desire, or is not structured or suppleted by a *sinthome*. These different orientations towards psychosis are manifested in how both parties make examples of writing, the creativity of an exemplary author coming to typify the creativity, the agency of the desire they endorse: for Lacan (1976) it is Joyce's *suppléance* of a latent psychosis, the *sinthome* of his "writing of epiphanies"; whereas for Deleuze and Guattari (1980) it is Kafka's minor literature that is a creative, expressive *becoming* that unintentionally destabilizes language and its majoritarian discourses in the name of a self-consistent *difference*. The recourse to literature and aesthetics is certainly not incidental for either party. Lacan (1992) establishes his ethics of desire within an ethico-aesthetic field of *erotics*. What he begins to intimate in this context, here, is that the *clinic* of desire, the facilitation of the desiring of the analysand, may rely upon the *experience* of the analyst. Experience informs a judgement that is both ethical and aesthetic: the two ideals of this judgement, that would orient desiring as a productive and authentic being-towards-death for the analysand, being heroic autonomy and beauty. The clinician, in this context, may encourage difference, the minoritarian, an open model of desiring at the same time as facilitating the subject's agency or intention in his desiring . . . if these are extraneous or superfluous to the expression of self-consistent desiring what harm could it do other than to, perhaps, alleviate suffering, passivity, fear. Perhaps to this degree, Deleuze and Guattari would not have opposed the clinician's facilitation of the *sinthomic suppléance* of the psychotic? If the psychotic is dancing between a state of breakdown and breakthrough, this experience has elements of both an unravelling lack as well as a minoritarian potential. Psychosis, then, is a most harrowing form of "make or break": in trying to elucidate a "subject" or "agent" in what they observe of the psychotic, clinicians behold a slippage between creative becoming and passive subjection. They have no authority to intervene in this process but may be available to listen, facilitate, offer their *experience*, whenever, however they are drawn in to that process. This offering of experience can be governed by an ethics of judgement which serves the name of difference.

FINAL COMMENTS: THE DEVELOPMENTAL ORIGINS OF DESIRE

In describing this complex array of conceptualizations developed by Lacan and placed in critical opposition to Deleuze and Guattari's thought, I have sought to describe an ineffable origin to desire founded in the Real, an origin which is defined by alterity and lack, where desire and *jouissance* are defined in terms of *sinthomic suppléance*, forms of symptomatic adjustment. In this, Lacan seems to remain committed to notions of sign, signification and other linguistic metaphors.

In the subsequent part, or "Clinical Frame," I will explore the manner in which philosopher and psychoanalyst, Julia Kristeva, engages critically with Lacan's linguistic emphasis by proposing the concept of the "semiotic" to designate other elements outside of language function, and, redressing what she sees as Lacan's overemphasis of the Symbolic and linguistic function rooted in de Saussurian linguistics.[14] What is of interest, here, is Kristeva's establishment of what she terms "The Semiotic," to define a realm of non-representational, non-linguistic, non-signifying drives and affects. Of especial interest is her descriptions of this realm made in relation to the discourse of the "borderline" subject, whom she feels is overlooked or excluded by the Lacanian. Suffice it to say, Kristeva's approach is an attempt to amend or address what she sees as an ongoing linguistic bias in the later Lacan's conceptualization of the Real, in the name of emphasizing the qualities of alterity and difference that are perhaps better characterized in her description of the Semiotic. In the clinical part of this work, I will refer to Kristeva's (1982, 1983, 1995) work to explore her conceptualizations around abjection and the borderline subject to see how much they can mediate or overcome some of the biases I have found in my analysis of Lacan's and Deleuze and Guattari's ideas about psychosis and desire, which may be clinically relevant in understanding the tension between creativity, expression and meaning, as opposed to degeneration and suffering that permeates the clinical and ethical engagement with borderline experience.

Chapter 9

Temporality
Seduction, Integration, and Translation

In the preceding philosophical part of this work, we arrived at a thinking of time that began with Heidegger's hermeneutic ontological orientation, where I elucidated concepts of Care, *Geworfenheit* (thrownness), *Entwurfen* (project) and being-towards-death before extending this thinking via Green's and Derrida's reading of Freud's oeuvre, in which *Nachträglichkeit*, *re-presentation*, bidirectional time, heterochronicity and, finally, *différance*, could be seen to permit a fuller understanding of historicity, facticity and potentiality that arguably remained consistent with the Heideggerian orientation.

Within the developmental context, here, I will attempt to explore notions of originary temporality further, where the conceptualizations of Jean Laplanche (otherness and the enigmatic signifier) and Donald Winnicott (unintegration and disintegration) introduce fundamentally *temporal* notions of developmental origins while maintaining, at the same time, a respect for limits and alterity. These notions will be seen to be in a sense originary or foundational limits that pervade infantile, child and adult experience, and will thus be relevant to our clinical approach in the final part, where a developmental orientation will be maintained.

LAPLANCHE: *NACHTRÄGLICHKEIT*, TRANSLATION, THE ENIGMATIC SIGNIFIER, AND THE THEORY OF GENERAL SEDUCTION

One of the central themes in Laplanche's (1987, 1990, 1992) writings is his attempt to retrieve elements of Freud's early writings about traumatic seduction and generalize these into a general theory of seduction where seduction is seen as foundational in the development of the unconscious. As such,

Laplanche is attempting to overcome the rupture in Freud's work following his abandonment of the seduction theory by universalizing the processes of seduction and sexualisation (as a form of traumatic process). This is something that will become relevant to the clinical part of the work below, when concepts of abuse and trauma are analysed critically. In his theory, Laplanche suggests that repression is a "failure of translation," occurring because of the asymmetry between the child and caring adult akin to Loewald's thinking on differentiality. In the transactions between adult and child, there is a surplus (of meaning or understanding) which is nevertheless retained by the child, where repression is a form of implantation and deferral. This surplus originating from the adult can be conscious or unconscious, but for the infant or child the remnants or traces are very much residually unconscious but reappear, in need of translation. Laplanche (1987, 1990, 1992) refers to these remnants as enigmatic signifiers or messages, the unconscious representing a surplus of untranslated communication.[1]

For Laplanche, the small child is dependent upon the care of the adult, and has limited capacity to communicate, reliant upon the attentive, receptive and projective capacities of the carer. For the child, the primitive communication received by the carer is related to survival, adjustment and adaptation; whereas from the carer, usually the maternal figure, there is a surplus of communication, verbally and non-verbally, consciously and unconsciously, where other key elements are present such as the sexual and love components of the carer's communication (the erotics of breastfeeding and physical nurturance, the love component of maternal investment and care) that the small child passively receives. Laplanche argues that at the broadest level this is a form of primal seduction.

Thus, Laplanche's project is to formulate a generalized theory of primal seduction which is cast in terms of foreign, enigmatic elements that the child is universally exposed to, beyond the more narrow focus of the abused child or the perverse patient, that were Freud's more specific psychopathological foci and beyond a normative sequence of psychosexual development where there is an interrelationship between sexual drive/excitement and self-preservative biological needs cast in a normative, intrapsychic development sequence. Laplanche would argue that Freud's radical discovery of infantile sexuality omits the relational components of otherness and differentiality at a primal or foundational level (presuming these emerge more significantly later in Freud's Oedipal complex). Seduction, as such, is no longer an abusive event, but a universal, primal one: "I am, then, using the term primal seduction to describe a fundamental situation in which an adult proffers to a child verbal, nonverbal and even behavioural signifiers which are pregnant with unconscious sexual significations (1987, 126)."

Seduction and enigmatic signification lay the foundations for future sexuality and other unconsciously driven activity in terms of untranslated signifiers that have as their origins the otherness and differentiality of the adult world of the carer (conscious and unconscious, verbal and nonverbal, affective and behavioural), and are implanted within the future-driven, drive-based developmental trajectory of the small child. Now, in this, *Nachträglichkeit* becomes the key concept in Laplanche's theory of primal seduction. Laplanche posits that Freud's concept of *Nachträglichkeit*:

> contains both great richness and great ambiguity between a retrogressive and progressive directions. I want to account for this problem of the directional to and fro by arguing that, right at the start, there is something that goes in the direction from the past to the future, and in the direction from the adult to the baby, which I call the implantation of the enigmatic message. This message is then retranslated following a temporal direction which is sometimes progressive and sometimes retrogressive (according to my general model of translation) (1992, 222).

Here, translation refers to a passive form of repression where undifferentiated, unassimilated "enigmatic messages" are retained and constitute the drive from without, sexual or otherwise. This radical reconceptualization of the drive is not in some essentialist, biological account being related to an originary somatic source so much as necessarily formed by implantations by the other. Every act of translation involves an incorporation or binding integration of the enigmatic signifier into the ego and its internal objects, where any untranslated remainder remains unconscious. In fact, Laplanche holds that there is always an unconscious surplus or excess, which he terms the *source-object*, an object which collapses the Freudian distinction between an external *object* of the drive (an external object that enables the drive to achieve cathexis and satisfaction) and its *source* (a stimulus or excitement in an erotogenic zone). Laplanche's *source-object* is a repressed, internalized fragment that becomes the source of the exciting, traumatizing drives pressing towards discharge, impinging the homeostatic body-ego from within. These drives are a combination of exogenous by-products of implantations that are residual secondary to the infants failed attempts at translation and binding leading to repression. The translation process partially alleviates repression as a process of sublimation.

As such, Laplanche's revision of Freudian metapsychology involves the seductive-traumatic action of the other as the foundational origin of the drive in infant development, as well as the defensive, metabolizing process of translation and binding of the other's implantations by the subject through processes of repression and sublimation, which are ego processes that bind and integrate. By linking translation and *Nachträglichkeit*, Laplanche conceptualizes a matrix of origins that are relational (in terms of differentiality and alterity) but also temporal, destined to be repressed and worked through, remaining residual as unconscious enigmatic signifiers and source-objects This process of translation, and the temporal function of *nachträglichkeit* in Laplanche's model of primary seduction, fits the descriptions of temporality derived in the philosophical part of this work above, referring to bidirectional time, *re-presentation* and *différance* (deferral, excess).

Also of significance, are Laplanche's descriptions of pathological forms of implantation, which will come to be of relevance in the clinical discussion of borderline experience below. In contrast with every day, normal implantation, Laplanche (1990) postulates a violent, pathological form he calls *intromission*:

> Implantation is a process which is common, everyday, normal or neurotic. Beside it, as its violent variant, a place must be given to *intromission*. While implantation allows the individual to take things up actively, at once translating and repressing, one must try to conceive of a process which blocks this, short circuits the differentiation of the agencies in the process of their formation, and puts into the interior an element resistant to all metabolisation. (1990, 136)

Intromission results in elements that cannot be subject to normal processes of repression-translation—Laplanche (1990) refers to these elements as *psychotic enclaves* of untranslatable parental elements (conscious and unconscious, actions, relations, wishes, fantasies) that persist as untranslatable, foreign, unmetabolisable.[2] In the following "clinical frame" of this work, this will be explored further insofar as such untranslatable elements can be seen to play a role in borderline experience, and how a notion of intromission can be expanded beyond early development and be seen to become an element of borderline and dissociative phenomena.

Ultimately, Laplanche's conceptualizations of the enigmatic signifier, repression-translation and *Nachträglichkeit* form part of a renewed, more encompassing theory of generalized seduction which includes the differential action of the other, unconsciously driven, on the origins of self or ego, in a form that develops the origins of the drive, in a relational and temporal situation that Laplanche refers to as the *fundamental anthropological situation.* And most importantly, Laplanche develops an understanding of the originary action of temporality in functions of *Nachträglichkeit* as bidirectional, involving *différance* and *re-presentation* through the action of repression-translation, an action which can be extended to thinking about trauma and psychopathology at a relational and temporal level, something that will be advanced in the clinical part of this work, below. What will be taken up now is some related thinking Winnicott (1971, 1974) developed in his thought around impingement, breakdown, unintegration, integration and disintegration, all of which has a fundamentally temporal character.

WINNICOTT: THE TEMPORAL ACTION OF INTEGRATION AND IMPINGEMENT

In the discussion of originary relationality in this developmental part of this work above, Winnicott's model of transitional phenomena was explored to highlight an understanding of early development being primarily relational prior to any sense of a differentiated ego with boundaries between inner and outer, self and other, and so forth. Importantly, Winnicott also developed fundamentally temporal notions in his model of transitional experience. As we saw, in what Winnicott called the *facilitating environment*, the infant fluctuates between states of primitive anxiety and feelings of omnipotence where there is no sense of inner or outer. Impingements or failures of the environment which the infant may experience as milder primitive anxiety (if gentle enough), lead to an engagement with the world in which transitional states emerge with the development of a sense of projective intentionality and subjective objecthood (the classical example being self-soothing with the transitional object). Progressively, play in the transitional space culminates in mature object relating (a mature sense of unitary self and world, self and others) but where there is still, for Winnicott, a privileging of play and transitional phenomena as being at the heart of mature health, creativity and vitality (aesthetic sensibility, intellectual endeavours, religious faith, other mature forms of pleasure and transcendence). As such, two notions of developmental time operate were seen to operate here: linear, progressive developmental time and regressive, unconscious time insofar as the self has a capacity to progress through different self-states— mature objecthood, play/creativity in the transitional space, primary narcissistic states (e.g., narcosis) and profound impingement and environmental failure creating primitive anxieties. At the broadest level, the transitional object and transitional phenomena may be conceived of in three ways: firstly, as typifying a phase in the child's normal emotional development in which processes of individuation are acted out in the process of play; secondly, where this play is used as a defense against separation anxiety (analogous with, but considerably developing, Freud's discussions of the *Fort-Da* game, for example); and, lastly, as an articulation of a more universal sphere of agency and creativity that is intrinsic to our sense of engagement, dwelling and agency in the world.

These Winnicottian conceptualizations illustrate a developmental component to the bidirectional temporality I described in the philosophical part of this work above. Here, temporality is constitutive of infant-caregiver interactional patterns where there is an unfolding of processes of identity and differentiation, continuity and change, mutuality and intersubjectivity leading to an integrated sense of self in the world of others and objects. Thus, even though Winnicott did not conceptually advance a broader notion of *Nachträglichkeit* or temporality, he certainly emphasized the importance of continuity in time, of the self and other, in ego integration and a sense of self and reality. Another key contribution, here, is his distinction between unintegration, integration and disintegration.

For Winnicott, unintegration represents a timeless, primal originary state that is immediately influenced by the facilitating environment in terms of environmental failures and impingements, leading to processes of transitional experience, potential space and ego integration. As such, unintegration could be seen to be an abstract or illusory origin for which there is a sense of nostalgia. In Winnicott's theory temporal processes become active and understood in relation to absence and frustration: in *Playing and Reality* (1971) Winnicott lists at least three aspects of the ego sense of time: the experience of a time limit to frustration; a growing sense of process and remembering; and the capacity to integrate past, present and future. An important instance of the failure of ego to integrate experience in time is seen in the clinical "fear of breakdown" (1974). Clinically, the fear of breakdown is experienced as the fear of a "breakdown that has already been experienced" although developmentally it relates to an "unthinkable anxiety" that could never be integrated in time as a transitory event in the present and then, contained within temporal ego function, so continues to be experienced as the trace of a futural prospect of annihilation. This relates to other self-states Winnicott describes under the rubric of *disintegration* where there is a loss of continuity in space and time, and the self is experienced as fragmented, annihilated, depersonalized or subjected to the most primitive anxieties such as a fear of falling forever. Experiences of disintegration and fear of breakdown relate to severe or cumulative environmental failures and Winnicott (1962) described the development of a *false self* structure to overcome disintegration, breakdown and other instabilities of self.[3] These forms of psychopathology, as well as the notions of integration and disintegration, will be relevant to my subsequent clinical discussion of borderline experience. What is of significance here, is the elucidation of the temporal qualities of Winnicottian concepts of *integration*, which relate to a differentiated, bound sense of time as an ego function; *unintegration*, as some form of illusory, atemporal origin for which there is idealization and nostalgia; and *disintegration*, as a form of unbinding and loss of self in which past experience seems immediately present or futural in fragmentary states of primitive anxiety.

FINAL COMMENTS

By exploring these conceptualizations of Jean Laplanche (generalized seduction, translation and the enigmatic signifier) and Donald Winnicott (unintegration and disintegration) I have sought to introduce fundamentally *temporal* notions of developmental origins while maintaining, at the same time, a respect for limits and alterity. These temporal conceptualizations were seen to be linked to originary or foundational limits that pervade infantile, child and adult experience, and will thus be relevant to our clinical approach in the final part of this work, where a developmental orientation will be maintained.

In the philosophical frame above, I advanced notions of *Nachträglichkeit*, *re-presentation*, bidirectional time, heterochronicity and, finally, *différance*, that could be seen to permit a fuller understanding of historicity, facticity and potentiality that arguably remained consistent with the Heideggerian orientation to temporality. Here, I have sought to expand upon this in the developmental context more fully: origins of seduction (Laplanche) and primary narcissism/dependence (Winnicott) permit the action of the other to occur over time with ineffable temporal rhythms (presence/absence, frustration/relief, unconscious implantation) where ego or self integration processes are developed that are temporal in nature in keeping with our understanding of *Nachträglichkeit* and bidirectional time—processes of translation-repression and movements between integration and disintegration. We saw that drives, as a form of project, are inextricably linked to this developmental context of the differential horizon, alterity and *Nachträglichkeit*.

We now also have the temporal foundations of an understanding of trauma, seen within a universal phenomenon of seduction as the imposition of the other upon the small child within the context of differential relating, which can in some way become excessive in the process of intromission of unassimilable, unmetabolisable experiences which will reside as unintegrated, psychosis-inducing fragments; as well as the notion of an excessive or cumulative experience of impingements (both as environmental failures and excessively active input from the care giver) that lead to self pathologies in terms of disintegration and defensive false self-structures. These ideas will be taken up in the clinical part of this work below in our approach to the understanding of borderline experience and clinical work.

What I will turn to, now, is an application of these developmental principles, concerning relationality, embodied affectivity and temporality, to the fields of infant, attachment and naturalistic developmental research that found some of the most prevalent clinical theories of developmental psychopathology and clinical treatment in borderline personality disorder.

Chapter 10
The Origins of Borderline Personality
Scientization, Technologies of the Self, and Cultural Disavowal

In the philosophical frame of this work, I focussed upon originary or foundational notions of temporality, relationality, embodied affectivity and technicity. From a hermeneutic ontological standpoint, we became aware of the existential horizon within which understanding and interpretation occur, and in this developmental frame I have elaborated upon notions of *developmental origins*, where an awareness is maintained of the limits, horizons and complexity in our understanding of the infant's relational, temporal, affective and embodied world. Developmentally, this is relevant when we approach infantile and childhood experience and the processes of individuation or subjectification that occur in development. This complexity, in a developmental sense, relates to the elaborate and sophisticated passage of progressive formation we undergo: there are phases of prolonged dependence beginning with maternalization but extending into all manner of familial, educational and other social or cultural contexts that permit the potentiation of complex forms of emotional relatedness, linguistic capacity, technical ability and complex embodied affectivity.

There is an attempt, here, to overcome a tendency to firstly envisage an endpoint, a modern, culturally specific adult individual, and then attempt to conceptualize this developmental complexity from the perspective of a putative endpoint. In doing this, one can conceptualize an individual with sophisticated intrinsic capacities (representational, linguistic, social, emotional) that are fixed and enduring. This loses the sense of ourselves as situated and thrown, always continuing to develop, form, evolve and *become*, with continuing transitions between potentiation and degradation where the complexity and ineffability of our horizon of existence forbids us from getting outside ourselves to attain the objectivity we seek. As such, in this part of the work, developmental origins have been described which maintain a critical outlook towards theoretical models that adultomorphize infantile subjectivity, or portray it as individualistic, or adopt descriptions that rely on modes of objective presence such as representational theories of consciousness or neurobiological models that correlate to developing neurocognitive capacities. In doing this, the unknowability of infant "experience," its alterity, and its inextricability from the relational, temporal, embodied, affective, and technical contexts, has been maintained. I want to suggest that there is no originary form of infant "experience" to be understood outside these contexts.

In terms of the relational theme, ideas around dialogicality, difference and alterity were discussed. I discussed the ideas of Winnicott, Bollas and Loewald in order to explore notions of originary, differential relationships which involve a dynamic progression from an infantile state of primary narcissism, a progression which explores the founding of consciousness, ego in terms that are by definition relational and overcomes any conceptual reference to causal objective presence. All of these conceptualizations carry through developmentally to adult relations and are consistent with the notion of bidirectional time I described earlier. Winnicott's explication of transitional phenomena, for example, carries through to adult life and exemplifies creative, agentic existence where engagement in the world and relations with others involves the reciprocity and simultaneity of the subject's work on the object and the object's work on the subject, what Winnicott called subjective objecthood. Bollas's notion of the transformational object describes the non-representational, immanent presence of the earliest relational systems which are maintained in one's relation to oneself and others, and are the source of complex, relationally based mood states and experiences throughout life. And Loewald describes the infantile origins of individuation (as agency, drive and so forth) as being immersed in differential relationships with the mother, language and the world all of which propel or drive development as a process of differentiation and internalization. All of these conceptualizations uphold the importance of originary relationality where individuation, the development of the sense of an agentic self, and a differentiated sense of self and other, inner and outer, mind and body and so forth, are products of relational processes which endure insofar as there always remain elements of differentiality, alterity, the implicit and immanent, the ineffable or the unrepresentable, that are more primary and originary and operate behind, within or outside the individual. This extends the sense of ourselves as situated and thrown, always continuing to develop, form, evolve and *become*, but with factical, contingent and finite developmental origins that are relationally based, and a differential horizon and a sense of alterity both within ourselves and without. I have wanted to emphasize these origins, and concepts that assist in describing the dynamics of originary relationality, because here I will want to contrast them with other relational concepts that are adopted in developmental psychopathological theories of borderline pathology: theories that refer to intrapsychic object relations (and primitive defences), cognitive and dialogical models, internal working models (and motivational systems), and developmentally acquired capacities such as "mentalization." I will hold that these models do not account for the aspects of relationality I have begun to describe here, and this will become relevant to the clinical work I pursue and articulate in the following "clinical" frame.

In terms of temporality, I have advanced ideas around care, bidirectional time, *Nachträglichkeit*, and heterochronicity. By exploring conceptualizations of Jean Laplanche (generalized seduction, translation and the enigmatic signifier) and Donald Winnicott (unintegration and disintegration) I sought to introduce fundamentally *temporal* notions of developmental origins while maintaining, at the same time, a respect for limits and alterity. Here, I sought to expand upon this in the developmental context more fully: origins of seduction (Laplanche) and primary narcissism/dependence (Winnicott) permit the action of the other to occur over time with ineffable temporal rhythms (presence/absence, frustration/relief, unconscious implantation) where ego or self-integration processes are developed that are temporal in nature in keeping with our understanding of *Nachträglichkeit* and bidirectional time—processes of translation-repression and movements between integration and disintegration. We saw that drives, as a form of project, are inextricably linked to this developmental context of the differential horizon, alterity and *Nachträglichkeit*. These temporal conceptualizations were seen to be linked to originary or foundational limits that pervade infantile, child and adult experience, and will thus be relevant to our clinical approach in the final part of this work, where a developmental orientation will be maintained. This understanding of temporality is seen to counter unidirectional models of staged, progressive, hierarchical developmental acquisition, where borderline pathology is seen to be a form of developmental deficit or failure such as it is found in the developmental models of the Mentalization and Kernbergian schools.

And in terms of embodied affectivity I developed ideas around the sub- and supra-individual processes of becoming and differentiation. In describing the complex array of conceptualizations developed by Lacan and placed in critical opposition to Deleuze and Guattari's thought, I sought to describe an ineffable origin to desire founded in the Real, an origin which is defined by alterity and lack, where desire and *jouissance* are defined in terms of *sinthomic suppléance*, forms of symptomatic adjustment. I also alluded to the way in which philosopher and psychoanalyst, Julia Kristeva, engages critically with Lacan's linguistic emphasis by proposing the concept of the "Semiotic" to designate other elements outside of language function, and, redressing what she sees as Lacan's overemphasis of the Symbolic and linguistic function rooted in de Saussurian linguistics. Of especial interest were her descriptions of this realm made in relation to the discourse of the "borderline" subject, whom she feels is overlooked or excluded by the Lacanian. Kristeva describes borderline discourse as chaotic, where language or symbolic function disintegrates, and is affected by a process Kristeva calls *abjection* entailing an absence or collapse of the boundaries that structure the subject. Kristeva (1982) describes the abject as a form of developmental origin, before individuation, or inception into the imaginary and symbolic, which can rupture and intrude into adult life, but is more pervasive for the borderline subject. Notions of abjection, *jouissance*, the Real and *sinthomic suppliance* will be seen to be placed in critical contrast to notions of selfhood that value the ideals of cohesion, integration, regulation and stability the lack of which is seen to define borderline pathology without an account of the universal place of difference, alterity and lack in desiring and embodied affectivity.

Now in turning to the technical and scientific theme, and any idea of originary technicity, I intend to expand this out to critically examine the uses to which a natural-scientific orientation is put in establishing a theory of borderline personality for developmental psychopathology and the clinic.

As I described in the philosophical frame, technology and technicity, in the theoretical conceptualizations of Bernard Stiegler, can be seen to constitute self-understanding, epistemology and becoming, where interiorisation and exteriorisation co-exist as worldhood. Examples here may be the earliest forms of technologies such as tools and mirrors (which in turn co-exist with us existing and conceptualizing ourselves as technical, reflective beings), techniques and practices that facilitate symbolic or representational art (from the most primitive forms), language itself (in its spoken and written forms) not to mention how these may interact in such sophisticated modern technologies as film and digital media and other forms of representation. All of these technical processes co-exist with self-representational interpretive processes. The artefactual technological world is an ineliminable part of temporality, not only as dead history but a living form of memory, as well as an instrumental aspect of our becoming. *Individuation*, for Stiegler, is a psychic, collective and technical *process*, the result of which is the hypothetical individual. This is the opposite of the humanistic doctrine and aligns with but considerably extends Heidegger's concerns about technology: a suspicion around technology reflects a suspicion of the kind of individual that is produced.

As such, Stiegler (1994) argues that it can be more useful to understand how technologies form a part of human becoming situated within existence, rather than assisting in the establishment of objective knowledge or understanding situated outside of existence (which is aporetic). From these perspectives we have to remind ourselves of the inherent limits of *thinking technologically* and the role that technological thinking can play in affecting or limiting *individuation*. This relates to the kinds of individuals that are constituted, normatively and pathologically, within a historico-cultural technological context. As such, how we conceptualize and constitute ourselves as healthy or sick individuals, is inextricably linked to our technicity and technological understanding.

Now in this respect I think the borderline concept can be seen to be a locus for these limits in psychiatry and psychotherapy. At the beginning of this work I drew reference to Derrida's (1998) description of the *borderline* as some form of limit:

> The borderline is never a secure place, it never forms an indivisible line, and it is always on the border that the most disconcerting problems of topology get posed. Where, in fact, would a problem of topology get posed if not on the border? Would one ever have to worry about the border if it formed an indivisible line? A borderline is, moreover, not a place per se. It is always risky, particularly for the historian, to assign to whatever happens on the borderline, to whatever happens between sites, the taking place of a determinable event. (1998, 77)

I think the most "disconcerting problem of topology" here is the area in which there is no metaphor, no *technological* metaphor to be used. Here, we return to the idea of limits and otherness which I think are fundamental issue for psychodynamic, psychoanalytic and most other psychological theories and their relationship to the borderline concept. Derrida's (1998) definition can serve to remind us to recognize the limits of meaning and signification, to have a sense of reservation and the appreciation of alterity (otherness) and complexity. A core issue for the borderline concept, then, is that it may represent a limit: it will be important to recognize the supplementarity of any technological metaphors used to explain or define it. The borderline concept then becomes a limit concept where many paradoxical ideas coalesce that fail to grasp or capture complexity or alterity: the relational paradox of projective identification; the temporal paradoxes of deferred action and recovered memory; the paradoxes of embodiment and identity identified in concepts such as somatoform dissociation, stimulus entrapment, fixed ideas and multiple personalities; and finally, paradoxes of agency and control, identified in concepts such as conversion and disavowal. In Stiegler's terms, there is a technological context in which this form of individuation has arisen which we may do better to try to understand; at the same time as being suspicious of the more *post hoc* (or supplementary) technological metaphors used to explain an originary or natural form of existence as if it were an object of scientific study.

This context can be seen to be a broader historical context, as well. As we saw in our discussion of Deleuze and Guattari's work (1972, 1980), psychoanalytic theory can be seen to fall within a historical movement in which subjectification occurs, the theory being situated within specific cultural and technical modes of construction of the individual that are related to sub- and supra-individual processes that are historically contingent both in a biological (evolutionary) and socio-political sense. In a related way, Michel Foucault used the concept of "technologies of the self" to describe subjectification occurring in historically specific modes of practice, modes of what he calls, in his later works, *power/knowledge*, in which scientific discourses, and discourses such as psychoanalytic and psychiatric discourse, very much fit within practices which control, order and constitute social and subjective experience, domesticate and structure it.[1]

Derrida (1998) is interested in Foucault's omission of a more direct or fuller engagement with psychoanalysis in *Folie et Deraison* (1961) and the *History of Sexuality* trilogy (1976–1984), and Derrida's (1996) explores and develops this in a piece published in his *Resistances of Psychoanalysis*. Here Derrida develops a Foucauldian critique of psychoanalysis which revolves around ideas of the technical and technologies of the self: Freud's revolutionary potential is undermined by the "thaumaturgy" of psychoanalytic clinical practice that is very much a part of the psychiatric tradition Foucault describes as forming in the modern era beginning with Tuke and Pinel.

> Psychoanalysis will never free itself from the psychiatric heritage. Its essential historical situation is linked to what is called the "analytic situation," that is, to the thaumaturgical mystification of the couple doctor-patient, regulated this time by institutional protocols . . . the thaumaturgical play whose techne Pinel would have passed down to Freud, a techne that would be at once art and technique, the secret, the secret of the secret, the secret that consists in knowing how to make one suppose knowledge and believe in the secret. (1998, 93–94)

This brings us to the idea of psychoanalytic treatment, psychotherapy and psychiatric practice as technical enterprises fitting within a very specific modern moral and cultural context. It can be argued that the borderline concept has necessarily arisen in this modern context as a central limit concept that exposes or challenges the limits of the contemporary schools of psychoanalytic, psychological and psychiatric theory and clinical practice. Much of the clinical part of this work will involve an attempt to critically understand and articulate an ethically and "therapeutically" sustainable standpoint to consider borderline experience whilst maintaining an understanding and appreciation of these limits. What I would first like to describe, here, are some of the "technological metaphors" that seem prevalent in theories of borderline developmental psychopathology that are seen to inform the dominant clinical schools.

In this developmental frame I have attempted to describe originary forms of relationality, temporality and embodied affectivity that reflect limits that are consistent with a hermeneutic ontological standpoint and maintain an openness to complexity, alterity and difference. Now I would like to describe some of the alternative "origins" used by these schools which, I feel, omit the type of broader historical–technological perspective and broader hermeneutic standpoint I have described. The most pervasive technological "origin metaphors" that I will now describe, relevant to this study of borderline experience, I have termed the "Attachment," the "Trauma" and the "Structural" metaphors. What is of primary interest, here, is the fact that these "technological" ideas of origins could be seen to have emerged after the "discovery" of borderline conditions, problems or personality disorders, as if they fitted within a scientific process of research and elucidation of a naturally occurring disorder. What I would argue is that these technologies actually form part of a process of *constituting* the disorder, forming part of a greater technological–cultural context in which the borderline problem has not only emerged but through which it is constituted.

THE ATTACHMENT METAPHOR

There has been increasing understanding of the necessary relational, linguistic and time-cued aspects of the development of selfhood (e.g., Stern, 1985, 2004). Clinical theorists have sought to integrate the many scientific fields in which development is studied such as ethology, developmental neuroscience, developmental psychopathology and attachment research to understand disorders such as dissociative disorders and borderline personality disorder. In the field of scientific consideration of early development, there has been increasing understanding of the necessary relational, linguistic and time-cued aspects of the development of "the self." Clinical theorists have sought to integrate the many scientific fields in which development is studied such as ethology, developmental neuroscience, developmental psychopathology and attachment research to understand disorders such as dissociative disorders and borderline personality disorder.

The attachment paradigm, developed from Bowlby's work by a range of researchers and clinicians including Ainsworth, Main, Lyons-Ruth, Crittenden and Holmes, is arguably the most developed of these naturalistic-scientific approaches. Furthermore, various groups have integrated attachment research with models of borderline pathology. Fonagy, Bateman, Jurist, Gergely and Target, for example, have integrated research on disorganized attachment to develop their theory of mentalization to explain borderline disturbances and a model of therapy for borderline personality disorder (Fonagy et al., 2002). They explore research that demonstrates the critical role of parental affect mirroring in the early development of interpersonal interpretative capacity to develop a social biofeedback theory of early subjective development which leads to mature capacity to mentalize, core disturbances of which underpin borderline disturbances. Liotti (1992, 1995, et al., 2000) has also advanced Bowlby's attachment paradigm, and more recent ethological and developmental research, to develop a Cognitive Evolutionary model of understanding disorders such as borderline personality disorder and dissociative disorders, which he would view as intrinsically developmental, attachment-based disorders. And Schore (1994, 2003) has reviewed developmental neuroscientific research concerning affect regulation and interpersonal relatedness to formulate a model of psychotherapy that addresses developmental deficits associated with borderline disturbance.

As such, the attachment paradigm incorporates a lot of groundbreaking and fascinating empirical research, but one can question the use to which this research is put, in establishing broad or foundational theoretical constructs about selfhood and subjectivity. In all of this work there is a privileging of the centrality of the formative influence of foundational dyadic attachment relationships in the achievement of selfhood, seen in naturalistic, evolutionary terms. There is often, in a sense, a considerable extrapolation of the research used to derive central theoretical constructs that, as a result, are potentially reductionistic and oversimplified, and influenced by implicit assumptions, or what I call forms of *metaphor*. In favoring such metaphors there is arguably a loss of complexity in how we understand the evolution of development, the complexity of self-experience in later development, and ultimately in what occurs in psychotherapy (and in particular the psychotherapy of individuals with borderline problems).

For the Mentalization Group (Fonagy et al., 2002) psychotherapy is described as an attempt to enhance mentalized affectivity. The development of the self is explained in terms of a social biofeedback theory. Fundamental early attachment experiences permit the infant to move from a mode of psychic equivalence through intense engagement in attachment relationships (through forms of mirroring and feedback) to more reflexively understand intentional engagement with the environment and others. This manner of engagement implies that the young child begins to internalize and represent their engagement, initially in a pretend mode (the mode of daydream, fantasy, imagination, play) but eventually in a metarepresentational stance that the group calls "mentalization" (Jurist, 2005, 2010). In this context, the norm of mature emotional life is what is called *mentalized affectivity* . . . there are no pure intrapsychic affects *per se,* affective consciousness is mostly already mentalized that's to say, having a metarepresentational or intentional quality to it (a background awareness of a reciprocal relation between self and other). The group's explanation of borderline states (and we can see these as analogous in many ways to Janet's hysterical states) is that they operate in the pretend mode and mode of psychic equivalence. There is no theory of trauma as external imposition so much as a limited capacity to deal with potentially traumatic experiences via mentalized affectivity: for the borderline individual the whole of development would be characterized as traumatic. And with regard to technique the crucial issue is that the analyst survives (resists destructive enactments, maintains a coherent identity), and manages to infer and help to create a coherent self by adopting a mentalistic elaborative stance, often dealing with the non-verbal and with enactments, carefully avoiding either hyperactively mentalizing what the individual expresses but without simply adopting an inactive supportive mode. This is with the purpose of encouraging inward affective identification, modulation and expression in a mentalizing mode.

Liotti (1992, 1995, et al., 2000) relates the disorganized/disoriented attachment category to borderline and dissociative disorders and has verified this association in longitudinal studies. He adds a description of self-representational configurations that children prone to dissociation conceptualize to symbolize their experience. Multiple representations, each dissociated from the other, are constructed in childhood as stereotypic roles of rescuer, persecutor and victim. These roles, Liotti believes, are likely to be reactivated and confirmed by traumatic experience and within relationships that, while nonabusive, activate aversive emotions. Once activated, the roles trigger dissociative experiences ranging from periodic states of detached confusion to the full fragmentation of multiple personality disorders. Liotti accepts the hypothesis of Mary Main and other attachment researchers that a source of the disorganization and dissociation lies in the child's attachment to a traumatized, frightened-frightening but not steadily rejecting caregiver ("D-category" attachment). Such an attachment will elicit in the child multiply varying internal working models (IWMs) as a rescuer of the fragile parent, as a powerful persecutory source of the caregiver's distress, and as a threatened, helpless victim of insensitive parenting. Liotti suggests that children who have had prior disorganizing experiences will later avoid seeking contact to relieve distress and instead have these forms of IWMs activated and will also activate motivational systems other than attachment. Liotti proposes a motivational systems theory based upon ethological–evolutionary assumptions. He has compared and critically evaluated Lichtenberg's motivational systems theory based upon observations of mother–infant interactions which found five motivational systems (the regulation of physiological requirements, and the attachment–affiliation, exploratory–assertive, aversive, and sensual–sexual systems). Liotti (1992, 1995, et al., 2000) looks at this theory in relation to ethological theories and McLean's tripartite brain theory. He describes four types of nonverbal emotional interactions, one of which is the attachment system related to careseeking and caregiving involving smiles, cries, clinging and seeking for attachment. The other three are the reciprocal roles of dominance and submission—grinding, frowning, threatening vocalizations and yielding postures; those of seduction and courtship—display of sexual appealing postures and body parts; and finally those involving cooperation towards a shared goal—smiles, relaxed posture, pointing to the goal. Liotti regards the careseeking, caregiving attachment to have preeminent importance as the first to be activated during infancy. Liotti makes the suggestion that when D-category children, adolescents or adults attempt to escape the disorganizing dilemma triggered by attachment, they may activate contact through sexuality, dominance struggles, or exploratory activity instead as a form of avoidance of the activation of attachment needs which trigger decompensation and dissociation.

And Schore (1994, 2003a and b) integrates attachment and developmental neuroscience research into a cognitive model of affect regulation that favours a model of right brain development in terms of cortical–subcortical neural networks that regulate affects and "social" emotions such as shame through the establishment of stable self-object representations worked through in affectively attuned, mirroring relationships between infant and mother/carer. These relational representations are stored as implicit memory systems activated in relationships and Schore uses this model of interaction to explain projective identification as a form of implicit "right brain-right brain communication." Borderline disturbance, in this system of ideas, is a form of self-disturbance arising from disorganized attachment (synonymous with early developmental trauma) and is characterized by affect dysregulation including excessive shame (and punitive superego) and relational disturbance. Interestingly Schore (2003a and b) concludes that self-psychological therapeutic approaches are confirmed by this theoretical model and, as such, his model of clinical treatment is in keeping with this tradition.

In all of these approaches, which I have subsumed under the description of the "Attachment Metaphor," we have a technological founding of borderline experience in aversive early development, or attachment, which is described in relation to observable natural-scientific studies of early mother–infant interaction, which can be related to other ethological forms of study and longitudinal follow-up studies of subsequent psychopathology. These approaches are used to found theories of borderline disturbance in terms of pathological attachment, which is described in terms of cognitive-representational deficits: dissociation or disorganization of internal working models; a deficit in a core interpersonal cognitive-representational capacity (*mentalization*); or affective dysregulation and relational disturbance based in deficits cortical–subcortical right brain networks. All of these approaches rely upon mother–infant research which emphasizes the importance of relational attunement and mirroring in caregiving, the development of implicit representations of relational patterns, and the disorganization or traumatisation that occurs if caregiving is disruptive, chaotic or excessively fear inducing. Observational studies (such as studies of marking, contingency detection, mirror neurons and so forth) are used to validate more broad and far-reaching integrative theories which have different emphases and theoretical constructions and clinical approaches.[2] Psychotherapy will become a reparative process for these developmental deficits.

THE TRAUMA METAPHOR

With the movement, in the past 30–40 years to focus upon posttraumatic stress (originally arising from the study and treatment of stress syndromes in rape victims and war veterans), a field of traumatology has emerged that combines information processing models of memory cognition, with neuroendocrine models of acute and chronic stress and models of loss of integration of psychological processes encapsulated within a recovery of Pierre Janet's conceptualizations around dissociation. This field of traumatology is best exemplified by the work of Bessel van der Kolk, Onno van der Hart, Alexander McFarlane and Ellert Nijenhuis (e.g., van der kolk, 1987; van der Hart et al., 1993 and 2006). It has also led to advancements such as Judith Herman's (1997) conceptualisation of complex posttraumatic stress disorder and more complex models of traumatic dissociation such as structural dissociation and somatoform dissociation. This study of traumatology, and the effects of "abuse," has merged with the literature on traumatic early development (as related to disorganized attachment), such that borderline disturbance, along with related disorders such as dissociative disorder, can be seen as after-effects of chronic or severe developmental traumatisation. Therapeutic approaches, here, focus upon improved integration of traumatic memories and related dissociative disturbances (somatic, affective and mnemic) and a reduction of autonomic and emotional dysregulation and are often eclectic insofar as they can involve a mixture of "trauma-focussed" therapeutic modalities (cognitive-behavioural, EMDR, mindfulness, "attachment-based" and so forth). Psychoanalytic clinicians such as Davies and Frawley-ODea (1994) have also described clinical work with adult abuse survivors in terms of specific forms of transference relationship and dissociative pathologies, developing a model of psychoanalytic trauma work.

In all of this, it can be seen that underlying the metaphorics of traumatology are the notions of wounding, scarring, surgical care and healing, all transposed or transferred onto technological conceptualizations of the traumatized psychic apparatus. The spread of influence and interest in traumatology, trauma, dissociation and abuse, has led to critical positions which describe the overreaching, over generalized and ambiguous nature of these concepts (Jureidini, 2004, for example), and their susceptibility to overzealous use and manipulations by clinicians (see Clancy, 2010 for example).[3]

Chapter 10

THE STRUCTURAL METAPHOR

One of Otto Kernberg's major contributions is his systematic developmental model of structural borderline personal organization which involves a rich fusion of ideas from object relations theory and ego psychology. Kernberg's theoretical writings are always sensitive to their historical influences and the dominant theoretical concepts from preceding psychoanalytic thinkers from which his own ideas are derived. In a range of writings in the 1960s and 1970s (e.g., Kernberg, 1975), structural borderline personality organization is described and seen in terms of developmental stages, drives, defenses and object relations. In this context, development is seen in terms of a sequential progression from undifferentiated infantile affective states in a primary autistic phase, to phases of symbiosis and differentiation where representations of self and other are differentiates and splitting of good and bad representations (and associated affects) are integrated and overcome.

Kernberg's model of self and object development rests on five stages that delineate the growth of internalized object relations "units" or "dyads" of representation. The final culminating stage occurs when the ego, superego and id are consolidated as intrapsychic structures. By successfully completing all the developmental tasks, the child has developed a neurotic personality organization, which is the strongest personality structure.

Kernberg's developmentally based theory of *Borderline Personality Organisation* is conceptualized in terms of "structural deficits" such as unintegrated and undifferentiated affects and representations of self and other. Kernberg identifies constitutional and environmental factors as the source of disturbance for these individuals and stresses the important role of the mother or primary carer who treats the child on the surface (callously) with little regard for the child's feelings and needs. In borderline pathology, the lack of integration of the internal object relations dyads corresponds to a "split" psychological structure in which totally negative representations are split off/ segregated from idealized positive representations of self and other (seeing people as all good or all bad). Whilst this summary does not do justice to the richness and sophistication of Kernberg's theoretical descritpins, it does highlight the principle aspects of his Structural model that became key referents for the model of manualised psychotherapy that was subsequently developed to treat borderline personality disorder.

The putative global mechanism of change in patients treated with this manualised therapy, "transference-focused psychotherapy," is the integration of these polarized affect states and representations of self and other into a more coherent whole. The effects of this approach are held to be better behavioral control, increased affect regulation, more intimate and gratifying relationships and the ability to pursue life goals. This is believed to be accomplished through the development of integrated representations of self and others, the modification of primitive defensive operations and the resolution of identity diffusion that perpetuate the fragmentation of the patient's internal representational world. To do this, the client's affectively charged internal representations of previous relationships are consistently interpreted as the therapist becomes aware of them in the therapeutic relationship, that is, the transference. Techniques of clarification, confrontation and interpretation are used within the evolving transference relationship between the patient and the therapist.

Kernberg's paradigm represents a move to describe borderline issues in systematic, foundational terms with reference to a structural personality organization founded in terms of developmental deficits (in relation to a linear, sequential normative developmental trajectory) which are understood in terms of primitive defences (splitting, primarily) and internal representations of object relations ("units" or "dyads") that reflect disturbed object relations. I have referred to this approach in terms of the "structural technology" because it establishes borderline experience in terms of an understandable organization of developmental psychopathology with an apparent conceptual and objective scientific rigour that can be distilled and operationalised into a manualised and researchable form of psychotherapy. I have described it in this way to highlight its nature as a therapeutic technology governed by a "structural metaphor."

THE CULTURAL AND TECHNOLOGICAL ORIGINS OF "BORDERLINE" PROBLEMS

The attachment, trauma and structural metaphors all involve an evocation of objective, naturalistic, observable, scientific understanding. In all contexts, references are made to forms of causal objective presence: cognitive representational and neurobiological modes (inner working models, mentalizing processes, traumatic memory systems, structural dissociation, units or dyads of internalized object relations) that are used to describe healthy and pathological individual psychological functioning. Developmental trajectories are described involving the acquisition of integrative, regulating functions the absence of which is the basis of borderline disturbance that is seen in terms of dysregulated and unintegrated psychic structures and functions in the individual.

I will not pursue a comprehensive critical analysis of these approaches and paradigms further, here.[4] I have introduced the idea of these different developmental "technologies," which I feel are operative in those theories I described which see borderline disturbance broadly in terms of disturbance in attachment, trauma or psychic structure, to contrast this to the forms of developmental origin I have described earlier in this part of the work where I attempted to maintain an awareness maintained of the limits, horizons and complexity of our understanding of the relational, temporal, affective and embodied components of early development.

The "technological" and "cultural" orientation here, not only serves to remind us of the ways in which our understanding is limited by our level of technological and scientific understanding, but also the manner in which our technicity and culture constitutes our understanding and way of being in historically specific modes of practice. Technicity, here, is a broad term that can encapsulate elements of our technical culture such as computational technology, digital representational media, modern biological and medical sciences (genetic, molecular, neuroscientific, evolutionary and so forth) and so forth. This technicity, which Stiegler understands in terms of exteriorisation and individuation, and Foucault understands in terms of power/knowledge and technologies of the self, also relates to our broader historico-cultural situation (industrial, developed, scientific, medicalized, individualistic and liberal-democratic). This situation is confronted by a horizon of alterity, difference and the unassimilable. In this case, the borderline concept has arisen with unstable, shifting meanings, presenting "problems of topology" where alteritous, differential and unassimilable experiences meet with the modern psychoanalytic or psychiatric clinic. Here, we can first identify the metaphorical strategies the clinics use to understand and relate to these experiences (medicalize, technologize or scientize them): they can become domesticated and *infantilized* in terms of an individual who has experienced or suffered aberrant developmental events (trauma, abuse), and exhibits subsequent developmental and structural psychological deficits that can be overcome and integrated.

Technical descriptions of borderline and dissociative phenomena mostly refer to absences or excesses of relational, temporal, embodied awareness: consider, for example, concepts such as derealisation, depersonalisation, disembodiment, amnesia, numbing, emptiness, overwhelming distress, anger, suicidality and self-loathing. All of these elements pose challenges to therapeutic work necessitating hospitality, understanding, a focus upon relatedness, care, avoidance of alienation, violence, stigmatisation and confusion. A technical-scientific orientation may represent a limited form of understanding not adequately respecting and engaging with elements of difference, alterity and unassimilable limits in the sense of an attempt to engage in dialogue and understanding.

FINAL COMMENTS TO CONCLUDE THE DEVELOPMENTAL FRAME (PART II)

All models of psychoanalysis and developmental psychopathology have what could be termed origin myths or metaphors that attempt to encapsulate what are seen to be the most crucial formative events, dynamics or elements of experience that form the basis of development of the self, ego or subject.

In advancing my hermeneutic ontological orientation in this developmental part of the work, I have attempted to describe developmental origins and limits that are fundamentally and inextricably relational, temporal, embodied, affective and seen within a historical and technological horizon of understanding. I described originary forms of relationality that are transitional, transformational and differential, referring to the work of Winnicott, Bollas and Loewald, respectively. I described originary forms of temporality extending the concepts of *Nachträglichkeit*, heterochronicity and bidirectional time to Laplanche's ideas of repression-translation and the enigmatic signifier and Winnicott's concepts of disintegration and integration. And in terms of originary forms of embodied affectivity I maintained an analysis of desire seen as founded in supra and sub individual processes, within organic and socio-political fields of articulation, exploring originary developmental forms arising in notions of abjection, *jouissance*, the Real and *sinthomic supplance* that can be seen to be placed in critical contrast to notions of selfhood that value the ideals of cohesion, integration, regulation and stability the lack of which is seen to define borderline pathology without an account of the universal place of difference, alterity and lack in desiring and embodied affectivity.

The critical standpoint of this hermeneutic ontological orientation thus seeks to undermine, overcome or contextualize approaches to thinking that assert numerous traditional errors or aporias that were seen to be encompassed by "traditional metaphysics": the representational model of consciousness, Cartesian dualism, as well as the favouring of modes of objective presence (objectivism, reductionism, essentialism, scientism and so forth) when approaching the understanding of existence, experience and the world. In my analysis of technicity and technology in this part of the work, I sought to situate the more objectivist and scientifically founded models of developmental psychopathology and borderline personality as technologically limited and historically situated.

Now clinically, this hermeneutic orientation is relevant when we approach the psychotherapeutic situation as a relational context of discourse and dialogue (both linguistically and practically mediated vis-à-vis actions, enactment and non-verbal expression) influenced by limits, horizons, differentiality and otherness. In what follows in the next part of the work, I will maintain a critical outlook towards clinical models that focus upon individualistic pathology outside of the relational contexts that ethically, socially and culturally embed the treatment situation. This critical outlook will be reflected in discussion of modalities of psychotherapy such as Linehan's Dialectical Behaviour Therapy, Kernberg, Clarkin and Yeomans's Transference-focused Psychotherapy and Fonagy, Bateman and Target's Mentalization-based Therapy. An emphasis on ethical, social and cultural embeddedness can serve to focus on the respect or hospitality of otherness, as well as the violence that can occur when individuals are medicalized or subjectified in the treatment context. The preceding philosophical and developmental analyses of relationality, temporality and embodied affectivity will thus also be utilized in a critical analysis of the fields of traumatology (e.g., Judith Herman, Bessel van der Kolk) and structural models of dissociation (Otto van der Hart and Ellert Nijenhuis) as they are applied to borderline phenomena, and commonly used terms such as abuse, trauma and dissociation. Importantly, comparisons will be made to some of the most prominent North American Intersubjective and Relational thinkers (especially Stolorow, Aron, Atwood, Orange, Frie, Bromberg, Donnel Stern) as well as Meares's work in his Conversational model, where all of these approaches are seen to attempt to be mindful of these issues when they pursue more a focus on humanistic, dialogical, perspectival and co-constructivist approaches that attempt to eschew authoritarian, medicalizing, objectifying or, indeed, *subjectifying* stances. Questions will be posed regarding the role of otherness and differentiality in the dialogue that unfolds in treatment: what role the authority of the therapist has, compared with the authority of the individual entering into therapy; and what ethical issues are pursued and what limits and boundaries are maintained.

In all of this, the ultimate endeavour will be to defining a clinical outlook to borderline experience that emerges out of, and encapsulates, as much as it can of a horizon of understanding that is mindful of the complexity of our experience in terms of its relatedness, temporality, embodiment, affectivity, technicity and, ultimately, its otherness to itself. The next clinical frame, then, will elaborate how this interpretive process can be adopted clinically where the patient and therapist dwell together more openly and attempt to understand and explore the alterity and difference in what is experienced without a reliance upon the inference of scientific causal mechanisms, definitive explanation or recourse to forms of objective presence. This process uses doubling or empathy but in a manner in which one could consider the work occurring in a transitional or transformational space (after Winnicott and Bollas) with a differential relational dynamic (after Loewald) but is also dialogical (after intersubjective and relational theorists such as Aron, Stolorow, Orange, Atwood, Frie, Mitchell, Bromberg and Donnel Stern). It entails an open understanding of the operation of time, its heterochronicity and bidirectional nature and its focus on project and potentiation (after Green and Laplanche). It also entails an awareness of embodied affectivity and desire founded in processes of alterity, difference and lack (after Lacan and Kristeva).

This process does not arrive at a transparent, equitable form of insightful relating. It seeks to interpret and share an understanding of unconscious phenomena in their fundamentally relational, lived, embodied and historical qualities with a descriptive orientation that will reveal the hidden and open up a space of potentiality in the field of relations, desiring and the movement of time.

Part III

CLINICAL FRAME

INTRODUCTION

In this final part, the *clinical frame*, I will develop the hermeneutic orientation already established in the philosophical and developmental parts, using it to describe a therapeutic stance that can be adopted in the treatment of an array of problems or disturbances that fall under what I have described as the field of borderline experience. As I have described to date, the borderline concept could be seen to be a limit concept where many paradoxical ideas and issues coalesce in the clinical fields of psychiatry, psychotherapy and psychoanalysis: for example, the relational paradox of projective identification; the temporal paradox of *Nachträglichkeit* as it is manifest in the deferred action and recovered memory in the context of trauma and abuse; the paradoxes of embodiment and identity identified in concepts such as somatoform dissociation, stimulus entrapment and multiple personalities; and finally, paradoxes of agency and control, identified in concepts such as conversion and disavowal. Many other complex phenomena also aggregate here: for example, the behaviour of self-mutilation that can enact or symbolize the boundaries between body and affect, control and dyscontrol, privacy and communication, dissociation and grounding; or, the phenomenology of overwhelming affective states, which form dynamic clusters such as the affects of shame, anger and the dynamics of internal discipline and external hostility.

In this part of the work I will elaborate upon a more complex model of therapeutic action, which will attempt to understand, incorporate or critically engage elements of other clinical approaches within a broader hermeneutic frame of understanding. I will describe how much of the literature on borderline experience idealizes, through notions of stability, cohesion, integration and regulation, the idea of an individualized, functional self, ego,

"I" or subjectivity that is unified and somewhat separated from its relational, temporal, embodied, affective, technical and cultural contexts. In this context, I will demonstrate how objectivist, reductionistic modes of thought (such as representational models of consciousness, Cartesian dualities) and categorical, synchronic, individualistic models of psychopathology are favoured and how these lose the depth and complexity of clinical experience. In all of this, the ultimate endeavour will be to defining a clinical outlook to borderline experience that emerges out of, and encapsulates, as much as it can of a horizon of understanding that is mindful of the complexity of our experience in terms of its relatedness, temporality, embodiment, affectivity, technicity and, ultimately, its otherness to itself.

This clinical frame, then, will elaborate how an interpretive process can be adopted clinically where the patient and therapist dwell together more openly and attempt to describe and explore the alterity and difference in what is experienced without a reliance upon the inference of scientific causal mechanisms, definitive explanation or recourse to forms of objective presence. This process uses doubling or empathy but in a manner in which one could consider the work occurring in a transitional or transformational space (after Winnicott and Bollas) with a differential relational dynamic (after Loewald) but is also dialogical (after intersubjective and relational theorists such as Aron, Stolorow, Orange, Atwood, Frie, Mitchell, Bromberg and Donnel Stern). It entails an open understanding of the operation of time, its heterochronicity and bidirectional nature and its focus on project and potentiation (after Green and Laplanche). It also entails an awareness of embodied affectivity and desire founded in processes of alterity, difference and lack (after Lacan and Kristeva).

A number of central, classical clinical issues will be explored in this approach. It will pay particular attention to issues around the conceptualization of dissociation, splitting and disavowal, as these have arisen from the work of Janet and Freud, and how tensions here relate to current clinical approaches to borderline experience that adopt models of dissociation (the traumatology movement with thinkers such as Bessel van der Kolk, Onno van der Hart, Ellert Nijenhjuis and Judith Herman, relational thinkers such as Philip Bromberg, and attachment-based theorists such as Giovanni Liotti). It will also review terms such as *abuse* and *trauma* in the context of earlier and historical usage, current research in traumatology, and a more complex analysis of how the therapist and patient work together "in time." It will also explore the ethical and interpretive agency of the therapist from a hermeneutic perspective (evoking concepts of fallibilism, prejudice, embeddedness and the sensibility to two-person dynamics). It will also explore clinical interpretative perspectives in light of preceding discussions about dialogue, conversation, narrative, differentiality and otherness.

Most broadly, it will be seen that the hermeneutic perspective can simultaneously permeate one's clinical approach to psychotherapy, one's orientation to theoretical thought within psychotherapy and developmental psychopathology, and offer a broader, personal interpretive orientation towards the situation of psychotherapy for the psychotherapist. Questions will be posed regarding the role of otherness and differentiality in the dialogue that unfolds in treatment: what role the authority of the therapist has, compared with the authority of the individual entering into therapy; and what ethical issues are pursued and what limits and boundaries are maintained. In this context, I will relate my hermeneutic ontological orientation with other clinical schools that attempt to be mindful of issues when they pursue more a focus on dialogical,[1] perspectival and co-constructivist approaches that attempt to eschew authoritarian, medicalizing, objectifying or, indeed, *subjectifying* stances, such as the work of the Intersubjective and Relational Schools with the work of Stolorow, Atwood, Orange, Aron and Frie focused upon in particular; as well as Meares's work in his Conversational model. In this project, I do not intend to establish a comprehensive analysis of or engagement with the thought of thinkers within the Relational and Intersubjective schools of psychoanalysis. It has been noted elsewhere that in the past 20–30 years the body of Relational and Intersubjective psychoanalytic theory and literature has grown increasingly broad, diverse and difficult to engage as a unitary field or paradigm.[2] Thus far I have already alluded to the engagement of intersubjective thinkers such as Stolorow, Orange, Atwood and Frie, with hermeneutic philosophy. In a broad sense, these thinkers, and many of the other Relational and Intersubjective thinkers, hold to the primacy of relationality, relatedness in therapeutic dialogue as well as in an understanding of subjectivity or, for that matter, primary intersubjectivity. In my approach, I have developed a specific form of hermeneutic ontological approach, and developed philosophical and developmental conceptualisations to adapt to the clinical field of borderline experience. Further exploration of affinities these conceptualisations have with these thinkers and schools may be advanced in the future but this is too big a task to develop further comprehensively in this work, even if I will make references or allusions to particular themes and ideas from these schools.

Part of what I will describe will be an attitude of openness and respect for complexity founded in the hermeneutic outlook that I have described. Much of this relates to an awareness of context, not just in terms of the situation of referral and the origins of the treatment for the individual, but also the situation of the practitioner and the treatment that the practitioner offers. This situatedness is complex for both parties, in terms of personal, familial, cultural and historical origins for the patients, and personal, professional and institutional origins for the practitioner, and influences the form of frame that is established. Part of this involves the clinician developing an ethico-critical stance with which to approach the treatment context. It requires empathy, relating, hospitality, a dialogical focus, a respect for complexity and difference as well as an awareness of the differentiality of the context. Many of these elements are very germane to the "borderline" presentation. I would argue, as many have done in the past (e.g., Fromm, 1995) that the borderline designation is often more readily adopted by the clinician than the patient, is often alienating, and can reflect a reductionism in the clinician's perspective in order to project, isolate or externalize the clinician's confusion or anxiety about their orientation to an individual that presents to them. This confusion and anxiety can relate to senses of urgency, being too involved or implicated, losing a sense of boundaries and controls. An ethico-critical stance may look towards sharing, empathy and kinship. It may engage in dialogue with a respect and acceptance of otherness, an attempt at hospitality and adjustment for the sake of the other. The practitioner may need to submit to experiences of helplessness and hopelessness in the face of the other individual, where the capacity to sit with and attempt to relate may be all that can be shared. At other times, the practitioner may have to overcome roles into which they did not expect or accept to be cast, more aware that the differential nature of the relationship and their authority has to be handled more actively and carefully so as to not be destructive.

But in terms of a broader ethico-critical stance and awareness of context, there are a range of clinical, cultural and technical factors that are relevant to the presentation of the "borderline individual." This stance must be aware of these factors, and the underlying constructivism and contextualism of the borderline field. In introducing this constructivist and contextualist orientation I referred to the work of Erving Goffman (1959, 1961, 1963, 1974) and Michel Foucault (1977, 1976–1984, 1961). In this respect, I have already alluded to, in my introduction to this work, the many elements of the *context* in which the borderline conceptualization emerged: its possible supplanting of the Victorian notion of hystericism; the convergence of psychoanalytic and orthodox psychiatric theory and research to focus on personality organization and pathologies of selfhood leading to the concept of "personality disorder" which in turn comes to fall within a scientific realm of empirico-objective study; borderline personality disorder then becoming an object of study within evidence-based clinical medicine, and specifically with regard to effective treatments in the form of manualized, protocol-based models of psychotherapy. I also described that along with this have arisen a group of related integrative theoretical models of borderline personality disorder which refer to developmental neuroscience, attachment disorder (attachment being operationalized and objectified in research protocols) and developmental psychopathology particularly in relation to variants of abuse and trauma.

Now, if we broaden our focus to consider the social and historical context of the appearance of the borderline concept there are other factors which can be introduced into our frame of consideration. Considering these factors may give us a certain critical outlook towards the seemingly objective, innocuous, scientific or taken-for-granted approaches of understanding borderline personality disorder. It may further destabilize them. Here, we can focus on a range of tensions, conflicts and discordant relationships that exist in our later twentieth- and now early twenty-first-century culture. This concerns the manner in which individuals interface with institutions, and are constituted by systems of scientific knowledge and technical practice. More broadly, it also reflects how the individual's experience is constituted by a broad range of clinical and cultural elements that organize self-experience. "Borderline" individuals may experience them-selves as rejected, disenfranchised, terrifyingly isolated, or controlled, brutalized and subjugated. Their sense of chaos and despair leads to desperate, random and destructive acts. In our era, this may all be a fragmented, chaotic expression of our loss of boundaries: the limits of our permissiveness, the after-effects of our openness to explicitness (sexual, violent, graphic) as well as frank problems of neglect, omission and maltreatment seen in the formative course of individuals' lives. This loss of boundaries is met with our high ambitions for individualism (individual rights and responsibilities) and for social cohesion and inclusion, seen in terms of our wish for the total reach or grasp of civility and the purported control of the law and human services. The "borderline", then, is the marginal terrain, a domain of omission, where the brutal, the savage, the rough, the bad and inhumane ways we treat each other, our children, are then related to by means of clinical sterilization, *clinicalization, medicalization or technologization.* Here, therapies could be seen as substitutive forms of care and factors such as "abuse" and "trauma" could come to be seen as "individualized" causative events that can potentially be prevented or repaired. In all of this, there is a risk of dehumanization and stigmatization of the individual.

As I have already said, I do not intend to develop a sociocultural critique of "borderline personality disorder" concept further. However I would argue that this contextualist and social constructivist understanding can be important to frame the ethical and critical orientation of the practitioner within their clinical work.[3] In what follows, though, I will focus primarily upon the clinical issues I have described, developing these under the existing headings already adopted in the previous parts: the relational themes, temporal themes, themes of embodiment and affectivity and, finally, technical themes.

Chapter 11

Relationality

Relations Within and Without

In the philosophical part of this work, I discussed the notion of originary relationality that can be seen to be derived from Heidegger's project insofar as human being is always already situated in a relational context, with concepts such as *Mitwelt*, *Mitsein*, *jemeinigkeit* and *Befindlichkeit* referring to being that is always already with others, where moodfulness is always seen dialogically in how one interprets oneself both to oneself (as another) and to others. This relationality was also seen to be embedded within a limited horizon beyond which otherness or alterity also intervenes and needs to be come to terms with, both in terms of an appreciation and respect for our limits and then in terms of ethical standpoints. I derived from Gadamer's and Ricoeur's thought that forms of the self, subject or individual are constituted by or secondary to relational processes: in particular, dialogue or conversation as well as the dialectic with otherness (the otherness of embodiment, of the other, of death, of conscience and so forth). This extends notions of selfhood into performative, ethical and existential domains. All of these elements considerably extend Heidegger's original thought but nevertheless both thinkers were seen to remain committed to Heidegger's hermeneutic ontological orientation in articulating these elements of selfhood as historically, linguistically and factically embedded or situated. We also saw that thinkers such as Levinas and Derrida emphasized notions of otherness and differentiality in order to limit or curtail our understanding and avoid metaphysical standpoints that oppress or alter the complexity and finitude of meaning or understanding, and that interpretation is always necessarily ethical in nature.

In the developmental part or "frame," I then discussed Winnicott, Bollas and Loewald in order to explore notions of originary, differential relationship which involve a dynamic progression from an infantile state of primary narcissism, a progression which explores the founding of consciousness, ego in terms that are by definition relational and overcomes any conceptual reference to causal objective presence (avoiding models that adultomorphize infantile subjectivity, or portray it as individualistic, or adopt descriptions that rely on modes of objective presence such as representational theories of consciousness or neurobiological models that correlate to developing neurocognitive capacities). All of these conceptualizations were seen to carry through developmentally to adult relations and are consistent with the notion of bidirectional time I described. Winnicott's explication of transitional phenomena, for example, carries through to adult life and exemplifies creative, agentic existence where engagement in the world and relations with others involves the reciprocity and simultaneity of the subject's work on the object and the object's work on the subject, what Winnicott called subjective objecthood. Bollas's notion of the transformational object describes the non-representational, immanent presence of the earliest relational systems which are maintained in one's relation to oneself and others, and are the source of complex, relationally based mood states and experiences throughout life. And Loewald describes the infantile origins of individuation (as agency, drive and so forth) as being immersed in differential relationships with the mother, language and the world all of which propel or drive development as a process of differentiation and internalization.

All of these conceptualizations uphold the importance of originary relationality where individuation, the sense of an agentic self, and a differentiated sense of self and other, inner and outer, mind and body and so forth, are products of relational processes which endure insofar as there always remain elements of differentiality, alterity, the implicit and immanent, the ineffable or the unrepresentable, that are more primary and originary and operate behind, within or outside the individual. This extends the sense of ourselves as situated and thrown, always continuing to develop, form, evolve and *become*, but with a factical, contingent and finite developmental origins that are relationally based, and a differential horizon and a sense of alterity both within ourselves and without.

This relational orientation, founded in hermeneutic ontology, can be contrasted with relational concepts that are adopted in developmental psychopathological theories of borderline pathology: theories that refer to intrapsychic object relations (and primitive defences), cognitive and dialogical models, internal working models (and motivational systems), and developmentally acquired capacities such as "mentalization." I will hold that these models do not account for the aspects of relationality I have described, and this will be seen to be relevant to the clinical work I will describe.

In general terms, the relational orientation I advance can be seen to influence a clinical or therapeutic stance. The clinical situation, the consulting room and the dyadic frame, can be seen as a transitional or transformational setting in the sense I described from the conceptualizations of Winnicott and Bollas. In this there is a differential relation, a potential space is formed and used by the patient, in interaction with the therapist (discursively, performatively and so on). But the therapist actively assists in this constitution, though remaining mindful of the need for space, reception and engagement for the patient. Bollas (1987) thus, accords importance to the abstinence or neutrality of the therapist, upholding the importance of free association in the presence of the attentive and receptive analyst. Green (1978) has used Winnicott's conceptualisations to describe the analytic object, the co-constructed and co-constituted product of the analytic encounter[1]: "the analytic object is neither internal (to the analysand or analyst), nor external (to either the one or the other), but is situated between the two. So it corresponds precisely to Winnicott's definition of the transitional object and to its location in the intermediate area of potential space, the space of "overlap" demarcated by the analytic setting (1978, 180)."

This notion of a therapeutic frame as a transitional, transformational or potential space may be seen to be especially important if much of the work with so-called borderline patients, involves the establishment and maintenance of a frame, of *frame-work*, so to speak. Fromm (1995) elegantly describes, in Winnicottian terms, this as a relational or dyadic problem, so that the borderline term cannot really be seen as anything other relational or dyadic in nature:

> Winnicott once wondered what would happen if the baby looked into his mother's eyes and did not see himself? What I suspect can happen is the simultaneous establishment of no-boundary and of enormous gap—the gap between an image held urgently by the mother and the child's felt potential in and of himself. The imposition of the former on the latter is the boundary violation. . . . Perhaps the *borderline* is the child's internalization of the no-man's-land between the parents or between image and inner experience, especially as parental figures receive and react to the child's developing personality and affectivity. This gap may also be the formative precursor of the fault lines in the treatment situation, which the patient must actively exploit rather than passively suffer. The actual meaning in the word *borderline* . . . may simply reflect the problems of people around borders or boundaries. For some people, the earliest efforts at contact and at separateness have encountered unbridgeable gaps, external then increasingly internal, brought both hopefully and assaultively to the therapist. (1995, 242)

If the therapist anticipates this, receives, expects and responds to this, this will amount to complex forms of transitional or transformational relating. The complexity of this lies in its construction in the frame or setting, where the therapist adopts a receptive, elaborative, attentive stance, but is also engaged, participates, and shares in a dialogical, interactive sense (encompassing all the discursive and performative levels of the relationship). It is a differential relationship, the setting is about care, treatment, assistance and so forth, the therapist is designated with some form of authority that the patient relates or reacts to, but this authority must be exercised with or based in reservation, respect, humility, and an atmosphere of hospitality. Boundaries and borders will be constantly negotiated and worked on in this form of potential space. The therapist must maintain a reflective voice and elaborative stance, attending to the nature and qualities of the relationship, but not from "outside" the relationship as if the therapist merely receives communications, and responds interpretively in terms of a form of response or reception, even if this is unconsciously generated in the manner described by Bollas (1987) in terms of his ideas about receptive capacity, linked, somewhat, to Winifred Bion's ideas about reverie, containment and linking, or Masud Khan's ideas about interpretation, lying fallow and so forth.

In this respect, the therapist cannot be too deliberative, passive or reflective, and is very much thrown into or situated within the relationship, even if the therapist wants to think about it. It may be helpful, here, to be reminded of those Heideggerian notions of *Mitwelt* and solicitude (being with another, leaping forward in either an anticipatory or intervening sense for another), within a dialogue of Care that is projective and futural, focussed upon the situatedness of moodfulness for the patient as it is shared with the therapist. This form of relational encounter is both discursive and performative in this regard, it is about utterances and gestures, and the therapist may in some way be therapeutic by being either exemplary or protective of the relationship, demonstrating a willingness to meet and engage, conveying a sense of hospitality and respect, and in the process constituting a space of potentiation. This is a process in and of itself, for the sake of itself, but also arises in some other form of context of help or assistance that I alluded to earlier as having, after Derrida (1996) a *thaumaturgical* element, because there is a faith, an expectation in both parties, that this process can be helpful, miraculous even, in its beneficial or curative effects.

Part of this also involves an appreciation of, and respect for, otherness, difference, complexity and limits and alongside this an appreciation of the art of experienced but intuitive engagement at a narrative and performative level. Part of my conceptual elaboration has been directed at an exploration of ideas about unconscious processes that are temporal, relational, and agentic insofar as they mediate linguistic, somatic, affective and technical expression. The challenge is to think about these processes from within (as a constructive and contextualized participant), without recourse to metapsychological theories, theories that reduce unconscious elements to modes of objective presence. An appreciation of primary or originary relationality serves to highlight the paradoxical or aporetic nature of concepts such as projective identification where specific forms of unconscious relationality and mutual influence are identified as distinct and anomalous processes, and where unconscious "communication" in general is seen as mysterious and magical. A hermeneutic ontological standpoint to relationality reminds us that an "individual" is never alone even when they are alone, in the sense of persisting narrative and performative elements that reside in a "self" that is by no means unified and singular. Underlying temporal, affective, somatic and technical elements can be thought about in constellations that combine in seemingly paradoxical presentations of conversion, multiple personalities, somatoform dissociation and so forth. These elements, even at the subtlest or most minute level, are engaged with and related to contextually and constructively by the therapist, who, through their own therapeutic experience, attends to these things within him or herself and within the work.

If we hold that processes of individuation and subjectification are secondary, and the self is constituted or contextualized in these relational, temporal, embodied, affective and technical processes, this will influence how we think about goals or maxims of psychotherapy that refer to or uphold as ideals, models related to stability, coherence, regulation, cohesion of the self (or ego or subject) as a unified, individual entity. In this context, relationality can be reduced to a form of individualistic cognitive capacity, this being seen in contemporary theory through the adoption of terms such as *mentalizing capacity*, *reflective function*, *theory of mind*, *metacognition* and so forth. Deficiencies in these can be seen as primary borderline problems. Relationality, in Kernberg's conceptualisation of borderline personality structure, can also be seen to be intrapsychically represented or inscribed in primitive or impaired modes of object relating. I have argued that these individualistic approaches lose something of the primary or originary relational aspects. This is relevant to understanding borderline experience where, as I have described earlier, many of the metaphors (attachment, trauma, structural) describe the borderline individual, self, or subject in terms of dysregulation, instability, lack of cohesion, disintegration[2] and so forth. One of the primary concepts that is being increasingly adopted in this context, by a diverse range of these thinkers from the traumatologists (van der Kolk, van der Hart, Nijenhuis) and attachment theorists (Schore, Liotti) is dissociation, which refers in a diffuse sense to a loss of integration, but generally in a sense which is intrapsychic and individualistic. I would here, like to explore this concept at this level, and assess the extent to which underlying relational (and temporal) and other hermeneutic ontological conceptualizations can assist in understanding the use of such a concept, and clarifying many of the ambiguities that come to problematize its usage. To do this, I would first like to undertake an historical analysis of the concept, and its links to Freudian concepts such as disavowal and splitting (which came to be adopted by Kernberg in his structural model of Borderline Personality Organization which fuses elements of ego psychology and object relations theory) before I then turn to more contemporary theories and relate these to my hermeneutic ontological approach.

It is important from the outset to acknowledge that a concept such as "dissociation" is comparable to "borderline" insofar as it is complex, ambiguous and laden with historical meanings. Dissociation, as such, could be seen to be a limit concept in an analogous way to how I have described the borderline concept. Dissociation can be seen as normal or pathological, adaptive or maladaptive, seen as a protective defence or a decompensating response when defences are breached. It can be seen to present as a distinct and uniform phenomenon or a spectrum of varied but related phenomena. In particular, I would like to look at the position dissociation holds and has held over the twentieth century moving from an *excluded* to an increasingly *included* position in psychoanalytic and psychodynamic thinking, possibly in correlation to the emergence of the centrality of the borderline concept, something described here by Bromberg (1995):

> If one wished to read the contemporary psychoanalytic literature as a serialized Gothic romance, it is not hard to envision the restless ghost of Pierre Janet, banished from the castle by Sigmund Freud a century ago, returning for an overdue haunting of Freud's current descendants. With uncanny commonality, most major schools of analytic thought have become appropriately more responsive to the phenomenon of dissociation, and each in its own way is attempting actively to accommodate it within its model of the mind and its approach to clinical process. (1995, 511)

I think it is useful to think about the history of this idea, and its roots in the works of Freud and Janet. It may be useful, though, to draw out some of the tensions that emerge when Freud's and Janet's respective theoretical systems enter into dialogue and similarities and differences are drawn out at certain points. Much has been made of the history Freud and Janet shared, such as their formative experiences treating hysteria under Charcot, the common intellectual heritage they shared in late Victorian Europe (the legacy of many traditions for example the emergence of the evolutionary perspectives of Darwin and then Hughlings Jackson) as well as the conflicts they had over the years. Here, I want to look mainly at the relationship between Janet's concept of dissociation and certain aspects of Freud's thinking (ideas around splitting and disavowal). I want to elaborate upon this before I return to more modern debates reviewing more current approaches as I think some of the core issues are crucial.

FREUD AND JANET: DISAVOWAL AND DISSOCIATION

To begin with Freud, it is interesting to note that he seemed more open to ideas relating to dissociation at the extremes of his working life . . . the pre-analytic period immediately after his time in Paris when he formulated his ideas with Breuer, and the times towards the end of his life. Many readings of Freud's early works would see a simultaneous suppression of his seduction theory and a move away from an interest in the ideas of splitting of consciousness, dissociation and hypnoid states as he began to formulate his own topographic model. However, in later works as he was formulating his structural model, a notion of splitting of the ego and disavowal (*verleugnung*), emerged, initially linked to fetishism (and explanation in terms of intrapsychic conflict and his psychosexual theory of castration) but broadened out be a universal pathological phenomenon:

> the childish ego, under the domination of the real world, gets rid of undesirable instinctual demands by what are called repressions. We will now supplement this by further asserting that, during the same period of life, the ego often enough finds itself in the position of fending off some demand from the external world which it feels distressing and that this is effected by means of a *disavowal* of the perceptions which bring to knowledge this demand from reality. Disavowals of this kind occur very often . . . and whenever we are in a position to study them they turn out to be half-measures, incomplete attempts at detachment from reality . . . and result in the situation of there being a splitting of the ego. (1937–1939, *SE 23*, 202–3)

Here Freud is returning to the idea of the pathogenic impact of contradictory, irreconcilable or unassimilable experience that occurs in reality, rather than the primary traumatic impact of intrapsychic conflict and the primary defensive mechanism of repression. The impact is a form of splitting of the ego. Freud also makes reference to how this traumatogenic or pathogenic impact, in the form of disavowal and splitting occurs unconsciously like repression:

> [Repression and disavowal] have the following important characteristic in common. Whatever the ego does in its efforts of defence, whether it seeks to disavow a portion of the real external world or whether it seeks to reject an instinctual demand from the internal world, its success is never complete and unqualified. The outcome always lies in two contrary attitudes, of which the defeated, weaker one, no less than the other, leads to psychical complications. In conclusion, it is only necessary to point out how little of all these processes becomes known to us through our conscious perception. *(1937–1939, SE 23, 203–4)*

So if the ego is split in the context of a response to real trauma through the process of disavowal, this process would occur unconsciously. It is to be distinguished from repression and also denial or negation (*verneinung*) which is apparently associated with the denial of what is repressed, but also of repression and conflict itself so that the psyche can deny its nature as an internally divided entity in order to perceive itself as an autonomous, integrated "I."

Janet, over the years, would state Freud had merely appropriated his own concept of the *subconscious* when Freud formulated his ideas of the unconscious. Many of the conceptualizations of *subconscious* pathological processes that Janet formulated relate to splitting off (dissociation) of subconscious systems from the self or ego. His work would be primarily concerned with understanding "hysteria," a broad term that would resemble today what psychiatrists might term posttraumatic stress disorder, somatoform dissociation, dissociative disorder, complex PTSD, as well as borderline and histrionic personality disorders. His general formulation of hysteria would be in terms of a malady of personal synthesis characterized by the narrowing of the field of consciousness and dissociation. That is, for Janet, personal consciousness, or "the self," is a synthetic unity arising out of subconscious systems and ideas. Interestingly, here, Janet felt that dissociation, in itself, was a universal pathological phenomenon that could feature in many psychological disorders. What was specific to hysteria (and our interests today) is, somehow, the preservation of systems of ideas and functions through the simultaneous retraction or narrowing of what can be held in consciousness, and the dissociation or *désagrégation* of functions.

> This preservation of functions in the dissociated state seems to me to be fundamental to hysteria and not found in other psychological disorders. It is here that more often memories, coordinated actions, habits will dissociate themselves, separate themselves into smaller and smaller elements that do not exist in any functional sense. . . . Hysteria is thus a malady of the personality in which there is a decomposition of functions and ideas which would ordinarily unify to constitute personal consciousness . . . These notions of the narrowing of the field of personal consciousness and of dissociation are parallel. They can be considered to relate to each other without one having priority over the other. . . . Hysteria thus becomes a form of mental depression characterized by the narrowing of the field of personal consciousness and by the tendency to dissociate and freeing the system of ideas and functions which in their synthesis would ordinarily constitute personality (1909, 291–2; my translation)

What results in hysteria, then, are pathological manifestations which emerge *outside of* personal consciousness. Janet would refer to concepts like *idées fixes* (literally fixed ideas or in everyday French meaning obsessions) and *automatisms* to understand hysterical phenomena which could become manifest as sensory perceptions, affect states, intrusive thoughts and behavioural enactments that somehow were held or expressed subconsciously and could emerge in a dissociated, non-integrated manner supposedly not unified within personal consciousness. Janet would state that these manifestations would have a traumatic origin, trauma being some situation which is unassimilable, not able to be held or synthesized within personal consciousness. As such, the manifestations, as symptoms, could be seen as a mixture of unassimilated responses, impressions, feeling states and so forth. These are seen as outside the workings of the normal conscious self seen as a fragile synthesized state which emerges as our sense of ourselves in present time, in the real world. Interestingly, or ambiguously, other elements of ourselves can be organized to some extent, be intentional to some extent, but remain subconscious, seemingly alien to or "other than" our present, conscious self. One of the tasks of psychological therapy for Janet is to address these unintegrated fragments, the fixed ideas, by bringing them into consciousness through some process of synthesis.

In loosely covering these ideas of Freud and Janet, I want to focus on ambiguities and tensions that arise when we think of ideas such as the splitting up of the self or ego, and the intentionality of unconscious or subconscious elements that form part of a response to trauma. I believe that there are certain tensions in these ideas that can be seen in the different approaches of Freud and Janet. Freud, later in his work, seemed to return to the idea that both repression and disavowal/denial were in some ways universal but also specifically pathological phenomena. In this sense, ambivalence, splitting and non-self-transparency are, in a sense, *universal* phenomena, though the processes can lead to distinct pathologies and symptom formations in part related to the health or weakness of the ego, defensive processes that are employed and the nature of the real traumata that are experienced. Freud in his later work, however, did not elaborate very much at all upon the therapy of this general form of disavowal. This is in contrast to Janet's tendency to hold that dissociation, and hysterical dissociation in particular, is of central concern to psychological therapy and is distinctly *pathological*. Unlike Freud he would seem to maintain that normal selfhood is based in some form of integrated self-transparent synthetic unity. The tension, here, comes when we question the extent to which this is realistic or achievable. If pathological dissociation needs to be overcome, how do we maintain the idea that other forms of unconscious or subconscious elements persist and how do we see these relating to the dissociated elements. For Janet, this question would relate to the limits of the assimilability of subconscious ideas and systems in personal consciousness. For Freud this would relate to the independent and primary status of the unconscious but also, perhaps, the intrinsic limits of the ego's capacities to assimilate all of the contradictoriness of reality (traumatic *or* universal elements of "reality"). As a prelude to *Civilization and Its Discontents* (*SE XXI*, 1930, 63–4) Freud briefly speaks about the relations of man to the universe as a whole. Evoking the concept of the oceanic experience—that "sensation of 'eternity'," that "feeling as of something limitless, unbounded"—he raises the question of the limits of knowledge and the need for religious faith. He posits that this feeling of oneness with the world is not a primary experience but a residue of the infant's absence of ego boundaries, of the archaic union with the world. These limits for Freud are necessary to posit for one's understanding of oneself and the cosmos.

At this point, I would return to my own notion of hermeneutic ontological *limits* found within the orientation introduced in the previous parts of this work. From within this standpoint, we are reminded that any thinking we might entertain, as theorists, clinicians or self-interpreting conscious individuals is only within a horizon of ambiguity, unknowability and facticity; a thinking where we will always be in conflict with ourselves. It is from this standpoint that we might think differently about how to approach the unconscious or subconscious domain, particularly if we want to be mindful of primarily relational, temporal, somatic, affective elements or processes that permeate it. I want to develop this more with reference to the notions of disavowal and dissociation I have just described (I will henceforth use them interchangeably, though I want you to remain aware of the tensions between Freud's and Janet's models that I have raised).

MODERN APPROACHES: SPLITTING, DISAVOWAL, AND DISSOCIATION IN THE BORDERLINE EXPERIENCE

To begin with I would like to orientate some current approaches to trauma work with the modern-day counterpart of the "hysteric," by thinking about work that attempts to retrieve the loss of synthetic self function while working with unconscious. I want to look at questions and problems that arise with individuals who are diagnosed with dissociative disorders, including dissociative identity disorder as well as borderline disorders. I think that in this clinical context, all of the tensions I have just alluded to present themselves in the form of very real and immediate questions arising in psychotherapy with those individuals. I have already alluded to different paradoxical features including conversion, somatoform dissociation, dissociative identity disorder, as well as distortions of memories of the past, or recent events, distortions of agency (issues of capacity and responsibility for behaviours out of "conscious control"), and complex forms of memory (somatic, affective, atmospheric and so forth) that are often seemingly fragmented, inarticulable elusive.

I would like to critically explore two current theoretical approaches which are especially relevant because of the central interest they have in borderline and dissociative pathology: firstly the approach of what I will call the Mentalization Group of Fonagy, Bateman and Target; and secondly the work of Meares and his school. I think both of these approaches are confronted by the dilemma of understanding the nature of therapeutic agency in a relational field in which unthinking elements dominate (relational expression which can be seen in terms of enactment, acting out, projective identification and other complex forms).

For the Mentalization Group, as described earlier, psychotherapy is seen as an attempt to enhance mentalized affectivity (Fonagy et al., 2002; Jurist, 2005; Jurist, 2010). The development of the self is explained in terms of a social biofeedback theory. Fundamental early attachment experiences permit the infant to move from a mode of psychic equivalence through intense engagement in attachment relationships (through forms of mirroring and feedback) to more reflexively understand intentional engagement with the environment and others. This manner of engagement implies that the young child begins to internalize and represent their engagement, initially in a pretend mode (the mode of daydream, fantasy, imagination, play) but eventually in a metarepresentational stance that the group calls mentalization. In this context, the norm of mature emotional life is what is called *mentalized* affectivity: there are no pure intrapsychic affects *per se,* affective consciousness is mostly already mentalized, that's to say, having a metarepresentational or intentional quality to it (a background awareness of a reciprocal relation between self and other). The group's explanation of borderline and dissociative states (and we can see these as analogous in many ways to Janet's hysterical states) is that they operate in the pretend mode and mode of psychic equivalence. There is no theory of trauma as external imposition so much as a limited capacity to deal with potentially traumatic experiences via mentalized affectivity. And with regard to technique the crucial issue is that the analyst survives (resists destructive enactments, maintains a coherent identity), and manages to infer and help to create a coherent self by adopting a mentalistic elaborative stance, often dealing with the non-verbal and with enactments, carefully avoiding either hyperactively mentalizing what the individual expresses but without simply adopting an inactive supportive mode. This is with the purpose of encouraging inward affective identification, modulation and expression in a mentalizing mode.

One could argue that, clinically, there is the risk that this description of technique and underlying disorder has too much explanatory power and too little specificity whereby every problem or phenomenon is always explained in terms of a deficiency in mentalization and every therapy justified as a cultivation of mentalization. There is also, arguably, too little attention paid to the mediating or constitutive role of language (not to mention other supraindividual social and cultural factors). A theory of affects as self-reflexive can also come to imply that emotions be in some way self-transparent to the normal individual, a goal or maxim which does not match our everyday experience. This seems to be a Janetian emphasis at odds with the group's analytic backgrounds. This may be a reason why one can see that in the group's clinical discussions object relations concepts are often invoked, concepts which may seem incommensurate with the model that is being explicitly promulgated (e.g., Fonagy et al., 2002, 444, 447, 465). This perhaps belies the idea that a broader notion of the Unconscious remains implicitly relied upon without necessarily being accounted for[3].

In contrast, Meares's (2000) "Conversational model" does invoke the primacy of language (*qua* conversation) as constitutive of self, where affects, meaning and language combine in a self-structure that is internalized from a developmental trajectory beginning with mother–infant attachment experiences, and cultivated in later self-directed play. Meares, too, emphasizes the internalization of dyadic relations in selfhood (such as self-other and intentional relations) in his notion of the duplex self. Invoking the Jamesian notion of the "stream of consciousness," self function is described like a personal idiolect, a sustained and cohesive conversation with the self. At this level, developmental failure is described in terms of a failure of personal synthesis, trauma and dissociation occurring when the self de-couples or breaks down. There is an associated loss of meaning and value . . . other more primitive forms of self-function, "trauma systems," are split off and are primed to re-emerge in present day relations, seemingly existing at the pre-conscious level of implicit and procedural memory. Repair in therapy occurs through the cultivation of narrative conversation that is at this personalized, intimate level of self-function. The therapist works at an intimate, implicit level, building resonances and complexity by relating to the intrusions of trauma-based systems, in turn restoring self-function. There is a Kohutian and Janetian emphasis, here, on self-cohesion, personal synthesis, and the internalization of self-functions through the therapy.

In both of these groups affects fall within a complex process of the doubling or synthesizing of the self which is not divorced from the existential situation involving other modes of being such as interpersonal relatedness, language, memory, embodiment. Affect becomes the tone, atmosphere of this binding, or failure to bind. This begins to approach Heidegger's notions of affect and personal synthesis in his hermeneutic ontological analytic elaborated earlier. In these models there seems to be a subversion of the more Freudian conceptualization of the dynamic Unconscious of intrapsychic depth or conflict to more of an implicit, procedural form of unconscious. To put it metaphorically, these forms of therapeutics may become more concerned with modification rather than awareness, form rather than content, engaging on operational surfaces rather than in archaeological depths. This could be exemplified in their conceptualizations of dissociation which are quite different in some ways but seem to emphasize repair occurring more in the potential space of overall self-function, without the potential for specific abreaction, catharsis or reintegration . . . dissociated memory is not reached for or worked through at a specific level, but is approached with a view to re-discovering or re-synthesizing the self when dissociation intrudes. However, one is still left to wonder, though, about the opaque background of our selves, a potentially more particulate, non-synthetic domain from where other aspects of ourselves, and our agency (sexuality, aggression, other forms of motivation or complex affective states) emerge and cannot be totally captured by synthetic, reflexive self-function. If this is subconscious or unconscious, what are the conditions of possibility for considering it or working with it therapeutically? In the context of traumatic dissociation or disavowal this becomes a problem, then, of the limits of self-transparency or the capacities to the ego to synthesize or integrate, and, in relational terms, of the limits of therapeutic mutuality or intimacy. These limits, again, go back to the questions I have raised about Janet in relation to Freud's own approach to disavowal. In this context, traumatic memories cannot simply be "re-integrated" as this is conceptualized by trauma theorists such as Herman (1997) or van der Kolk (1987). If traumatisation operates at the level of loss of synthetic self-function, and the operation of an unbound, non-mentalized implicit unconscious this has implications for how we see ourselves working within the transference and what the role of interpretation might be. The idea of assigning to therapy a cognitive function, valuing the idea of mastery conferred by self-knowledge, no longer applies. The primary purpose is no longer to extend self-awareness, pushing back the bounds of one's ignorance and misunderstanding of oneself. The traditional notion of Strachey's mutative interpretation, is supplanted by a working more at an implicit, minute, subtle level. This is with a view to the retrieval of a certain type of presence of mind as it is described in concepts such as mentalized affectivity and the duplex self.

Consider, for example, clinical scenarios[4] in which individuals with severe forms of dissociative and borderline disturbance present with issues related to dissociation or disavowal. Such patients, for example, can present with inexplicable somatic symptoms, pseudo-seizure and other conversion-type problems, and repetitive re-traumatization experiences before it even dawns upon them or others around them to address or confront any distant, developmental trauma issues. They may be referred after a period of several months of gross disturbance (suicidality, overwhelming intrusive experiences of fragmentary sensorial and somatic symptoms or memories which filled them with anxiety and fear). Initially there may be great difficulties maintaining a frame in which to work due to intrusive violations of the frame, all sorts of "enactments" within and outside the frame that challenge the work, and so forth. There may be a great sense of risk, leading to fear, demoralisation and despair in the therapist. The therapist is aware many of the elements (seen in terms of enactment, projective identification, splitting and so forth) may be trauma based but it is difficult to introduce a conversation or dialogue about this initially. Gradually in psychotherapy the therapist and patient may begin to work through an array of developmental experiences characterized by sexual "abuse" and other sadistic or protracted forms of "abusive" treatment if a working alliance is formed and two can think about and reflect on these. Significant therapeutic developments occur when they confront intolerable, unacceptable ideas, very much resembling Janetian "fixed ideas," which the patients are often profoundly ambivalent about and begging you as the therapist to renounce as false or fantastical. It is this level of ambivalence that is easily manipulated in the context of reinforcing denial of previous trauma, or in the cultivation of false memories. It is a challenge, and a necessity for the therapist to adopt an open-minded, accepting attitude, with no suggestion of any capacity for omniscience or arbitration of truth. Often, the intolerable, irreconcilable idea will relate to very alien, indigestible fragments indicating memories of disturbing, irreconcilable experiences. The holding of these ideas in their conscious minds, in the session, initially has an overwhelmingly catastrophic effect but the experience of surviving this, and the containment in the therapeutic setting, is incredibly powerful and strengthening. This could be seen as a working through of the denied or disavowed experience (Freud), or an addressing of the subconscious fixed idea (Janet). In this work an insight can be developed into the relational determinants of the denial/disavowal which are so pathogenic in the developmental context. Not only are the experiences, for the child, so confusing, so irreconcilable or incomprehensible that they are disavowed or dissociated, but we come to understand how the perpetrators actively relate to the patients in a manner which negates any sense of reality to what is occurring to the patients as they experience it. The perpetrators look through the patient, discuss the patients in front of them as if they are a non-conscious object; and most crucially, the perpetrators may at other times have another form of relationship with the patients. At other times they may be an authority figure who treats them in a most dismissive, moralistic, judgemental manner, and in subtle ways, we come to recognize, monitors and controls the patients in how they express themselves and their emotions to others, making the patients call themselves into question and be timid and self-effacing. They may also deceptively portray themselves as caring and intimate, seemingly seeking to introduce the idea that any other behaviour on their part would be impossible; and furthermore, the perpetrators can imply that the acts or events are consensual, or intended on the patients' part, inferring that they are consensually engaging, colluding or actively participating in what occurs.

All of these behaviours on the part of perpetrators impose and potentiate the action of disavowal or dissociation on the profoundly disturbing experiences. This indicates a *relational* basis rather than a purely unconscious, *intrapsychic* basis to the disavowal/dissociation.

As these experiences are worked through and understood over a number of sessions the patients often experience more of a sense of self-awareness and reflectiveness, and a gradual recovery of themselves as not overcome by the endless, intrusive repetition of the event of re-traumatization and the unpredictable intrusions of fragmentary somatoform/affective/sensory elements. There is a sense of a return of balance and cohesion to themselves in terms of time (distinguishing what was then and what is now) and relatedness (what are my feelings, who other people are). As this occurs, we are more able to articulate the complex moods and feelings—senses of violation, self-loathing, shame, disgust, anger—linking these to the described past and present events and occasions which are acknowledged to be only partially apprehended or understood as "memories." There is no sense that this is fully resolved or worked through so much as a sense that they have somehow recovered themselves to go on with the work of the therapy in all its complexity, openness and potentiality.

This, in a sense, speaks of the relational processes occurring in a therapy of traumatisation. It can be, though, that we can generalize such processes to refer to all manner of unconscious, unintegrated elements that are potentiated and worked through in the therapy, where a literal or concrete origin (abuse events, early experiences) may be more elusive or subtle, and the relating may be contextualized and constructed more in the present relationships (within the therapy reflecting current-day extratherapeutic relationships).

FINAL COMMENTS

I would say that a therapeutic outcome is not an achievement of total self-transparency or mutuality with the therapist. The sense of "reality" achieved is complex and tenuous. Janet referred to this sense of reality with terms like *la fonction du réel* and *presentification*, referring primarily to the idea of being able to situate oneself back in common-sense realty, working in present time, having a hold of oneself. This is consistent with the ideas of the mentalization group and Meares which refer to the aims of restoring synthetic self-function, self-transparency and self-awareness. This does not account for the ongoing processes of what the unconscious or subconscious realm might continue to "throw up" whether it is disavowed or dissociated elements, or other demands.

Donnel Stern (1997) nicely develops Freud's ideas about disavowal and splitting and Janet's ideas about dissociation by referring to disavowed elements as *unformulated* and, as such, being "not me" or of not having a quality of being "mine," which, in turn can lead to intrusive experiences feeling other than me, not real, not true. Working with *unformulated experience* involves a process of formulating, acquiring and personalizing the experience (consistent with Freud's famous expression: *wo Es war, soll Ich werden*). Stern (1997) is relational in his thinking and holds to the primacy of therapeutic conversation and dialogue, where latent meaning and understanding are constructed dialogically in the session and therapeutic relationship. This process, in trauma or other analytic work, may be interminable in the sense that there will always be ongoing unconsciously determined processes of articulation. The idea, here is that dialogicality is enhanced and "not me" or "unformulated" elements (dissociated and disavowed) are overcome. In a sense this is consistent with Fonagy's group speaking of enhancing mentalizing function in the process of working through unmentalized content, the alien self and pretend mode functions, but the emphasis, perhaps more in keeping with Meares's Conversational model, is on the primary role of relationality. What I would add is the sense of limits (difference, alterity and otherness) that remains, without a maxim of achievable, total mutuality, relatedness and correspondingly, cohesion and self-transparency[5].

The trend to formulate the "relational self" began with Freud and has a long history evolving with conceptualizations of internal object relations: "The ego can take itself as an object, can treat itself like other objects, can observe itself, criticize itself, and do heaven knows what to itself. In this, one part of the ego is setting itself over and against the rest. So the ego can be split; it splits itself during a number of its functions—temporarily at least (1933, *SE* 22, 58).

Modern day relational and intersubjective theorists may infer more dialogical, conversational or more implicit, attachment-based forms of the self's relationship to itself (and others) as fundamentally dyadic, duplex or relational. I would like to maintain, through the philosophical and developmental conceptualizations I have developed, that this clinical situation remains limited and complex in its situatedness where unconscious processes are decentred, the "unconscious" being somehow outside itself and unobjectifiable. Loewald uses the concept of *differentiality* to describe the mode of relating in the therapeutic session. The experience and knowledge of the therapist, much of which may be implicit and objectively unknowable, can guide the dwelling in and open exploration of the therapeutic work, dialogically and performatively. Again there is a focus on openness to possibility and the conversational nature of this process. Loewald's conceptualization of the "internalization of a differential" helps us to arrive at a developmental notion of the temporal nature of the Heideggerian Care and Solicitude where there is a form of thrownness (the infant/patient in the differential setting) that is moved forward by projection (through the movement to internalization as a form of self-sufficiency and cohesion). I acknowledge but actually enjoy bringing to light this contradictory linking of temporal projection and relational internalization. The notion of a differential relationship is suited to the hermeneutic ontological frame for understanding philosophically the individual's worldhood, the developmental frame of the infant, as well as the therapeutic frame for the patient. For example, we can see how in the therapeutic setting the temporal-projective elements of the differential relationship are internalized in the sense that the patient can internalize implicitly what the therapist projects or holds in mind for them. We can see the therapeutic setting as developmentally based but future-focussed (constructive as a potentiating field of becoming) where the relational encounter at a performative and narrative level is instrumental in a process of change although this change will always be complex, insofar as it is founded in otherness and difference, as well as being factically arbitrary insofar as it is limited and situated.

The differential element contradicts any aspiration to an empathic process in which two equal minds meet consensually to explore and mutually derive a common understanding and descriptive language to work through the patient's problems. This lacks a sense in which the patient may actually need to rely upon this sense of a differential relationship. What is important here is that the patient relates to the therapist in this differential setting, is contained within it and a space is maintained where there is enough room for transition, transformation and potentiation—for the therapist, this involves the combination of a more receptive, elaborative and reflective stance, and efforts to be actively present and real for the patient, in the manner of constructing and contextualizing the relationship. Through the internalization of the differential the patient comes to have a sense of containing and interpreting *for themselves*.

Beginning with Freud and Janet's work with hysteria, there has remained a focus upon integration, stabilitization and unification of the ego or personality in the overcoming of dissociation, disavowal and splitting. I have alluded to and elaborated to a small extent, the modern counterparts of these early trends which continue to focus upon transparency, cohesion, regulation and integration in the self as well as transparency and mutuality in the relational encounter. I have upheld the idea of a relational background that mixes with a complexity of temporal, affective, somatic and technical articulation and expression. If this is a variation, or a different platform for thinking the unconscious in hermeneutic ontological terms, we can consider a change in Freud's maxim *Wo Es war, soll Iche Werden* (traditionally translated as "Where Id was there Ego shall be")[6]. In talking about the goal of therapy as the development of a sense of stability, uniformity or cohesion (in oneself, in reality) we must remain appreciative of the complexity of an underlying background of becoming understood in terms of otherness and differentiality. This background has the elusiveness not of a singularity but of a complexity of differentiating elements of existence that are relational, temporal, affective, somatic and technical. This could be encapsulated in a simple variation of the Freudian maxim by instead saying: "Where it becomes, I shall be." In saying this, "I" must maintain a concern and respect for what "It" is, in all of its complexity.

Chapter 12

Embodied Affectivity
Borders, Bordering, and the Abject

In the philosophical part of this work, I explained how *Being and Time* (1928) includes an analysis of mood and affectivity as *befindlichkeit*, but that any analysis of embodiment on Heidegger's part was limited. I explored Derrida's (1983) deconstructive analysis of the related issue of sexuality, around the use of the German word "Geschlecht," an analysis which intended to uncover that the neutrality of *Dasein* does not so much represent a negative resistance to sexual differentiation (rendering it secondary, ontic) so much as a primal source of every sexuality, a form of elusive potency and multiplicity. As such, this type of deconstructive argument confirms the idea that the relative impoverishment of Heidegger's own ontological development of sexuality, and in a broader sense embodied affectivity, arguably belies a potentially fertile ontological foundation.

From this foundation, I explored the ontology of desire established by Gilles Deleuze and Felix Guatarri (1972, 1980), which developed conceptualizations of desire as

> as *difference*, *becoming* and *potentiation*, encapsulated within a broader ethical and political critique of psychoanalysis, seeking to avoid conceptualizing the familial constitution of a unified self by focussing upon a sub-individual realm of body parts, or "libidinal intensities," and their supra-individual interconnections in the social, thus providing a single system of configurations of "desiring-production," a system which can be analysed with the critical aim of, at once, overcoming both the Freudian approach to subjectivity and the Marxist approach to sociality. Loosely, Deleuze and Guattari (1972, 1980) held *subjectification* and *individuation* (as well as familialisation) as secondary processes that emerge from these supra and sub individual processes, within an organic and socio-political field of articulation. The importance of this conceptualization of desire for us related to its emphasis upon firstly the positivity, the productivity,

the *exercise* of power in desire; and secondly, the multiplicity, the specificity, the perversity of the assemblage of enunciation that is desire. This type of desire as *enunciation* and *becoming*, a desire as *chaos* and multiplicity favours *difference*. For Deleuze and Guattari (1980), "multiple sexualities," perversity and sexual difference, are the key productive elements of desire. I concluded that this ethics encourages the *exercise* of desire as power but, it seems, fails to analyse the degree to which psychotic states are an active *exercise* of desire, a *productive, creative desire*, or merely an *enunciation* of a *disempowered experience*. In abandoning an individuated conception of self-hood we are often unsure as to where the *exercise* of power lies. The psychotic's desire, here, may not be exercised by an empowered agent, and is perhaps only a suffering experienced and enunciated under the gaze of clinicians and theorists.

In the developmental part or "frame," I advanced some of Lacan's developmental conceptualizations of desire before I then turned to contrast and juxtapose these with the work of Deleuze and Guattari (1972, 1980). In the broadest and loosest sense, Lacan sought to decentre subjectivity throughout his works by situating processes of individuation or subjectification "outside": developmentally the reflective process occurs when the infant identifies itself as whole firstly through the reflection outside of itself in a mirror, the so-called "mirror phase" of imaginary identification, the *Imaginary Order*, in which the ego and the imaginary relationship with one's body is constituted. The infant or child is also subject to the dialogical process that occurs when the child is initiated as a speaking subject and is dependent upon language, in the *Symbolic Order*, where the "I" of speech is situated. As such, individuation or subjectification is seen as decentred, a form of lack or alienation in which the ego, subject or self is produced without, or from the exterior reference of the image and the word. This alienation is seen as originary, insofar as there is no pure or non-alienated origin prior to this. The third or other Order or register, *the Real*, may represent this origin but only as the unknowable pre-Symbolic, pre-Imaginary reality, which can drive need, anxiety, dread, but remain ineffable or non-representable, only understood in terms of any experiential residue or secondary effect.

In my analysis, we saw how Lacan described embodied affectivity, in the concepts of *desire* and *jouissance* with reference to these three Orders or Registers. What was of especial interest, there, was Lacan's later developmental formulation of *desire*, as the primary and originary form of embodied affectivity, and how this linked to his later formulation of psychosis. I emphasized the possibility that Lacan's later ideas around psychosis could potentially be related to the borderline concept, although Lacan and Lacanians mostly reject the latter concept.[1] What was significant to note, there, is that Lacan remains committed to a deficit model of psychosis, in fundamental distinction to Deleuze and Guattari's (1972, 1980) formulations of schizophrenia as a form of creative potentiality. Also, Lacan's latter ideas about psychotic desire become more originary and radical, involving developments of his theories of the Real, *jouissance*, the Thing and extimacy into pre-Symbolic concepts of meaning such as *lalangue*.

I contrasted and explored how the ideas of Lacan and Deleuze and Guattari impact upon an ethics of the clinic. I described that Deleuze and Guattari's (1980) notions of desire, enunciation and becoming are based upon a theory of expression which favours minoritarian, machinic heterogenesis and which relies upon an ethics of *difference*. This ethics endorses the *exercise* of power away from homogeneity and hegemony, a power that *produces difference*; but ignores the degree to which this is an active *exercise, creative* and *intentional*, or merely a more *passive experience, a subjection to heterogenesis* in which expression or enunciation result as a by-product. It would seem that in abandoning an individuated conception of "subject," Deleuze and Guattari (1980) avoid any theory of agency, of active organization or structure in subjectivity, in the name of selfless heterogenesis and machinic multiplicity. And by linking psychosis to *becoming* as a polymorphous, pre-Oedipal origin of multiplicity, fragmentation and perversity, this approach may indeed represent, to the Lacanian, a nostalgia for an illusory original satisfaction of the pre-Oedipal drive, but also may, in actuality, derive from a state of potential even topologically prior to the imaginary setting of this nostalgia (the mirror stage). Desire here is a *universalized sexuality* of perversion: multiple sexualities or *assemblages* are encouraged to emerge, defined by symbiotic relations of machinic heterogenesis where libidinal intensities or "thresholds" interact and combine to form unique and specific assemblages. In endorsing such a free-play of the becoming of desiring there is little room for a clinical pathologizing of desire. This is in fundamental opposition to the references Lacan makes throughout his work to a *lack* of structure, formation and volition to the psychotic's desiring whether this be Schreber's transsexuality, a passive disempowered *jouissance* of the Other that the psychotic suffers or the *sinthome-less, jouissance-less* unravelling of the psychotic. In this context, I argued that it is not inappropriate to ask whether Deleuze and Guattari (1972, 1980) may have overlooked the kind of clinic Lacan's (1992) ethics of desire would endorse, a clinic in which the analyst had the one primary calling to advocate the subject's pursuit of his own desire . . . set in the context of Lacan's later developments of a desire/*jouissance* structured by multiplicitous *sinthomes*.

Desire itself can be interpreted as a sublation of the Freudian death drive, culminating in a limit or antiproductive moment, for both Lacan (the *jouissance* of the Real *Thing*) as well as Deleuze and Guattari (*schizophrenia*, *chaos*). Multiplicitous desiring may take different forms for the subject: for Lacan, it becomes the variable structures of the *sinthome*, a form of binding *suppléance* of a lack; and for Deleuze and Guattari it is the expression of *machinic assemblages* of becoming. Deleuze and Guattari's (1972, 1980) conceptualization is based upon perverse, fragmentary machinic assemblages of affects, a *becoming* the Lacanian may arguably feel is harking nostalgically back to a pre-structural, psychotic unconscious as illusory origin. If becoming is a melding of form and content for Deleuze and Guattari, then psychosis remains an exemplary and self-consistent form of becoming. Lacan's conceptualizations are different at this level: they involve a fallibilization of man, the structuring or organization of *jouissance*, by the signifier or the *sinthome*, which is necessary for desire to be accessed and articulated but at the same time defines man to be necessarily alienated from the Real, even if it is held by man to be the ultimately desirable origin, however illusory or unobtainable. For Deleuze and Guattari, this formulation is just another neurotic repression of the most self-consistent form of becoming. Lacan's orientation was always to hold that this is the most that desiring can be, the goal being to at least have access to this limit as a creative, volitional, directive pursuit and not a subjection, a victimization, or something leading to an unravelling.

Thus, I saw that there was a fundamental incommensurability in the relation between these theorists' conceptualizations of psychosis: for Deleuze and Guattari it is an exemplary form of *breakthrough*— it is creative, productive, self-consistent, expressive; whereas for Lacan it is a pathological form of *breakdown*—unformed, passive, subjected, lacking. Hence Deleuze and Guattari would say that Lacan's conceptualizations are unified by a neurotic attempt to reterritorialize or repress the exemplary type of becoming that is psychosis; while Lacan would say that Deleuze and Guattari are reactionaries that naïvely celebrate a psychotic pathology that doesn't yield a creative *jouissance* or a stable, meaningful subjectivity because it alternatively lacks a discourse with the Other, does not search out a Thing of desire, or is not structured or suppleted by a *sinthome*. A resolution to this would involve some form of dialectic between breakdown and breakthrough, which may, in turn, hark back to the forms of dialectical relations I have mentioned elsewhere such as Freud (1920, 1923) referring to the movements between binding and unbinding, *Eros* and *Thanatos*, or Winnicott's (1971) conceptualisations of the movements between integration and disintegration. Two thinkers I will now describe here, Julie Kristeva and Andre Green, have developed ideas about these dialectics, but, importantly, have articulated the different sides in terms of "borders," linking this to borderline experience or pathology. I intend to develop this thinking around "borders" to explore issues of embodied affectivity as they relate to borderline experience.

BORDERLINE PATHOLOGY: KRISTEVA AND "ABJECTION," GREEN AND "BORDERS"

Philosopher and psychoanalyst Julie Kristeva has developed a range of ideas focussing upon originary desire and pre-Symbolic development that are directed more explicitly to borderline pathology, and seem to mediate or overcome this tension between breakdown and breakthrough, or creativity and destruction or degeneration. Kristeva (1982, 1983, 1995), engages critically with Lacan's linguistic emphasis by proposing the concept of the "semiotic" to designate other elements outside of language function, and, redressing what she sees as Lacan's overemphasis of the Symbolic and linguistic function rooted in de Saussurian linguistics.[2] What is of interest, here, is Kristeva's establishment of what she terms "The Semiotic," to define a realm of non-representational, non-linguistic, non-signifying drives and affects. Of especial interest is her descriptions of this realm made in relation to the discourse of the "borderline" subject, whom she feels is overlooked or excluded by the Lacanian.

Kristeva (1982, 1983, 1995) describes borderline discourse as chaotic, where language or symbolic function disintegrates, and is affected by a process Kristeva calls *abjection*. Put simply, abjection entails an absence or collapse of the boundaries or *borders* that structure the subject. In the *Powers of Horror*, Kristeva (1982) defines abjection as "what disturbs identity, system, order," including the boundaries or borders of subject and object, inner and outer, or, in Lacanian terms, processes of imaginary identification (ego formation) or Symbolic discourse as subjectification. The primary example for what causes such a reaction is the corpse (which traumatically reminds us of our materiality and blurs subjectivity and objectivity). Kristeva (1982) describes the abject as a form of developmental origin, before individuation, or inception into the imaginary and symbolic. For the infant, this earliest stage of development is referred to as the *chora* and is dominated by non-subjective, non-boundaried, chaotic experience of affects, drives and percepts. For the adult, and especially the borderline adult, the abject is associated with the eruption of the Real into our lives, and Kristeva links it to shame, primitive fear and *jouissance*. Kristeva (1982) describes that the discourse of the borderline subject is dominated by these eruptions, and associated experiences of boundless shame, fear and loss of self. These are related to the overwhelming, unbounded intrusion of Otherness, alterity, into experience, far beyond the bounds of a secondary reflective or dialogical (or Imaginary and Symbolic) relationship with oneself or others. The challenge in the therapeutic situation, here, is how to resituate this in reflection and dialogue, promote these and in turn mediate these experiences (in subjective or individuating terms).

In a related way, Green (2000) approaches these dilemmas when he describes the "central phobic position" of some borderline patients, a central defensive position which involves the destruction or degeneration of the individual's psychic functioning that affects the relational and temporalizing work in the session. This fits with Green's (1986) description of the borderline subject in terms of a broader notion of *borders* related to instincts which exist on the border between mind and body, between energy and symbolization, such that the borderline concept in a sense reflects the most basic or primary form of "pathology" in terms of unstable or moving borders, which could relate to me/not-me, self and other, mind and body, yes or no, inside or outside. The borderline subject, influenced by this central form of phobia, negates these relations, relations which, in Winnicottian terms, afford the opportunity for transitional experiencing. Developmentally, excessive forms of loss and intrusion, unmediated experience, rupture, impingement and failure of whatever kind, have led to these difficulties with "bordering." Therapeutically, according to Green (1986), the challenge of borderline work is that it is *inductive*, as opposed to the *deductive* work that occurs with neurotic problems. Somehow, the therapist needs to induce transitional, transformational experience and relating, *facilitate* it. In Bionian terms, Green reflects that this may be work more on the container more than the contained. Green (2000) describes subtle forms of evocative relating, mutual resonance, retroactive reverberation and heralding anticipation which enhance the relational and temporal therapeutic processes of the clinical work. The efforts made, here, are to re-situate and re-contextualize the individual, with themselves, with others, and in time.

I would expand on this by stating that the role of the therapist in this situation is to "complicate" the individual's expressions, relate to them, temporalize them in the sense of performative gesture and narrative dialogue where the sense of timing and sharing are "induced" within the differential context of the therapeutic work. The unbordered, the alteritous, the unmediated will be related to and thought about to facilitate and enhance forms of individuating, subjectifying, that occur with oneself and others.[3] The ethical stance, here, involves a respect for autonomy, complexity, the freedom to differentiate and develop in one's desiring in all of the multiplicitous complexity as it is described by Lacan and Deleuze and Guattari. The "frame-work," or work around boundaries and bordering, is simultaneously constitutive and productive as well as limiting and containing. In terms of embodiment and affectivity, this may involve work around many of the elements that typically coalesce in what is characterized as borderline work: unmediated, intrusive, impinging affective and somatic states—Kristeva's abject shame states, the forms of somatoform dissociation (van der Hart et al., 2006) describes, the satellites of trauma and stimulus entrapment Meares (2000) describes, or the conservative moods Bollas (1987) describes—are overcome through recontextualizing, resituating, mediating, subjectifying and *complicating* these experiences in the therapeutic work. The work here is inductive, the efforts the therapist makes to work with, understand and relieve these elements operates in subtle ways, in terms of "how I respond to them," "how I handle them" and the links I make to other relational, temporal and technical processes. The relational processes can be introduced into the situations in which these unbounded elements arise, what is seen to relationally trigger or evoke them, what connections and links there may be to other relational elements within the therapy, as well as extratherapeutically in present, past and future relationships; the temporal components may relate to understanding these elements as complex mnemic traces (affective, somatic, gestural and so forth); and the technical components may relate to whatever implicit or explicit techniques one may have to handle or overcome these elements as isolated, impinging and unmediated (ushering in the broad range of attitudes, skills, strategies and know-how that pervades this field encapsulating approaches that are pharmacotherapeutic or skills-based such as the dialectical behaviour therapy approach of Marsha Linehan).

The relationship with the otherness of oneself, (the performative, dialogical, temporal, and technical processes of self-relationship), becomes more mediated and "complicated."[4] The borders are strengthened, here, in terms of processes that are reinforced in the therapeutic work. I would emphasize, as I have elsewhere, that in this work one cannot aim for total self-legislation, total self-mediation, total self-transparency in the patient. It is a bordering, a relating to otherness dialogically, performatively, temporally and so forth, where these borders with otherness relate to the body, the other person, the otherness of death and so forth. This form of "bordering" experience, as opposed to "borderline experience," can relate to what I have elsewhere described in terms of transitionality (Winnicott), transformation (Bollas) and differentiality (Loewald). In terms of embodied affectivity, I think the borders relate to desiring processes that are heterogonous, multiplicitous and complex, where the dialectic with otherness relates to movements between creative and destructive processes of becoming and potentiation. Nowhere is this more the case than in the domains of sexual and aggressive experiences and behaviours where processes of articulation will only ever be mediated to an extent, where one will always have the opportunity to be "beside oneself," "to lose oneself, to be taken up by or overcome by the Otherness of the process.

Therapeutically, the aspiration is to overcome unmediated and archaic, un-bordered, remnants. Abject shame, here, can be overcome if it is related to in the manner I describe, through contextualisation, empathy and handling. Primitive, archaic forms of self relationships can be overcome, here. For example, what Kernberg (1975) referred to as the action of the archaic, punitive superego, which could be seen to be a simultaneously fragile and weak but overly violent and domineering form of self-relationship (self-scolding, self-punishing, self-disciplining) can be challenged and overcome.

Phenomena and experiences that coalesce around this idea of the punitive superego are not simply explained in terms of the internalization of an abusive figure, not simply a hyperbolic reaction to shame and guilt secondary to traumatisation. It could relate to all manner of formative experiences where there is a very fragile attempt at bordering, at controlling and organizing oneself, in the face of overwhelmingly abject, traumatizing, unmediated experience. In this way, it could be seen to be a primitive archaic remnant of self-relationship.[5] To this degree, many other forms of experience and behaviour that fall under the borderline concept could be analysed here: suicidal gestures and cutting could be seen as literal, immediate, archaic attempts at bordering: not simply a "primitive" or "maladaptive" attempt at the grounding of dissociation; not simply the "enactment" of a punitive superego; not simply the "physicalizing" of psychic pain. These behaviours represent all of this and more: they are *complicated* and the role of the therapist is to respect, respond to and relate to the complexity of these borders (mind and body, past and present, presence and absence, inner and outer, whatever they may be) and in doing so, facilitate more of a sense of understanding, containment and mediation, of context and control. And perhaps one of the most complicated "afflictions" of all, in this regard, are the array of difficulties that fall within the rubric of "multiple personality disorder," where borders and boundaries between an array of performative, affective, mnemic and narrative modes of being are experienced as too pronounced, too limited, too rigid and frozen, where there may be a phobic resistance to exploration, reflection, mediation, change and so forth. And then there are related "bordering complexes," obsessive compulsive, bulimic, impulsive, that also have affinities with "borderline experience" or pathologies of bordering.

All of this work is directed at further contextualizing, mediating, binding, and, ultimately, *bordering* experience as it arises in the therapeutic work. The individual and therapist are bound together in a complex context and share the constitutive process together. It is helpful for the therapist to articulate the limits of this work, the boundaries and borders, in terms of the limits of capacity, vision, reach and so forth that they have. As such, it is just as important for the therapist to maintain a distance, a sense of difference and otherness, as it is to assert a presence, an intimacy, and a sense of mutuality. The border between these two domains, of identity and difference, of repetition and change, of fusion and alienation, is where the action of the therapy occurs. This then, can become a space of articulation, performative and dialogical, that limits and mediates desiring in all of its complexity, working on the frames, the boundaries and borders of experience, in the face of the full force and breadth of complex desiring processes. . . .

Chapter 13

Temporality
Play, Care, and the Work of Trauma

In the initial philosophical part of this work, we arrived at a thinking of time that began with Heidegger's hermeneutic ontological orientation, where I elucidated concepts of Care, *Geworfenheit* (thrownness), *Entwurfen* (project) and being-towards-death before extending this thinking via Andre Green's and Jacques Derrida's reading of Freud's oeuvre, in which *Nachträglichkeit*, *re-presentation*, bidirectional time, heterochronicity and, finally, *différance* could all be seen to permit a fuller understanding of historicity, facticity and potentiality that arguably remained consistent with the Heideggerian orientation.

Then in the developmental context, I explored notions of originary temporality further, where the conceptualizations of Jean Laplanche (otherness and the enigmatic signifier) and Donald Winnicott (unintegration and disintegration) introduce fundamentally *temporal* notions of developmental origins while maintaining, at the same time, a respect for limits and alterity. These notions were seen to be in a sense originary or foundational limits that pervade infantile, child and adult experience (in forms of play, creativity, and potentiation in a rich array of experiences), and were thus seen to be relevant to the clinical approach here in the final part of this work, where a developmental orientation will be maintained. I also sought to expand upon this in the developmental context more fully: origins of general or universal seduction (Laplanche) and primary narcissism/dependence (Winnicott) permit the action of the other to occur over time with ineffable temporal rhythms (presence/absence, frustration/relief, unconscious implantation and impingement) where ego or self-integration processes are developed that are temporal in nature in keeping with our understanding of *Nachträglichkeit* and bidirectional time—processes of translation-repression and movements between integration and disintegration. We saw that drives, as a form of project, are inextricably linked to this developmental context of the differential horizon of relationality, alterity and *Nachträglichkeit*.

I sought to describe these as the temporal foundations of an understanding of trauma, seen within a universal phenomenon of seduction as the imposition of the other upon the infant or small child within the context of differential relating, which can in some way become excessive in the process of intromission of unassimilable, unmetabolisable experiences which will reside as unintegrated, psychosis-inducing fragments; as well as the notion of an excessive or cumulative experience of impingements (both as environmental failures and excessively active input from the care giver) that lead to self-pathologies in terms of disintegration and defensive false self-structures. These ideas will now be taken up and expanded upon in this clinical "frame" in our understanding of developmental trauma and borderline experience in clinical work.

In the clinical chapter on relationality above, I discussed the therapeutic situation as a transitional, transformational and differential space, referring to Winnicott's idea of the potential space and Green's extension of this into thought around the analytic object. In Winnicott's (1971) thinking around the potential space of psychoanalysis, he also describes elements of the *temporality of play* in this potential space:

> I make my idea of play concrete by claiming that playing has a place and time. It is not inside by any use of the word (and it is unfortunately true that the word inside has very many and various uses in psychoanalytic discussion). Nor is it outside, that is to say, it is not part of the repudiated world, the not-me, that which the individual has decided to recognize (with whatever difficulty and even pain) as truly external, which is outside magical control. To control what is outside one has to do things, not simply think or wish, and doing things takes time. Playing is doing. (1971, 41)

Within the Winnicottian metaphorics of the clinical encounter, play occurs both within a relational and a *temporal* field. We are reminded of Winnicott's (1971) developmental ideas about the timing of presences and absences, senses of integration and disintegration, effects of failure and impingement, leading to traumatic effects (impingements, loss of a sense of self and the real, false self-structures and so on). Green (2002, 110–130) extends the notions of the symbolization of play, reflecting on Freud's ideas about the *Fort/Da* game, traumatic enactment and symbolization, expanding these ideas to a much broader field of "traumatic play" that occurs within the therapeutic space, in all manner of performative and narrative based expression and symbolization.

Green (2002), here, develops a sophisticated theory of drive and object relations (the *drive-object*, "objectalizing") based upon many of the ideas Freud (1920–1922) develops in *Beyond the Pleasure Principle*, simultaneously linking and relating the Freudian conceptualizations of the pleasure and reality principle, *Eros* and *Thanatos*, *Binding* and *Unbinding* with more Winnicottian conceptualizations of play and trauma. Underlying this is a commitment to reinstate a drive theory, a commitment I do not necessarily share in the form it takes in Green's (2002) theoretical elaboration, where I would see that there remains a risk of maintaining some form of deterministic, essentialistic or reductionistic system of energetics. Ricoeur's (1965) work *Freud and Philosophy* conducts a careful analysis of the Freudian hermeneutic realm where the causal energetics of the drive become inextricably linked to the domain of symbolic interpretation for the analyst, a hermeneutic link between energetics and meaning. In this work Ricoeur (1965) does repeatedly note the significance of Freud's assertions of the timelessness of the unconscious and the Id, but Ricoeur does not undertake a broader analysis of Freudian time or temporality within this project.[1]

What is relevant for us, here, is the temporal element to traumatic play that Green develops from Winnicott's work. This can be melded with the broader field of relational, somatic, affective and technical elements I have elaborated upon within my hermeneutic ontological framework. If we adhere to ideas of traumatic elements re-emerging repetitively, seemingly in an unthinking, compulsive sense, we can use notions of temporal rhythmicity (binding/unbinding, discontinuities/fragmentation) and the idea of these elements being somehow dissociated, unintegrated or outside time, in order to understand the requirement of a *temporal* quality to therapeutic action. Here, therapeutic work may relate to the "temporalizing" of traumatic elements as they are constructed, contextualized and worked through in the therapeutic relationship.

Green (2002), aptly describes the challenges of work with borderline cases, or even defines borderline cases, in temporal terms:

> With borderline cases, the compulsion to repeat has revealed a psychic vocation whose purpose is *anti-time*. Everything has to return to the point where it began; it is not possible to consider any conflict with the minimum degree of suspension required for it to be elaborated, and then, perhaps, overcome. Everything has to be actualized and exhausted on the spot; not only to prevent any progression, but also to prevent anything new from emerging. (2002, 121)

I would add, here, further Winnicottian elements to the atemporal traumatic elements: features such as severe unthinkable acute psychic pain (as a form of archaic disintegration experience), suicidal thinking, other overwhelming states described as affective (pain, anxiety, horror, despair) or dissociative (depersonalized, derealized, absent and so forth), experiences of psychic death that are also performatively expressed and thus highly dangerous insofar as they entail self-harming or suicidal impulses. These elements, which seem so immediate and overwhelming, are difficult to work with, *play* with (saying this, in itself, seems glib or antithetical), re-temporalize or contextualize. All of the contextual, constructive work therapeutically (the relationship developed, the concern, the boundaries and limits, the empathic gestures) might have at their heart an attempt at establishing an enduring and intact temporal continuity in the therapeutic relationship. In Winnicott's terms, the good-enough mother survives. In broader terms, the therapist maintains the context of the work, the good will and attempt to meet and engage in a working, constructive dialogue, a dialogue where it is necessary for the patient to see how he or she is held in mind, thought about, related to, responded to over time. All of this work has a temporal quality (the rhythm/ regularity of the work, the reliable presence and absence of the therapist), all of the temporal elements to distinguish boundaries and borders around me and not-me, related to in terms of actions and utterances, and discourse concerning the somatic and affective elements alluded to in the chapter on embodied affectivity immediately above.

We can add to this a consideration of our earlier discussion of Laplanche's (1990, 1992) formulation of a general theory of seduction, where his theorization of the formative impact of enigmatic signifiers, the impact of the other in the differential relationship as universally seductive and traumatic, and the ongoing temporal modes of translation-repression, all fit within a theory of bidirectional developmental time. In the clinical setting, this enigmatic otherness constitutes an invitation to seduce or be seduced (with all of the "sexual," "aggressive," abusive," "traumatic" or other overtones this may engender) both directed towards the patient and the therapist alike. It constitutes the general field of traumatic enactment and play that is relationally based and constituted by the therapist and patient alike. To maintain a differential orientation, the therapist must maintain a thoughtful stance giving him or herself the opportunity ("giving him or herself *time*") to think temporally from within the field, with and for the patient so that the patient can come to do this more so with and for themselves. And this process is not merely a past-focussed, reconstructive, insight-forming process. It is a process of potentiation and becoming that hopefully facilitates broader growth and change for the patient.

Loewald (1980), in papers such as "The Experience of Time" and "On the Therapeutic Action of Psychoanalysis" was keenly interested in the futural focus of the psychoanalyst in what he termed the "teleological" aspects of psychoanalysis. In his view, the process is always guided by the analyst's awareness of the patient's true form or "emerging core." The analyst must hold this in trust to steer the process: "It is this core, rudimentary and vague as it may be, to which the analyst has reference when he interprets transferences and defences, and not some abstract concept of reality or normality (1980, 229)."

In a broader field than the traditional analytic field of one-person interpretation what does this mean? If we hold to Loewald's idea of the differential setting and internalization of the differential, how do we understand the therapist's *temporalizing* stance. The therapist somehow maintains a temporal focus, working with the patient within a space of potentiation to construct, contextualize, constitute and understand the therapeutic process in a temporal sense: a broad field of discussing, reflecting upon, differing about "what you're doing," "what I'm doing," "what we're doing" where "doing," in the broadest sense of *play*, refers to a whole experiential-relational field of narrative and performative expression. It fits into and melds with the context, what the therapist does and says, what can and can't be offered and so forth. The therapist thinks about those alteritous, enigmatic elements that impact upon the space. In a traumatic sense, these are important to think about and this requires some restraint and maintenance of a space for the patient to articulate, work on and play with these elements, and for the therapist to think about and respond to them from within a differential relationship. The therapist must be mindful of this, and this requires an awareness of and cultivation of a differential setting within which this can occur (a setting of thought, observation, consideration and deliberate responsiveness). As such, this is not just a therapeutic process of therapist and patient meeting in the here and now, where the therapist attempts to attune to and connect with their patient without a sensibility to temporal elements.[2]

The therapist does and must take up the opportunity to engage with, play with and change with their patient in the present moment, but also, at the same time, in an enigmatic way influence their patient where a significant part of this influence involves a number of temporal actions with and for the patient: *reflection upon*, *coming to terms with*, *working through*, *anticipating*, *projecting* and so forth. In the sense of trauma, this temporalizing action may take the form of restoring elements to their place in the past, or it may be an attempt at restoring a futural focus. If this refers to understandable, discrete, traumatic events it can be a sense of the balance between "getting over" something and "getting on with life" in a process of restoring some sense of temporal balance alongside balance in the other aspects of being described in my hermeneutic ontological framework. However many elements are more enigmatic, less understandable in that literally traumatic sense, and the therapist cannot claim to arbitrate and interpret all of these with an objective or omniscient stance. Chronologically, the earlier the "events," the more implicitly, enigmatically retained or understood they may be. There is no sense that one can reliably attempt to reconstruct a reality or an insight in this. In spite of the many vacillations and complex statements Freud made about actual trauma, intrapsychic trauma, seduction, phantasy and wish, which have become a core element of the controversial heritage and contestability of his body of work, Freud (1917) did hold to the ambiguity between truth and falsehood in "traumatic experience":

> If infantile experiences brought to light by analysis were invariably real, we should feel that we were standing on firm ground; if they were regularly falsified and revealed as inventions, as phantasies of the patient, we should be obliged to abandon this shaky ground and look for salvation elsewhere. But neither of these things is the case: the position can be shown that the childhood experiences constructed or remembered in analysis are sometimes indisputably false and sometimes equally certainly correct, and in most cases compounded of truth and falsehood (*SE 15–16*, 367)

Elsewhere, Freud, also, described hysterical symptoms as being more than just traumatic remnants in a mnemic sense: "Hysterical symptoms are not attached to actual memories, but to phantasies erected on the basis of memories" (1900, *SE 4–5*, 491).

If, in my analysis, I extend this notion of hysterical symptoms being based in phantasy to all manner of processes of expression or articulation that are relationally, temporally, somatically, affectively and technically derived, it becomes evermore complex. In this hermeneutic ontological framework, I have upheld ideas of alterity, limits, and differentiality. What the therapist can hope to do is establish a sense of relatedness, dwelling and sharing in this context of limits, alterity and differentiality. What therapist can be mindful of, here, is the manner in which the temporalizing function creates room or space for this relating, for dreaming and thinking, interpreting and understanding where previously there wasn't.

Thinkers of the Intersubjective School have articulated some related ideas in their writings on trauma work. Stolorow (2011a & b, 2009), for example, elaborates his own conceptualization of relational trauma and relational work that establishes kinship-in-finitude: he uses the philosophical conceptualisations of Critchley and Derrida on death and mourning, and adapts the Heideggerian concept of *Mitsein* (and in particular, being-towards-death, solicitude and authenticity), to articulate how relational work can re-establish a sense of temporal and relational functioning after trauma. Orange (2011) describes how dialogue, in all of its metaphorical complexity, can help to understand and overcome the most complex or inarticulable elements of traumatic "experience," where creative dialogue and metaphoric play can form a part of therapeutic work. In thinking at this level, we are aware of the limits of explicit, conscious work on identifiable traumatic elements (imaginal re-exposure, integration work, and so forth): some of the work may simply be levelled at attempts at re-establishing temporal, relational, affective and somatic links. In doing this, we have an orientation for approaching unconscious work with the traumatized unconscious that is much broader, temporally and relationally attuned and able to approach the complexity of the action of trauma which may become manifest in all manner of atemporal, non-relational, unresolved, unformulated, dissociated, psychotic, unsymbolized, somatic, and affective fragments of expression or gesture.

I believe that many of the problems around understanding the temporality or historicity of what I loosely call the traumatized unconscious may be addressed using this type of relational, temporalizing therapeutic stance grounded in my hermeneutic ontological approach. This can be considered, for example, in cases of brief reactive psychosis, dissociative psychosis, or what since the mid to late nineteenth century have been known as hysterical psychosis (see van der Hart et al., 1993). In some ways, hysterical psychosis could be described as involving forms of splitting and fragmentation that lead to personal modes of expression (acting, speaking, self-interpreting) which rely on fragmentary experiences, descriptions or expressions which seem narrow and limited, often with a literal and concrete quality, which can be overcome through the kind of therapeutic work I am describing. Often these presentations seem to relate to an event of re-traumatization, sometimes with a "determined" feel to it (linked to repetition compulsion) in which the subsequent decompensation may have psychotic elements (persecutory and grandiose) as well as more dissociative elements related to a disjointed sense of self, time, others and so forth. There may be concrete and fragmentary symptoms (conversion symptoms, symptoms akin to somatoform dissociation) that seem to have a mnemic or symbolic quality that the patient cannot acknowledge. The present interpersonal situation (therapeutically or extratherapeutically) can be responded to as a form of "re-traumatization" leading to a sense of fragmentation or dissociation, somatic and affective experiences that feel real and in the present, and interpretations of occurrences that meld the past and the present in a narrowed down, collapsed form of temporality as if it were all appearing in a fragmentary form in the present-day.

Interpretively, repetitive efforts made at linking the re-traumatizing event to the concrete psychotic state (referring to splitting and projective mechanisms) would not lead to an "ahah" moment where an insightful awareness crystallizes and the psychotic state resolves, losing its "literal realness." Rather than asserting an explanation or a causal understanding the therapist opts for exploring the experiences and events in a more open approach, dialogically, facilitating a dwelling in and reflecting upon the experiences together, describing them together and exploring them for their possibilities. The therapist actively attempts to disentangle what is past and what is present, what is attributable to the patient or to the other (which could be the therapist him or herself), defining borders and boundaries in the work, relationalizing and temporalizing the work in the manner I have already described above. In doing this, there may be a gradual restoration of a sense of self and place and time, and with this is a gradual working through of what begin to crystallize as "memories" as if from the current day viewpoint what couldn't be comprehended is now "seen."

As this process develops, the patient experiences the return of a sense of self-awareness and reflectiveness, a capacity to self-interpret and a gradual recovery of themselves as not overcome by two separate forms of objective presence: the event of re-traumatization and the psychotic state. They feel they can descriptively explore the complex moods and feelings—they may be senses of violation, self-loathing, shame, disgust, anger—and link these to the described past and present events and occasions which are acknowledged to be only partially apprehended or understood as memories. Here, we may be dealing with complex interpersonal experiences and events, with no objectifiable truth or understanding, and with the possibility of limits of understanding, memory or comprehensibility. There is no sense that this is fully resolved or worked through so much as a sense that the patient has somehow recovered themselves to go on with the work of the therapy in all its complexity, openness and potentiality.

This kind of case can be explored in such a way in order to elaborate upon how a therapeutic process in which the patient and therapist dwell together more openly and attempt to experience, relate to, describe and explore the hidden and concealed in what the patient experiences without the inference of causal mechanisms, definitive explanation or reference to forms of objective presence leads to the sense of a more complex self-structure which is analogous in some ways to Heidegger's Care structure in its relationality and temporality. This is the case because it involves an overcoming of self-splitting which features modes of self-interpretation which have recourse to objective presence. Other modes of self-functioning, what Heidegger might call more authentic modes, are recovered and these relate to aspects of the Care structure in its temporal historicity (how thrownness and projection are implicated in a present moment that seemed seized by the past re-traumatizing event and the continuously "present" dissociative or psychotic states). This recovery is facilitated by the reciprocal process of dwelling together which facilitated mutual awareness (what Heidegger called doubling or empathy) something recovered after relational events in which doubling or empathy do not feature.

I have deliberately spoken about this in general and abstract terms in order to encapsulate this type of work in a way that encompasses many different iterations and forms of complexity. One can think of cases of hysterical psychosis one has seen, or even generalize this type of relational and temporalizing stance to many other forms of clinical situations or clinical work where the expression of apparently enigmatic unconscious, dissociative or psychotic elements are worked through, understood and contextualized in a relational and temporalizing therapeutic process. It can incorporate all manner of complex and fragmentary affective, somatic disturbances, relational problems and dissociative disturbances featuring discontinuity and disintegration.[3] An important emphasis has been placed upon a broad notion of play which encapsulates more discursive and performative elements than Winnicott (1971) originally described. These elements, unconscious, enigmatic and traumatic, become temporalized in such a way as the patient is more open to the complexity of their being, less affected by the intrusive, fragmentary, disintegrating and unbound elements that had existed without a temporalizing, restorative function found in play with others. This is what is therapeutically discovered as a form of true self found in dialogue and relationship with the therapist. The temporal movement in this work helps to re-situate the individual in a space of care with the therapist, which becomes an expressive and performative *microcosm* of a broader horizon of care in life outside the consulting room. What the patient may gain is more of a sense of themselves, their own being, and authenticity in their relationship with themselves and others. The intrusive, enigmatic and fragmentary unconscious intrusions or impingements are less narrowing, alienating or destabilizing, as these have been shared and contextualized so as to create a clearing, a space from which to consider the future as an horizon. The patient is no longer confronted by death (psychic death, suicide) as an immediate prospect or already experienced annihilation, so much as an horizon of finality and alterity that can be comported towards, related to with others within the project of life, but thankfully deferred.

Chapter 14

Technicity and Technique

Conclusion to the Clinical Frame

What does it mean when psychoanalysts and psychotherapists state that the borderline patient is the "patient of our time"?

In the philosophical part of this work, I described how technology and technicity, in the theoretical conceptualizations of Bernard Stiegler, can be seen to constitute self-understanding and becoming, where interiorisation and exteriorisation co-exist as worldhood. Examples here may be the earliest forms of technologies such as tools and mirrors (which in turn co-exist with us existing and conceptualizing ourselves as technical, reflective beings), techniques and practices that facilitate symbolic or representational art (from the most primitive forms), language itself (in its spoken and written forms) not to mention how these may all be implicated and advanced in such sophisticated modern technologies as film and digital media and other forms of *representation*. All of these technical processes co-exist with self-representational interpretive processes. The artefactual technological world is an ineliminable part of temporality, not only as dead history but as a living form of memory, as well as an instrumental aspect of our becoming. *Individuation*, for Stiegler, is a psychic, collective and technical *process*, the result of which is the hypothetical individual.

As such, Stiegler (1994) argues that it can be more useful to understand how technologies form a part of human becoming situated within existence, rather than assisting in the establishment of objective knowledge or understanding situated outside of existence (which is aporetic). From these perspectives we have to remind ourselves of the inherent limits of *thinking technologically* and the role that technological thinking can play in affecting or limiting *individuation*. This relates to the kinds of individuals that are constituted, normatively and pathologically, within a historico-cultural and technological context. As such, how we conceptualize and constitute ourselves as healthy or sick individuals, is inextricably linked to our technicity and technological understanding. And it is from this perspective that we can consider why and how the borderline category has arisen.

Subsequently in the developmental part of this work, I argued that the borderline concept can be seen to be a locus for limits and tensions in psychiatry and psychotherapy, where many paradoxical ideas coalesce that fail to grasp or capture complexity or alterity. I referred to the relational paradox of projective identification, the temporal paradoxes of deferred action and recovered memory, the paradoxes of embodiment and identity identified in concepts such as somatoform dissociation, stimulus entrapment, fixed ideas and multiple personalities as well as, finally, paradoxes of agency and control, identified in concepts such as conversion and disavowal. Now the "borderline" category, historically, emerged in this context of limits and tensions. It was only in a *post hoc* fashion that it crystallized into a discrete "diagnostic category," an identifiable syndrome or pathology, which could then be a locus of a diverse range of psychopathological theories and treatment paradigms. In Stiegler's terms, there is a technological context in which this form of individuation has arisen which we may do better to try to understand; at the same time as being suspicious of the more *post hoc* (or, in Derridean terms, "supplementary") technological metaphors used to explain it as if it were an originary or natural form of existence or an object of scientific study. Here, I discussed and referred to what I described as attachment, structural and trauma metaphors. What is of primary interest is the fact that these "technological" metaphors could be seen to have emerged after the "discovery" of borderline conditions, problems or personality disorders, as if they fitted within a scientific process of research and elucidation of a naturally occurring disorder. What I would argue is that these technologies actually form part of a process of *constituting* the disorder, forming part of a greater technological-cultural context in which the borderline problem has not only emerged but through which it is constituted.

I have also elaborated that this technological context can be seen to be a broader *historical* context as well. As we saw in our discussion of Deleuze and Guattari's work (1972, 1980), psychoanalytic theory can be seen to fall within a historical movement in which *subjectification* occurs, theory being situated within specific cultural and technical modes of construction of the individual that are related to sub and supra individual processes that are historically contingent both in a biological (evolutionary) and socio-political sense. In a related way, Michel Foucault used the concept of "technologies of the self" to describe subjectification occurring in historically specific modes of practice, modes of what he calls, in his later works, *power/knowledge*, in which scientific discourses, and discourses such as psychoanalytic and psychiatric discourse, very much fit within practices which control, order and constitute social and subjective experience, domesticate and structure it. Foucault does not have a humanist emancipatory agenda or conspiratorial focus in this: following Nietzsche, his critical historicization of modern scientific discourses and institutional practices (and other aspects of modernity) has an antihumanist orientation, seeking to undermine any universalist, humanistic and objective scientific pretensions to these discourses and practices for the purpose of greater critical awareness and ethical lucidity.

This brings us to the idea that psychoanalytic treatment, psychotherapy and psychiatric practice are technical enterprises fitting within a very specific modern moral and cultural context. It can be argued that the borderline concept has necessarily arisen in this modern context as a central limit concept that exposes or challenges the limits of the contemporary schools of psychoanalytic, psychological and psychiatric theory and clinical practice. Much of the clinical part of this work has involved an attempt to critically understand and articulate an ethically and "therapeutically" sustainable standpoint to consider borderline experience whilst maintaining an understanding and appreciation of these limits.

The "technological" and "cultural" orientation here, not only serves to remind us of the ways in which our experience and understanding is limited by our technicity, but also the manner in which our technicity and culture constitutes our understanding and way of being in historically-specific modes of practice. Technicity, here, is a broad term that can encapsulate elements of our technical culture such as computational technology, digital representational media, modern biological and medical sciences (genetic, molecular, neuroscientific, evolutionary and so forth) and so forth. This technicity, which Stiegler understands in terms of exteriorisation and individuation, and Foucault understands in terms of power/knowledge and technologies of the self, also relates to our broader historico-cultural situation (industrial, developed, scientific, medicalized, individualistic, anomic and liberal-democratic). This situation is confronted by a horizon of alterity, difference, and the unassimilable. In this case, the borderline concept has arisen with unstable, shifting meanings, presenting "problems of topology" where alteritous, differential and unassimilable experiences meet with the modern psychoanalytic or psychiatric clinic. Here, we can first identify the metaphorical strategies the clinics use to understand and relate to these experiences (medicalize, technologize, or scientize them): they can become domesticated and *infantilized* in terms of constructing an individual who has experienced or suffered aberrant developmental events (trauma, abuse), and exhibits subsequent developmental and structural psychological deficits that can be overcome and repaired. Clinically, though, there is the possibility that these experiences become transformed behaviourally into the identifiable borderline syndrome (even if this varies subtly in type from practitioner to practitioner or model to model) when the "borderline individual" comes to interact with the clinical setting. Brandchaft and Stolorow (1984), for example, have argued how a clinical practitioner's model of borderline pathology or treatment can actually produce or reinforce its own certain type of "borderline patient."

At an individual and historico-cultural level, alterity, difference and the unassimilable, here, may refer to all manner of margins of experience, some related to aspects of gender difference, sexuality, cruelty, aggression, excessive passion and violence for example. The experiences, at the individual level, become constructed within a symbiotic relationship with the clinical and cultural elements of the organization of self-experience. These experiences become manifest in a historically specific manner. Wirth-Cauchon (2001), for example, argues that the borderline construct situates itself within conflicts around gender and sexual difference, taking over from hysteria which was a related limit concept in the Victorian era. In the age of hysteria, the hysteric may have appeared out of the dynamics of the inability to express the unthinkable, the will to implicit silencing, the action of taboo, privacy and secret. In the "borderline era," the borderline may be a fragmented, chaotic expression of the limits of our permissivism, the after-effects of our openness to explicitness (sexual, violent, graphic) and the collision of our high ambitions for individualism (individual rights and responsibilities) with frank problems of neglect, omission and maltreatment seen in the formative course of individuals' lives. In the borderline era, these individual and cultural elements reflect the terrain of the failed reach or grasp of our civility in terms of the purported control of the law and human services. Democratic rights to universal care and support become a mirage or unreachable horizon, the "borderline" individual instead experiencing a morass of isolation, neglect, stigmatisation and abusive re-traumatization. Protests are then made to the clinical practitioners and therapeutic services that would offer sanctuary and technological forms of (substitutive) care. Here, there is a risk of dehumanization, stigmatization and disenfranchisement of the individual.

Technical descriptions of borderline and dissociative phenomena mostly refer to dysregulation of relational, temporal, embodied or affective experience or awareness: consider, for example, concepts such as derealisation, depersonalisation, impulsivity, disembodiment, amnesia, numbing, emptiness, overwhelming distress, anger, suicidality and self-loathing. All of these elements pose challenges to therapeutic work necessitating hospitality, understanding, a focus upon relatedness, care, avoidance of alienation, violence, stigmatisation and confusion. A technical-scientific orientation may represent a limited form of understanding not adequately respecting and engaging with elements of difference, alterity and unassimilable limits in the sense of an attempt to engage in dialogue and understanding. The borderline concept may function, for the therapist, as a defensive "bordering off" of the relationship, of the interaction, a process of delimiting that may potentially be alienating, stigmatizing or demoralizing for the patient.

This would be the reservation, the ethical and critical standpoint, that I would adopt in considering the most objectifying, manualized, models of psychotherapy that have been articulated to treat borderline personality disorder, such as Linehan's (2006) Dialectical Behaviour Therapy, Fonagy, Bateman and Target's "Mentalization-based Treatment" (Fonagy et al., 2002), "Transference-Focussed Psychotherapy" which is a modified form of Kernberg's original approach (Clarkin, Yeomans and Kernberg, 2006), Ryle's Cognitive Analytic Therapy (Ryle 1997), Meares's Conversational Model (2000), Supportive Psychoanalytic Psychotherapy (Appelbaum, 2006), Schema-Focused Therapy (Giesen-Bloo et al., 2009) and Systems Training for Emotional Predictability and Problem Solving (or "STEPPS," Blum et al., 2008). All of these approaches have emerged from a technological culture of operationalized technical skills, evidence-based protocols, economically defensible managed care, and specialized research paradigms.

All of these approaches justify their efficacy in terms of objective measures (rates of self-harm, suicidality, hospitalization, rating scales with indices of symptom disturbance and quality of life). In contrast to this, I have attempted to articulate a therapeutic stance in which the identity of the therapist, as a technically and culturally defined expert, is aware of their complicity in the creation of the borderline diagnosis or identity, and maintains something of a knowing and critical stance towards it in their interactions and relationships with individuals designated as borderline. The position of the therapist is to respect the uniqueness, the complexity, the autonomy, the otherness of the person presenting for therapeutic work. The therapist understands the limits and differentiality of the therapeutic situation, and adopts an openness to the enunciation of the relationship through a form of hospitality. In the establishment of a form of differential relationship, the therapist is aware of the culture-boundness of the therapeutic situation, the thaumaturgical legacy, and adopts this with a wary and critical stance with a view to enhancing the patients own openness to potentiation, becoming and change.

Much of this relates to an awareness of context, not just in terms of the situation of referral and the origins of the treatment for the individual, but also in terms of the situation of the practitioner and the treatment that the practitioner offers. This situatedness is complex for both parties, in terms of personal, familial, cultural and historical origins for the patients, and personal, professional and institutional origins for the practitioner, and influences the form of frame that is established. Part of this involves the clinician developing an ethico-critical stance with which to approach the treatment context. It requires empathy, relating, hospitality, a dialogical focus, a respect for complexity and difference as well as an awareness of the differentiality of the context.

Many of these elements are very germane to the "borderline" presentation. I would argue, as many have done in the past (e.g., Fromm, 1995) that the borderline designation is often more readily adopted by the clinician than the patient, is often alienating, and can reflect a reductionism in the clinician's perspective in order to project, isolate or externalize the clinician's confusion or anxiety about their orientation to an individual that presents to them. This confusion and anxiety can relate to senses of urgency, being too involved or implicated, losing a sense of boundaries and controls. An ethico-critical stance may look towards sharing, empathy and kinship. It may engage in dialogue with a respect and acceptance of otherness, an attempt at hospitality and adjustment for the sake of the other. The practitioner may need to submit to experiences of helplessness and hopelessness in the face of the other individual, where the capacity to sit with and attempt to relate may be all that can be shared. At other times, the practitioner may have to overcome roles into which they did not expect or accept to be cast, more aware that the differential nature of the relationship and their authority has to be handled more actively and carefully so as to not be destructive.

In this clinical "frame" I have also elaborated in some depth upon elements of therapeutic work that are best understood within the hermeneutic ontological framework I established earlier in philosophical and developmental terms, where there is a focus upon the relational, temporal, somatic and affective elements or contexts of experience.

Firstly, I developed the idea of the therapeutic situation as a *relational* context affording time and space for transformation, transitionality, potentiation and becoming, with reference to the ideas of Winnicott, Bollas, Loewald and Green. In applying this to borderline experience, I sought to understand limit concepts that are related to the borderline concept, those of "trauma" and "dissociation," in relational terms. I pursued a historico-critical analysis of Janet's concept of dissociation, and Freud's concepts of splitting and disavowal, and the manner in which these conceptualisations become unstable if they are not understood within a broader unconscious field of temporal, relational, somatic and affective elements considered from a hermeneutic ontological orientation. Specifically, I sought to describe how intrapsychic and intersubjective elements of trauma and dissociation (and related concepts of splitting and disavowal) may collapse within a broader understanding of a relational field. And I developed this relational understanding by discussing the relational work that occurs around complex forms of dissociative, traumatic or borderline disturbance.

Secondly, I re-articulated the complex philosophical and developmental conceptualisations of desire derived from Deleuze and Guattari's (1972, 1980) thought about desiring (as a process of differentiation, becoming, individuation and machinic heterogenesis) and its relationship to Lacan's notions of desiring in relation to extimacy, *jouissance*, the Real and Lacan's later elaborations of pre-Symbolic desiring (in relation to *lalangue* and the *sinthome*). I explored their different conceptualisations of psychosis as creative or destructive, and sought to re-situate this tension between breakdown and breakthrough, between productive becoming and destructive disintegration both historically dating back to Freudian dichotomies (*Eros* and *Thanatos*, Binding and Unbinding) and Winnicott's distinctions between integration and disintegration. If there is a temporal rhythmicity between these poles that founds a productive movement of becoming, then psychotherapy can be understood in terms of a complex field of performative, dialogical, temporalizing and technical processes of enunciation and articulation. Therapeutic work can involve mediating processes of enunciation and articulation. Borderline experiences, here, can be understood as unmediated, and in this sense I drew upon Kristeva's (1982) conceptualisation of the *abject* and Green's (1986, 2000) conceptualisation of the unbordered and atemporal elements of borderline experience. Psychotherapy in this context becomes a constructive process of mediation, overcoming abject states of shame (and other unmediated, archaic, traumatic remnants), where time and relationship are re-established, along with other borders of experience (self and other, inner and outer, mind and body, and so forth). In Green's (1986, 2000) terms, this overcomes the atemporal and central phobic position of borderline experience. I emphasized the constructive nature of this work lies in the *complicating* of and *bordering* of experience.

And thirdly, I applied the temporal conceptualisations I had developed in the philosophical and developmental parts of this work to describe the *temporalizing* function of clinical work in the borderline field. I described how Green (2000) developed Winnicott's concepts of potential space and play to describe forms of traumatic play (narrative based, performative) that can be part of the transitional work of the psychotherapy. I discussed traumatic elements that appear in traumatic play in narrative and performative elaborations with reference to Laplanche's (1990, 1992) concepts of enigmatic signification and translation, where complex and fragmentary unconscious elements (somatic, affective, mnemic and so forth) re-present, consistent with the notion of therapeutic time as bidirectional. The establishment of space in the differential setting permits traumatic play to occur where traumatic elements (intrusive, impinging and repetitive) can be worked with, becoming temporally contextualized or *timed*.

Concluding this clinical "frame," the main point to make is that a heterogeneity of theoretical concepts and technical approaches can meld with practical wisdom, based in experience which is understood often more at the implicit level, or retained at an unconscious level, rather than a more conceptual or cognitive level. There will always be limits to the insight and experience of the therapist, a sense of their fallibility, prejudice and situated perspective. And there will always be limits to the situation and the context that therapy can occur within. Different theoretical approaches may have widely divergent descriptions of their therapeutic approaches . . . these all may converge to an extent in the individual setting with the obvious influence of the therapist's own experience in the face of the client in front of them and the exigencies and contingencies of the therapeutic situation for them both. A hermeneutic framework reminds us of the contingent, immediate elements of the therapeutic encounter that defy explanation but rely on our implicit understanding. Here, experience and understanding often coexist with but come before knowledge and explanation. What the patient may experience is an active, responsive listener, someone who is able to relate to them, facilitate and contextualize the work, and is able to ultimately remain with the patient—be with the patient—in a way that becomes paradigmatic for the patient in their own development of ways of being *with themselves* as well as being with others. This hermeneutic framework reinforces the ethical and critical position that the therapist adopts where notions of complexity, otherness, limits and differentiality may help to orientate us to working with the unconscious or subconscious as something we cannot theoretically conquer so much as apprehend, respect and be mindful of—but only to an extent.

Conclusion

Where have we arrived at, in this exploration and reinterpretation of the borderline concept? How do we now understand the paradox, that a term once used to designate approaches to theoretical and clinical ambiguities, now objectively designates a collective of uniform individuals? What is there that is problematic or ethically ambiguous when these individuals are seen to be suffering with a definable range of dysregulations, instabilities, impulsivities and impairments, that can be rectified in the clinical encounter with experts who practice technical, researched treatments that work towards the ideals of regulation, stability, cohesion, integration and control? If we expose the borderline concept, or open up the borderline individual, to a broader interface of concerns about the body and affect, about time and relationship, about culture and technology, what new horizons or frontiers are discovered?

In the beginning, I contextualized the "borderline" concept in relation to the history of its usage and application referring to a rich and complex history in psychodynamic, psychoanalytic and psychiatric theory over the past 70 years or so, also giving consideration to the concept's prehistory, extended back to the types of hysterical problems Charcot, Freud, Breuer and Janet treated and wrote about. I argued that the term "hysteria," in its time, was a similarly complex, broad-ranging, far-reaching term; and that it is interesting to contemplate how the borderline concept itself may have supplanted this earlier concept of hysteria where both concepts, perhaps, share analogous forms of culturally laden and historically specific complexity. I observed that the borderline concept now is over-represented in clinical research and practice in comparison to other so-called personality disorders, and it has many more complex affinities than these other personality disorders within debates and controversies in fields as diverse as gender studies, developmental research, forensic science and cultural studies exploring phenomena such as self-harm, sexualisation, sexual abuse and other complex or prolonged forms of trauma.

If the borderline concept occupies an increasingly *central* place in what is a discontinuous and mobile field of ideas and clinical movements in psychoanalysis, psychology, psychodynamic theory and orthodox psychiatry, it is because the concept has become a *limit concept*, aggregating many of the elements that psychological, psychiatric and psychoanalytic systems grapple with or have failed to come to terms with elsewhere. I argued that this dominance and centrality relates to the concept's designated capacity to capture, incorporate or enfold many of the clinical phenomena, or conceptualizations in psychopathological theory that do not fit anywhere else due to limitations or restrictions in these systems. I argued that this relates to many of these systems being dominated by, while at the same time often attempting to overcome, tendencies towards categorical, individualistic, synchronic (nontemporal) and intrapsychic approaches to understanding, favouring these over the dimensional, relational, diachronic (temporal) and interpersonal approaches to understanding.

My project, then, became an undertaking to reinterpret the borderline concept not simply as a psychopathological term but more broadly as a historical concept we are confronted by as clinicians, implicated in responding to and addressing in our activity and work. I referred to "borderline experience" as a form of experience and encounter that the suffering individual and the concerned clincian are both affected by and implicated within. My project would attempt to analyse borderline experience from this perspective, both as it pertains to an individual's subjectivity as well as a clinician's understanding. In fact, I argued that the two coexist and are always already embedded within a whole series of historically derived clinical and cultural practices. As such, borderline "experience" was to be treated as a form of "found object" that is analysed and related to in this work, not theorized or derived in a foundational sense. It is seen as a form of self-experience and clinical experience that occurs within a particular historical and socio-culturally determined context.

In describing my methodology or approach, I used the concepts of *frames*, *framing* and the novel term *frame-work* to introduce the notion that this type of analysis is simultaneously a form of theoretical contemplation outside the clinical field and a mode of intervention within the field, something analogous to the action of psychotherapy outside the field of everyday relations, or the action of philosophical contemplation outside the field of everyday thought and experience. The primary framework I chose to adopt involved a *hermeneutic ontological* orientation based on the work of Martin Heidegger and certain philosophical thinkers after Heidegger who developed and advanced this orientation. My methodology involved advancing a description of this orientation thematically in terms of notions of *relationality*, *temporality*, *embodied affectivity* and *technicity*. I would then attempt to apply this orientation to developmental and clinical fields of approaching and understanding borderline experience.

THE PHILOSOPHICAL FRAME

In the *Philosophical Frame* (Part I), a central theme was the elaboration of a hermeneutic orientation that emerged from the work of Martin Heidegger in the first half of the twentieth century but was then elaborated by some of his followers and subsequent philosophers influenced by him. I was careful to specify, here, that some of the ideas I incorporated and developed in my *hermeneutic ontological* orientation would be derived not only from Heidegger's original project, but also his own later developments of and departures from this project and then also from other thinkers, such as Hans-Georg Gadamer, Paul Ricoeur, Emmanuel Levinas, Jacques Derrida as well as Gilles Deleuze and Felix Guattari, who all either engaged with but departed significantly from Heidegger's work or critically engaged it. I chose this approach of critically analysing and adopting a diverse array of thinkers from a certain tradition of modern European philosophy, in order to describe, delineate and define my own broader *hermeneutic ontological* orientation, which would be seen to emerge from a Heideggerian tradition of philosophizing, but could then be systematized according to four novel themes that I would develop myself, those of *relationality*, *embodied affectivity*, *temporality* and *technicity*. This thematic system would then be employed to analyse the borderline concept and field of borderline experience from a hermeneutic ontological orientation.

In Heidegger's principle early work *Being and Time* (1928), the discipline of hermeneutics was extended beyond the study of interpretation as it is applied to written texts or forms of methodology in the human sciences (philology and historiography, for example). For Heidegger (1928) it became an *ontological* undertaking, now concerned with the interpretation and understanding of Being in general, and the conditions of man's being in the world in particular. The hermeneutic frame of reference, here, involves considering man as intrinsically self-interpreting, and any movement towards the understanding or interpretation of the world or Being in general beginning with the fact that man is always already in the world, moving towards an interpretation and understanding of it from a position of already being there. This means the mode of interpretation is already enfolded within a *frame* or *hermeneutic circle*. The *Philosophical Frame* then detailed some foundational descriptions of Heidegger's (1928) approach to hermeneutic ontology exploring concepts of selfhood, interpersonal relatedness, temporality, moodfulness and language within a broader hermeneutic orientation that would subsequently be related to theories of developmental psychopathology and psychotherapeutic action, in the hope of overcoming some of the individualizing, non-temporal, categorical, intrapsychic approaches to understanding, compensating for these with the dimensional, relational, diachronic, embodied and technical approaches to understanding and experience. The hermeneutic ontological orientation situates thought, meaning and understanding within the existential embeddedness and situatedness of Being in general, encapsulated in Heideggarian concepts such as "worldhood," "care" and "thrownness."

I then critically explored, in some depth, the work of psychiatrist Ludwig Binswanger, who attempted to apply and develop Heidegger's thought to the clinic (Chapter 2, Part I). I attempted to elaborate some of the difficulties and tensions that arise when Heidegger's philosophical approach to hermeneutic ontology is brought into engagement with a clinical realm of understanding. This involved an appreciation and analysis of what Heidegger termed *Ontological Difference*, a difference that marks a divide between *ontic* fields of understanding (concerned with concrete beings, their properties and understanding derived in an empirico-objective sense) and ontology (concerned with *Being* itself, understood in hermeneutic terms). Through an exploration of Binswanger's project, and Heidegger's (1959–1969) responses and broader engagement with psychiatrists and psychoanalysts in his Zollikon Seminar, I concluded that Heidegger seems to have encouraged a notion of ontological difference that does not represent a complete divide, where ontological understanding can potentially influence or permeate a practical activity such as psychiatry or psychotherapy. And this would not be a purely critical influence, seeking to undermine so many of the dominant biologistic, cognitivist or humanistic approaches within psychiatry, all of which interpret human being ontically. Psychiatry and psychotherapy, understood in the broadest of terms, is a practical field concerned with individuals whose Being is *especially* at issue for itself or others—Being that is problematized. When a psychiatrist or psychotherapist is enlisted to assist another individual in orienting himself towards his own Being, the psychiatrist, of necessity, is called upon to operationalize and apply an understanding of health or normativity in selfhood. In this field, Heideggerian authenticity may constitute a goal of treatment or an ethical orientation for the clinician, and hermeneutic ontology may assist in determining the extent but also the limits of understanding in treatment, and the horizon within which ontical concepts operate in practically driven therapeutic activity.

The space, or borderline if you will, between the ontic and the ontological, and the utility of developing hermeneutic ontology as an orientation that can potentially inform clinical approaches, was then taken up further by exploring some of the key philosophical themes that can be extracted from Heidegger's (1928) project that have been taken on, developed and deviated from in subsequent philosophical thinkers who have all, importantly, adopted psychoanalytic or psychiatric clinical concepts to assist in the development of their thought. This makes us aware of how germane the clinical is, or can become, to the Heideggerian project, when issues emerge about the tensions raised by the concept of *Ontological Difference*. Such tensions include the extent to which various elaborations of ontology incorporate elements of existence or experience such as broader, deeper and more complex forms of affectivity, memorality, relationality as well as embodiment and ethical concern than was envisaged by Heidegger himself in his early project. The later Heidegger, who became increasingly focussed upon language and thought as the foci of the understanding of Being, distanced himself further from affinities with humanistic approaches or philosophical anthropology. However, later philosophers influenced by Heidegger engaged with the early Heideggerian project to develop hermeneutic ontology further in this direction, while others explored the progression of Heidegger's thought and analysed the sustainability or complexity of ontological difference. I chose to elaborate upon these issues in terms of four thematic headings where Being and existence are understood in terms of *relationality*, *embodied affectivity*, *temporality* and *technicity* (Chapters 3–6, Part I).

I discussed the notion of originary *relationality* that can be seen to be derived from Heidegger's project insofar as human being is always already situated in a relational context, with concepts such as *Mitwelt*, *Mitsein*, *jemeinigkeit* and *Befindlichkeit* referring to Being that is always already with others, where moodfulness is always seen dialogically in how one interprets oneself both to oneself (as another) and to others (Chapter 3, Part I). This relationality was also seen to be embedded within a limited horizon beyond which otherness or alterity also intervenes and needs to be come to terms with, both in terms of an appreciation and respect for our limits and then in terms of ethical standpoints. I derived from Gadamer's and Ricoeur's thought that forms of the self, subject or individual are constituted by or secondary to relational processes: in particular, dialogue or conversation as well as the dialectic with otherness (the otherness of embodiment, of the other, of death, of conscience and so forth). Nevertheless both thinkers were seen to remain consistent with Heidegger's hermeneutic ontological orientation in articulating these elements of selfhood as historically, linguistically and factually embedded or situated. We also saw that thinkers such as Levinas and Derrida emphasized notions of otherness and differentiality in order to limit or curtail our understanding and avoid metaphysical standpoints that oppress or alter the complexity and finitude of meaning or understanding, and that interpretation is always necessarily ethical in nature.

I then discussed notions of *embodiment* and *affectivity* that can be seen to depart from a neutral and somewhat ill-defined potentiality in Heidegger's ontology (Chapter 4, Part I). I justified the inclusion and incorporation of some of the most rich and productive conceptualisations that have emerged since Heidegger's project, that can nevertheless be seen to be consistent with my broader orientation of *hermeneutic ontology*. Here, I explored *L'Anti-Oedipe* and *Mille Plateaux*, where Deleuze and Guattari (1972, 1980) develop a theory of desire that elevates the social over the familial, where the best model for social desire is seen to be the schizophrenic unconscious. This model, which underpins their approach of schizoanalysis as an overcoming of psychoanalysis, avoids the familial constitution of a unified self by focussing upon a sub-individual realm of body parts, or "libidinal intensities," and their supra-individual interconnections in the social, thus providing a single system of configurations of "desiring-production," a system which can be analysed with the critical aim of, at once, overcoming both the Freudian approach to subjectivity and the Marxist approach to sociality (making schizoanalysis, in a sense, a critical fusion of historical materialism and semiotic psychoanalysis). We saw that the rich conceptualization of desire, in Deleuze and Guattari's (1972, 1980) work, emphasizes those elements of ontology that relate to becoming, potentiality and differentiation, as well as productivity and creativity in the enunciation and differentiation of *desire* as process. Loosely, Deleuze held subjectification and individuation (and familialisation) as secondary processes that emerge from these supra and sub individual processes, within an organic and socio-political field of articulation. The critical, *schizoanalytic* orientation sought to historicize and polemically engage current manifestations of subjectivity, laying the possibility of further application of their orientation to the borderline field of experience in subsequent frames, where modes of oppression, repression or limitation may be operating within systems of *subjectification*.

I then proceeded to develop some of Heidegger's (1928) thinking about *temporality* that began with his hermeneutic ontological orientation, and in particular his concepts of Care, *Geworfenheit* (thrownness), *Entwurfen* (project) and being-towards-death (Chapter 5, Part I). I used this understanding of temporality to explore the problematic issue of unconscious time in Freud's oeuvre, and tensions that arise between Freud's references to the timeless Unconscious and his elaboration of the concept of *Nachträglichkeit*. I explored the analyses of Green and Derrida who have critically engaged Freud's work and thinking of time, leading to the development of radical temporal concepts such as *re-presentation*, bidirectional time, heterochronicity and, finally, *différance*, all of which could be seen to permit a fuller understanding of temporal Being in terms of its historicity, facticity and potentiality. I argued that these temporal concepts remain consistent with but extend the Heideggerian orientation to temporality in forms of Care, *Geworfenheit* (thrownness), *Entwurfen* (project) and being-towards-death.

I argued that these temporal concepts potentially allow further consideration of developmental and clinical issues in any individual's temporal trajectory. Establishing this temporal ontological theme, then, could permit further analysis of the intrinsically temporal nature of Being in development, and the fundamentally temporal work of psychotherapy.

And finally, I described *technicity* further from a Heideggerian point of view in how we articulate ourselves and come to understand ourselves through our technological engagement, such that technology and science are embedded within our field of existence as becoming (Chapter 6, Part I). Here, technology and technicity, in the theoretical conceptualizations of Bernard Stiegler, can be seen to constitute self-understanding, epistemology and becoming, where interiorisation and exteriorisation co-exist as worldhood within an individual and cultural lifeworld that is technically derived and engaged. Examples here may be the earliest forms of technologies such as tools and mirrors (which in turn co-exist with us existing and conceptualizing ourselves as technical, reflective beings), techniques and practices that facilitate symbolic or representational art (from the most primitive forms), language itself (in its spoken and written forms) not to mention how these may interact in such sophisticated modern technologies as film and digital media and other forms of representation. All of these technical processes co-exist with self-representational interpretive processes. The artefactual technological world is an ineliminable part of temporality, not only as dead history but a living form of memory, as well as an instrumental aspect of our becoming. *Individuation*, for Stiegler, is a psychic, collective and technical *process*, the result of which is the hypothetical individual. This is the opposite of the humanistic doctrine and aligns with but considerably extends the later Heidegger's concerns about technology: a suspicion around technology reflects a suspicion of the kind of individual that is produced. As such, Stiegler (1994) argues that it can be more useful to understand how technologies form a part of human becoming situated within existence, rather than assisting in the establishment of objective knowledge or understanding situated outside of existence (which is aporetic). From these perspectives we have to remind ourselves of the inherent limits of *thinking technologically* and the role that technological thinking can play in affecting or limiting *individuation*. This relates to the kinds of individuals that are constituted, normatively and pathologically, within a historico-cultural technological context. As such, how we conceptualize and constitute ourselves as healthy or sick individuals, is inextricably linked to our technicity and technological understanding. As such, problems with the "borderline" cocnet could be better understood through a critical exploration and analysis of technical processes of individuation in our contemporary culture, both specifically in clinical practice contexts and also more broadly in a range of other social contexts.

In summary, then, what I established, in the *Philosophical Frame* were the foundations of a hermeneutic ontological orientation which departs from Heidegger's foundational work *Being and Time* (1928) but loosely encapsulates philosophical advances made both subsequently by Heidegger's writings after his *Kehre*, as well as by some subsequent philosophers who I have labelled post-Heideggerian, who have variably taken up issues developed in Heidegger's thought, and developed them in directions that I have seen to be useful for the developmental and clinical analyses I planned to undertake. The critical standpoint of this hermeneutic ontological orientation seeks to undermine, overcome or contextualize approaches to thinking that assert numerous traditional errors or aporias that were seen to be encompassed by "traditional metaphysics": the representational model of consciousness, Cartesian dualism, as well as the favouring of modes of objective presence (objectivism, reductionism, essentialism, scientism, etc.) when approaching the understanding of existence and the world. I developed a range of concepts related to the themes of relationality, embodied affectivity, temporality and technicity that I then moved to employ and develop further in the *Developmental* and *Clinical Frames* of my study where I would explore the problematics that arise concerning the borderline concept and borderline experience.

THE DEVELOPMENTAL FRAME

All models of psychoanalysis and developmental psychopathology have what could be termed origin myths or metaphors that attempt to encapsulate what are seen to be the most crucial formative events, dynamics or elements of experience that form the basis of development of the self, ego or subject. In advancing my hermeneutic ontological orientation in the *Developmental Frame*, I attempted to describe developmental origins and limits that are fundamentally and inextricably relational, temporal, embodied, affective and seen within a historical and technological horizon of understanding. The structure of this frame involved the description of originary forms of relationality, embodied affectivity and temporality that were seen to be radically different to the typical models of early development that are invoked by prominent theories of borderline personality disorder. In the chapter on technology and technicity, I would go on to describe these prominent theories in terms of a series of "technological metaphors" which I would contextualise in historical and cultural terms along the way to critically appraising them in contrast to the forms of developmental origins I had elucidated within my hermeneutic ontological orientation.

Firstly, I described originary forms of relationality that are *transitional, transformational* and *differential*, referring to the work of Winnicott, Bollas and Loewald, respectively (Chapter 7, Part II). I discussed Winnicott, Bollas and Loewald in order to explore notions of originary, differential relationships that involve a dynamic progression from an infantile state of primary narcissism, a progression which explores the founding of consciousness or ego in terms that are by definition relational and overcome any conceptual reference to causal objective presence (avoiding models that adultomorphize infantile subjectivity, or portray it as individualistic, or adopt descriptions that rely on modes of objective presence such as representational theories of consciousness or neurobiological models that correlate to developing neurocognitive capacities). Winnicott's explication of transitional phenomena, for example, carries through to adult life and exemplifies creative, agentic existence where engagement in the world and relations with others involves the reciprocity and simultaneity of the subject's work on the object and the object's work on the subject, what Winnicott called subjective objecthood. Bollas's notion of the transformational object describes the non-representational, immanent presence of the earliest relational systems which are maintained in one's relation to oneself and others, and are the source of complex, relationally based mood states and experiences throughout life. And Loewald describes the infantile origins of individuation (as agency, drive, etc.) as being immersed in differential relationships with the mother, language and the world all of which propel or drive development as a process of differentiation and internalization.

All of these relational terms (*transitionality*, *transformationality* and *differentiality*), imply that individuation, the sense of an agentic self, and a differentiated sense of self and other, inner and outer, mind and body and so forth, are products of relational processes which endure throughout life. If subjectivity is always first relationally derived, there wil always remain elements of otherness (alterity), the implicit and immanent, the ineffable or the unrepresentable, that are more primary and originary and operate behind, within or outside the individual's subjectivity. This extends the sense of ourselves as situated and thrown, always continuing to develop, form, evolve and *become*, but with factical, contingent and finite developmental origins that are relationally based, and a differential horizon and a sense of alterity both within ourselves and without. These relational elements, in a way, represent margins or "borderlines" of subjectivity. As such, all of these elements of originary relationality would come to be seen as beneficial concepts for understanding relational issues in the clinic of the borderline patient, as it would be explored in the *Clinical Frame*.

Secondly, I explored the developmental origins of embodied affectivity by developing some of Lacan's developmental conceptualizations of desire before I then turned to contrast and juxtapose these with Deleuze and Guattari's ontology of desire (Chapter 8, Part II). In the broadest and loosest sense, Lacan sought to decentre subjectivity throughout his works by situating processes of individuation or subjectification "outside": developmentally the reflective process occurs when the infant identifies itself as whole firstly through the reflection outside of itself in a mirror, the so-called "mirror phase" of imaginary identification, the *Imaginary Order*, in which the ego and the imaginary relationship with one's body is constituted. The infant or child is also subject to the dialogical process that occurs when the child is initiated as a speaking subject and is dependent upon language, in the *Symbolic Order*, where the "I" of speech is situated. As such, individuation or subjectification is seen as decentred, a form of lack or alienation in which the ego, subject or self is produced without, or from the exterior reference of the image and the word. This alienation is seen as originary, insofar as there is no pure or non-alienated origin prior to this. The third or other Order or register, *the Real*, may represent this origin but only as the unknowable pre-Symbolic, pre-Imaginary reality, which can drive need, anxiety, dread, but remain ineffable or non-representable, only understood in terms of any experiential residue or secondary effect.

In my analysis, I demonstrated how Lacan described embodied affectivity, in the concepts of *desire* and *jouissance* with reference to the three Orders or Registers. What was of especial interest, there, was Lacan's later developmental formulation of *desire*, as the primary and originary form of embodied affectivity, and how this linked to his later formulation of psychosis. I emphasized the possibility that Lacan's later ideas around psychosis could potentially be related to the borderline concept, although Lacan and Lacanians mostly reject the latter concept. What was significant to note, here, is that Lacan remains committed to a deficit model of psychosis, in fundamental distinction to Deleuze and Guattari's (1972, 1980) formulations of schizophrenia as a form of creative potentiality. Also, Lacan's later ideas about psychotic desire become more originary and radical, involving developments of his theories of the Real, *jouissance*, the Thing and extimacy into pre-Symbolic concepts of meaning such as *lalangue* and the *sinthome*.

I contrasted and explored how the ideas of Lacan and Deleuze and Guattari around desire and psychosis impact upon an ethics of the clinic. Desire itself can be interpreted as a sublation of the Freudian death drive, culminating in a limit or antiproductive moment, for both Lacan (the *jouissance* of the Real *Thing*) as well as Deleuze and Guattari (*schizophrenia, chaos*). Multiplicitous desiring may take different forms for the subject: for Lacan, it becomes the variable structures of the *sinthome*, a form of binding *suppléance* of a lack; and for Deleuze and Guattari it is the expression of *machinic assemblages* of becoming. Deleuze and Guattari's (1972, 1980) conceptualization is based upon perverse, fragmentary machinic assemblages of affects, a *becoming* the Lacanian may arguably feel is harking nostalgically back to a pre-structural, psychotic unconscious as illusory origin. If becoming is a melding of form and content for Deleuze and Guattari, then psychosis remains an exemplary and self-consistent form of becoming. Lacan's conceptualizations are different at this level: they involve a fallibilization of man, the structuring or organization of *jouissance*, by the signifier or the *sinthome*, which is necessary for desire to be accessed and articulated but at the same time defines man to be necessarily alienated from the Real, even if it is held by man to be the ultimately desirable origin, however illusory or unobtainable. For Deleuze and Guattari, this formulation is just another neurotic repression of the most self-consistent form of becoming. Lacan's orientation was always to hold that this is the most that desiring can be, the goal being to at least have access to this limit as a creative, volitional, directive pursuit, and not a subjection, a victimization, or something leading to an unravelling. I saw that a resolution to this conflict would involve some form of dialectic between breakdown and breakthrough, which may, in turn, hark back to the forms of dialectical relations Freud (1920, 1923) refers to when he describes the movements between binding and unbinding, *Eros* and *Thanatos*, or Winnicott (1971) conceptualizes when he described the movements between integration and disintegration, these ideas subsequently planned to be taken up in the discussion of temporality that followed as well as in the discussion of borderline forms of somatic and affective "instability" in the *Clinical Frame*.

Thirdly, I described originary forms of temporality by extending the concepts of *Nachträglichkeit*, heterochronicity and bidirectional time by thinking about the developmental origins of time (Chapter 9, Part II). I explored notions of originary temporality further, where the conceptualizations of Jean Laplanche (otherness, repression-translation and the enigmatic signifier) and Donald Winnicott (unintegration and disintegration) introduce fundamentally *temporal* notions of developmental origins. These notions were seen to be in a sense originary or foundational limits that pervade infantile, child and adult experience (in forms of play, creativity and potentiation in a rich array of experiences), and were thus seen to be relevant to the *Clinical Frame*, where a developmental orientation would be maintained. I also sought to expand upon this in the developmental context more fully: origins of general or universal seduction (Laplanche) and primary narcissism/dependence (Winnicott) permit the action of the other to occur over time with ineffable temporal rhythms (presence/absence, frustration/relief, unconscious implantation and impingement) where ego or self-integration processes are developed that are temporal in nature in keeping with our understanding of *Nachträglichkeit* and bidirectional time—processes of translation-repression and movements between integration and disintegration. We saw that drives, as a form of project, are inextricably linked to this developmental context of the differential horizon of relationality, alterity and *Nachträglichkeit*. I also sought to describe these as the temporal foundations of an understanding of trauma, seen within a universal phenomenon of seduction as the imposition of the other upon the infant or small child within the context of differential relating, which can in some way become excessive in the process of intromission of unassimilable, unmetabolisable experiences which will reside as unintegrated, psychosis-inducing fragments; as well as the notion of an excessive or cumulative experience of impingements (both as environmental failures and excessively intrusive input from the care giver) that lead to self-pathologies in terms of disintegration and defensive false self-structures. These ideas would be taken up and expanded upon in the *Clinical Frame* in our understanding of developmental trauma and borderline experience in clinical work.

And finally, in my analysis of technicity and technology in this part of the work, I sought to situate the more objectivist and scientifically founded models of developmental psychopathology and borderline personality as technologically limited and historically situated, and critically engaged with and potentially better framed by my hermeneutic ontological orientation (Chapter 10, Part II). This discussion made reference to developmental theories derived from infant and attachment research (Daniel Stern, 1985; Schore, 1994, 2003; Liotti, 1992, 1995; Fonagy et al., 2002, for example), traumatology (van der Kolk, 1987; van der Hart et al., 1993, 2006) and psychoanalytic psychotherapy (Kernberg, 1975). I referred to all of these models as adopting and utilizing forms of *technological metaphors* (Attachment, Trauma and Structural metaphors) in an uncritical way. In my discussion, I referred tosome biases in these models which are, no doubt, self-serving biases which favour certain kinds of therapeutic intervention: models of borderline pathology which focus on forms of early development (pre-oedipal, mother–infant, attachment based) often favour forms of dyadic therapy which see the therapy metaphorically as a form of reparation of neurodevelopmental deficit; models of borderline pathology which focus on forms of abuse and trauma often favour models psychotherapy which rely on traumatic integration and catharsis (e.g., Bessel van der Kolk, Ellert Nijenhuis, Onno van der Hart); models of structural personality deficit which focus on pragmatic psychotherapies that rely on the acquisition of ego or self-functions (Peter Fonagy and Anthony Bateman's mentalization based psychotherapy, Otto Kernberg, John Clarkin and Frank Yeomans's transference-focused psychotherapy; and Marsha Linehan's dialectical behaviour therapy). Ultimately, I attempt to contextualize or situate these approaches within a broader technological and socio-cultural context from which "borderline experience" has emerged, a context that the clinician is also embedded within and must come to terms with to avoid clinical biases and ethical risks.

THE CLINICAL FRAME

In the third and final part of the work, the *Clinical Frame*, I developed the hermeneutic ontological orientation already established in the *Philosophical* and *Developmental Frames*, using it to describe a therapeutic stance that can be adopted in the treatment of an array of problems or disturbances that fall under what I have described as the field of borderline experience. I described the borderline concept as a form of limit concept where many paradoxical ideas and issues coalesce in the clinical fields of psychiatry, psychotherapy and psychoanalysis: for example, relational phenomena or experiences described in terms of "projective identification"; temporal phenomena encapsulated by terms such as *Nachträglichkeit* as it is manifest in deferred action and recovered memory that is experienced in the context of histories of "trauma" and "abuse"; complex disturbances of embodiment and identity encapsulated in concepts such as somatoform dissociation, stimulus entrapment and multiple personalities; and finally, disturbances of subjective agency and control, identified in concepts such as conversion and disavowal. Many other complex phenomena also aggregate here: for example, the behaviour of self mutilation that can enact or symbolize the boundaries between body and affect, control and dyscontrol, privacy and communication, dissociation and grounding; or, the phenomenology of overwhelming affective states, which form dynamic clusters such as the affects of shame, anger and the dynamics of internal discipline and external hostility. The approach, in the *Clinical Frame*, was to demonstrate how the hermeneutic ontological orientation, and ideas advanced in the preceding two frames within this framework, could help to elucidate a better understanding of these phenomena in terms of relationality, embodied affectivity, temporality and technicity.

A number of central, classical clinical issues were explored in this approach. I paid particular attention to issues around the conceptualization of dissociation, splitting and disavowal, as these have arisen from the work of Janet and Freud, and how tensions here relate to current clinical approaches to borderline experience that adopt models of dissociation (the traumatology movement with thinkers such as Bessel van der Kolk, Onno van der Hart, Ellert Nijenhjuis and Judith Herman, relational thinkers such as Philip Bromberg, and attachment based-theorists such as Giovanni Liotti). I also reviewed terms such as *abuse* and *trauma* in the context of earlier and historical usage, current research in traumatology, and a more complex analysis of how the therapist and patient work together "in time." And finally, I also attempted to describe and explore the ethical and interpretive agency of the therapist from a hermeneutic perspective evoking concepts of fallibilism, prejudice, embeddedness, and the sensibility to two-person dynamics, as well as ideas about dialogue, conversation, narrative, differentiality and otherness described in the earlier frames.

Most broadly, it was shown that the hermeneutic perspective can simultaneously permeate one's clinical approach to psychotherapy, one's orientation to theoretical thought within psychotherapy and developmental psychopathology, and offer a broader, personal interpretive orientation towards the situation of psychotherapy for the psychotherapist. Part of what I describe is an attitude of openness and respect for complexity founded in the hermeneutic outlook already established. Much of this relates to an awareness of context, not just in terms of the situation of referral and the origins of the treatment for the individual, but also the situation of the practitioner and the treatment that the practitioner offers. This situatedness is complex for both parties, in terms of personal, familial, cultural and historical origins for the patients, and personal, professional and institutional origins for the practitioner, and influences the form of frame that is established. Part of this involves the clinician developing an ethico-critical stance with which to approach the treatment context. It requires empathy, relating, hospitality, a dialogical focus, a respect for complexity and difference as well as an awareness of the differentiality of the context.

Many of these elements are very germane to the "borderline" presentation. I argue that the borderline designation is often more readily adopted by the clinician than the patient, is often alienating, and can reflect a reductionism in the clinician's perspective in order to project, isolate or externalize the clinician's confusion or anxiety about their orientation to an individual that presents to them. This confusion and anxiety can relate to senses of urgency, being too involved or implicated, losing a sense of boundaries and controls. An ethico-critical stance may look towards sharing, empathy and kinship. It may engage in dialogue with a respect and acceptance of otherness, an attempt at hospitality and adjustment for the sake of the other. The practitioner may need to submit to experiences of helplessness and hopelessness in the face of the other individual, where the capacity to sit with and attempt to relate may be all that can be shared. At other times, the practitioner may have to overcome roles into which they did not expect or accept to be cast, more aware that the differential nature of the relationship and their authority has to be handled more actively and carefully so as to not be destructive. This can also be understood in terms of a broader ethico-critical stance and awareness of context, where there are a range of clinical, cultural and technical factors that are relevant to the presentation of the "borderline individual." This stance must be aware of the underlying social construction and historical context of the borderline field, in terms of its "technological" constitution and culture-boundedness. From this standpoint I went on to focus primarily upon specific clinical issues developing these under the existing headings already adopted in the previous frames: the relational themes, temporal themes, themes of embodiment and affectivity, and, finally, technical themes.

Firstly, I developed the idea of the therapeutic situation as a *relational* context affording time and space for transformation, transitionality, potentiation and becoming, with reference to the ideas of Winnicott, Bollas, Loewald and Green (Chapter 11, Part III). In applying this to borderline experience, I sought to understand in relational terms, limit concepts that are related to the borderline concept, and specifically those of "trauma" and "dissociation". I undertook a historico-critical analysis of Janet's concept of *dissociation*, and Freud's concepts of *splitting* and *disavowal*, and the manner in which these conceptualisations become unstable if they are not understood within a broader unconscious relational field seen from a hermeneutic ontological orientation. Specifically, I sought to describe how intrapsychic and intersubjective elements of trauma and dissociation (and related concepts of splitting and disavowal) may be understood and worked with relationally. I developed this relational understanding by discussing the work that occurs around complex forms of "dissociative," "traumatic" or "borderline" disturbance. I drew theoretical comparisons with the manner in which relational work is conceptualized by the Mentalization group and Meares's Conversational model, attempting to highlight the importance of an horizon of complexity, alterity and differentiality that remains in the relational context, overcoming aspirations to achievements of individual self-transparency, or total relational mutuality. I also spoke favourably about Donnel Stern's conceptualization of unformulated experience, and the affinities his relational model may have with mine.

Secondly (Chapter 12, Part III), I re-articulated the complex philosophical and developmental conceptualisations of desire derived from Deleuze and Guattari's (1972, 1980) thought about desiring as a process of differentiation, becoming, individuation and machinic heterogenesis and its relationship to Lacan's notions of desiring in relation to extimacy, *jouissance*, the Real, and Lacan's later elaborations of pre-Symbolic desiring (in relation to *lalangue* and the *sinthome*). I explored their different conceptualisations of psychosis as creative or destructive, and sought to re-situate this tension between breakdown and breakthrough, between productive becoming and destructive disintegration both historically dating back to Freudian dichotomies (*Eros* and *Thanatos*, Binding and Unbinding) and Winnicott's distinctions between integration and disintegration. If there is a temporal rhythmicity between these poles that founds a productive movement of becoming, then psychotherapy can be understood in terms of a complex field of performative, dialogical, temporalizing and technical processes of enunciation and articulation. Therapeutic work can involve mediating processes of enunciation and articulation. Borderline experiences, here, can be understood as unmediated, and in this sense I drew upon Kristeva's (1982) conceptualisation of the *abject* and Green's (1986, 2000) conceptualisation of the unbordered and atemporal elements of borderline experience. Psychotherapy in this context becomes a constructive process of mediation, overcoming abject states of shame (and other unmediated, archaic, traumatic remnants), where time and relationship are re-established, along with other borders of experience (self and other, inner and outer, mind and body, and so forth). In Green's (1986, 2000) terms, this overcomes the atemporal and central phobic position of borderline experience. I emphasized the constructive nature of this work lies in the *complicating* of and *bordering* of experience.

And thirdly, I applied the temporal conceptualisations I had developed in the philosophical and developmental parts of the work to describe the *temporalizing* function of clinical work in the borderline field (Chapter 13, Part III). I described how Green (2000) developed Winnicott's concepts of potential space and play to describe forms of traumatic play (narrative based, performative) that can be part of the transitional work of the psychotherapy. I discussed traumatic elements that appear in traumatic play in narrative and performative elaborations with reference to Laplanche's (1990, 1992) concepts of enigmatic signification and translation, where complex and fragmentary unconscious elements (somatic, affective, mnemic and so forth) re-present, consistent with the notion of therapeutic time as bidirectional. The establishment of space in the differential setting permits traumatic play to occur where traumatic elements (intrusive, impinging and repetitive) can be worked with, becoming temporally contextualized or *timed*. I attempted to make links, here, to thinkers of the Intersubjective tradition, such as the work of Stolorow (2011a and b, 2009) who describes the temporalizing function of establishing kinship-in-finitiude, and Orange (2011) who describes the temporalizing function of dialogue and metaphor in analytic work.

The overall achievement of the *Clinical Frame*, then, was to elaborate how an interpretive process can be adopted clinically where the patient and therapist dwell together more openly and attempt to describe and explore the alterity and difference in what is experienced without a reliance upon the inference of scientific causal mechanisms, definitive explanation or recourse to forms of objective presence. This process uses doubling or empathy but in a manner in which one could consider the work occurring in a transitional or transformational space (after Winnicott and Bollas) with a differential relational dynamic (after Loewald) but is also dialogical (after Intersubjective and Relational theorists such as Aron, Stolorow, Orange, Atwood, Frie, Mitchell, Bromberg and Donnel Stern). It entails an open understanding of the operation of time, its heterochronicity and bidirectional nature and its focus on project and potentiation (after Green and Laplanche). It also entails an awareness of embodied affectivity and desire founded in processes of alterity, difference and lack (after Lacan and Kristeva). The central aim was to define a clinical outlook to borderline experience that emerges out of, and encapsulates, as much as it can of a horizon of understanding that is mindful of the complexity of our experience in terms of its relatedness, temporality, embodiment, affectivity, technicity, and, ultimately, its otherness to itself. This led to the development of some novel conceptualisations of work in the borderline field in terms of *relating, desiring, temporalizing, complicating* and *bordering*. And the broader novel conceptualisation that has structured this work, and characterized its approach, I have referred to as *frame-work*.

This, then, was the culmination of an approach which began with the elaboration of an interpretative framework, referred to as a *hermeneutic ontological orientation*, that was used to explore and elucidate the "borderline concept," which I argued had become a problematic limit concept. Throughout this approach I have historicised and critically appraised the borderline concept, and other implicated concepts (such as "abuse," "trauma," "personality disorder" and so forth), and attempted to contextualise them within a more open and complex field of understanding that favours approaches to interpretation that focus upon the fundamentally relational, temporal, embodied, affective and technical aspects of our existence. I used the concept of *frames*, *framing* and *frame-work* to introduce the notion that this type of analysis is simultaneously a form of theoretical contemplation outside the clinical field and a mode of intervention within the field, something analogous to the action of psychotherapy outside the field of everyday relations, or the action of philosophical contemplation outside the field of everyday thought and experience. And I developed an open frame-work in terms of four themes, *relationality*, *temporality*, *embodied affectivity* and *technicity*, through which to advance the understanding of developmental and clinical issues that are implicated in the field of borderline experience. It is hoped that the outcome of this approach has not been another closed, reduced or objective explanatory concept or system of concepts, so much as an open, interpretative framework that has been established in philosophical terms, then elaborated in developmental and clinical terms, according to those hermeneutic ontological themes.

FINAL COMMENTS

In reviewing the outcomes of this study, and making some concluding comments about future directions this kind of work might take, I would emphasize some of the challenges and limitations of adopting the kind of methodology used here. In pursuing a multidisciplinary approach where complex and sophisticated systems of thought in one field, such as philosophy, are interrelated and then applied to a related field such as psychoanalytic theory, there is a risk of an unwieldy eclecticism, a confusion of tongues, or a sterile and inauthentic hybridization. In this study, I have attempted to avoid these problems by contextualizing the works and thinkers historically, highlighting the links that existed both in terms of the training of the thinkers and the affiliations that the philosophers and psychoanalysts acknowledged themselves, as well as referring to any precedents that already exist in the literature regarding multidisciplinary or cross-disciplinary approaches such as mine. I noted at the beginning of the work that Heidegger (1959–1969) himself was both sceptical of attempts to apply his work to related disciplines or clinical fields, but also, contradictorily, engaged in such attempts in his *Zollikoner Seminare*. I then followed a path of thought, which I defined as a *hermeneutic ontological* orientation, in which a range of post-Heideggerian philosophers advanced Heidegger's thought and engaged with psychoanalytic theory. This enabled me to establish a range of ideas and concepts that could be systematized in terms of four themes, those of *relationality, embodied affectivity, temporality* and *technicity*. I then applied and elaborated upon this hermeneutic ontological orientation in the developmental and clinical domains with a focus on understanding borderline experience.

In following this kind of approach, I have also attempted to find the balance between exegesis and explanation of the theoretician's original thought, and adaptation and application of it to a new context, consistent with Nietzsche's exhortation that opened the *Philosophical Frame*. This requires a sensitive balancing of a sensibility to context in the history of ideas, with an ambition for innovation and application to problematics in new fields. I have also attempted to meld this kind of adaptation and application with my own creative development of concepts and ideas in each of the *Philosophical, Developmental* and *Clinical Frames*. I engaged in this approach in a spirit of exchange, creativity and dialogue, where the type of open interpretative framework I have established, and the ideas and relationships I have mapped out, can continue to be pursued and elaborated.

In philosophical and psychoanalytic theory alike, much is made of the complexity and diversity of models, schools and approaches that exist, and there are concerns about the "babelization" of theory. An alternative ideal to homogenization, universalisation, and the pursuit of absolute objectivity is a respect for and appreciation of diversity, difference, multiplicity, complexity and alterity. Here dialogue, hospitality, respect of the other's authority, creative dialogue and productive exchange can all be favoured and advanced. I have attempted to emphasize that these processes can form the basis of an ethical stance in theorizing and clinical work alike. I have also attempted to emphasize that historical, cultural and technological awareness can form the basis of a critical stance in both theoretical and clinical work.

By adopting a multidisciplinary or cross disciplinary approach there is the possibility of opening channels of exchange and dialogue, fertile seams that can lead to new thought and approaches, with the ethical and critical underpinnings I have described. This can also overcome problems of school-based insularity, dogmatism and stagnation. Psychotherapy, psychoanalysis and psychiatry are clinical fields that are so complex in terms of their historical, cultural and technological embeddedness, as well as their affinities with numerous other fields including the basic and human sciences (developmental neuroscience, attachment research, linguistics and so forth) and other disciplines (anthropology, sociology, history and, yes, philosophy). There is great scope for further developments and applications where a hermeneutic ontological orientation may help to frame or contextualize these exchanges between and advances in these fields. Also, the everyday work of the psychotherapist or psychoanalyst requires the maintenance of a range of relationships not only with clients and with oneself in one's professional identity, but also at other levels both more personally and privately, and also in more theoretical, scientific or technical levels. And again, a hermeneutic ontological orientation may help to frame or contextualize these relationships.

In terms of more specific directions that this kind of work may take in the future, there are a number of directions, or "lines of flight," that could be pursued. This work could be considered to offer a broad structure, and broad lines of association, with room for further application and elaboration.

Firstly, there is further room to develop and explore the affinities this application of hermeneutic ontology has with thinkers of the Intersubjective School such as Stolorow, Orange, Frie, Aron and Atwood. I have explored, to a limited extent, some of their applications of Heideggerian philosophy that are akin to mine, but there is much room for a fuller exploration and engagement with their conceptualisations of relationality, relatedness, therapeutic work in intersubjective terms, as well as their use of phenomenological philosophy (emerging from Husserl and Heidegger) and the philosophy of contemporaries of Heidegger such as Merleau-Ponty, Buber and subsequent philosophers (Gadamer and Levinas in particular). Their conceptualisation of "life worlds," "experiential worlds" and "worlds of experience" (e.g., Orange, 2001; Stolorow et al., 2001; and Stolorow et al., 2002) could be explored for the conceptual and historical affinities these have with concepts such as "world designs" that Binswanger developed. Frie's (e.g., 1997) sophisticated exploration and revival of Binswanger's project could be engaged with to this degree. Stolorow's (e.g., 2007, 2011, et al., 2002) rendition and application of Heideggerian thought could also be engaged with, given the broad extensions and applications I have mapped out in this project. And Orange's (e.g., 2010, 2011, et al., 1997) engagement with and development of the thought of a range of hermeneutic philosophers could also be further engaged with in its affinities with and differences from the type of hermeneutic ontological approach I have begun to articulate. In particular, certain points of difference could be explored that relate to themes of antihumanism, nihilism, destruction/deconstruction and critical history that form part of a *Nietzschean* legacy that could be seen to not only influence (implicitly or explicitly) Freud's and Heidegger's projects, but also many of the other thinkers explored in this project including Foucault, Derrida, Deleuze and Guattari and Stiegler, all of whom could potentially be brought into fuller productive dialogue with thinkers of the Intersubjective School.

Secondly, there is also further room to engage with other schools of psychotherapy and psychoanalysis and other theorists that have only been mentioned in passing in this work, due to limitations of space and time. This would include Relational theorists such as Bromberg and Donnel Stern, and the Conversational theorist Meares, who all develop conceptualisations that have affinities with my hermeneutic ontological orientation, and apply their ideas to the field of borderline experience. It would also include the work of exponents of the Mentalization school who have advanced theoretical and clinical ideas around mentalization beyond the original works that described it a decade ago (for example, Jurist, 2010 and Jurist et al., 2008). And it would include orthodox and arguably more insular schools of theory, such as contemporary Lacanian (Miller, Laurent) and *Daseinsanalytic* (Boss, Condrau) schools, which could potentially benefit from dialogue and engagement with other contemporary psychoanalytic theories and approaches from other disciplines.[1]

Finally, many of the philosophical and psychoanalytic theorists I have engaged with in this work have been demanding to engage within a broader project of my own. The philosophers I have described who have developed and departed from Heidegger's thought such as Derrida, Levinas, Ricoeur, Gadamer and Stiegler, all fall within a European tradition of philosophizing that has a historical sensibility (the history of philosophy and the history of ideas), where the innovation and creativity of the master thinker or *auteur* critically meets the tradition of thought head on, seeking to establish an authority to occupy prominence at the forefront of change. This is in a manner akin to the range of psychoanalytic thinkers I have engaged, such as Green, Kristeva, Laplanche and Deleuze and Guattari, who were of French origins, and who in some sense all sought to articulate their positions as post-Freudian or post-Lacanian. All of these thinkers look at their predecessors, the previous generation of thinkers, with an attitude of critical appraisal and revisionism. They engage with and look to other fields and disciplines to invigorate their approach. In adopting this style of work, there are multitudes of directions that can be taken in further revising and amending my adaptation of the work of Heidegger and these post-Heideggerian philosophers as well as engaging further with these psychoanalytic theorists.

As such, some of the engagement in this work is introductory or schematic and can be developed further. Examples of this would include a more systematic and inclusive engagement with Andre Green's work, cultivating an understanding of its relationship with Winnicott's work. Green's (1986, 2002, 2008) attempts to reinstate or revitalize drive theory could be critically engaged, particularly in relation to other schools such as the Intersubjective school whose thought has a complex engagement of its own with drive theory (e.g., Stolorow, 2002). Also, the work of analyst and Derridean scholar, Alan Bass, could be engaged with in terms of its more refined development of a specific line of thought that crosses Nietzsche, Heidegger and Derrida, to engage Freudian theory, and, in particular, Freudian notions of interpretation and resistance, and confront these with philosophical notions of difference and destruction/deconstruction. My broader and more schematic *frame-work* of hermeneutic ontology could benefit from this refinement, but conversely Bass's system of ideas could potentially engage with the broader field of thinkers and clinical issues I explore. And finally, more comparisons could be made with the work of clinician and theorist Louis Sass (1989, 1992, 1994), who has engaged the thought of a number of the philosophers explored in this work (especially Heidegger, Gadamer, Derrida and Ricoeur) to examine and explore schizophrenic experience in a manner that is arguably related to the approaches adopted in this work.

In all of this, I would endorse the idea of maintaining the openness, complexity and differentiality of the field of thought in this domain. As such, in its broadest terms, this project has been an attempt to critically engage with the borderline concept and field of experience with this idea in mind. But I have also attempted to develop an orientation, my *hermeneutic ontological* orientation, where constructive interpretative elements are developed. The novelty of this approach is the development of such a systematic orientation, as well as a philosophical engagement with and analysis of a number of independent psychoanalytic theorists leading to a broader conceptual, developmental and clinical approach to the borderline field.

Behind this field of thought and relationships, what remains is the unthought, the alteritous, the liminal, which gets related to and thought about and in the process changed, homogenized, constructed. We have to acknowledge a background of archaic, brutal, chaotic movements and forces that remain inarticulable. There is a borderline, here, that is unstable, shifting, in dialectical tension between organization and disorganization, creativity and destructivity, breakdown and breakthrough. If we have to engage at this borderline, we need to maintain a productive tension, and an ethical and critical sobriety to avoid the extremities on each side of the border: either engaging in excessively closed, reductionistic or restrictive thought or, alternatively, being swept up in boundless, unmediated or brutal activity.

Notes

INTRODUCTION

1. Sass (1982) made related arguments in a *New York Times Magazine* article as early as 1982.

2. With this work, and certain other earlier philosophical and psychoanalytic works of historical significance, I will refer to the original date of publication rather than the date of the more updated or translated edition. This is in order to preserve a sense of chronological history when referring to those works.

CHAPTER 1

1. Page references are to the original 1928 German edition of *Being and Time* as these are given in the margins of all translated versions.

CHAPTER 2

1. Indeed part of the later Binswanger's turning away from Heidegger arguably relates to criticisms Heidegger, and a student of Binswanger, Medard Boss, made when Heidegger and Boss collaborated in the Zollikon Seminars. Later, this led to Boss and a colleague, Condrau, further developing *Daseinsanalysis* into a psychotherapeutic school quite separate from the original work Binswanger undertook. This form of psychotherapy, which still exists today in a small but diverse international federation of practitioners, will be discussed in the final clinical part of this work.

2 In this way, the ontical does have a kind of *ontological* viewpoint. Here, Being is understood in terms of a natural world of beings, or entities—individual human beings in their natural, objective environment, the domain of empirical scientific understanding.

3. And it was written at a time when the early Foucault identified with an existential-phenomenologial approach. Indeed, he applied such an approach to the practical field of historiography... hence his interest in Binswanger. It would be interesting to explore the reasons why Foucault abandoned this form of approach in favour of his consequent *structural, archaeological* and *genealogical* approaches.

4. Although the delineation between the role of this tradition and Dilthey's hermeneutics is complex and arguably quite ambiguous for Heidegger.

5. One could think about this in terms of the multiple uses to which English speakers put the word *affect*: *Dasein* can be seen as *affected* by its past in such a manner that its *affect* in relation to its current world is determined.

6. This analysis expands the notion of forgetting into the social and moral spheres, in which *Dasein flees* from its open potentiality-for-being into a self-conception aligned with the "they-self," i.e. with community norms, public standards, the current *mode*; and suffers pangs of guilt and conscience. Authenticity, here, becomes more of a quest for individuality and personal meaning. This analytic of social and moral authenticity explores *Dasein*'s temporality, and specifically its *being-towards-death*, in a manner quite akin to Kierkegaard and was, no doubt what the "existentialist" approaches of French thinkers such as Sartre, Camus and de Beauvoir drew upon....

7. This analytic can be expanded into the social and moral fields, where *inauthentic* abandonment and *authentic* resoluteness pertain to *Dasein*'s relation to the "they-self" and the guilty "appeals" of its conscience.

8. Medard Boss would come to assemble and edit the transcripts culminating in a 1987 publication, translated into English in 2001. Segments of this transcript are discussed by Dallamyr, 1993.

9. Page references are to the original 1987 German manuscript as these are given in the margin of the translated version.

10. Indeed, Frie (1997, 2003) extends this exploration to include the manner in which Binswanger, and others may, indeed, redeem various individualistic (and other) biases which appear inherent in Heidegger's analyses in *Being and Time* (1928) in spite of its appeals to the fundamentally relational nature of existence encapsulated in concepts such as *Mitwelt* and *Mitsein*. Frie (1997, 2003) is able to establish this in a much broader analysis of Binswanger's original writings. A critical analysis of Heidegger's conceptualization of *Mitsein*, and its interpretation by Frie and another philosophically trained analyst, Robert Stolorow, will be included in the chapter below which explores, more broadly, issues of relationality and otherness emerging from Heidegger's hermeneutic ontological project.

11. Sass (1992) advances an analysis of these issues around Ontological Difference in order to elucidate a more authentic understanding of certain forms of schizophrenic phenomenology.

CHAPTER 3

1. Frie (pp. 77–85, 1997) contextualizes Binswanger's critique within a broader philosophical debate around Heidegger's analyses of sociality, authenticity and death and correctly casts these as having a central role in Heidegger's *Kehre*, in which Heidegger distances himself from more anthropological or existential-humanistic

interpretations of his work and begins to, in his own subsequent work, focus on language and thought, rather than *Dasein*, as ontologically primary elements.

2. By elaborating his own conceptualization of relational trauma and kinship-infinitude, and using the philosophical work of Critchley and Derrida on death and mourning, Stolorow (2011a and b, 2009) makes a concerted attempt to faithfully redeem or amend some of these biases in his critical analysis of Heideggerian *Mitsein*, and in particular, being-towards-death, solicitude and authenticity.

3. Simondon's theory of individuation was an important influence on the thought of Gilles Deleuze and Bernard Stiegler, both of whom will be discussed below.

4. Importantly, Levinas's work is often seen in relation to his biography, and often in contrast to Heidegger's biography. Levinas himself was of Jewish background and a student of Heidegger's who became subject to Nazi captivity for the majority of World War 2. Prior to this, Levinas had witnessed Heidegger's professed affiliation with National Socialism as a University Rector and thus distanced himself from Heidegger's thought. For Levinas and many others who study Heidegger, the question of an ethical stance in relation to approaching and understanding his work, remains an important and valid issue to address, particularly given further historical findings about Heidegger's complicity and involvement in Nazi activities in the early-mid 1930s, and how these relate to other biographical details, including Heidegger's long term relationship with prominent Jewish thinker Hannah Arendt, his later difficulties with depression and a suicide attempt, amongst other things (see Farias, 1987; Rockmore, 1991 and Wolin, 1991, for example).

5. Indeed, debates generated between all of these thinkers, Derrida, Levinas, Ricoeur and Gadamer have been a great source of intellectual interest, exemplified by collections such as Pirovolakis (2011), Michelfelder and Palmer (1989), and many others.

CHAPTER 4

1. This is what was taken up, and developed by contemporaries of Heidegger such as the Merleau-Ponty of *Phenomenology of Perception*.

2. I also believe that to engage with these works, one has to enter into them, inhabit them, as they defy easy summary and lose their critical and subversive action if abbreviated or domesticated too much. In this respect, I have been inspired by the approach in Goodchild's (1996) excellent analysis of the "politics of desire" in Deleuze and Guattari's *Anti-Oedipus* (1972) and *A Thousand Plateaus* (1980).

3. This term is loosely adapted from a Lacanian usage, something that will be discussed in the final section of this chapter.

4. The complexity of the conceptualizations that establish these paralogisms is prohibitive: the arguments will be summarized here without delineating five specific paralogisms.

5. Desiring-machines are also referred to as *partial-objects*, borrowing from Melanie Klein's characterization of infantile object-relations in the paranoid position.

6. A contradicition in terms in logic, it represents a disjunction which is inclusive and affirmative "without restricting one by the other or excluding the other from the one" (1972, 76).

7 And these results of the transcendental process, hallucinosis and delusion, fit with an ego which is apparently experiencing profound disorganization, paranoia, exaltation, perplexity in its attempt to extract itself from the immanent field.

8. In the case of *nomadism/schizophrenia* and *repression* alike, subjectivity is something extracted from the immanent plane of production; it is, in itself, "transcendent" and unproductive. The extremity of *nomadism* is the immanence of the experience, the experience of immanence, before it is extracted, articulated, or transcendentalized as a subjectivity.

9. Inclusive disjunctive synthesis is the opportunity of the most productive desiring-production within the field of the plane of immanence: it is the nomadic act of the schizophrenic which most represents an unmediated unconscious; but Deleuze and Guattari (1972) will also try to elaborate a nomadic sociality in the *socius*—the two, ultimately, being continuous. Nomadism is the truest, most immanent experience of "reality."

10. At the ontological level of the field of immanence of desiring-production, that which is whole, representational and transcendental is referred to as *molar*; whereas that which remains partial, non-representational and immanent is referred to as *molecular*. The complexity of these ontological concepts, as types of *consistency*, cannot be explored here other than to highlight this specific application. These designations must be kept in mind for they will be elaborated upon further on towards the end of this chapter.

11. Deleuze and Guattari (1972) say that in *lack*, the paralogism of "extrapolation" occurs. The phallic signifier is extracted from the chain of signification to define the Oedipal situation: it becomes a transcendental, despotic signifier "on which the entire chain thereafter seems to depend, assigning an element of lack to each position of desire, fusing desire to a law" (1972, 110).

12. This Marxist account has not been elaborated upon here.

13. And the authors' emulation of this experience in their text seems to threaten its own validity and coherence to readers anticipating a well-elaborated and developed form of traditional scholarship!

14. In the chapter "One or several wolves," Deleuze and Guattari (1972) seek to show that Freud's "Wolf Man" enunciates a desire of multiplicity, of becoming-a-pack-of-wolves. They argue that Freud misinterprets these enunciations back to a pathological state where the Wolf assumes a singular Oedipal symbolism. Thus, in Freud's analysis, the Wolf-man is only permitted to make Oedipal statements about himself—his desire becomes repressed. The authors summarize Freud's flaw: "We are not just criticizing psychoanalysis for having selected Oedipal statements exclusively . . . We are criticizing psychoanalysis for having used Oedipal enunciation to make patients believe they would produce individual, personal statements, and would finally speak in their own name" (1980, 38).

CHAPTER 5

1. Green (2002) also highlights the significance of *Mourning and Melancholia*, where Freud differentiates between mourning and melancholia through a more articulated theory of intrapsychic object relations, which can be the site of forms of pathological memory. This links object relations to another form of *re-presentation*. He also

refers to socio-cultural memory, primal fantasy (the Freud of *Totem and Toboo* and Group Psychology and the Analysis of the Ego) having birectional quality.

2. What is paradoxical about death is that as we have seen with the early Heidegger it may represent an ultimate horizon of non-relational, non-temporal individualization but within the existential context, it is something that is projected towards, it forms a *temporal* horizon. We see death figuring as a temporal concept in Heidegger's notion of *Dasein* as being-towards-death, projecting towards death, finding its individual authenticity in this relation to death. Extending this, there is room to analyse the creative potential of the Freudian death instinct and this may fit within the problematic of the absence of temporality in the Freudian Unconscious.

3. Ironically, his thinking of time, as Green (2002) has established it from Freud's work, itself has a bidirectional nature to it: Green is retroactively establishing a meaning and cohesion in Freud's work around time, where there wasn't one.

CHAPTER 7

1. Green certainly repeatedly acknowledges Winnicott as a central influence on his work and this influence, no doubt, would be found in his thinking on temporality.

2. Comparisons could be made with Lacan's notion of capture in the imaginary relationship with the mother, or Bion's container-contained relationship.

3. This is obviously different to the Lacanian distinction between the imaginary and symbolic orders. Interestingly theorists such Andre Green have argued the complementarity of Winnicott's and Lacan's approaches: in spite of Winnicott's failure to adequately explore the linguistic nature of selfhood, Winnicott's transitional space and self-development do undermine the overemphasis on abstract linguistic conceptualization in Lacan's theorization of the unconscious, anticipating, perhaps Kristeva's own focus on a pre-Symbolic Chora and Semiotic Order in her critical appraisal of Lacan. The views of these latter thinkers will be explored below and reference will be made to these contrasts with the Winnicottian orientation.

4. His notions of relationality in treatment, both in *The Shadow of the Object* (1987) and a subsequent work, *Being a Character* (1992) will be explored in the clinical part of this work below.

5. This will be especially relevant to our analysis of developmental theories of borderline pathology that hold to the acquisition of relational abilities such as mentalization and capacities for conversation and dialogue whilst ignoring the formative and original relationality that occurs.

6. This process is of great philosophical and scientific interest, arguably beginning with nineteenth-century analyses of history and evolution that occur in a wide range of theorists including Hegel, Marx, Darwin, and Nietzsche.

CHAPTER 8

1. I will refer to the years of publication of the Lacanian translations I refer to: many of Lacan's writings were based upon seminars that were only assembled from

transcripts for publication much later so it is difficult to refer to an original publication date that coincides with the timing of the seminar.

2. Subsequent Lacanian ideas about *untriggered psychosis* and *ordinary psychosis* found in the work of Jacques-Alain Miller, Russell Grigg and Eric Laurent, amongst others, could be analysed in their affinities with formulations of borderline pathology but this will not be undertaken in this work.

3. This is a locus of many aspects of Lacanian theory . . . the origin of the Freudian superego begins here; desire as inscribed in the Symbolic begins here, with its inextricable relations with the Law, where the Father represents initially the Law as prohibition of incest.

4. Although it is inextricably linked to these stimuli and in a sense depends on them, it does not *arise* from them. It is always difficult to know just how much can be read into the specific behaviours or roles of a real mother or father in the upbringing; just how literal or concrete one can interpret the setting of the complex. This difficulty, and the lure of the simplicity of being concrete, to which Lacan (1977, 218–19) succumbs like so many others, is especially dangerous when one comes to consider the aetiologies of neurosis and psychosis in the clinic—interpretations of which, offered at this level, can leave parents with debilitating feelings of guilt and self-recrimination.

5. The symbolic Father, the paternal signifier, is the primordial, symbolic Other.

6. Grigg (1998, 56–7) is apt to point out how this Subject-Other relationship appears, at once, as the symbolic nature of the Subject's interpersonal relationship to others through speech (emphasized more in the Seminar) as well as to language *per se* (emphasized more in the *Ecrits* piece).

7. Provisional in the multiplicity of meanings of the two concepts, and the ways in which these meanings would change with time for Lacan, something that will be developed more in Part III below. Similarly, a full elaboration of just how the Symbolic, Imaginary and Real interact is beyond the scope of this piece.

8 The seminar on ethics is strange for its adoption of the concept of *jouissance*: it makes little effort to define it clearly in relation to the theory and ethics of *desire*. Desire as a concept becomes unstable because it shifts between being limited by the Law (in opposition to *jouissance*) and being a transgression of the Law (in union with *jouissance*).

9. In the article "The subversion of the subject and the dialectic of desire in the Freudian Unconscious" in the *Ecrits* (1977, pp. 292–325).

10. The ambiguity of this surplus *jouissance* of loss seems to relate somehow to what Lacan (1992) earlier called the extimacy of the Thing. Lacan would come to refer to it as *plus-de-jouir*, both "more *jouissance*" and "no longer *jouissance*." This kind of *jouissance* as a frustrated nostalgia, repetitively searched for in desire, parallels the way in which the illusory pre-Symbolic drive relates to the symbolic Thing of desire through the relationship of extimacy. Here, the elusive Thing can assume an endless array of (metonymic) forms, all of which are adequate to desire but are only a (metaphoric) substitute for the original object of the drive. Both notions capture the ambivalence of *signification* insofar as metaphor is *substitutive*, that which is substituted for is always lost and unavailable, prior, only alluded to.

11. We are ignoring, here, any distinctions Lacan may have made between desire and drive, the former relating to the Law/Other and the latter the Thing/Real, for the sake of parsimony.

12. This, at least, avoids having to problematize the clinical relevance of an analysis of a *famous* psychotic who was neither widely recognized as psychotic nor analysed clinically or even biographically by Lacan in any detail.

13. Thought they would have described as "oedipalized" in the first work.

14. This discussion refers to her conceptualizations in *Powers of Horror: An Essay on Abjection* (1982), *New Maladies of the Soul* (1995) and an essay directly engaging with Lacan's ideas: "Within the microcosm of 'The Talking Cure'" (1983).

CHAPTER 9

1. Aulagnier (1975) could be seen to establish a similar "primordial psyche," with her theorisation of the constitution of the unconscious through repression and the primal pictograms it is constituted by.

2. Interestingly, at points Laplanche does allude to the possiblity of the superego, universally, as such a psychotic enclave which acts on the ego, while at other times he is referring to it more as a specifically pathological form of disturbance.

3. Khan (1960, 1983, 1974) would develop these ideas into a theory of cumulative trauma.

CHAPTER 10

1. Foucault does not have a humanist emancipatory agenda or conspiratorial focus in this: following Nietzsche, his critical historicization of modern scientific discourses and institutional practices (and other aspects of modernity) has an antihumanist orientation, seeking to undermine any universalist, humanistic and objective scientific pretensions to these discourses and practices for the purpose of greater critical awareness and ethical lucidity.

2. Green (2000) and Orange (2003) have also critically reviewed these theoretical paradigms and the incorporation of infant research, drawing similar conclusions to mine.

3. Interestingly, Leys (2000) mounts a Foucauldian critical history of the concept of trauma on the way to maintaining that it is a fundamentally unstable, ambiguous and dissonant concept that oscillates between opposing "mimetic" and "antimimetic" models which hold, respectively, that the subject is unable to integrate the trauma into the cognitive or perceptual system leading to forms of hypnotic imitation, or that the trauma is a completely external event that the patient, with the proper handling, can always recall and master.

4. For example, there have been widespread criticisms levelled at the traumatology and attachment-based theories, in terms of pseudo-empiricism and reductionism that is produced through the bolstering of psychoanalytic or psychodynamic theory with

the findings of neurobiological, behavioural and ethological research (e.g., Green, 2000; Orange, 2003). In this context it is argued that the complexity of psychoanalytic conceptualization, the richness of language, meaning, experience and later or more advanced developmental problems are all omitted.

PART III

1. I can only briefly, here, refer to the origins of models of the "dialogical self" coming from thinkers such as William James and Mikhail Bakhtin that have been adopted and directly elucidated in developmental models of psychotherapy used in an understanding Borderline Personality Disorder by theorists such as Meares (the Conversational Model), as well as Anthony Ryle (in his cognitive-analytic model) and practitioners influenced by "Dialogical Self" theorists Hubert Hermans and Harry Kempen (e.g., Giancarlo Dimaggio).
2. Indeed, it has proven difficult to review and critique this field in any form of inclusive or summary approach. Mills's (2005) critical review, for example, led to numerous responses and challenges.
3. Indeed it may motivate them to be more politically active or socially engaged in a broader way in domains such as health economics, social services and welfare advocacy.

CHAPTER 11

1. Unfortunately I cannot attempt, here, to describe how this relates to ideas of thirdness in the relational and intersubjective tradition, in thinkers such as Thomas Ogden and Jessica Benjamin.
2. Limitations prevent me from elaborating upon another fouindational thinker of borderline pathology, Jean Bergeret (1974), who links borderline pathology to astructuration, arising from disturbances in early object relations and psychosexual development.
3. This idea, and a more comprehensive analysis of the concepts of mentalization and mentalized affectivity, will not be developed further here. The complexity of these concepts, and a diversity of critical approaches to them, is well covered in Jurist, Slade and Bergner (2008), for example.
4. In this clinical part of the work I have chosen not to describe specific clinical cases of my own both due to ethical reasons and due to my reservation, in alignment with thinkers such as Green (1986), about the utility of this methodology for a theoretical exposition such as this. Instead, I have elected to discuss general clinical encounters or scenarios which may be representative or demonstrative for the clinical issues I am addressing, and which may be, in turn, reflected upon or adopted by readers for their own clinical work.
5. This point is not inconsistent with Stern's own attempt at distinguishing his approach from the approach of the mentalization group (in Jurist, Slade and Bergner, 2008).

6. A psychoanalytic tradition has arisen from this maxim, a tradition of retranslations and reinterpretations by many famous analysts (Lacan and Green, for example), adapting it to their own theoretical models.

CHAPTER 12

1. Lacan had originally commented upon clinical work with the borderline as psychotherapy conducted in the imaginary order, a psychotherapy of illusion not grounded in language or discourse, cut off and ungraded in a larger symbolic order of task and meaning and hence with no place for both parties to become subjects within a matrix of social reality. This, as such, would not allow the borderline concept to be seen as a coherent clinical concept or commensurate with Lacanian analytic work. Subsequent Lacanian ideas about *untriggered psychosis* and *ordinary psychosis* found in the work of Jacques-Alain Miller, Russell Grigg and Eric Laurent, amongst others, could possibly be analysed in their affinities with formulations of borderline pathology but this will not be undertaken in this work.

2. This discussion refers to her conceptualizations in *Powers of Horror: An Essay on Abjection* (1982), *New Maladies of the Soul* (1995) and an essay directly engaging with Lacan's ideas: "Within the microcosm of 'The Talking Cure'" (1983).

3. This could be seen to relate to but extend the forms of mentalization described by Fonagy's group and conversation and the duplex self-described by Meares's group, outlined in the chapter immediately above.

4. Although I cannot expand upon it here, Bromberg's relational model of multiplicity, dissociation, and trauma could be criticized, at this level, for not being "complicated" enough. Fredrickson, in Frie and Orange (2009) ably criticizes the limits of Bromberg's model, using a Heideggerian approach to critique Bromberg's over-reliance upon representational modes of understanding that are limited and are, in a sense, complicit with the afflictions such as multiple personality disorder, that Bromberg engages with.

5. This idea is presented by many theorists. Indeed Ricoeur (1965) goes so far as to state that the superego represents a form of archaic remant in an evolutionary sense, an instinctualized 'premorality'. Elsewhere, Freud and Lacan focus on the archaic collective history of the superego, for example, in the myth of the primal horde. Whereas Schore (1991) details the emergence of shame and superego development in early misattunement experiences in attachment relationships, in his theoretical contribution to linking borderline experience with disorganized attachment.

CHAPTER 13

1. Also, I would argue that Ricouer's (1965) thinking about time and narrativity are not developed to the extent of his later works and that, along with the favouring of Husserlian and Kantian philosophy (in contrast to Heideggerian or the establishment of his own fuller philosophical anthropology and hermeneutics in his later works).

2. Although this kind of present-focused process is important, and it is articulated well by Daniel Stern (2004) describing moments of meeting, attunement, and implicit relational processes that assist in the development of a sense of relational self, even Stern (2004, pp. 197–218) does not hold to ignoring the action of the past on the present in the therapeutic processes he describes in his own work and the work described by the Boston Process Change Study Group.

3. In the chapter on embodiment and affectivity, immediately above, I briefly referred to Bromberg's (1995, 1998) conceptualization of multiple selves, traumatisation, and the understanding of dissociative identity disorder or multiple personality disorder being seen as an extreme variant of selfhood which is universally conceptualized as multiplicitous, the norm of which involves "standing in the spaces." One can apply the temporalizing form of relational work I describe here to this domain, where stable, self-attributed identities can be seen as a developmentally appropriate but restrictive forms of trauma response that require validation and empathy but also understanding and contextualisation with a view to working through and overcoming.

CONCLUSION

1. Frie (2001), for example, reviewed a work of Gion Condrau and ably demonstrates the potential for the modern *Daseinsanalytic* group to engage in debate with modern schools of psychoanalytic theory as opposed to critically engaging a more anachronistic form of traditional Freudianism.

Bibliography

Aulagnier, P. 1975. *The Violence of Interpretation: From Pictogram to Statement*. Trans. Sheridan, A. 2001. London: Brunner-Routledge.

American Psychiatric Association. 2000. *Diagnostic and Statistical Manual of Mental Disorders, Fourth Edition*, Text Revision. Washington, DC, American Psychiatric Association.

Applebaum, A. 2006. "Supportive psychoanalytic psychotherapy for borderline patients: an empirical approach." *Amercian Journal of Psychoanalysis*, 66(4): 317–322.

Atwood, G.E., Orange, D.M., & Stolorow, R.D. 2002. "Shattered Worlds/Psychotic States: A Post-Cartesian View of the Experience of Personal Annihilation." *Psychoanalytic Psychology*, 19:281–306.

Bass, A. 2000. *Difference and Disavowal: The Trauma of Eros*. Palo Alto: Stanford University Press.

Bass, A. 2006. *Interpretation and Difference: The Strangeness of Care*. Palo Alto: Stanford University Press.

Bateman, A., & Fonagy, P. 2004. *Psychotherapy for Borderline Personality Disorder: Mentalization Based Treatment*. Oxford: Oxford University Press.

Bergeret, J. 1975. *La Dépression Et Les États-Limites*. Paris: Payot.

Binswanger, L. 1963. *Being-in-the-World. Selected Papers of Ludwig Binswanger*. Trans. Needleman, J. London: Souvenir Press. Includes: "Heidegger's Analytic of Existence and its Meaning for Psychiatry," pp. 206–222; "Dream and Existence," pp. 222–249; "Introduction to *Schizophrenie*," pp. 249–266; "The Case of Lola Voss," pp. 266–341; "Extravagance," pp. 342–351.

Binswanger, L. 1958. *Existence. A New Dimension in Psychiatry and Psychology*. May, R., Anger, E., & Ellenberger, H. (Eds). New York: Touchstone. Includes: "The Existential Analysis School of Thought," pp. 191–213; "Insanity as Life-Historical Phenomenon and Mental Disease: The Case of Ilse," pp. 214–236; "The Case of Ellen West," pp. 237–365.

Blum N., St. John D., & Pfohl, B. 2008. "Systems training for emotional predictability for problem solving (STEPPS) foe outpatient with borderline personality disorder: a randomized controlled trial and 1-year follow-up." *American Journal of Psychiatry*, 165:468–478.
Bollas, C. 1987. *The Shadow of the Object: Psychoanalysis of the Unthought Known.* New York: Colmbia University Press.
Boss, M. 1979. *Existential Foundations of Medicine and Psychology.* Trans. Conway, S. & Cleaves, A. Northvale: Jason Aronson.
Boss, M. 1963. *Psychoanalysis and Daseinsanalysis.* Trans. Lefebre, L. New York: Basic Books.
Brandchaft, B., & Stolorow, R. 1984. "The borderline concept: Pathological character or iatrogenic myth." In *Empathy*, Vol. 2, J. Lichtenberg, M. Bornstein & D. Silver (Eds.). Hillsdale, NJ: Analytic Press, pp. 333–358.
Bromberg, P.M. 1995. "Psychoanalysis, dissociation, and personality organization reflections on Peter Goldberg's essay." *Psychoanalytic Dialogues: The International Journal of Relational Perspectives*, 5:511–528.
Bromberg, P.M. 1998. *Standing in the Spaces: Essays on Clinical Process, Trauma, and Dissociation.* New Jersey: Analytic Press.
Clarkin, J., Fonagy, P., & Gabbard, G. (Eds). 2010. *Psychodynamic Psychotherapy for Personality Disorders: A Clinical Handbook.* Washington DC: American Psychiatric Publishing.
Clarkin, J., Yeomans, F., & Kernberg, O. 2006. *Psychotherapy for Borderline Personality Disorder: Focussing on Object Relations.* Washington DC: American Psychiatric Publishing.
Clancy, S. 2010. *The Trauma Myth: The Truth about the Sexual Abuse of Children and its Aftermath.* New York: Basic Books.
Critchley, S., & Bernasconi, R. (Ed.) 2002. *The Cambridge Companion to Levinas.* London: Cambridge University Press.
Dallamyr, F. 1988–1989. "Heidegger and psychotherapy." *Review of Existential Psychology and Psychiatry*, XXI(1–3):9–35.
Davies, J., & Frawley-O'Dea, M. 1994. *Treating the Adult Survivor of Childhood Sexual Abuse.* New York: Basic Books.
Deleuze, G., & Guattari, G. 1972. *Anti-Oedipus. Capitalism and Schizophrenia.* Trans. Hurley, R., Seem, M., & Lane, H. 1984. Minneapolis: University of Minnesota Press.
Deleuze, G., & Guattari, G. 1980. *A Thousand Plateaus. Capitalism and Schizophrenia.* Trans. Massumi, B. 1988. London: The Athlone Press.
Derrida, J. 1972a. "Freud and the Scene of Writing." Trans. Mehlman, J. *Yale French Studies* 48:74–117.
Derrida, J. 1972b. "La différance." *Marges de la philosophie.* Paris: Editions de Minuit.
Derrida, J. 1978. *Writing and Difference.* Trans. Bass, A. London and New York: Routledge.
Derrida, J. 1981. *Positions.* Trans. Bass A. Chicago: University of Chicago Press.
Derrida, J. 1983. "*Geslecht I*: Sexual difference, ontological difference." *Psyche: Inventions of the Other.* Trans. Benezdivin, R., & Rottenberg, E. 2008. Stanford: Stanford University Press.

Derrida, J. 1987. *The Post Card: From Socrates to Freud and Beyond.* Trans. Bass, A. Chicago & London: University of Chicago Press.
Derrida, J. 1996. *Résistances de la psychanalyse.* Trans. Kamuf, P., Brault, P., & Naas, M. *Resistances of Psychoanalysis.* Stanford: Stanford University Press.
Deutsch, H. 1934. "Über einen Typus der Pseudoaffektivität ("Als ob")." *Internationale Zeitschrift für Psychoanalyse*, 20:323–335.
Deutsch, H. 1942. "Some forms of emotional disturbance and their relationship to schizophrenia." *Psychoanalytic Quarterly*, 11:301–321.
Eickhoff, F. 2006. "On Nachträglichkeit: The modernity of an old concept." *International Journal of Psycho-Analysis*, 87:1453–1469.
Farias, V. 1987. *Heidegger and Nazism.* Philadelphia: Temple University Press.
Fonagy, P., Gergely, G., Jurist, E., & Target, M. 2002. *Affect Regulation, Mentalization and the Development of the Self.* New York: Other Press.
Foucault, M. 1977. *Discipline and Punish.* Trans. Sheridan, A. London: Allen Lane.
Foucault, M. 1976–1984. *History of Sexuality*, 3 Volumes: *Introduction, The Uses of Pleasure, and Care of the Self.* Trans. Hurley, R. 1988–1990. New York: Vintage Books.
Foucault M. 1961. *History of Madness.* Trans. Murphy, J., & Khalfa, J. 2009. New York: Routledge.
Foucault, M. 1984–1985. "Dream, imagination and existence. Introduction to *Rêve et Existence.*" *Review of Existential Psychology and Psychiatry*, XIX(1):29–79.
Freud, S. *The Standard Edition of the Complete Works of Freud.* Trans. Strachey, J. 1953–1966.
———. 1955. Volume II (1893–1895): Studies on Hysteria.
———. 1962. Volume III (1893–1899): Early Psycho-Analytic Publications.
———. 1953. Volume IV (1900): The Interpretation of Dreams (First Part).
———. 1953. Volume V (1900–1901): The Interpretation of Dreams (Second Part) and On Dreams.
———. 1960. Volume VI (1901): The Psychopathology of Everyday Life.
———. 1953. Volume VII (1901–1905): A Case of Hysteria, Three Essays on Sexuality and Other Works.
———. 1960. Volume VIII (1905): Jokes and their Relation to the Unconscious.
———. 1959. Volume IX (19061908): Jensen's "Gradiva" and Other Works.
———. 1955. Volume X (1909): Two Case Histories ("Little Hans" and the "Rat Man").
———. 1957. Volume XI (1910): Five Lectures on Psycho-Analysis, Leonardo da Vinci and Other Works.
———. 1958. Volume XII (1911–1913): The Case of Schreber, Papers on Technique and Other Works.
———. 1955. Volume XIII (1913–1914): Totem and Taboo and Other Works.
———. 1957. Volume XIV (1914–1916): On the History of the Psycho-Analytic Movement, Papers on Metapsychology and Other Works.
———. 1963. Volume XV (1915–1916): Introductory Lectures on Psycho-Analysis (Parts I and II).
———. 1963. Volume XVI (1916–1917): Introductory Lectures on Psycho-Analysis (Part III).
———. 1955. Volume XVII (1917–1919): An Infantile Neurosis and Other Works.

———. 1955. Volume XVIII (1920–1922): Beyond the Pleasure Principle, Group Psychology and Other Works.
———. 1961. Volume XIX (1923–1925): The Ego and the Id and Other Works.
———. 1959. Volume XX (1925–1926): An Autobiographical Study, Inhibitions, Symptoms and Anxiety, The Question of Lay Analysis and Other Works.
———. 1961. Volume XXI (1927–1931): The Future of an Illusion, Civilization and its Discontents, and Other Works.
———. 1964. Volume XXII (1932–1936): New Introductory Lectures on Psycho-Analysis and Other Works.
———. 1964. Volume XXIII (1937–1939): Moses and Monotheism, An Outline of Psycho-Analysis and Other Works.
Frie, R. 1997. *Subjectivity and Intersubjectivity in Modern Philosophy and Psyhco-analysis: A Study of Sartre, Binswanger, Lacan and Habermas*. London: Rowman and Littlefield.
Frie, R. 2001. "Review: *From Psychoanalysis to Daseinsanalysis—A Discussion of Martin Heidegger's Impact on Psychotherapy* by Gion Condrau." *Contemporary Psychoanalysis*, 37:153–167.
Fromm, G. 1995. "What does *Borderline* mean?" *Psychoanalytic Psychology*, 12: 233–245.
Gadamer, H. 1960. *Truth and Method*. Trans. Weinsheimer, J. & Marshall, D. 1989. New York: Crossroad.
Gadamer, H. 1976. *Philosophical Hermeneutics*. Trans. Linde, D. Los Angeles: University of California Press.
Giesen-Bloo, J., van Dyck, R., Spinhoven P., van Tilburg W., Dirksen, C., van Asselt, T., Kremers, I., Nadort, M., & Arntz, A. 2009. "Outpatient Psychotherapy for Borderline Personality Disorder: a randomized trial of Schema focused therapy versus Transference focused therapy." *Archives of General Psychiatry*, 63(6):649–658.
Goffman, E. 1959. *The Presentation of Self in Everyday Life*, University of Edinburgh Social Sciences Research Centre: Anchor Books.
Goffman, E. 1961. *Asylums: Essays on the Social Situation of Mental Patients and Other Inmates*. New York: Doubleday.
Goffman, E. 1963. *Stigma: Notes on the Management of Spoiled Identity*. New York: Prentice-Hall.
Goffman, E. 1974. *Frame Analysis: An Essay on the Organization of Experience*. London: Harper and Row.
Goodchild, P. 1996. *Deleuze and Guattari: An Introduction to the Politics of Desire*. London: Sage Publications.
Green, A. 1978. "Potential Space in Psychoanalysis: The Object in the Setting." In *Between Reality and Fantasy: Transitional Objects and Phenomena*. Grolnick, S. and Basrkin, L. (Eds). New York and London: Jason Aronson.
Green, A. 1986. *On Private Madness*. London: Hogarth Press.
Green, A. 1995. "An Interview with Andre Green." *New Formations*, 26:15–35.
Green, A. 2002. *Time and Psychoanalysis*. London: Free Association Books.
Green, A. 2008. "Freud's Concept of Temporality: Differences with Current Ideas." *International Journal of Psychoanalysis*, 89:1029–1039.

Green, A. 2000. "Science and science fiction in infant research." In Sandler J., Sandler A-M., & Davies R. (Eds), *Clinical and Observational Psychoanalytic Research*. London: Karnac Books, 41–73.
Grigg, R. 1998. "From the mechanism of psychosis to the universal condition of the symptom: On foreclosure." In Nobus, D. (Ed.), *Key Concepts of Lacanian Psychoanalysis*. London: Rebus.
Gunderson, J., & Singer, M. 1975. "Defining borderline patients: an overview." *American Journal of Psychiatry*, 132:1–10.
Gunderson, J., Kolb, J., & Austin, V. 1981. "The Diagnostic Interview for Borderline Patients." *American Journal of Psychiatry*, 138:896–903.
Heidegger, M. 1928. *Sein und Zeit*. Translated as *Being and Time* by Macquarrie, J., & Robinson, E. 1978. Oxford: Basil Blackwell.
Heidegger, M. 1928b. *The Essence of Reasons*. Trans. Malick, T. 1969. Evanston: Northwestern University Press.
Heidegger, M. 1929. *Kant and the Problem of Metaphysics*. Trans. Taft, R. 1990. Bloomington: Indiana University Press.
Heidegger, M. 1959–1969. *Zollikon Seminars: Protocols, Conversations, Letters*. Trans. F. Mayr. 2001. New York: Northwestern University Press.
Heidegger, M. 1954. "The Question Concerning Technology." In *Martin Heidegger: Basic Writings*, (Ed.) David Ferrell Krell, 1977, repr. New York: Harper Collins Publisher, 1993.
Heidegger, M. 1947. "Letter on Humanism." In *Wegmarken* (1919–58). Translated as *Pathmarks*. Ed. McNeill, W. 1998. Cambridge: Cambridge University Press.
Herman, JL. 1997. *Trauma and Recovery: The Aftermath of Violence from Domestic Abuse to Political Terror*. NY: Basic Books.
Howell, E. 2005. *The Dissociative Mind*. Hillsdale, NJ: The Analytic Press.
Janet, P. 1909. *Les Nevroses*. Paris: Ernest Flammarion.
Jureidini, J. 2004. "Does dissociation offer a useful explanation for psychopathology?" *Psychopathology*, 37:259–265.
Jurist, E. 2005. "Mentalized Affectivity." *Psychoanalytic Psychology*, 22:426–444.
Jurist, E. 2010. "Mentalizing Minds." *Psychoanalytic Inquiry*, 30:289–300.
Jurist, E., Slade, A., & Berger, S. 2008. *Mind to Mind: Infant Research, Neuroscience and Psychoanalysis*. New York: Other Press.
Kernberg, Otto F. 1975. *Borderline Conditions and Pathological Narcissism*. Northvale, NJ: J. Aronson.
Khan, M. 1960. "Clinical aspects of the schizoid personality: Affects and technique." *International Journal of Psycho-Analysis*, *41*, 430–437.
Khan, M. 1983. *Hidden Selves: Between Theory and Practice in Psychoanalysis*. London: Hogarth.
Khan, M. 1974. *The Privacy of the Self*. London: Hogarth.
Kohut, H. 1971. *The Analysis of the Self*. New York: International Universities Press.
Knight, R.P. 1953. "Borderline states." *Bulletin of the Menninger Clinic*, XVII:1–12.
Kristeva, J. 1982. *Powers of Horror: An Essay on Abjection*. New York: Columbia University Press.
Kristeva, J. 1995. *New Maladies of the Soul*. New York: Columbia University Press.

Kristeva, J. 1983. "Within the Microcosm of 'The Talking Cure.'" Trans. Gora, T., & Waller, M. *Interpreting Lacan.* Ed. Smith, J., & Kerrigan, W. New Haven: Yale University Press, pp. 33–48.
Kuypers, J. 2009. *Rhetorical Criticism: Perspectives in Action.* Lanham, MD: Lexington Press.
Lacan, J. 1986. *The Ethics of Psychoanalysis (1959–1960). The Seminar of Jacques Lacan, Book VII.* Ed. J. Miller, tr. D. Porter. London: Routledge. 1992.
Lacan, J. 1932. *De la psychose paranoïaque dans ses rapports avec la personnalité.* Paris: Seuil.
Lacan, J. 1976. *Le Sinthome. Seminaire XXIII* (1975–76), *Ornicar? 6–11.*
Lacan, J. 1977. *Écrits: A Selection.* Tr. Sheridan, A. London: Tavistock.
Lacan, J. 1992. *The Ethics of Psycoanalysis. The Seminar of Jacques Lacan—Book VII 1959–60.* London: Routledge.
Lacan, J. 1993. *The Psychoses. The Seminar of Jacques Lacan—Book III 1955–1956.* Trans. Grigg, R. London: Routledge.
Lang, H. 1997. *Language and the Unconscious.* Trans. Brockelman, T. Leiden: Brill Academic Publishers.
Langs, R. 1979. *The Therapeutic Environment.* New York: Jason Aronson.
Laplanche, J. 1987. *New Foundations for Psychoanalysis.* Trans. Macey, D. Oxford, England: Basil Blackwell.
Laplanche, J. 1990. *Essays on Otherness.* Ed., Fletcher, J. London: Routledge.
Laplanche, J. 1992. *Jean Laplanche: Seduction, Translation, Drives.* Fletcher, J. & Stanton, M. (Eds). Trans. Stanton, M. Psychoanalytic Forum, Institute of Contempary Arts London.
Levinas, E. 1961. *Totality and Infinity: An Essay on Exteriority.* Trans. Lingis, A. Pittsburgh: Duquesne University Press.
Levinas, E. 1974. *Otherwise than Being, or Beyond Essence.* Trans. Lingis, A. Pittsburgh: Duquesne University Press.
Leys, R. 2000. *Trauma: A Genealogy.* Chicago: University of Chicago Press.
Linehan M.M., Comtois K.A., Murray A.M., Brown M.Z., Gallop R.J., Heard H.L., Korslund K.E., Tutek D.A., Reynolds S.K., & Lindenboim N. 2006. "Two-year randomized controlled trial and follow-up of dialectical behavior therapy vs therapy by experts for suicidal behaviors and borderline personality disorder." *Archives of General Psychiatry,* 63:757–766.
Liotti, G., 1992. "Disorganised/disoriented Attachment in the Aetiology of the Dissociative Disorders." *Dissociation,* 5:196–204.
Liotti, G., 1995. "Disorganised/disoriented Attachment in the Psychotherapy of the Dissociative Disorders." In S. Golberg, R. Muir & J. Kerr (Eds), *Attachment Theory: Social, Developmental, and Clinical Perspective.* Hillsdale, NJ: The Analytic Press.
Liotti, G., Pasquini, P., & The Italian Group for the Study of Dissociation, 2000. "Predictive factors for borderline personality disorder: Early traumatic experiences in the patient and losses suffered by the attachment figure." *Acta Psychiatrica Scandinavica,* 102:282–289.
Loewald, H. 1978. *Psychoanalysis and the History of the Individual.* New Haven: Yale University Press.

Loewald, H. 1980. *Papers on Psychoanalysis*. New Haven & London: Yale University Press.
Loewald, H. 1988. *Sublimation*. New Haven: Yale University Press.
Luepnitz, D. 2009. "Thinking in the space between Winnicott and Lacan." *International Journal of Psychoanalysis*, 90:957–981.
Meares, R. 2000. *Intimacy and Alienation: Memory, Trauma and Personal Being*. London: Routledge.
Michelfelder, D., & Palmer, R. 1989. *Dialogue and Deconstruction: The Gadamer-Derrida Encounter*. New York: SUNYP.
Mills, J. 2005. "A critique of relational psychoanalysis." *Psychoanalytic Psychology*, 22(2):155–188.
Mills, J. 1997. "The false Dasein: From Heidegger to Sartre and psychoanalysis." *Journal of Phenomenological Psychology*, 28(1), 42–65.
Mills, J. 2014. "Truth." *Journal of the American Psychoanalytic Association*, 62(2): 267–293.
Nietzsche, F. 1886. *Human, All Too Human*. Trans. Hollingdale, R. 1986. Cambridge: Cambridge University Press.
Orange, D. 2001. "From cartesian minds to experiential worlds in psychoanalysis." *Psychoanalytic Psychology*, 18:287–302.
Orange, D. 2003. "Antidotes and alternatives: Perspectival realism and the new reductionisms." *Psychoanalytic Psychology*, 20(3):472–486.
Orange, D. 2011. "Speaking the unspeakable: 'The implicit,' traumatic living memory, and the dialogue of metaphors." *International Journal of Psychoanalytic Self Psychology*, 6:187–206.
Orange, D., Atwood, G., & Stolorow, R. 1997. *Working Intersubjectively: Contextualism in Psychoanalytic Practice*. Hillsdale, NJ: Analytic Press.
Orange, D. 2011. *The Suffering Stranger: Hermeneutics for Everyday Clinical Practice*. New York, NY and Hove, East Sussex, UK: Routledge (Taylor & Francis Group).
Orange, D. 2010. *Thinking for Clinicians: Philosophical Resources for Contemporary Psychoanalysis and the Humanistic Psychotherapies*. New York, NY and Hove, East Sussex, UK: Routledge (Taylor & Francis Group).
PDM Taskforce. 2006. *The Psychodynamic Diagnostic Manual*. Silver Spring, MD: Alliance of Psychoanalytic Organizations.
Pirovolakis, E. 2011. *Reading Derrida and Ricoeur: Improbable Encounters Between Deconstruction and Hermeneutics*. New York: SUNY Series, Insinuations: Philosophy, Psychoanalysis, Literature.
Pontalis, J-B. 1981. *Frontiers in Psychoanalysis: Between the Dream and Psychic Pain*. London: Hogarth Press.
Richardson, W.J. 1963. *Heidegger: Through Phenomenology to Thought*. Preface by Martin Heidegger. The Hague: Martinus Nijhoff.
Richardson, W.J. (With Muller, J.). 1982. *Lacan and Language, Reader's Guide to Ecrits*. New York: International Universities Press.
Richardson, W.J. 1988. "Lacan and non-philosophy." In Silverman, H. (Ed.), *Philosophy and Non-philosophy since Merleau-Ponty*. New York: Routledge.
Ricoeur, P. 1965. *Freud and Philosophy: An Essay on Interpretation*. Trans. Savage, D. 1970. New Haven: Yale University Press.

Ricoeur, Paul. 1978. "The question of proof in Freud's psychoanalytic writings." In Reagan, C., & Stewart, D. (Eds.), *The Philosophy of Paul Ricoeur*. Boston: Beacon Press.

Ricoeur, P. *Time and Narrative (Temps et Récit)*, 3 vols. Trans. Kathleen McLaughlin and David Pellauer. Chicago: University of Chicago Press, 1984, 1985, 1988 (1983, 1984, 1985).

Ricoeur, P. 1981. *Hermeneutics and the Human Sciences: Essays on Language, Action and Interpretation*. Ed. and Trans. John B. Thompson. Cambridge: Cambridge University Press.

Ricoeur, P. 1981. "Narrative time." In Mitchell, W. (Ed.), *On Narrative*. Chicago: University of Chicago Press.

Ricoeur, P. 1986. "The self in psychoanalysis and in phenomenological philosophy," *Psychoanalytic Inquiry*, 6:437–458.

Rockmore, T. 1991. *On Heidegger's Nazism and Philosophy*. Los Angeles: University of California Press.

Rorty, R. 1979. *Philosophy and the Mirror of Nature*. Princeton: Princeton University Press.

Ryle, A. 1997. "The structure and development of borderline personality disorder: A proposed model." *British Journal of Psychiatry*, 170:82–87.

Sass, L. 1982. "The borderline personality." *New York Times Magazine*. New York: New York Times.

Sass, L. 1989. "Humanism, hermeneutics, and humanistic psychoanalysis: Differing conceptions of subjectivity." *Psychoanalysis and Contemporary Thought*, 12:433–504.

Sass, L. 1992. "Heidegger, schizophrenia and ontological difference." *Philosophical Psychology*, 5(2):109–132.

Sass, L. 1994. *Madness and Modernism: Insanity in the Light of Modern Art, Literature and Thought*. New York: Basic Books.

Sass, L., & Woolfolk, R. 1988. "Psychoanalysis and the hermeneutic turn: A critique of narrative truth and historical truth." *Journal of the American Psychoanalytic Association*, 36:429–454.

Schore, A.N. 1991. "Early superego development: The emergence of shame and narcisstic affect regulation in the practicing period." *Psychoanalysis and Contemporary Thought*, 14:187–250.

Schore, A.N. 1994. *Affect Regulation and the Origin of the Self: The Neurobiology of Emotional Development*. Mahwah, NJ: Lawrence Erlbaum.

Schore, A.N. 2003a. *Affect Dysregulation and Disorders of the Self*. New York: W. W. Norton & Company.

Schore, A.N. 2003b. *Affect Regulation and Repair of the Self*. New York: W. W. Norton & Company.

Simondon, G. 1958. *Du mode d'existence des objets techniques*. Paris: Aubier.

Simondon, G. 1989. *L'individuation psychique et collective*. Paris: Aubier.

Stern, A. 1938. "Psychoanalytic investigation and therapy in the borderline group of neuroses." *Psychoanalytic Quarterly*, 7:467–489.

Stern, Daniel. 1985. *The Interpersonal World of the Infant: A View from Psychoanalysis and Developmental Psychology*. London: Karnac.

Stern, Daniel. 2004. *The Present Moment in Psychotherapy and Everyday Life*. New York: WW Norton.
Stern, Donnel. 1997. *Unformulated Experience: From Dissociation to Imagination in Psychoanalysis*. Hillsdale, NJ: The Analytic Press.
Stiegler, B. 1994. *Technics and Time, I: The Fault of Epimetheus*. Trans. Collins, G., & Beardsworth, R. 1998. Stanford: Stanford University Press.
Stiegler, B. "Desire and knowledge: The dead seize the living." *Ars Industrialis*. Created 15/5/2009. http://arsindustrialis.org/print/3181. Accessed 30/9/2011.
Stolorow, R., Atwood, G., & Orange, D. 2002. *Worlds of Experience: Interweaving Philosophical and Clinical Dimensions in Psychoanalysis*. New York: Basic Books.
Stolorow, R. 2002. "From drive to affectivity: Contextualizing psychological life." *Psychoanaytic Inquiry*, 22:678–685.
Stolorow, R. 2007. *Trauma and Human Existence: Autobiographical, Psychoanalytic, and Philosophical Reflections*. New York: Routledge.
Stolorow, R. 2011. *World, Affectivity, Trauma: Heidegger and Post-Cartesian Psychoanalysis*. New York: Routledge.
Stolorow, R., Orange, D., Atwood, G. 2001. "World horizons: A post-cartesian alternative to the Freudian unconscious." *Contemporary Psychoanalysis*, 37:43–61.
Thoma, H., & Cheshire, N. 1991. "*Nachträglichkeit* and deferred action." *International Journal of Psychoanalysis*, 18:407–427.
Tversky, A., & Kahneman, D. 1981. "The framing of decisions and the psychology of choice." *Science*, 211:453–458.
van der Hart, O., Nijenhuis, E., & Steele, K. 2006. *The Haunted Self: Structural Dissociation and the Treatment of Chronic Traumatization*. New York: W.W. Norton & Co.
van der Hart, O., Witztum, E., & Friedman, B. 1993. "From hysterical psychosis to reactive dissociative psychosis." *Journal of Traumatic Stress*, 6(1):1–13.
Van Der Kolk, B. 1987. *Psychological Trauma*. New York: American Psychiatric Press.
Winnicott, D. 1974. "Fear of breakdown." *International Review of Psychoanalysis*, 1:103–107.
Winnicott, D.W. 1971. *Playing and Reality*. London: Hogarth.
Winnicott, D.W. 1962. "Ego distortion in terms of true and false Self." In Khan, M. (Ed.), *The Maturational Processes and the Facilitating Environment*. 1965. London: Hogarth and the Institute for Psycho-Analysis, 140–152.
Wirth-Cauchon, J. 2001. *Women and Borderline Personality Disorder: Symptoms and Stories*. New Jersey: Rutgers University Press.
Wolin, R. 1991. *The Heidegger Controversy*. Cambridge, MA: The MIT Press.
Zanarini, M., Frankenburg, F., Dubo, E., Sickel, A., Trikha, A., Levin, A., & Reynolds, V. 1998. "Axis I comorbidity of borderline personality disorder." *American Journal of Psychiatry*, 155:1733–1739.

Index

abject, abjection, 152, 164, 175, 205–8, 225, 241–2, 255, 257
abuse, 1, 5–8, 10–1, 18–20, 112, 154, 171–4, 176, 180–1, 196–7, 228, 238–9
aggression, 195, 222
alterity, 16, 20, 75, 78, 117–8, 121, 131–4, 151–3, 156, 159, 162–7, 174–8, 205–10, 213–7, 221–2, 235, 241–4
Aristotle, 30–1, 70, 93, 103
Aron, Lewis, 14, 20–1, 27, 113, 176, 178–9, 242, 245
attachment, 4, 10, 17–20, 109, 112, 116–9, 159, 167–73, 178, 180, 187, 193–4, 198, 220, 238–9, 245, 255, 257
    disorganized attachment, 169–71
Atwood, George, 14, 20–1, 27, 113, 176–9, 242, 245
authenticity, 51–8, 60–9, 140–2, 151, 214–7, 230

Bass, Alan, 15, 27, 247
becoming, 16, 60, 65, 78, 83, 89–91, 99, 103–11, 117, 129–30, 133–4, 140–51, 163–4, 199–207, 219, 223–5, 233, 236–7, 241–2

befindlichkeit, 32–3, 51–6, 64, 67, 70, 77, 121, 126–7, 183, 201, 231
Being and Time, 13, 25, 29–45, 48–51, 56, 63, 67–72, 77, 94, 106, 111, 201, 229, 234
being-towards-death, 54–6, 67, 99–101, 151, 153, 209, 214, 232, 250–3
Bergeret, Jean, 2, 256
bindung, 97–8, 129
Binswanger, Ludwig, 14–5, 26–7, 46, 47–64, 67–9, 230, 245, 249–50
Bion, Winifred, 129, 186, 206, 253
body without organs, 82–3, 88–91
Bollas, Christopher, 18, 20, 112, 118, 122, 125–30, 162, 175–8, 183–6, 206–7, 224, 234–5, 241–2
border, v, 185–6, 204–8, 212, 215, 225, 242
Boss, Medard, 14, 26–7, 62, 246, 249–50
boundaries, 19–21, 84–5, 157, 164, 176–80, 185–6, 192, 205–8, 212, 215, 224, 239–40
Bowlby, John, 4, 116, 167–8
breakdown, 43, 146–7, 150–1, 157–8, 204–5, 225, 237, 241
Breuer, Josef, 1, 189, 227

269

Bromberg, Philip, 4, 8, 20, 113, 127, 176, 178, 188, 239, 242, 246, 257–8

Care Structure. *See* sorge
Charcot, Jean, 1, 5, 188, 227
cohesion, 2, 19, 98, 124, 129, 146, 164, 175, 177, 187, 194, 197–200, 227
complication, 101, 206–8, 225, 242–3
Condrau, Gion, 14, 246, 249, 258
containment, 9, 77, 129, 186, 196, 199, 206–8, 253
conversation, 4, 20–1, 71–3, 121, 127, 176, 178–9, 183, 194, 196, 198, 223, 231, 239, 241, 246, 253, 256
culture, 9–10, 21, 105, 108–9, 123, 174, 181, 221–3, 227, 233, 240

dasein, 29–70, 78, 93–4, 104, 106–7, 127, 201, 246, 249–51, 258
Daseinsanalyse, 49, 51, 56–8, 60–4
death, 29–30, 54–6, 67–9, 72–3, 88–91, 93, 97–9, 101, 121, 140, 142–3, 150–3, 183, 203, 207, 209, 211, 214, 217, 231–2, 236, 250, 251, 253
  death instinct/death drive, 88–9, 97–8, 140, 142, 150, 203, 236, 253
deconstruction, 73–5, 246–7
defer, deferral, 19, 74, 85, 87, 96, 99–101, 154, 156, 165, 177, 220, 239
Deleuze, Gilles, 14, 16, 69, 78–91, 133–4, 143, 147–52, 163, 165, 201–6, 220, 224, 229, 232, 235–7, 241, 246, 251–2
denial, 5, 140, 190–1, 196
Derrida, Jacques, v, 14, 16, 72–8, 99–101, 121, 153, 165–6, 183, 186, 201, 209, 214, 229, 231–2, 246–7, 251

desire, 20, 78–91, 101, 133–52, 163, 175–8, 201–5, 224, 232, 235–7, 241–2, 251–5
desiring machine, 82–4, 88–90, 251
deterritorialization, 81, 106, 147–8
Diagnostic and Statistical Manual (DSM), 3–5
Dialectical Behaviour Therapy (DBT), 3, 18, 112, 175, 207, 223, 238
dialogue, 20–1, 26, 67–75, 101, 111–3, 121, 138–9, 174–80, 183, 186–8, 196–8, 205–6, 212–7, 222–4, 231, 239–44, 253
différance, 73–4, 99–101, 153, 156, 159, 209, 232
differentiation, 16, 78, 91, 111, 117, 129–33, 156–8, 162–3, 172, 184, 201, 224, 232, 235, 241
disavowal, 5, 19–20, 96, 161, 165, 177–8, 188–99, 220, 224, 239, 241
dissociation, 1, 4–5, 8, 19–22, 112, 165, 169–73, 176–8, 187–99, 206, 208, 215, 220, 224, 239, 241, 257

ego, 18–9, 34, 37–8, 44–5, 51–2, 64, 73, 84–7, 97–9, 109, 118, 122, 126–30, 134, 155–9, 162–3, 172, 174, 177, 184, 187–92, 195, 198–9, 202, 205, 209, 234–8, 252
enigmatic signifier, 153–6, 159, 163, 175, 209, 212–3, 21–7, 225, 237, 242
entwurf, 34, 42–5, 58, 77, 93, 98, 101, 108, 129, 153, 209, 232
eros, 97, 204, 211, 225, 237, 241
ethics, 26, 70, 73–5, 91, 103, 140–9, 151, 202–3, 236, 254
existenz, 38, 44–5
existenziale, 33, 51–2, 64, 127
exterior, exteriorisation, 16, 83, 89–90, 103–8, 117, 124, 142, 164, 174, 219, 221, 233

Index

extimacy, 135, 140–2, 203, 225, 236, 241, 254

facilitating environment, 123–5, 157–8
false self, 2, 158–9, 210, 238
Fonagy, Peter, 4, 8, 17–8, 109, 112, 116, 118, 167–8, 175, 193–4, 198, 223, 238, 257
la fonction du réel, 197
forgetting, 30, 54–5, 93–4, 98, 250
Foucault, Michel, 9–10, 47–57, 69, 166, 174, 180, 220–1, 246, 250, 255
frame, frame-work, 7–22, 25–7, 115–6, 179–81, 184–5, 196, 199, 206–8, 223, 226, 228–9, 240, 243–5
Freud, Sigmund, 1, 5, 14–5, 20, 47, 79–81, 90, 93–101, 109, 124, 128–9, 133, 135–7, 14–5, 142, 149–50, 153–7, 166, 178, 187–200, 203–4, 209–14, 224–7, 236–41, 246–7, 252–8
Frie, Roger, 14, 20–1, 27, 47, 176, 178–9, 242, 245, 250, 257, 258

Gadamer, Hans-Georg, 14, 16, 27, 70–2, 75, 121, 183, 229, 231, 245–7, 251
Goffman, Erving, 9–10, 180
Green, André, 18, 20, 27, 95–8, 112, 118, 153, 176, 178, 185, 204–11, 224–5, 232, 241–2, 246–7, 252–7
Guattari, Felix, 14, 16, 69, 78–91, 133–4, 143, 147–52, 163, 165, 201–6, 220, 224, 229, 232, 235–7, 241, 246, 251–2
Gunderson, John, 2

Herman, Judith, 1, 5, 14, 20, 112, 171, 176–8, 195, 239
heterochronicity, 16, 20, 98, 101, 117, 153, 159, 163, 175–8, 209, 232, 237, 242
historicity, 41, 71–2, 93–5, 101, 153, 159, 209, 215–6, 232

horizon, 12, 16–9, 29, 34–7, 45, 53–5, 63–71, 75, 93, 98, 107, 111–3, 115–8, 121–2, 129–31, 159, 161–3, 173–8, 217, 221–2, 227, 230–1, 234–5, 238, 241, 243, 253
horizontverschmelzung, 71

Id, 199
imaginary, 134–9, 141–9, 164, 202–5, 236, 253–4, 257
impingement, 124–5, 157–9, 206, 209–210, 217, 237–8
integration, 18–9, 97, 110, 153–9, 163–4, 171–2, 175–7, 187, 195, 199, 204, 209–211, 214, 225, 227, 237–8, 241
interior, interiorisation, 16, 83, 103, 106–8, 117, 124, 141–3, 156, 164, 219, 233
internalization, 84, 109, 124–5, 128–131, 162, 168, 172–3, 184–5, 193–4, 198–9, 209, 213, 235
Intersubjective School, 14, 20–1, 27, 113, 176–9, 198, 214, 242, 245–7, 256
intimacy, 140, 142, 195, 208

Janet, Pierre, 1, 5, 20, 60, 168, 171, 178, 188–99, 224, 227, 239, 241
jemeinigkeit, 38, 40, 55, 67, 70, 99, 121, 183, 231
jouissance, 91, 134–5, 140–51, 163–4, 175, 202–5, 225, 236–7, 241, 254

Kant, Immanuel, 31–2, 63, 78, 93, 97, 257
Kehre, 25, 69, 70–1, 111, 234, 250
Kernberg, Otto, 2, 4, 7–8, 112, 118, 163, 172–5, 187–8, 207, 223, 238
Khan, Masud, 2, 186, 255
Knight, Robert, 2
Kohut, Heinz, 2, 194

Kristeva, Julie, 18, 20, 112, 131, 135, 151–2, 163–4, 176, 178, 204–6, 225, 241–2, 246, 253

Lacan, Jacques, 14, 18, 20, 27, 79, 88, 91, 112, 118, 131, 133–52, 163–4, 176, 178, 202–6, 224, 235–7, 241–2, 246, 251, 253–7
Laplanche, Jean, 18, 20, 112, 118, 153–6, 159, 163, 175–8, 209, 212, 225, 237, 242, 246, 255
law, 11, 49, 84–7, 115, 137–40, 145, 181, 222, 252, 254–5
Letter on Humanism, 69, 104–5
Levinas, Emmanuel, 14, 16, 73–4, 121, 183, 229, 231, 245–6, 251
Linehan, Marsha, 3, 18, 112, 175, 207, 223, 238
Liotti, Giovanni, 4, 17–20, 109, 112, 116, 118, 168–70, 178, 187, 238–9
Loewald, Hans, 14, 18, 20, 27, 112, 118, 122, 128–30, 154, 162, 175–8, 183–4, 198, 207, 212–3, 224, 235, 241–2

das Man, 68
Meares, Russell, 4, 8, 21, 127, 176, 179, 193–4, 197–8, 206, 223, 241, 246, 256–7
mentalization, 4, 18, 109, 112, 116, 118, 131, 163, 167–70, 173, 175, 184, 187, 193, 195–8, 223, 238, 241, 246, 253, 256–7
Merleau-Ponty, Maurice, 14, 29, 245, 251
metaphor, 12, 41–2, 74, 99–100, 109–10, 117, 128, 140–6, 151, 165–76, 187, 194, 214, 220–1, 234, 238, 242
Mills, Jon, 14, 256
Mitchell, Stephen, 20, 176, 178, 242
mitsein, 67–8, 121, 183, 214, 231, 250–1
mitwelt, 67, 94, 121, 183, 186, 231, 250

mundanization, 59–64
Mystic Writing Pad, 99–101

nachträglichkeit, 19, 96–101, 153–4, 163, 175, 177, 209–10, 232, 237–9
Nietzsche, Friedrich, 15, 25, 30, 72, 75, 77, 80, 86, 88, 93, 221, 244, 246, 247, 253, 255
Nijenhuis, Ellert, 18, 112, 118, 171, 176, 187, 238

object relations, 2, 26, 90, 98, 118, 122–3, 131, 135, 138, 140, 163, 172–3, 184, 188, 194, 198, 210, 251–2, 256
Oedipus, 80, 87, 136–8
  Oedipal Complex, 81–7, 136–8, 145, 154
  l'Anti-Oedipe, 79–81, 133, 143, 148, 232
ontic, 15, 37–59, 62–9, 93, 101, 104, 201, 230, 249
Ontological Difference, 15, 33–4, 44–6, 62, 65–6, 69, 104–7, 230–1, 250
Orange, Donna, 14, 20–1, 27, 113, 176–9, 214, 242, 245, 255–7
The Other, 51, 68, 73–5, 90, 136–50, 155–8, 203–4
otherness, 20, 69, 72–5, 78, 101, 111–3, 121, 153–5, 165, 175–80, 205–9, 223–6, 231

paralogisms, 79–82, 86, 251
phallus, 86, 136–8
play, 109–10, 123–5, 128, 157–8, 168, 193–4, 209–17, 225, 242
Pleasure Principle, 97, 140, 210
présentification, 197
projective identification, 19, 26, 165, 170, 177, 187, 193, 196, 220, 239
psychiatry, 2–3, 6, 9–10, 15, 19, 27, 46, 49, 56, 62–5, 165, 220, 228, 230, 245

psychoanalysis, 2, 6, 8, 14–6, 19, 26–7, 46, 75–88, 133, 140, 166, 179, 201, 210, 228, 239, 245–6
psychosis, 2, 59–64, 82, 134–7, 141–7, 149–52, 159, 202–4, 210, 215–6, 225, 236–8, 241

Question Concerning Technology, 105–7, 110
Question of Being, 30–7, 45, 48, 70, 93

The Real, 134–46, 150–2, 163–4, 175, 202–5, 225, 236–7, 241
rede, 33, 52, 55, 64, 67, 127
reflective function, 187
Relational School, 27, 179
re-presentation, 96–101, 153, 156, 159, 209, 232, 252
Richardson, William, 14
Ricoeur, Paul, 14, 16, 70–2, 75, 77, 121, 183, 211, 229, 231, 246–7, 251, 257

Sartre, Jean-Paul, 104, 250
Sass, Louis, 14, 247, 249, 250
schizoanalysis, 79–81, 85–7, 133, 232
seduction, 5, 95, 153–6, 159, 163, 169, 189, 209–13, 237–8
self-harm, 1, 3, 19, 177, 212, 223, 228, 239
sexuality, 50, 64, 78, 89–96, 137–8, 149, 154–5, 170, 195, 201–3, 222
sinthome, 143–50, 203–4, 225, 236–7, 241
sorge (Care Structure), 33–4, 44–5, 67, 72, 77, 94, 108, 216
splitting, 3, 20, 110, 172–3, 178, 188–92, 196–9, 215–6, 224, 239, 241
Stern, Adolph, 2
Stern, Daniel, 17, 167, 238, 258
Stern, Donnel, 20, 113, 127, 176–8, 198, 241–2, 246, 256

Stiegler, Bernard, 16, 104–10, 124, 164–5, 174, 219–21, 233, 246, 251
Stolorow, Robert, 14, 20–1, 27, 113, 176–9, 214, 222, 242, 245–7, 250–1
subjectification, 17, 20, 69–70, 91–2, 111–3, 117, 133–4, 161, 166, 175–9, 187, 201–6, 220, 232, 236
subjection, 74, 143, 148–51, 203–4, 237
suicide, 3, 217, 251
superego, 170, 172, 207–8, 254
supplement, 74, 100–1, 110, 165, 220
symbol, symbolic, 19, 59–60, 86, 90, 95–7, 108, 125, 128, 134–47, 151, 163–4, 169, 177, 202–6, 210–1, 215, 225, 236, 241, 252–3

Thanatos, 204, 211, 225, 237, 241
thrownness, 16, 46, 52–8, 64, 67, 93–4, 98, 105, 115–7, 128–9, 153, 199, 209, 216, 230, 232
Transference Focused Psychotherapy, 18, 112, 172, 175, 238
transitional (phenomena, experience), 20, 122–6, 129–30, 157–8, 162, 175–8, 184–5, 206–7, 210, 224–5, 234–5, 241–2, 253
translation, 153–6, 159, 163, 175, 190, 209, 212, 225, 237, 242
trauma, 1–11, 17–22, 95–8, 110–2, 118, 127, 153–9, 167–81, 187–98, 205–17, 220–8, 238–43, 251, 255, 257–8

umsicht, 34, 42–5, 108
unformulated experience, 127, 198, 241
unthought known, 125–8

Van der hart, Onno, 5, 18, 20, 112, 118, 171, 176, 178, 187, 206, 215, 238–9
Van der Kolk, Bessel, 18, 20, 112, 118, 171, 176, 178, 187, 195, 238–9
verstandnis, 42, 44–5

verstehen, 33, 42, 52–5, 64, 127
vorhanden (*-heit*), 41, 43, 52

Winnicott, Donald, 2, 17–20, 112, 118, 122–30, 153, 157–9, 162–3, 175–8, 183–5, 204, 206–12, 217, 224–5, 234–7, 241–2, 247, 253
Wittgenstein, Ludwig, 29, 71

world and worldhood, 15–6, 33, 37–9, 51–8, 72, 105–8, 115–7, 124–6, 129, 164, 199, 219, 230
world design, 51, 56, 58–65, 245

Zollikon Seminar, 15, 26, 62, 67, 230, 244, 249
zuhanden (*-heit*), 41, 51

About the Author

Paul Cammell MA MBBS (Hons) FRANZCP PhD is an Australian psychiatrist, academic and psychoanalytic psychotherapist who originally trained in philosophy. He is Binational Chair of Advanced Psychotherapy Training for the Royal Australian and New Zealand College of Psychiatry. He has recently been a Visiting Fellow at the Personality Disorders Institute, Cornell University, New York. He is interested in relating contemporary philosophy to theories and clinical approaches in psychiatry, psychotherapy, and psychoanalysis.

Lightning Source UK Ltd.
Milton Keynes UK
UKHW010153070223
416581UK00001B/8